Jim Haynes was born in Sydney, attended Sydney Boys' High School and Sydney Teachers' College and then went bush to teach in towns like Menindee, on the Darling River, and Inverell in northern New South Wales. In between stints 'in the bush' he spent several years working in Britain and also gained two masters' degrees in literature, from the University of New England and the University of Wales.

Throughout his teaching career, Jim was usually in a band or group as a singer. He started the Bandy Bill & Co Bush Band in 1977 and also worked in radio on 2NZ Inverell and the ABC's popular *Australia All Over* program.

A major career change in 1988 saw him signed as a solo recording artist to Festival Records. Other record deals followed, along with hits like 'Mow Ya Lawn', 'Since Cheryl Went Feral' and 'Don't Call Wagga Wagga Wagga'. He created the first morning variety shows at the Tamworth Country Music Festival and toured his own shows, as well as touring with artists like Slim Dusty, Melinda Schneider and Adam Brand. He has hosted the Pat Glover Memorial Story Telling Awards at the Port Fairy Folk Festival for almost twenty years.

Jim has written and compiled over twenty books and released many albums of his own songs, verse and humour. He still works as an entertainer and has a weekend Australiana segment on Radio 2UE's long running *George and Paul* show.

Jim lives at Moore Park in Sydney with his wife, Robyn. He collects colonial art, plays tennis twice a week, supports the Sydney Swans and can walk to Randwick Racecourse in ten minutes.

THE BEST AUSTRALIAN YARNS

... AND OTHER TRUE STORIES

JIM HAYNES

ALLEN&UNWIN
SYDNEY · MELBOURNE · AUCKLAND · LONDON

Published by Allen & Unwin in 2013

Allen & Unwin
83 Alexander Street
Crows Nest NSW 2065
Australia
Phone: (61 2) 8425 0100
Fax: (61 2) 9906 2218
Email: info@allenandunwin.com
Web: www.allenandunwin.com

Cataloguing-in-Publication details are available
from the National Library of Australia
www.trove.nla.gov.au

ISBN 978 1 74331 683 2

Set in 12/15 pt Minion Pro by Bookhouse, Sydney
Printed and bound in Australia by Griffin Press

10 9 8 7 6

The paper in this book is FSC® certified.
FSC® promotes environmentally responsible,
socially beneficial and economically viable
management of the world's forests.

THIS BOOK IS DEDICATED TO THE MEMORY OF THE LATE
PAT GLOVER 1915-2005 - THE PORT FAIRY SHANAKEE

CONTENTS

Real Aussie Characters   47

Aussie Myths and Mysteries   93

Drinking Yarns 141

Yarns from Our Past 189

Aussie Icons   283

INTRODUCTION

The term 'yarn spinning' comes from the days when threads of wool or cotton were hand spun into yarn—which was a more substantial product and could be used to make cloth.

So, like the real yarn spinners, the person telling a yarn takes some threads of a story and makes something substantial or meaningful from them.

There is a clue in our language that tells us that most yarn spinners in olden times were female. The word 'spinster' means an unmarried woman. This was because in the days before the Industrial Revolution many single females earned their living by spinning yarn—and probably told stories as they did it. So 'occupation, spinster' came to mean 'unmarried woman'.

Yarns are not really full-blown stories, because they are usually about one single incident or event and don't have to have a beginning, middle and end—although some do.

Yarns are not really jokes. They don't have to have a punch line or be funny, though many are. People expect a good yarn to be at least entertaining and interesting, but not necessarily funny. It is true, however, that yarns are the way we have preserved and developed our Australian sense of humour.

If there is an Australian sense of humour, it seems to me to be about laughing at ourselves and supporting the underdog, but it's hard to say exactly where the Australian sense of humour came from.

Obviously Irish and Cockney elements were very strong in the development of our sense of humour. Word play and alcohol have played a large part in what Australians have found funny over the past two hundred years. The more dry, deadpan humour that is also found in our favourite yarns might have come from the settlers and convicts who hailed from Yorkshire, Lancashire, the West Country and other rural areas of Britain.

What is often forgotten in discussions about the Australian sense of humour is that Indigenous Australians have a wonderful and unique sense of humour and are among the most amusing people I know to sit and yarn with. Aboriginal humour is mostly broad, self-deprecating and ironic. It is often very 'in-house' and sometimes delightfully rude.

The naming of the yearly festival, held in Melbourne since the 1950s, is a case in point. The festival is called Moomba and the story goes that original organisers wanted a new and unique name, so they asked local Aboriginal elders to suggest something and received the reply 'Moomba', which they were assured meant 'let's get together and have fun'. Years later someone finally let the cat out of the bag and confessed that 'Moomba' in the local dialect actually means 'up your bum'!

This type of payback humour is nothing new. There is another example from the Brisbane area where, in colonial times, white settlers pushed out the Aborigines, cleared the bush and formed a farming settlement. When the settlers asked the dispossessed Indigenous Australians what the place was called they were told 'Goona'. Only years later did the settlers discover that 'goona' was the local Aboriginal word for shit.

According to Indigenous writer Tyson Yunkaporta, the town's leading citizens then decided to insert a 'd' and thus make the name incorporate the positive English word 'good'—and 'Goodna' it has remained to this day, an outer suburb of Brisbane.

Often Indigenous Australian humour is about the underdog who may not win in the end but has the last laugh. I am sure that this is where we get some of that element of self-deprecating deadpan humour, which is part of the 'Aussie' character, although I think the Irish also added to that sense of supporting the underdog in our culture.

Interestingly, some yarns which turn up often in our folklore have an interchangeable hero, sometimes an Irishman and at other times an Aboriginal Australian. Here is an example that I first heard as an Irish–Australian yarn but which is also now commonly told with an Aboriginal hero.

> The fishing inspector catches Paddy putting a mud crab into the boot of his car.
>
> 'Hey! You can't do that! I saw what you have there. It isn't mud crab season. I'll have to fine you!' he says.
>
> 'Hang on,' says Paddy, 'it isn't what it looks like. This mud crab is my pet. His name is Marty. Everyday I bring him down here for a swim.'
>
> 'A pet mud crab?' replies the inspector, 'Never heard of such a thing!'
>
> 'It's true, mate,' says Paddy, taking the mud crab from the boot and stroking it. 'Look, I'll show you.'
>
> Before the inspector can get his thoughts together, Paddy takes two steps to the edge of the mangroves and puts the mud crab gently into the water.
>
> 'Go on, Marty,' he says, 'have another swim.'
>
> The mud crab slides into the muddy water and disappears.
>
> Paddy stands silently, arms folded, as the minutes tick by. Finally the inspector asks, 'Well, when is he coming back? Where is he?'
>
> 'Where's what?' asks Paddy, innocently.
>
> 'The mud crab.'
>
> Paddy frowns at him quizzically and asks, 'What mud crab?'

Our sense of humour and love of a yarn has no doubt something to do with the Irish heritage in Australia. Over one third of convicts and early settlers were Irish and the tradition of yarn spinning is very strong in Irish areas of Australia such as the Warrnambool, Koroit and Port Fairy district.

The folk festival held at Port Fairy is the biggest and best in Australia and the tradition of 'shanakee' or village storyteller was alive and well until recently at Port Fairy in the guise of the late Pat Glover, after whom the annual storytelling competition, held at the Port Fairy Folk Festival, is named and to whose memory this book is dedicated.

The yarns we tell every day at the dinner table or in the workplace are not usually well-constructed stories like the mud crab joke. They are mostly anecdotes from life. When we have a good story to tell, something unusual or amusing or quirky, we often say we will 'dine out on that yarn' for a period of time. This refers to the fact that a good yarn spinner is popular as a guest. Someone with amusing or entertaining anecdotes to tell will be invited to more dinner parties than a boring person. So, being a good yarn spinner makes you popular and in demand among your peers.

We all love amusing or strangely coincidental stories, whether they be family yarns or work-related anecdotes. If you have ever socialised with a group who are all from one profession, you have no doubt heard their yarns. Teachers' reminiscences, doctors' stories, truckies' stories, builders' experiences—every profession or sport or hobby has its own store of folklore and yarns. Anything amusing or strange or salacious gets passed around the office or workplace or social group fairly quickly.

Human beings have a need to communicate and yarn spinning is one way of building the bond we all desire to form between individuals—that thing that makes each social group unique.

Shared yarns help us to become a group—a family, good neighbours, a team, a profession . . . friends.

Among Australian men, the social group was often the drinking group, and yarn spinning in the pub after work was a very strong Australian tradition. In the bush, men yarned around the camp fire or in the pub, while women formed informal groups for afternoon teas or yarned at the CWA hall, or over the back fence in the town and city. Families shared anecdotes and amusing stories about work or school or relatives at dinner or after dinner. In a more formal way, the art of after-dinner speaking was a very important element of the semiofficial meetings and celebrations and fundraising events of community or professional groups.

While there are millions of good yarns, not everyone is a good yarn spinner. Those who have 'the gift of the gab' or the ability to tell a yarn in a well-structured and entertaining fashion are highly regarded in most social groups.

The word 'raconteur' is not so common these days but we all know someone who is 'the life of the party' and can entertain when appropriate. We also all know those who cannot tell yarns well, or who think something is amusing or worth hearing when everyone else realises it is not. So, just as we value good yarn spinners, we will avoid at all costs those who are poor yarn spinners!

Some yarns are generic. Urban myths and gossip spread fast and the same stories come around again and again. In the world of journalism these can be useful when it is a slow news week or during the 'silly season'.

The 'silly season' in Australia is the period immediately following Christmas. During this time there is not as much real news because the whole nation shuts down and politicians and businesses and the entertainment industry are not issuing any media releases. After Christmas, advertising is slow due to everything having been done before Christmas. Permanent staff from newspapers and radio and television stations are on annual leave and stand-in presenters and journalists are left with little to talk about or write about. This is the season for recycled urban myths and apocryphal stories.

The newspapers drag out the old furphies about sightings of Tasmanian tigers or mysterious large beasts, such as the Emmaville panther or yowie. Poltergeist stories appear, or that yarn about the fish falling from the sky, or the one about the pelican that takes the family chihuahua from the wharf at Coffs Harbour, or Kingston, or Albany—or somewhere. These are 'generic' yarns, designed to interest and fascinate anyone.

Many yarns are, however, more specifically related to a group, a family or a profession, or a group of friends. Most of us think our profession or family have the best stories and yarns. Many of the best yarns are only meaningful if you know the character in the story, or the jargon of the profession or group, and its past history and folklore.

Most families have a few characters whose eccentricity or meanness or ability to get into crazy mix-ups is legendary—within the family at least.

Often a good family yarn just appears from nowhere but is worth telling, at least to other family members. Those outside the family group can also often relate to a family yarn or anecdote that contains a poignant human truth or circumstance.

My dad passed away while I was working on this collection. He was one of those blokes who never talked about his experiences in World War II. He served in the British Navy and I knew he'd been on a destroyer in the North Sea and the Mediterranean in the early years of the war and on a troopship that was torpedoed and almost sank limping back to Gibraltar over Christmas 1943. Later, he was on an aircraft carrier that was part of the final thrust against Japan and was twice hit by kamikaze suicide planes.

He never talked about any of that, but my mum, a great yarn spinner, used to tell us things about the war. Dad had sent her photos of the damage after the kamikaze attacks. She kept them with other wartime photos in a small Globite school bag and I'd look through them now and then as a kid.

After I wrote a book about the Australian experiences in World War II several years ago, I was trying to make conversation with my dad at the nursing home, never an easy thing to do. I started telling him I was working on a book about Australians at war and researching the events at Tobruk. He let me talk, as he always did, so I went on telling him how ships on their way to Tobruk with supplies, or returning with wounded were constantly pummelled from the air and raided by German U-boats.

After enemy propagandists on Radio Berlin called the supply-line ships 'a pile of scrap iron', Australian troops christened them the 'Scrap Iron Fleet'.

'You Brits used the term the "Tobruk Ferry",' I told him, 'But the Aussies called it the "Scrap Iron Fleet".'

'Being part of the Tobruk Ferry was no picnic,' I told my dad. 'Lost on the supply run in the eight months of the siege were two destroyers, three escort vessels and twenty-one other ships.' He appeared vaguely interested in my chat for once, so I went on, happy to find any topic to engage him in conversation.

'You were on a destroyer in that first part of the war, weren't you?' I asked.

'The *Antelope*,' he said, quietly.

'Ahhh, that's right, I remember now,' I said smiling, 'you were in the North Sea at that time, weren't you?'

'No,' he said, 'we were on the bloody Tobruk Ferry for seven months!'

I didn't realise I'd researched and written an account of something my dad actually lived through. That yarn will be part of our family history from now on.

Some family yarns involve uncanny coincidences. My wife's family had been trawler men for several generations and her parents built a state-of-the-art, sixty-foot trawler in the 1970s and named it the *Lauryn G.*—after their three kids, Laurence, Robyn and Garth. The *Lauryn G.* was the family business for thirty years, but was sold when my wife's parents retired.

Now, my brother-in-law, Garth McMillan, is a paramedic who sometimes worked the Westpac Rescue Helicopter. A trained diesel fitter, ambulance officer and surf lifesaver, Garth once received the Royal Humane Society Medal for bravery for jumping from a helicopter, swimming to a disabled yacht in a severe storm, reviving and administering first aid to the solo yachtsman who had been injured, fixing the yacht's diesel engine and taking it to shore. He was the right man for the job, you might say.

Garth happened to be on call one night in 2006 when there was a report that a vessel was in trouble out to sea off Noosa Heads. A trawler had suffered a hook up on an unknown object while trawling and the vessel overturned and sank. As it turned out later, the boat was lost and the skipper drowned, but two crewmen were rescued and survived. None of this was known as the helicopter flew to the scene, but more information came to hand via radio. When Garth heard the description of the vessel he went rather quiet and then asked its name. It was the *Lauryn G.*

If a family or a group of professionals spends a lot of time together, the yarns seem to multiply and become more a part of the social fabric of the group. Touring with groups of entertainers, musicians and crew in the 1980s and 1990s was a rich source of yarns and show business folklore for me. Every show provided some hilarity or calamity or situation that was worth yarning about, and was often recalled years later.

Of course the yarns are embellished and retold and become funnier over time. Col Joye and Frank Ifield are two characters who stand out to me as being fabulous yarn spinners with limitless stores of amusing and nostalgic yarns to tell backstage.

Frank, who is no longer able to sing due to a serious lung operation in the 1980s, now has a show where he yarns about his past, while Wayne Horsburgh sings the famous songs and I provide Aussie humour.

Col is so fond of yarning that he often forgets the purpose of an interview or media appearance. One Christmas he was supposed to be promoting an album of rock and roll Christmas songs on my 2UE spot with George Moore and Paul B. Kidd. We had yarned and taken calls from fans for almost half an hour when George, looking at the big hand of the studio clock approaching news time, became worried and tried to get Col focused on what the record company and publicist wanted from the interview.

'Now, you have a new album of rock and roll songs out for Christmas,' said George, the ultimate radio professional, prompting Col to wax lyrical about the album.

'Do I?' said Col. 'Oh, yes, that's right. I've heard it too—it's good.'

The late Slim Dusty, Leonard Teale and Smoky Dawson were all a treasure trove of great yarns and stories. Often it was all you could do to drag yourself away from the dressing room and onto the stage—the best show was the one going on backstage.

I suppose everyone thinks that their profession has the best yarns and the best yarn spinners, but I think showbiz people are the best; most of them are natural show-offs and many can talk underwater. 'Vaccinated with a gramophone needle' was what my mum used to say.

I tour now and then with a variety show called *Back to the Tivoli*. It's owned and hosted by my mate Wayne Cornell, who has been in show business for most of his life and sang in the Delltones years ago. Wayne could fill ten books with stories about entertainers and touring. He told me a story about asking a famous entertainer for a tip to help him succeed as a young aspiring singer. While young Wayne waited expectantly, the legend put his hand on his shoulder and said, 'Never leave your wallet backstage.'

For some reason, certain trades and professions seem to have more yarns than others. As you will find reflected in this collection, horseracing people and railway workers seem to be especially good at remembering and passing on great yarns from their work.

Of course, war always creates great yarns, not always amusing but often fascinating and redolent of great heroism and sacrifice. Often these are infused with the black humour that comes in the face of great danger or suffering. Digger yarns from both World Wars have always been favourites with the Australian public.

We all love ghost stories and tales of supernatural or at least mysterious and inexplicable events. Sitting around a camp fire as kids taking turns to shine a torch into our own faces and tell scary yarns was a great source of pleasure when I was growing up.

I have attempted to make this selection a varied and entertaining collection of yarns related mostly to Australian history and events. This means that most of the yarns are of the more generic type, not too specifically related to one group or section of the population.

There are sections devoted to horseracing and railways and war, but I have tried to make the yarns in those sections the type that have an element of amusement or interest that will appeal to most people who just like a good yarn.

I have tried to avoid those yarns that are really just jokes with a local twist. I have heard thousands of jokes in my time and very few of them make good yarns. Hosting the Pat Glover Story Telling and Yarn Spinning Awards at the Port Fairy Folk Festival for almost twenty years has been a great pleasure for me. It has made me realise that a true yarn is a very different thing to a joke.

Jokes are mostly brief, momentary entertainments and a few are usually enough in a social gathering. Yarns, however, can be spun for hours around a camp fire or dinner table and the conversation will never become boring, especially if most people around the table can pick up a thread and make something from it by adding an experience or story.

I would love to make a collection of real family yarns one day, but I have no idea how to go about collecting them. There are hardly any in this selection because most families never write them down. They remain as part of the family folklore and are rarely passed on to outsiders.

The internet seems overloaded with meaningless, useless and trivial information and unfunny generic 'jokes', but it should be possible to start using it to collect and share the yarns that all families have stored in their collective memory banks—the meaningful stories and memories that make us who and what we are. But I am not the man for the job.

We need more blokes like my mate Frank Daniel who has spent most of his life remembering and writing down the yarns and stories that he has heard and experienced from childhood to the present. In lieu of this collection having a whole section of family yarns, I'll just end this introduction with one of Frank's family yarns.

A Family Memory by Frank Daniel
The Daniel family was well-known in the Southern Tablelands as sawmillers, blacksmiths, carriers, and farmhands, as well as being good drinkers, musicians and storytellers. The first Daniel family set up a sawmill at Holroyd Park in the suburb of Ashfield, Sydney.

They were cedar cutters, and when their original source of supply depleted they went in search of new millable timber south of Goulburn to a place known as Bungendore. Here the so-called 'good timber' that they were told about was of no value at all; so they moved further south to Rossi in the Black Range, a part of the Great Divide, where they pioneered the sawmilling industry in that area.

They were an industrious lot and keen on progress, never taking time off for trivial matters, but they all had big families and the birth of new offspring, no matter which side of their family tree, was always an occasion to celebrate.

Weddings were the next best reason for celebration, as long as there was plenty of liquid refreshment to go with the yarning and the music.

Funerals were another good reason for a day off. You never knew what you might buy or trade at a funeral, plus there'd always be plenty of cups of tea and scones as well as a good supply of grog on hand to see the dearly beloved on his or her way and it was a good chance to catch up with distant relatives.

When my grandmother Lilian passed away in her late nineties, her funeral was set for the Friday afternoon, which happened to coincide with the ninety-sixth birthday of old Auntie May. It so happened that two travellers were passing through town the same day and asked the publican at the Lake George Hotel if there was any chance of a bit of entertainment in town. He mentioned Granma's funeral and stated, 'You just wouldn't know what might happen at one of them Daniels "turnouts".'

So the two blokes went to the funeral, the wake at the pub, and the birthday party in the Daniel Farm Building Workshop. They had a beaut time and next morning they asked if there was likely to be another such occasion in the near future.

AUSSIE HUMOUR

The one thing I always say, when asked what makes Australian humour different from other types, especially American humour, is that we like to laugh at ourselves. Old-fashioned Australian humour is all about mocking pretension and laughing at our own quirks and characteristics in a gentle, often deadpan way.

The homogenisation of Western civilisation, due to television and the internet and other technology, is gradually destroying the unique nature of what makes Australians laugh, but we still have some identifiable traits to our sense of humour. As our humour loses its unique character, due to the effect of American entertainment dominating our lives, it is ironic that the cartoon often touted as the funniest example of Australian humour was actually drawn by a man born in the USA.

Stan Cross was born in Los Angeles in 1888. His family were British and moved to Perth in Western Australia in 1892. After school, he worked on the railway and studied art at night until a wealthy brother sent him to London to study and there he began drawing cartoons for *Punch*.

He returned to Australia and worked on *Smith's Weekly* from 1919 for £5 a week. He drew a number of comic strips, including *The Potts*, *Dad and Dave* and *Wally and the Major* and, in July 1933, drew what is said to be the funniest joke ever produced in Australia, with the caption, 'For gor'sake stop laughing, this is serious!'

The words are spoken by a workman clinging to a girder at the top of a skyscraper. Another bloke is clinging to his trousers, which have fallen down around his ankles. The bloke hanging close to death is laughing uncontrollably.

Cross continued to draw *Wally and the Major* until he retired to Armidale in northern New South Wales in 1970. Cross died there in 1977. His gravestone is engraved, 'Stop laughing, this is serious!'

I think the funniest Australian cartoon ever is one Norman Lindsay drew for *The Bulletin*. An old cocky and his rather large missus are leaning on the pigpen and she says, 'It's our golden wedding anniversary soon, dear, will you be killing the pig?'

The old cocky answers, 'Why should an innocent animal suffer for something that happened years ago?'

Cartoons are not yarns, of course, but that one demonstrates the real understated humour and practical view of the world that seems to me typically Australian.

Real-life situations are often funnier than fiction and the amusing incidents that brighten our day-to-day lives often make the best yarns and become part of our family history to be shared between friends over a dinner or a few drinks.

This section begins with some gentle, everyday, amusing yarns, but also contains some examples of typical Aussie male humour and also some zany Australian humour from the likes of Lennie Lower and Henry Horne.

KING KONG'S BUM

Travelling with my two young nieces on a Sydney bus one hot afternoon, I witnessed one of the funniest confrontations I have ever had the pleasure to observe. My nieces were around eleven and nine years old at the time and having a day out in the city with Uncle while on a holiday from Adelaide. A Sydney bus trip from the city to Nana's place out at Banksmeadow turned out to be as much of an adventure as a ride on the Manly ferry.

A rather strange-looking fellow boarded the bus at Central Railway Station. He was a short man with a goatee wearing an oddly old-fashioned three-piece suit and a trilby hat, and carrying a very old suitcase. He paid his fare and sat in the disabled seat right at the front of the bus, leaving his suitcase in the aisle. He was quite odd to look at and rather eccentric in his deliberate mannerisms and movements and my nieces giggled silently at his appearance and behaviour, as kids often do at anything out of the ordinary.

The other main character in the drama was a rather large bloke who had obviously had just one beer too many after work and was on his way home standing up, strap-hanging, although there were still several seats available.

An elderly woman with a walking stick boarded the bus and, the disabled seat being occupied by the eccentric little chap, stepped awkwardly past his suitcase and looked for a seat.

'Hey, mate!' the big bloke said loudly. 'Get out of that seat and get your port out of the way, that's for old and disabled people.'

The small man with the goatee ignored the comment and the elderly lady found a seat further down, but the large tipsy bloke was not going to let it go at that. He began to aim a tirade of abuse at the little man in the suit.

'Are you deaf as well as stupid, mate?'

'What's that growing on your chin? Looks like it belongs on a billy-goat.'

'What's in the suitcase? You taking your brain to the cleaners in that?'

'Hey, mate, that seat is for the physically handicapped, not the mentally handicapped.'

Finally, the response came. It was rather prosaic and disappointing.

'You should drink less and mind your own business,' said the small man primly as he stood to get off the bus.

The whole bus was shaking with suppressed merriment and it was one of those moments when you daren't look at whoever you are with for fear of bursting into laughter. Everyone was amused except the small man with the suitcase, but nobody laughed out loud.

'I'd need to drink a lot more to be as stupid as you,' the big man replied.

The small man left the bus by the front door but the middle doors were also opened and the bus was stopped at a red light which coincided with the bus stop. The small man walked a few steps along the pavement until he was level with the middle doors of the bus which remained open for a few seconds. He was now directly adjacent to his strap-hanging nemesis and the two made eye contact for a split second.

It was in the few seconds before the doors closed that the small man, now safely off the bus, fired his only real shot in the verbal battle.

With his suitcase in his hand, he stood staring at the big man and then said, quite casually but in a loud, clear voice, 'What are you going to do for a face when King Kong wants his bum back?'

The doors closed and the lights changed and the bus moved off.

The big man said, 'Smart arse,' dismissively and the bus broke into snorts and laughter.

My nieces were giggling like crazy, and when the big bloke got off a few stops later, I said, 'That was funny, wasn't it?'

'Yes,' my oldest niece replied quite seriously, 'that doesn't happen on buses in Adelaide.' **JH**

IF YA CAN'T CATCH 'EM, SHOOT 'EM!

I have a mate who is a great yarn spinner and we were swapping stories of things we had witnessed on bus trips around Sydney when he came up with a beauty that topped mine.

According to my mate, he was on a bus travelling out to the western suburbs from Railway Square many years ago. Somewhere near Annandale, a rather large woman ran to catch the bus, struggling with shopping in those old-fashioned string bags women used before the advent of plastic shopping bags.

The bus driver kindly waited for her and she struggled onto the bus, all red-faced and panting heavily. She fumbled with her purse and paid her fare and attempted to move down the bus. The strain on her shopping bags as she juggled them with her purse, plus the movement as the bus pulled away from the bus stop, caused her to stumble. She grabbed a seat to steady herself but her string bag broke and several large oranges rolled along the aisle of the bus.

The poor woman bent forward and chased the oranges down the aisle but the effort of bending forward after the exertion of running for the bus, and all the stress she was under carrying her shopping, caused her to break wind violently as she chased the oranges.

'Most people on the bus were too polite to laugh out loud,' my mate said, 'but there was a lot of snickering and a general murmur of suppressed laughter at the poor woman's plight.'

Eventually one of the passengers—there's always one—probably a bloke who'd had a few beers after work, broke the whole bus up into gales of laughter when he said loudly, 'That's the way, love, if you can't catch 'em—shoot 'em!'   **JH**

'IT'S NOT SYDNEY, YOU KNOW!'

There is a very mild kind of humour in this next story, more amusement than humour. Still, it's a very 'Aussie' story and Melinda and I have laughed about it for years. We use the phrase as a kind of catch cry when anything doesn't come up to expectations. I think it's the fact that we all know the situation and this type of character; we have all met her somewhere!

Touring shows into rural areas is always a good way to get some 'city versus the bush' yarns. City dwelling musicians and entertainers often have no idea about how things work in the bush and it used to be a great source of fun for those of us who have lived in the bush to watch the city slickers cope with things like no shops open after six o'clock and no room service in country motels. These days, things have changed. You can get a decent coffee in a country town and most towns of some size have the obligatory Maccas and Red Rooster and Kentucky Fried Chicken outlets open until midnight.

I remember touring back in the 1980s and 1990s when you would shudder when one of the musicians ordered a coffee in an outback town. Back then most country towns had never seen a real coffee machine and it was wise to order a pot of tea and not risk whatever sad excuse for real coffee might arrive in the form of instant or, even worse, hours-old pot coffee.

'Stick to tea,' I'd often whisper to musicians or entertainers on their first rural tour, when a request for 'latte' or even 'cappuccino' met with a blank look. 'They know how to make tea!'

It is still great fun to find that there remains, even in recent years, a certain lack of sophistication in country cafés. It's amusing to be an observer when a city slicker meets a relatively unsophisticated bush attitude head on.

Touring with Melinda Schneider was always great fun. Melinda was a country music superstar in Australia before she branched out and became an all-round musical theatre and television performer and personality.

Although she has great empathy with country people, Melinda is very much a city girl and my funniest memory of my years touring as her opening act was an incident that occurred in Griffith. Now, Griffith is a town very well supplied with good cafés and it's certainly not a town where you would hesitate to order a coffee.

The normal routine when touring is to rise late the morning after a show, leave the motel, have breakfast somewhere in the town and then drive to the next town. Often it is hard to sleep late due to the 'trolley gestapo' wanting to clean rooms and get you out of their hair, and it's no good driving to the next town too early because the rooms at the 'moey' (motel) are never ready until afternoon and the sound check isn't until two or three o'clock.

Griffith has a number of very fine cafés with alfresco dining on the wide pavements of the main street and it was in one of these that the classic confrontation occurred—between the sophisticated city entertainer and the young, gum-chewing fifteen-year-old country waitress.

Various breakfasts were on the menu but Melinda couldn't find exactly the right one for her.

'Can I have this breakfast but without the bacon and with poached eggs?' she enquired politely.

This seemed to be a huge imposition on the young waitress. She sighed, took the menu, pocketed her pencil and rolled her eyes. 'I'll go and ask,' she said with the stoicism of one who had just been asked to undertake a polar expedition without a dog team.

After the appropriate interval, she returned, took out her pencil and order book and said, 'The cook says "yes", you can have that. Wattle ya have to drink?'

Oblivious to the great difficulty she had already caused to the entire establishment, Melinda asked innocently, 'Do you have Earl Grey tea?'

That was the final straw. The waitress's hands went onto her hips, her eyes rolled, her shoulders drooped and her whole body was involved in one enormous sigh of exasperation and disbelief as she informed Melinda of a fact she probably already knew.

'It's not Sydney, ya know!'   **JH**

COLOGNE OR DUBBO

Another wonderful memory of touring with Melinda Schneider comes from the days when Adam Brand was the hottest thing in country music and he and Melinda and I were touring a show called *Good Friends*, which happened to be the name of Adam's latest hit song.

Part of the tour involved a concert at the Dubbo Show, where the audience sat in an uncovered wooden grandstand and we performed on that most hated by performers of all stages—the back of a truck, converted into a temporary stage. We were right next to the cattle stalls and it was drizzling rain. The organisers had kindly set up a small tent beside the stage, but it was not really weatherproof and the floor was muddy and getting muddier by the minute.

While Melinda and I were attempting to dress in our stage clothes without getting mud all over them, her mobile phone rang and it was soon obvious she was chatting to her famous mum, the great cabaret performer and yodeller, Mary Schneider.

After the usual 'mother–daughter' chat, Melinda said, 'Jim's here, Mum, I'll put him on to say hello, I'm changing.'

Backstage phone chat with Mary was not unusual. She and her daughter talk daily and Mary and I had recorded a song together years before and often had a catch-up phone chat.

'Hello, Mary,' I started out, 'are you on tour, too?'

'Yes, darling,' came the reply.

'Where are you?' I asked, innocently.

'I'm backstage at the Opera House in Cologne, Germany, darling. José Carreras is on and I'm on next. There's a hundred-piece orchestra and I'm all frocked up. Where are you and Melinda?'

'We're standing in mud and cowshit at the Dubbo Show.' I told her. 'It's raining and we're about to perform on the back of a truck.'

Ahhhhh—showbiz! **JH**

EL DUBBO
JIM HAYNES

Dubbo is a beaut town really, one of the most progressive rural cities in Australia. Like Wagga Wagga, however, the name 'Dubbo' just sounds funny to many Australians and always seems to get a laugh when it's used in a yarn or joke.

This next piece is a send up of Marty Robbins' classic song 'El Paso'. I have been doing this onstage for years. The tune is obviously missing but you can sing along to yourself. Those of you who know the original words to 'El Paso' might find it vaguely amusing.

When you go west in the USA, there are mountains and lone riders on the horizon and girls dancing in cantinas. When you go west from Sydney—there's just Dubbo!

Out in the west New South Wales town of Dubbo,
I fell in love with a sheila called Maude.
Night time would find us all down at the pub, oh
We'd sit there all evening and get really bored.

One night just one other drinker came in,
He had a bad case of wi i i i ind.
Dashing and daring, with us he was sharing
The results of the baked beans he ate from a tin.

Just for a moment I stood there in silence,
Shocked by the foul, evil deed he had done.
No one was breathing, 'twas time we were leaving.
We had but once chance and that was to run.

Out through the back door of that place I ran.
I had to make it outsi i i i ide!
He dropped such a good one, I left while I could run,
But poor Maude fell over, and inhaled and died.

Lost my love to pollution, there was just one solution.
I wrote this sad song about it, of course.
Then I galloped and galloped, until I reached Tamworth
It took a long time—'cos I don't have a horse!

LUNCH FOR DIPSO DAN
JIM HAYNES

Here is a yarn I heard years ago and turned into a poem. It's one of the funniest stories I ever heard based on horses' names. The central idea of a drunk confusing a horse's name with the advertised lunchtime in a pub was how the joke worked when I heard it. I added a few twists and turns and it took me a while to think up the final tagline. Then I put the whole thing into rhyme so I could copyright it. You can't copyright a joke, but you can copyright a poem.

Dipso Dan is the town drunk in my 'perfect country town', Weelabarabak.

Dipso Dan is a man who can strike any time,
You rarely get any warning,
He's thrown out of the pub as the minister passes
Late one Saturday morning.

'G'day there, Reverend,' says Dipso Dan,
'Got any good tips today?'
'Well, Dan,' says His Reverence, 'Lunch might be
A good thing for you, I'd say.'

'Thanks for that, Reverend, good on ya,' says Dan,
'I never forget what I'm told.'
To himself, he mutters, 'Never heard of Lunch,
It must be a two year old.'

Back in the pub goes Dipso Dan,
The drinking day is still young.
And the first thing he sees is a sign that says,
'Lunch is 12 to 1'.

'Look at the odds!' says Dipso Dan,
'That's gotta be worth a chance!'
But a firm hand grips his collar
And another the seat of his pants.

He's back on the street, but now he's obsessed,
'That Lunch might be a goer.
I'll go down the Royal and back it,' says Dan,
'Before the odds get any lower.'

So Dan staggers off to the other pub,
At the other end of the shops.
Halfway down there's the Chinese restaurant—
That's exactly where Dan stops.

And he stares at the sign in the window.
It says, 'Lunch is 11 to 2'.
'They're backing the thing for a fortune,' says Dan,
'That minister musta knew!'

'Fancy missin' out on 12s,
That's just the thing to spoil
Me afternoon, I'll hurry up,
I'll back it at the Royal.'

Dan staggers on and he's almost there
When he stops with a strangled yell.
'Lunch 1 to 2', says the blackboard sign
At the door of the Royal Hotel.

'Bloody odds-on, I've missed it,' says Dan,
'Me chance of a fortune is wrecked!'
Then he slides down the wall of the Royal Hotel,
Booze and exercise take their effect.

He sleeps through the paddy-wagon ride
But he wakes when they lock the cell.
He hears them walking away with the keys
And he knows he'll have to yell.

'I wanna know about Lunch,' yells Dan,
'And I've got a terrible thirst.'
'Bad luck about lunch,' the sergeant yells back,
'Cos I'm telling ya, sober up first.'

'Sober Up first, eh,' says Dipso Dan,
'So much for the minister's hunch.'
He lies down on the bed, 'Sober Up first, eh,
Thank gawd I didn't back Lunch!'

BE CAREFUL WITH BABIES
LENNIE LOWER

Lennie Lower was, to my mind, the funniest and most Australian of all humorists. His humour has a zany and often black feel to it and it was way ahead of its time. It's the kind of politically incorrect stuff that Australians really laugh at, but it seldom gets written down.

Babies are in again. It is in a spirit of kindness that we proffer instruction and advice, which follow:
    The top part of the baby is the part with the knob on it.
    The ends which wave about are the legs.
    It is not generally known that the baby must be held knob part up if the thing is to make any progress.
    Babies on the bottle should be taught to use an opener at about three months. The label should be removed, so that the child will not form any prejudices against a certain brand which may affect him in later life.
    At about six months, chewing should commence, either on a bone ring or on the doctor's bill. Things being as they are, we recommend the doctor's bill, because a bone ring is just about finished in two years.

At two years, the child's left leg should be tightly lashed to its left ear and rapidly whirled around. This will give it a good idea of what constitutes a good citizen and taxpayer. It will probably kill the kid, but everything is for the best.

THE BACHELORS' GUIDE TO THE CARE OF THE YOUNG
LENNIE LOWER

I have noticed with astonishment the absolute ignorance of bachelors in regard to the care of the young.

To begin at the beginning. It will be noticed in a fresh baby that it is of a pale, prawn-like colour, and is bald and toothless, exhibiting all the evidences of senility. This is the usual thing, and the minder is not to be alarmed.

The first thing noticeable about the baby is the yowl. This must be stopped at all costs. There are various methods, but the principle to keep in mind is ... 'at all costs'. Watches are very good; a firm hold must be kept on the chain, however, as I have on two occasions lost a perfectly good watch through the child swallowing it.

This mania for swallowing and sucking things may be indulged to an almost unlimited extent. Doorknobs are excellent, though the holding of the baby to the knob is somewhat tiring. This may be overcome by unscrewing the hinges of the door and placing it in an accessible position.

Babies of an artistic nature or of practically any nature, may be left with a tin of stove polish or a bottle of red ink or any other medium for an almost indefinite period.

In cases of persistent howling, a belt passed over the top of the head and buckled securely under the chin is an infallible remedy. This must be used only in extreme cases.

In handling, care must be taken that the baby is held in a more or less vertical position, the head being uppermost. The child at times has a tendency to jerk from the holder, and in the case of a beginner this may lead to disastrous results. Sticking-plaster and other first-aid appliances will be found to be very useful on these occasions, and a supply should always be kept on hand.

Where a baby has to be held for any length of time, a short loop of stout twine passed around the neck, and fastened to the wrist of the holder, will prevent contact with the floor.

Never allow a dog to lick the face of a baby, as any number of diseases may be communicated, and, in the case of a valuable dog, this is most serious, and may lead to its loss, or, at the best, a falling-off of condition, and an absence of lustre in the coat.

On two or three occasions I have found the addition of about one third of a cupful of rum to the feeding milk very effective. Only the best OP rum may be used, as babies are very delicately constituted internally. A better way is for the minder to have four or five cupfuls himself, when it will be found that an extraordinary number of ways of amusing the child will suggest themselves.

Should the little one inadvertently eat anything it shouldn't, thoroughly rinse or gargle the mouth with phenol, lysol, or any other good disinfectant.

In undressing the baby for the purposes of putting it to bed, bathing, etcetera, the beginner will find great difficulty in undoing the numerous buttons, tapes and various other fastenings with which it is lashed. An efficient and obvious method is to insert a penknife between the skin and the clothing and peel the mass off in one operation.

In bathing the child, never fill the bath right up, as it is only in exceptional cases that it will float. A cold shower and a brisk rub down with a stiff towel will have an invigorating and tonic effect.

In conclusion, a little helpful advice to the unwilling minder will not be amiss. Should you have been lured into minding a baby before, and wish to escape a second demand, a convincing excuse must be made. Lodge meetings and appointments, business or otherwise, are received with suspicion. By far the best is the statement that you feel your diphtheria coming back, and that you seem to be breaking out in funny red spots all over the body. This may be said in a conversational manner just as the request is about to be sprung. I have used this or something similar for some time now, and it has never failed yet.

THE MUTE BOY
JIM HAYNES

This is a version of a very common yarn about the stoic nature of the Aussie bloke who never speaks unless there's a reason to. I put it to rhyme.

The boy had never said a word, his mother was distraught.
He'd been at school almost a year—how could the lad be taught?
A mute for all of his six years—not one word had he spoken,
He seemed okay in other ways but his mother's heart was broken.

Then one day from his breakfast plate he slowly raised his head,
Flexed his lips a few times and—'This toast is burnt,' he said.
His cocky dad stared at the lad and slowly shook his head,
'Well, I'll be buggered,' were the words his startled father said.

His mum was overcome with joy and clasped him to her breast,
'My darling boy, my dearest joy! You speak like all the rest!
Why did you never speak before, dear lad, if you knew how?'
'Well,' he observed, 'everything was quite all right 'til now!'

TOO MUCH ARGUMENT

This is often quoted as the 'great Australian joke'—it's the forerunner of many jokes, including the previous piece of verse. Supposedly it shows the deadpan stoic nature of the typical Aussie male or, more accurately, the typical Aussie bushman.

Two swaggies had been tramping the long roads that stretch away to the horizon for many months, sharing tucker and working together when there was a bit of work, sharing their few pennies and buying tobacco and never bothering about which one had the most tea or smokes or made the camp fire each night.

One day, they tramped past a very dead animal lying several dozen yards off the track but swarming with flies and smelling like your worst nightmare. The object was black and putrid and they hurried on past it as quickly as possible.

That night in their camp, one bloke lit his pipe and remarked, 'That dead ox was the worst thing I've smelled in a long time, didn't it pong?'

'It wasn't an ox,' replied his mate, 'it was a horse.'

With that he turned in and was soon asleep in his swag.

Next morning he wakes to find his companion of many months gone, along with his swag and billy and half the rations.

Under a rock near the camp fire he finds a note which reads, 'I'm humping bluey on me own from now on; there's too much argument in this camp.'   **JH**

AUSSIE SPORTING CLANGERS

I have always loved those stupid things that commentators say in the heat of the moment. When you are not working to a script, as you never can be when commentating live sport, it's so easy to shove both feet into your mouth!

When I was at university in Britain, we'd always note down the funniest radio and television sports commentary blunders and share them at the dinner table.

Even the best and most famous commentators drop wonderful clangers. Back when colour television was coming in, snooker commentator Whispering Ted Lowe once whispered, 'He's going for the brown—which for those of you watching in black and white is the ball directly behind the pink.'

Famous Rugby League broadcaster Eddie Waring once said, in a moment of excitement, 'There's only one minute and sixty seconds left to go!' while legendary motor racing commentator Murray Walker said, 'Excuse me while I interrupt myself to give you the lap times.'

Believe it or not, when I was at university in Wales, we used to listen to Irish radio and they had the snooker on radio. One night, the commentator was so excited he said, 'And he's lining up dis very difficult shot and . . . oh, you shoulda seen dat!'

My favourite comment from that time wasn't from a broadcaster. The Welsh have a wonderful way of putting things and it was the president of the Welsh Rugby Union who said, in his annual speech, 'Well, we didn't have a very successful year internationally. We only beat Western Samoa, and it's a good thing we weren't playing all of Samoa!'

But I digress. Australian sports commentators are as good as any in the world at saying really stupid things on air. Rugby League broadcaster Rex Mossop was famous for getting tongue-tied when things became exciting. I remember poor Rex having to commentate a surfing competition, of all things, in his early days on television. He wasn't sure of the terminology and had probably never heard of a wipeout. A spectacular fall from a large wave was described by Rex as, 'Oh, no, he's had a prang!'

Rex's forte was saying the same thing in different ways. My favourite example was the time Cronulla half-back Perry Haddock scored and Rex explained, 'A great try by Haddock, and he's only a small, diminutive, little fellow.'

Stating the 'bleeding obvious' is a thing that we all do when we put our mouths into gear before our brains. After the adrenalin rush of winning, it's hard to focus on speeches. Greg Norman once announced at a presentation, 'I owe everything to my parents— especially my mother and father.' Richie Benaud's classic was, 'That slow motion replay doesn't show how fast the ball was travelling.'

Norman 'Nugget' May was renowned for being excitable and ignoring all athletes but the Australians. We all know his 'Gold, gold, gold for Australia!' commentary, but once at an Olympics he completely ignored the winner and runner up and called, 'Bronze—bronze for Australia!'

Nugget's best example of stating the bleeding obvious was when he announced, on the first night of an Olympics, 'Michelle Forde wins Australia's first Olympic Medal in four years!'

Veteran ABC radio 'sports-caster' David Morrow added to the list of classics when he announced, towards the end of a rugby game, 'It's very hot and I bet some of these forwards are really looking forward to relieving themselves in the bath.'

That's a case of not realising that certain words have different meanings. Some blunders, however, are just weird. Let's end with this one, from ABC's Peter Wilkins, which just makes no sense at all! 'The half time score is a great one in favour of Australia . . . Scotland nil, Australia nil.'

Errr—right!   JH

HARE TODAY, GONE TOMORROW
JIM HAYNES AND PADDY RYAN

Now, I know this is a true story because Paddy Ryan told it to me himself, and I helped him to write it all down, just as it happened. As you can see, it happened in rhymed verse.

We've got real beaut neighbours, we help each other out,
Last June I went and worked for them when they were short a
     rouseabout.
So, when they took a holiday to the Gold Coast for a week,
They asked if I'd drop in each day to feed their chooks and sheep.

Now, I had this border-collie pup that I was trying to train
He'd yelp and jump and piddle when you let him off the chain.
So I let him run beside me bike when I went next door to see
That things there at the neighbour's place were satisfactory.

I checked the sheep for water while the pup yapped round my legs,
Then I went down to the chookhouse to pick up any eggs.
I was only gone a minute and yet, when I came back,
I saw a scene of devastation, 'twas an unprovoked attack!

You see, the neighbour's daughter had a rabbit for a pet,
And what I saw in their backyard—it gives me nightmares yet!
A rabbit hutch turned upside down and you could guess the cause
'Cos that pup stood in a fresh dug hole with something in his jaws.

I nearly died right on the spot! How could that mongrel do it?
I quickly grabbed the rabbit before he had a chance to chew it!
Right away I saw it was too late—the thing was dead.
I coulda kicked myself—but I kicked the dog instead!

The dog shot through and left me with that bunny on me hands,
To stay cobbers with our neighbours I'd have to make some plans.
As I tucked the bunny in me shirt and pedalled down the track
I thought, 'I'll just fill the hole in, clean him up and put him back.'

No one was home at our place so I washed him in the tub,
Took Mum's loofah from the shower and gave him a good scrub.
He seemed to have a lot of dirt stuck to his fur and claws,
So I scrubbed him with Dad's toothbrush and I combed his little paws.

He was starting to look better—but before I took him back
I thought I'd take a look at all those bottles on the rack.
The shampoo sure improved him, so I thought, 'Ahh, what the hell—'
I grabbed the other bottle and conditioned him as well.

He only needed drying now—the end was getting near,
So I hung him on the clothes line by a peg on either ear.
An hour later he was dry—I thought, 'That's nearly it.'
But I got Mum's new hair dryer and I fluffed him up a bit.

He was clean and dry and fluffy—it was probably enough,
But to finish off I touched him up with our gran's powder puff.
I hid him safely in the shed where he'd be out of sight.
Next day I filled the hole in and I sat the hutch upright.

The day they were due home I slipped the body in the cage.
They'd think he died of natural causes—heart failure, old age.
I checked the stock and tidied up then I was on me way.
Of course, as you'd expect he would, my neighbour rang next day.

He thanked me for me trouble, 'But here's something weird . . .' he said.
'We found our rabbit in his hutch really clean . . . and dead!
'His location and his freshness have us puzzled . . . not his health!
See, he died the day before we left . . . I buried him myself!'

APRIL FOOL!

On the morning of 1 April 1978, a barge appeared in Sydney Harbour towing a giant iceberg. Retailer and adventurer Dick Smith had been propounding his scheme to tow icebergs from Antarctica to solve the water shortage, and he had apparently succeeded. The radio stations were full of the news and a large crowd gathered.

Dick moored the iceberg near the Opera House and said he would sell ice cubes called 'Dicksicles' for ten cents each to improve the flavour of any drink they cooled. Phone calls started pouring into radio stations and more crowds gathered along the shore. Then it began to rain and the fire fighting foam and shaving cream that the 'iceberg' was really made of washed off, exposing the white plastic sheets beneath.

Dick also announced on another April Fool's Day, when the tunnel sections were being towed into the harbour, that it wasn't a tunnel after all, but a road, and that it floated during peak hour and sank during the rest of the day.

On 1 April 1975, Adelaide's *This Day Tonight* news program revealed that the country would soon be converting to metric time—100 seconds to the minute, 100 minutes to the hour, and 20-hour days. Furthermore, seconds would become millidays, minutes become centidays, and hours become decidays. The report included an interview with Deputy Premier Des Corcoran, who had agreed to give credence to the hoax. He praised the new time system and said South Australia was leading the way with decitime.

One viewer wanted to know how he could convert his newly purchased digital clock to metric time.   **JH**

POOR OL' GRANDAD
GRAHAME WATT

Toilet humour is very popular in Australia. This poem by my good mate Grahame Watt is one of the best examples. Long-drop dunnies were once very common in rural areas. You dug a hole and moved the dunny over it. The dunny was built on sleepers and could be moved with a certain amount of effort every decade or so.

Poor ol' Grandad's passed away, cut off in his prime.
He never had a day off crook—gone before his time.
We found him in the dunny, collapsed there on the seat,
A startled look upon his face, his trousers round his feet.

The doctor said his heart was good—fit as any trout.
The constable, he had his say, foul play was not ruled out.
There were theories at the inquest of snake bite without trace,
Of redbacks quietly creeping and death from outer space.

No one had a clue at all—the judge was in some doubt,
When Dad was called to have his say as to how it came about.
'I reckon I can clear it up,' said Dad with trembling breath,
'You see it's quite a story—but it could explain his death.

'This here exploration mob had been looking at our soil,
And they reckoned that our farm was just the place for oil.
So they came and put a bore down and said they'd make some trials,
Drilled a hole as deep as Hell, they said about three miles!

'Well, they never found a trace of oil and off they went, post haste,
And I couldn't see a hole like that go to flamin' waste!
So I moved the dunny over it—real smart move I thought,
I'd never have to dig again—I'd never be caught short.

'That day I moved the dunny it looked a proper sight,
But I didn't dream poor Grandad would pass away that night!
Now I reckon what has happened—poor Grandad didn't know,
The dunny was re-located when that night he had to go.

'And you'll probably be wondering how poor Grandad did his dash—
Well, he always used to hold his breath—until he heard the splash!'

A TALL TALE OF TAGGED TROUT
PAUL B. KIDD

This tale was told to me by a local down the Snowy Mountains way and he believed it to be true. But for all of my enquiries I couldn't find anyone who knew anything about a four-day fish festival in the district, either still running or in the past, with tagged trout. Could I have been deceived? You decide for yourself.

The annual four-day fish festival was shaping up to be a beauty. The big cash prizes on offer were attracting anglers from all over the country and although there were some notorious cheats among them, the organisers didn't seem to care. With around 5000 anglers at $10 a pop, they stood to make a killing, so a little fudging here and there wouldn't hurt. In fact, the rules almost encouraged it. The boundaries were anywhere within 30 kilometres of the starting point and they weren't policed. The area included four dams and several rivers.

The big prizes were for the capture of Terry, the Tagged Trout. There were four Terrys—one for each dam. They were trout of about a kilo, imported from a trout farm and branded with an identifying tag stapled to the tail.

Amid much fuss and press coverage, each year the Terrys were released into their new homes the day before the event. The release spots were kept secret so as not to give anyone an advantage.

The four Terrys were worth $50,000 each and even the village idiot could tell you that the organisers were in deep trouble if they were all captured. For that matter, only one had to be taken to prove embarrassing. Plus there were prizes of $10,000 each for the biggest Murray cod and yellowbelly.

You didn't need a degree in mathematics to work out that the difference in prize money on offer and the entry fees collected was minus $170,000—and that was without running costs. There had to be some skullduggery afoot.

The organisers maintained that the prize money for a Terry was underwritten by a big insurance company. But it wasn't because they knew that a tagged trout would never be caught.

In the five years of the Fish Fest, no one had ever caught a Terry and the organisers had walked away with a bundle. To ensure that no one came up with the goods, the Terrys were all orally fed a slow-acting poison before release. While they looked healthy enough when photographed being thrown into the dam, they were as stiff as a board in a matter of hours.

What the organisers did not count on was one of their own being more corrupt than them. He was known as The Moth because he was attracted to the light. He would get legless at the fishing club or the local and stagger home. If he saw a light on, he would invite himself in for a drink and there was no getting rid of him. He was a dreadful pest drunk, but sober he wasn't a bad bloke at all.

Being an official assistant-organiser and Terry-releaser, The Moth had been entrusted with the secrets of the villainy that went on. For his silence, he picked up a small share of the returns. But The Moth had got into big trouble on the punt and, with the heavies breathing down his neck for the money, he decided to out-cheat the cheats.

The only bloke he could trust with his life was an old mate of his in Sydney called Bill 'The Dago' Oliver. They called him The Dago because he never stopped whingeing about the fact that his missus spent her entire life in front of the TV watching the soapies. It had been going on for years and his constant grizzle was, 'There's not a day goes by without her watching that crap. There's not a day goes by when she does anythin' around the house. There's not a day goes by when I get a meal at home. Fair dinkum, there's not a day goes by . . .' That was The Dago.

Rocket scientists they were not. But between them, The Moth and The Dago devised a scheme that would scoop the pool . . .

Admittedly the rules of the tournament were loose, but a couple were hard and fast. There was absolutely no berleying allowed before the event and all fish had to be weighed by six o'clock sharp. Apart from that, it was open slather.

'We'll wrap up the cod and yellowbelly sections,' The Moth had told The Dago on the phone. 'I know an old cod hole about 50 kilometres out of town. When you arrive a day before the comp, I'll have 'em boilin' on the surface. Oh! And don't forget to bring your snorkel and flippers. You'll need them to catch Terry.'

The Moth drove out to the cod hole that was on a big corner in a bend in the river and hung six sheep heads from the branch of an overhanging tree. He made sure to keep them hidden well within the leaves.

He returned a week later to find his self-berleying device working a treat. The sheeps' heads were well and truly flyblown and the maggots were dropping into the water at a steady pace.

A week later, every fish within a hundred kilometres was waiting underneath with its head sticking out of the water and mouth open. The Moth knew that the smaller fish like the redfin and silver perch would attract the bigger cod and yellowbellies, which would eat them all, and then The Dago could catch them the first day of the comp at his leisure.

Snookering Terry the Tagged Trout wasn't so simple. It wasn't until four days before the comp that The Moth and The Dago devised a plan. And even then it was by a stroke of luck.

To add some authenticity to their shonky contest, the organisers announced that, due to being hounded by cheating anglers with binoculars, they would now secretly release the four Terrys without any press in attendance. The media spewed. 'How do we know that you will release any fish at all?' they barked.

Amid cries of deception and fraud, the organisers agreed to let the media photograph the four boats leaving with the Terrys on board and also arranged for a trusted observer to go out with each fish releaser.

The observers were selected from the town's most prominent and honest citizens—the police chief, the headmistress, the head of the Chamber of Commerce and the mayor. The Moth couldn't believe his luck. He drew his old mate the mayor, alderman Clarrie 'Carbuncle' Carr.

The mayor was as bald as Kojak and the locals called him Carbuncle because they reckoned he was shiny on the outside and inside he was full of shit.

Carbuncle loved nothing more than a bottle of Scotch and a friendly ear. The Moth had such an ear. It would be no trouble to get Carbuncle well and truly under the weather and carry out his deception.

At the releasing of the Terrys on the eve of the comp, the cameras flashed as Carbuncle and The Moth held Terry up in his plastic bag full of water for all to see. 'Take your time', the organisers had told The Moth. 'Don't make it obvious where you're heading to let the trout go. And don't let Carbuncle see you give it the poison. Otherwise we'll be paying him blackmail forever.'

The Moth putt-putted a couple of kilometres around the lake before he pulled in at Knot's Pier for the couple of bottles of Scotch he had hidden there the previous day. He primed Carbuncle with one and it wasn't long before the mayor was dribbling and showing off about all the bribes he'd taken over the years.

The Moth then loaded a block of concrete with a wire handle on board, explaining to his drunken friend that it was ballast in case a breeze came up. And off they went, straight to Mackenzie's Flats, the shallowest and sandiest part of the dam where no one had caught a fish in years. Here the Moth tied a hundred metres of sash cord to the concrete block and lowered it over the side.

When it hit the bottom a few metres down, he removed Terry from its bag, tied the other end of the sash cord through its gills, stuffed the poison capsule up its backside and threw it overboard for The Dago to find in the morning.

Carbuncle was oblivious to all of this because he was out cold on the bottom of the boat. The Moth got stuck into the other bottle of scotch and, by the time Carbuncle woke from his drunken stupor, The Moth was skiting about the exact location of the maggot-berleyed cod hole, the tethered trout and how clever he and The Dago were. The cunning old mayor, now sober, listened intently.

When the cops hauled The Moth in the following day and questioned him about the body they had found that had apparently drowned when it got tangled up in a length of sash cord at Mackenzie's Flats, he denied any knowledge of it.

Apparently the victim, complete with flippers and snorkel, had been diving towards the bottom and had become entangled in the cord because whoever had tied the fish to the end of it had jammed something up its backside causing it to blow up with air and float to the top.

'That explains why they told me ten times to shove the poison capsule down its gob,' The Moth thought to himself as he examined the trout the police had found attached to the sash cord. 'But that's funny', he thought to himself, 'where's the tag?'

The Moth was puzzled and upset. His partner in crime was dead and the tag was missing. What was going on?

'Had they seen anything that night,' the cops asked? After all, he and Carbuncle had headed out in that direction.

'No, sir,' The Moth replied and Carbuncle backed him up.

The cops didn't connect The Moth with the drowned Dago Oliver and Carbuncle wasn't saying anything. By a strange coincidence, the brother of the guy who found Dago's body, who by an even stranger coincidence happened to be Carbuncle's nephew, turned in a Terry that very afternoon and claimed the fifty grand.

Seeing as the tag was only just stuck to the tail and not stapled on like the originals and the trout was only about a half a kilo instead of a kilo like the original Terrys, the organisers smelt a giant rat, but couldn't do a thing about it. They had to mortgage their houses and come up with the money.

And by an even more extraordinary coincidence, Carbuncle's son weighed in a huge cod and a yellowbelly that same day and picked up a cool twenty grand. No one could figure out why maggots kept dropping out of the fishes' mouths at the weigh-in.

The organisers were out of pocket and the cops had an unexplained corpse. Carbuncle came into a lot of money all of a sudden and The Moth left town. They say he's been sighted around Bondi these days where the lights are on twenty-four hours a day.

ONE WISH
FRANK DANIEL

We had fished with little luck out on Lake Burrinjuck,
And Jack, me mate, said, 'Hell, we're out of grog.'
We hadn't had much fun, just sittin' in the sun,
And now we had to row ashore, a tidy slog.

We each reeled in our line, there was a jug attached to mine,
While my cobber only had a wormless hook.
As the sun continued glaring, we both just sat there staring
At the only catch we'd made we couldn't cook.

When I gave the thing a rub, so help me, from the jug,
A spook appeared before us in a cloud.
And both us fishin' blokes yelled, 'Holy flamin' smokes,
We'll have three wishes now if we're allowed.'

But the genie said, 'Oh, no, you only get one go.
I'm just a learner, I can't grant you three.
But with one I'll do my best, it'll be a little test,
And with one wish you'll surely have a spree.'

But me mate, perhaps remissful, was a little over-wishful,
And he said, 'I wish this lake was full of beer.'
In a flash, to our surprise, the lake turned amber 'fore our eyes,
And we watched that novice genie disappear.

I was cranky with old Jack; I wished the genie would come back,
Though my mate, now in his element, did gloat.
But I reckon Jack disgraced us, 'cos the problem now that faced us,
Was that we'd both have to pee inside the boat!

A GRAVE MISTAKE

Graveyard humour is popular in most countries; it's a way of relieving the terror of our own mortality and lessening the depth of grief and fear we associate with graveyards. When I was a kid, I heard the yarn about the bloke who gets drunk and takes the short cut home through Botany Cemetery and falls into a freshly dug grave and can't get out.

He rests for a while and dozes a bit and wakes to hear footsteps. Someone else is coming along the short cut.

'Hey, mate,' he calls, 'can you help me get out of here?'

A terrified scream is followed by the sound of the other bloke running for his life back to the main road.

This example of graveyard humour is nicely understated in the true laconic Aussie style.

A bloke of Scottish descent is the local bagpipe player and is always asked to play on Anzac Day and at other community events.

One day he gets a call from a women living in one of the new estates on the edge of town. Her father, who migrated from Scotland decades ago, has passed away and she wants bagpipes played at the funeral.

The piper says he'd be proud to do it for his usual nominal fee and the woman tells him how to find the cemetery.

'It's a new lawn cemetery that is just being developed and its a bit hard to find up here in the new section of town,' she tells him. 'There are a lot of new estates and cul-de-sacs, are you sure you will find it okay?'

He assures her he will find it and they discuss the tunes he will play and the time of the burial and the order of the service.

On the day, the bloke has a phone call as he is about to leave and that makes him a little late, but he has enough time to make it and heads off into the new area of town and gets completely bushed.

He drives around and up and down and discovers he is way off track. He starts again in a different direction, but all the streets and parks look the same and he eventually realises he has missed the ceremony.

Filled with guilt and shame, he is trying to find his way back to the part of town he knows when he sees two blokes filling in a hole in an area of lawn and landscaped ornamental trees.

'There it is!' he says to himself, 'And I've missed the service as I feared.'

He drives over to the fence near where the blokes are shovelling and grabs his pipes and strides over.

'Sorry, fellas,' he says, 'but I have to do this, it's very important.'

He plays 'Amazing Grace' and 'Scotland the Brave' and stands head bowed for two or three minutes before walking solemnly back to his car.

The two blokes digging stand silently and watch and listen.

As he walks off, one says to the other, 'Well, Nugget, I've been putting in septic tanks for years, and that's the strangest thing that ever happened to me while on the job!' **JH**

MILES FROM SYDNEY

Two swaggies camp in the bush, just off the road near a cemetery. After getting stuck into the rum they take a walk through the gravestones and look at the epitaphs and discuss the lives they see depicted—carved on the headstones.

They are swigging away at the rum and getting drunker and drunker and they drift apart as they meander among the graves.

'Struth, Harry,' one of the now drunk swaggies calls to his mate, 'there's a bloke here called Thompson who lived to be 102!'

His mate, who has wandered off towards the road, yells back, 'Thash nothin', there's a bloke here who was 155!'

'Blimey!' the other yells, 'What was his name?'

'Some bloke called Miles,' comes the reply, 'from Sydney.' **JH**

TALE OF A TOOTH
HENRY E. HORNE

I love this tall tale of a dental procedure in the days when the local blacksmith was also the town dentist. It should be in the 'Bush Yarns and Tall Tales' section, but the way the verse rhymes gives it a unique feeling of fun. It is slapstick comedy, but also has a touch of that very Aussie, understated humour.

Big Billy Bull
Of Bungendore
He used to pull
Our teeth before
The railway come;
And strike me dumb
And dead
Your head

'Ud fairly hum,
When Billy's pincers grabbed your gum,
While 'cross your chest
His weight he pressed
And pushed your 'pendix outa plumb.

But once a bloke
Named Johnny Jupp
Came down and broke
Our blacksmith up.
It turned him grey.
He tried all day
To lift
And shift
One tooth away;
Until, at last, in his dismay,
What does he do
But ties it to
The tailboards of me new spring dray.

And then we got
Into the cart
And at a trot
We made a start;
The bloke behind
He didn't mind
Becos
It was
Intended kind.
Though, till he sorta grew resigned,
He yelled, of course,
To stop the horse,
And cursed us black, and blue and blind.

So by the tooth,
Along the dust,
We dragged that youth

Till something bust;
And then we swore
And chucked it, for
There hung
And swung
Our tailboard, or
The most of it, to Johnny's jaw
Which snapped at us
With vicious cuss,
And said, 'You crimson cows, no more!'

THE BARREL OF BRICKS

This is one of the oldest tall stories around and has been popular in Australia for at least fifty years. There are many versions, but most concern a migrant worker, a 'New Australian', who gets a job working on a building site as a brickie's labourer. He explains to the boss why he isn't at work and how he managed to have a broken arm, a fractured skull, a broken nose, cracked ribs and a broken ankle.

I was a'workin' on a four-storey buiding anda the brickie he wanna the leftover bricks uppa the top to be bringa down to the bottom, but itsa too far to carry them bricks alla the way down!

So I getta the bright idea anda I make a pulley and I getta bigga bucket and haul him up to the roof and tie the rope to a railing down on the ground and I climb up and loada the bricks into the bucket. Then I go backa down to the ground, wrappa the rope around my hand a couple times and untie the end of the rope with my other hand.

Well, them bricks they heavier than me—so I shoot up in the air likea the space ship!

Halfa the way up, I meeta the barrel as she's a comin' down, and thats whena my arm she's a broke.

When I reacha the top, I hitta the pulley with my head, and that'sa when I fracture the skull.

Then the bucket she hit the ground and fall over and alla the bricks they fall on the ground. Now the bucket she'sa lighter than me, so she'sa comin' up and I'ma going down.

I hitta the bucket again, and that's when I breaka the nose.

I hitta the ground and land on the bricks, and that's when I cracka the ribs.

Then I letta go of the rope and the bucket she comin' back down and that's when I breaka the ankle.

And that's why I no more worka for you today!   JH

THE GOAT MACHINE

My favourite migrant yarn is the story of the poor refugee from Eastern Europe who comes to Australia destitute as a young man with his new wife.

Although he has an engineering degree from his own country, he has poor English and has to work as a labourer and cab driver to make ends meet.

Sadly, his wife is poorly and they have trouble having children but finally, after many years of struggle and working long into the night, he succeeds in making a wonderful invention. Then his wife announces she is pregnant at last. Things are looking up!

The invention the refugee has been working on is an application of a machine to make sausages from goat meat. It does the whole process, from slaughtering to skinning, boning, cutting and making the sausages.

It's a marvellous invention and the refugee forms a company to round up feral goats in South Australia, truck them down to Port Augusta where he has his factory, process them using his marvellous machine and sell the sausages in the Adelaide Markets.

Soon he is exporting and becomes a rich man.

The child is spoiled and adored and, although he is not the sharpest tool in the shed, his parents lavish upon him every possible thing a child could need or want and pay for extra tuition and, after several attempts and more tuition, he just makes it to university.

He doesn't have the marks needed to get in to study engineering, so he chooses to do a degree in marketing.

The kid is a spoiled brat and a real smart arse.

After one year of studying business and marketing, he comes home and says to his father, 'You are a fool, Pop, you have it all wrong in your business plan!'

'How is that?' asks his long-suffering and hardworking father.

'Well,' says the boy, condescendingly, 'you spent all your life making a machine that is wasteful. You put a goat in one end and a sausage comes out the other. What you should have worked on and invented is a device where you put in a sausage and a goat comes out!'

The old man looks at him sadly for a moment and then says, 'I think your mother already has one of those.'   JH

THAT CRAMMING FEELING OF SCHOOL DAYS
LENNIE LOWER

Lennie Lower was able to take a news item and create a funny yarn out of it—he made a living doing it. His humour was so Australian and his ability to extrapolate word play and mental images out of banal and prosaic everyday events was unsurpassed!

A terrible thing has happened at East Maitland Boys' High School.

The school is so crowded that four classes have been forced to take a week's holiday. We presume that all the boys' protests were in vain.

'Just give us a few mathematical problems—a logarithm—anything!'

'No!' said the headmaster. 'Here's your fishing rod. Go!'

Awful thing to do to a boy just when the locust and beetle season is coming on. That's what comes of overcrowding.

Right from a child we were against overcrowding of schools. We always had a feeling that we were one too many.

Us by ourself, or the teacher by himself—yes. But the pair of us by ourselves—no.

As a boy, we were brilliant at school. We shone at hi-cock-alorum; our locusts squeaked more loudly than any of the other pupils' locusts. Dunno how it came about; we just seemed to be able to get more out of them.

At tearing lumps out of our trousers we were absolutely on our own. We can't claim any credit for it. It was a gift. We held the flyweight record for window-smashing.

Our teacher got muscle-bound rewarding us for our prowess at hurling the ink-pellet.

At arithmetic and such we were fair, but uninterested. We knew that two and two made four, and were satisfied with that. If we were told that eight and eight made sixteen we accepted it philosophically.

But why anyone should need to know the result of buying 11 dozen cabbages at 8d, another 7½ dozen at 6½d, and how much profit would be made if he was 36 years of age and his father didn't come home till 11 o'clock—this always left us with a deep feeling of contempt.

We passed through school loaded with information and marbles.

The fact that Captain Cook won the battle of Trafalgar in 1876 has changed our whole life. This much we can say for the benefits of education.

But we still think that that school was overcrowded. Sort of crammed in.

THE WEELABARABAK BUGLE
JIM HAYNES

Local newspapers are a great source of hilarity in most small towns. Everything in this yarn comes from things I have read in local newspapers—honest!

The *Weelabarabak Bugle*, that's the paper in our town,
It's the method by which all the news is spread around.
Each Monday and each Thursday the *Bugle* hits the street
And if you've never read it, you've missed out on a treat.

The editor, Old Jonesy, puts most of it together.
He does the features, the photos, the farm news and the weather.
But, as it's only twice a week, the weather's yesterday's.
Mrs Phillips does fashion news and reviews the local plays.

On Thursday, it'll tell you the weekend netball draw,
And you read it on a Monday if you want to know the score.
How did footy go on Sunday? What's news down at the school?
Call it 'two minutes silence' and you're only being cruel!

Sure Jonesy sometimes rushes and small mistakes occur.
The CWA President's mad at what he did to her!
It was underneath a photo of her with a champion scone.
Well, a name like 'Mrs Tucker' is a bad one to get wrong!

Even headline spelling errors are not difficult to find,
'Members Active in the Loins Club' is one that comes to mind.
Like, 'Councillors Pass Motions on Brand New Town Hall Roof',
And 'Surveyor Leaks on Subdivision our Photo Shows the Truth!'

Though the news that's in the *Bugle* is always based on fact,
The editor's prejudices—they remain intact.
And Jonesy was a decent, well-meaning country bloke,
Who hated unions, Pommies, and all them 'city folk'.

One day he had a message, O'Shea's pig dog had gone wild!
Broke its chain and tried to maul the O'Sheas' youngest child,
Who no doubt had been tormenting it, as he was wont to do,
But the child had been saved by a stranger passing through.

He'd pulled up, grabbed a tyre lever, dashed into the fray,
Took the brunt of the attack, killed the dog and saved the day!
Jonesy soon was on the scene and the bloke was interviewed,
(While waiting for the ambulance, 'cos he was badly chewed.)

He said he lived in Sydney, but he was born in the UK.
He was a trade union organiser visiting branches up our way.
And the headline for our hero is Jonesy's best one yet,
'City-Based Pommy Communist Kills Local Kiddy's Pet!'

HOME BEAUTIFUL
LENNIE LOWER

Lennie Lower hated pretension. One very Aussie element of his humour was that notion of the battlers acting just like the toffs. Here he is taking the piss out of the middle class magazine articles about stylish living.

The charming home of Mr and Mrs John Bowyang, tucked away in Pelican Street, Surry Hills, is a revelation in piquancy. From the backyard one has a view of every other backyard in the street, and the tall chimney-stack of Tooth's Brewery looms majestically in the distance.

An antique casket, known to connoisseurs as a 'dirt-tin', stands by the back entrance. It is one of Mrs Bowyang's great sorrows that the lid has been pinched.

Mrs Bowyang has an artistic taste and an eye for effect. Two lines have been stretched between long poles at either end of the yard, and when these lines are full of clothes, the sight is bewitching in the extreme.

Empty salmon tins, kindly thrown over the fence by the next-door neighbours, and a worn-out bath and a coil of wire netting on top of the washhouse roof complete the picture.

Fascinating though the yard is, it is not until one enters the house itself that one gets a glimpse of the interior.

The motif throughout the whole house is one of antiquity. The wallpaper is mellow with age, and the ceilings have not been kalsomined for forty-seven years.

Hardly any of the doors shut properly, and the windows are held open by bright clean lemonade bottles.

Mrs Bowyang points with pride to an old meat safe which hangs in the drawing room, where the lodger sleeps.

There is a history attached to the old safe.

It was rescued from Mark Foy's big fire many years ago, and for a long time the parrot lived in it; but as the family grew the parrot had to be given away and the infant Bowyang sleeps in it now.

The old clock is another interesting relic. It was given to Mrs Bowyang by her mother, who was one of the Maloneys—the Woolloomooloo Maloneys who were so prominent in society a few years ago when the younger set ran a two-up school down at the wharves.

Though it has been in the family for many years—excepting occasional visits to the pawnshop—the alarm still works.

The bedroom furnishings are symbolic of that affectionate family life which seems to be fading into oblivion in these modern times. There are two double beds and a stretcher in the room, cleverly arranged so that one may walk from one bed to the other without climbing over.

Mr and Mrs Bowyang and little Jacky sleep in one double bed, the three youngest girls in the other, and Mr Bowyang's brother-in-law, who is out of work, sleeps in the stretcher.

Mrs Bowyang's hobbies are washing and mending, and some of the mending she does is nothing short of marvellous.

Business takes Mr Bowyang away every morning at 6.30, he being engaged in the sewer-digging profession; but he still finds time for his diversions, namely, washing up and placing tins where the rain comes in.

The younger children have a magnificent playground in Pelican Street, where they have a jolly time daubing themselves with mud, eating stray apple cores, and escaping being run over by passing lorries.

Viewed from the front, Mrs Bowyang's home is extremely attractive. It seems to attract all the dust in the streets, and although it has never been renovated since it was built, it is remarkably cheap for 25d a week, and the brass doorknob takes an excellent polish.

The writer was intrigued by the quaint, old world, worn-out, bashed-in atmosphere of the locality, and it was with great reluctance that he left. He lingered for a while, hoping to see the owner of Mrs Bowyang's residence, with the idea of strangling him when he saw him, but realising the futility of the idea he left.

SOLACE
FRANK DANIEL

Mary Martha Regan held her dying husband's hand.
Some forty years her senior, a proud and modest man.
For twenty years in wedded bliss he loved his Mary so—
This union saw a family—four sons were seen to grow.

The first three boys were big and strong, tall, solid and stout.
The fourth and youngest was a wimp, in looks he had missed out.
The old man cast a trusting eye towards his loving wife
And feebly whispered thanks to her for the good times in his life.

'But tell me—darlin' Mary, —please lay it on the line.
That skinny little bloke of ours—is he really mine?'
Mary squeezed his trembling hands then whispered in his ear.
'Yes, my love, he is your son, rest assured and have no fear.'

Old Regan closed his dimming eyes—life faded from his face,
Mary took a long deep breath and sighed, 'Oh, Saving Grace.
Thank God! He's gone with peace of mind, still with faith in me
And thank the Lord he didn't ask about the other three!'

DAD AND DAVE

No discussion of Aussie yarns and humour would be complete
without reference to Dad and Dave.

The iconic country bumpkins began life as much more serious
characters in the whimsical yarns about life on a selection on the
Darling Downs, written by Steele Rudd. His stories were so popular
that he had his own magazine, called simply *Steele Rudd*.

As time went by, Dad and Dave became caricatures and the Dad
and Dave yarns developed into more coarse and crude schoolyard
jokes. The radio program was set in Snake Gully. The southern
New South Wales town of Gundagai became associated with Dad
and Dave and Mum and Mabel due to the theme tune of the radio

show being the very popular song 'Along the Road to Gundagai' by Jack O'Hagen.

The Snake Gully version of Dad and Dave was more broadly humorous than the short stories, though not as crude and vulgar as the Dad and Dave jokes that we loved as kids.

An example of the middle ground type of Dad and Dave yarn is Dave saying to Dad, 'I met a beaut little bloke called "Thirty Mile in a Day Mick", Dad. He's a bullocky bloke.'

''Strewth, Dave,' says Dad, 'that's a helluva long name for a little bloke.'

'Well,' says Dave, 'they sometimes call him sumthin' else for short.'

'What do they call Thirty Mile in a Day Mick for short?' Dad asks.

Dave replies, 'They call him "Twenty-nine Mile in a Day Mick".'

JH

REAL BEAUT NEWS

Here is a Dad and Dave radio script, part of a series that Dennis O'Keefe and I presented at the Port Fairy Folk Festival a few years ago. For some strange reason, Dennis played the part of the stoic and sensible Dad and I played the idiotic Dave!

DAVE: G'day, Dad, I got some real beaut news.

DAD: Well, don't just stand there. What's the news?

DAVE: Well—Mabel's had a baby.

DAD: Well, stone the crows, Dave! You shoulda told me that straight off!

DAVE: Yeah, I know, but I was too excited.

DAD: Well, that's great news, Dave.

DAVE: Yeah, Dad, it's beaut—and 'ave a guess what kind she had.

DAD: Geez, Dave, I dunno—was it a boy?

DAVE: No. 'Ave another guess—

DAD: Strike a light, you're a fool, Dave! What was it then?

DAVE: 9 pound 10 ounces.

DAD: Was she in labour long, Dave?

DAVE: Aww, geez, Dad, don't be silly. She's always voted Country Party!

DAD: I give up! And, speaking of voting, don't forget the council elections today. You have to vote.

DAVE: Do I, Dad?

DAD: Of course you do, you damn fool. Don't you know voting's compulsory in Australia?

DAVE: Geez, Dad, is it? The man on the wireless said it was preferential.

DAD: Your mother and I raised an idiot! Of course you have to vote. You can vote down at the school.

DAVE: But me and Mabel are in another electrate, Dad.

DAD: You can still vote 'ere Dave—absentee.

DAVE: Geez, I dunno if I got time for tea, Dad. I gotta go and vote down at the school!   **JH**

GRAND FINAL DAY

Aussie yarns and humour contain a fair amount of racism and misogyny. I have avoided the racist yarns altogether, apart from a few mild migrant stereotypes, and I tried to avoid the more vulgar and crass misogynous ones, of which there are thousands. Hopefully, the few I have included here also have something to say about the nature of typical Aussie male attitudes and priorities. I hope readers will see that Aussie men, and their attitudes, are being made fun of in these yarns.

It's grand final day at the MCG.

The biggest sporting event of the year, with the obvious exception of the Melbourne Cup, is about to start. The umpire is about to bounce the ball.

Fred has been lucky enough to get a seat. He is excited and feeling pretty smug; seats are hard to get.

Yet, there beside him is an empty seat. He keeps looking at it and waiting to see who is running late for the big game and will be sitting beside him.

The hooter sounds twice, one minute to the bounce! There's still no one sitting beside him.

Fred looks across at the bloke one seat over. He looks a bit serious for Grand Final day, not as excited as the rest of the crowd.

'Nervous about his team's chances,' thinks Fred.

He smiles and the bloke smiles back weakly.

'I can't believe this,' says Fred, making conversation. 'The game is about to start and there's a spare seat!'

'Oh, I can explain that,' says the bloke two seats away. 'You see, that seat was for my wife. We bought two seats for the Grand Final at the start of the season but, sadly, she passed away.'

'Oh, that's terrible,' says Fred, 'so sorry to hear that, mate, but surely someone you know would have wanted the seat! How about your family members? All your friends? Even a neighbour?'

'No,' says the bloke sadly, 'not one of 'em wanted to come. They're all at the funeral.'   JH

EVERY CLOUD HAS A SILVER LINING

This one is even worse!

A retired bloke and his wife, the Johnsons, are doing the 'grey nomad' thing, travelling around in a campervan towing a small runabout fishing boat.

One day, while they are camping at a lovely isolated beach on the Western Australian coast, the wife takes a swim and goes missing while he's out in the boat fishing.

A distraught Mr Johnson searches and calls frantically and then drives to the nearest town and reports the tragedy to the local police sergeant in the little two-man police station.

Grief stricken, he returns to the campervan and drinks himself silly for a few days and nights.

One morning, a few days later, there's a knock at the campervan door. There is the sergeant in uniform and a younger constable in scuba gear.

The sergeant says, 'Mr Johnson, we have some news for you.'

'Oh,' says the old bloke, 'I guess it's all bad.'

'Well, yes,' says the sergeant slowly, 'unfortunately, some of it is really bad news, but some might be seen as good news, and maybe there will be some more good news.'

'Well,' says Mr Johnson stoically, 'I guess you'd better give me the bad news first.'

'I'm really sorry to inform you,' says the sergeant formally, 'that your wife is dead. The constable here found Mrs Johnson's body a few hours ago. It was caught in a cleft in the reef not far offshore in about 12 metres of water.

'We got a line around her and pulled her up to the surface. Of course there was nothing we could do, as she was quite dead.'

Mr Johnson sits for quite a while with his head bowed and sobs quietly. Then he makes an effort, shakes himself and pulls himself together and asks, 'You mentioned good news. What on earth could the good news be, Sergeant?'

'Well,' says the old copper slowly, 'when we got your wife up, there were quite a few really good sized crayfish and some nice crabs attached to her, so we've brought you your share.'

Then he goes to the police car and opens the boot, takes out a sugar bag and comes back and hands Mr Johnson the wet bag, which has a couple of nice crayfish and four or five crabs still alive inside.

'Well, thanks for that,' Johnson says, a little lost for words. 'That's very thoughtful of you. I haven't eaten in days. They are real beauties, too.'

'Well', says the sergeant slowly, 'there's a bit more good news, if you're interested.'

'Really, what's that?' asks Mr Johnson, still holding the bag.

'Well, if you're up for a boat ride, me and the young constable here get off duty in a few hours and, if the sea's calm enough, we thought we might shoot over there and pull her up again!'

JH

ARITHMETIC
TRADITIONAL/JIM HAYNES

Out on the side verandah, she tried to make her phone work,
To get the neighbour's son to come and do a bit of homework.
He soon got the message, and quickly sent a text to her,
Got on his bike quick as you like and soon was sitting next to her.

He said, 'Let's do mathematics.' He moved into position.
He kissed her once, he kissed her twice and said,
   'Now, that's addition.'
She thought she'd take those kisses back and get into the action,
She kissed him once, she kissed him twice and said,
   'Now that's subtraction.'

Then he kissed her and she kissed him, there was no hesitation,
You could tell that they were getting close to multiplication.
Then suddenly her dad arrived and made a quick decision.
Said, 'On your bike and take a hike!' and taught them
   long division.

'Hit the track and don't come back!' said Father with derision.
Kicked the boy's arse down the garden path and taught them
   long division.

DESERT ISLAND 1

One of those live sheep export boats sinks in the Indian Ocean
and only one crew member, one sheep dog and one sheep, a ewe,
survive. They are all washed up on a small atoll with grass and
coconut trees and birds and lots of fish to help them stay alive.

   The bloke builds a hut and finds food easily and starts to think
about the ewe in his lonelier moments. But every time he tries to
get the ewe alone and grab her, the dog moves between them and
snarls at him. This goes on for two years. The bloke is well fed
and sheltered but he keeps trying to get to the ewe, and the dog
never lets him.

One day, a pleasure boat is wrecked outside the reef in a storm, a swanky yacht with an all-girl crew.

There is just one survivor, a beautiful young woman who makes it onto the reef and collapses a few hundred metres from shore with the tide coming in fast.

The bloke swims out through the huge surf and manages to bring her back to life. Then he carries her back to shore, almost drowning in the process. He warms her and feeds her and nurses her back to health, finding food and caring for her day and night until she is well again.

When she has recovered enough to get up and walk about the island, she is so grateful she tells him,' You saved my life and I'll do anything I can to make you happy.'

'Anything?' he asks, surprised. 'Anything at all?'

'Yes,' she says, standing there in her torn shorts and bikini top, 'anything at all!'

'Gee, that's great!' says the bloke, 'because there is one thing you could do for me.'

'Gladly,' says the beautiful young woman, 'what is it?'

"Well,' says the bloke enthusiastically, 'you could take that dog for a long walk to the other end of the island.'   JH

DESERT ISLAND 2

A light spotter-plane flying around a desolate area of the Great Barrier Reef crashes into the sea and only one of the two customs officers on board survives.

He swims to a small atoll with grass and coconut trees and birds and lots of fish to help him stay alive, builds a hut and, after six months, he realises he is presumed dead and there's no chance of rescue.

One day, a cruise ship passes outside the reef in the dark and a famous entertainer on board is accosted by an obsessed and drunken fan. In a mad bid to escape sexual assault, she jumps overboard and her cries go unheeded as the ship sails on. It is Kylie Minogue!

When dawn breaks, she sees the island in the distance and swims towards it, yelling for help as her strength fails.

The bloke on the island hears her faint cries. He swims out through the surf and finds her just afloat. He pulls her back to the island, almost drowning in the process, carries her back to shore, warms her and feeds her and nurses her back to health.

Kylie recovers and is so grateful to him for saving her life that they form an immediate bond. They sit and talk and fall deeply in love.

Theirs is a perfect existence, they have food, shelter, love and companionship, but one day Kylie finds him sitting on the rocks by the beach, sadly staring out to sea.

She is worried and asks what is wrong.

'Oh, it's nothing, really,' he replies sadly, 'my life is perfect here with you, except . . .'

'What is it then?' asks a concerned Kylie.

'Well, I am an Aussie bloke, and there is one thing I really miss,' he says despondently.

'What is it that you need?' asks Kylie. 'I'll do anything to make you happy.'

'Well, there is one thing you could do, if you don't mind,' he says hesitantly.

'Anything, just ask,' says Kylie.

'Well, could you dress up like a bloke for me? Put on my clothes and paint on a charcoal moustache?'

'Sure,' says Kylie, 'whatever your desires are, darling, that's okay with me. Don't be ashamed or shy, just tell me what you want.'

'Well, could you go into those trees and then wander out and pretend to be a mate of mine?' he asks.

'Of course, that's easy,' says Kylie.

So, she does just that. Dressed as a bloke she walks into the trees and then strolls out and says, 'G'day, mate. How are ya going?'

The bloke walks to her briskly and says, 'G'day, mate, I'm terrific . . . and guess who I'm rooting!'

JH

THE LIARS
HENRY E. HORNE

Ten boys sat in a ring and played at telling lies,
An outback pastime, with a strayed young dog for prize.
The parson they informed, who strolled to see their fun,
The pup was for the cove who told the biggest one.

The good old man looked upon that ring of boys and sighed.
'I'm sorry to hear such a thing as this,' he cried.
'I never dared to tell a lie, nor ever knew,
Such sinful sport, my lads, when I was young like you.'

Ten faces fell, not from shame, but sheer defeat;
Ten little liars dropped the game, for they were beat.
Ten boys arose—a sullen band—quite broken up;
And Jim, the judge, said, 'Billy, hand the bloke the pup.'

REAL AUSSIE CHARACTERS

Whatever the group doing the yarn spinning, it's funnier if you know the character involved, whether it's a grumpy old uncle, or a nervous young nephew, or crazy old auntie, a legendary old character in your workplace or the office sad sack!

The best yarns are those about great characters, people with strong or unusual elements to their nature—things that often lead them into conflict with more mainstream elements of society.

This is my personal favourite of all the sections in this book, because all the characters in the yarns here are people for whom I have a great deal of affection or respect. This section is really made up of a collection of my personal heroes from our past.

Some, like William Dawes, I consider to be true heroes, men of principle who stood up against the odds and conventions of the time and achieved great things in spite of being ahead of their time.

Others are heroes of mine because of what they achieved, like Annette Kellerman, Hubert Wilkins, J.F. Archibald, Barney the Builder and Francis Greenway. Those last three, and many of the others in here, were all odd characters in some way with a Shakespearian character flaw or two that made them truly fascinating people.

Some, like Sam Poo, John Knatchbull and Henry Despard did such stupid things that you would shake your head and wonder what on earth they were thinking when they did the things that make them so sadly memorable generations later.

Some of these characters simply had personality to burn and achieved wonderful things—like Larry Foley, Billy Hughes and Smoky Dawson. Others were true eccentrics whose lives seem bizarre to us merely 'normal' people.

Most Australians are fairly conventional in social attitude and find characters who live their lives to a totally different set of rules fascinating. We love reading yarns about unconventional people like Billy Blue, Quong Tart and Breaker Morant.

When it comes to the true eccentrics, like Bea Miles, Arthur Stace and Percy Grainger, I think we find their lives so weird compared to ours that yarns about their odd lives are really interesting. We all have a certain affection, I think, for the truly eccentric people who brighten up, and help to shake up, the societies in which we live.

All these characters are real and the yarns are all true. They all fascinate and amuse me and a few of them have inspired me. I wish I had met them all but I only ever met two of them.

Smoky Dawson was one of them. He was a good mate and it was a pleasure and a privilege to know him.

And, when I was a small boy, Bea Miles travelled on a tram with my mother and me and told Mum that I was a 'lovely little boy with a bright future'. I remember seeing her on trams quite a few times with her sign around her neck that said she'd recite lines from Shakespeare for threepence and whole speeches for ninepence. Needless to say, she never paid her tram fare.

WILLIAM DAWES

The Man Who Wouldn't Collect Heads

Dawes Point, in Sydney Harbour, is named after a remarkable man.

William Dawes was born in Portsmouth in 1762 and joined the Royal Marines at seventeen. He was wounded in the battle of Chesapeake Bay during the American War of Independence.

Dawes was a self-taught astronomer and was recommended by the Astronomer Royal, Reverend Nevil Maskelyne to join the First Fleet. He helped navigate during the voyage and set up an observatory in a hut on what is now Dawes Point.

The Aboriginal name for Dawes Point, Tullagalla, was at first changed to Point Maskelyne in honour of the Astronomer Royal. It was the site of the first guns mounted in Sydney, which were carried out on HMS *Sirius*, and was the site of the first observatory and the first cemetery.

Dawes was the first European to explore the Blue Mountains and the first to make extensive written records of Aboriginal languages, and to realise that each tribe had a separate language.

He was also the first European on record to defend Aboriginal rights. In December 1790, in retribution for the killing of his gamekeeper, Governor Arthur Phillip ordered several marines, including Dawes, to capture two Aborigines from the Bideegàl tribe and to sever the heads of ten males.

The gamekeeper, McIntyre, had reputedly killed and mistreated some Aborigines. Dawes refused to participate in the retaliation and was arrested for disobeying the order.

Phillip then changed the order to the 'capture of six men, to be shot if they could not be captured'. After talking with the Reverend Richard Johnson, Dawes took part in the expedition, which failed to find any Aborigines.

Dawes subsequently declared to Phillip that he regretted taking part and would never 'collect heads' for anyone. He refused to make the apology demanded by Phillip and was not granted leave to remain as a settler in New South Wales.

He was given no land and was sent back to England in December 1791. Dawes applied for positions in the colony of New South Wales several times, but was never allowed to come back. He went to Africa and was three times governor of the colony of Sierra Leone where he became involved in the campaign to abolish slavery.

He later moved to Antigua, undertook unpaid work for the Church Missionary Society and established schools for the children of slaves. He died there in 1836.   **JH**

FRANCIS GREENWAY

The Arrogant Convict

Francis Greenway was born near Bristol in 1777 into a family of masons, architects and builders. He was 1.6 metres tall, broad, with hazel eyes, auburn hair and a ruddy complexion. He oozed self-confidence, was artistic, temperamental and quick to take offence and to anger. He seems to have been the epitome of a bloke with 'small man syndrome'.

Greenway became an architect 'of some eminence' in Bristol and nearby Bath. His only remaining building in the United Kingdom is the magnificent Clifton Club. He also designed Christ Church, Downend.

In 1809, Greenway and his brothers became bankrupt over a failed housing development and, in 1812, he pleaded guilty 'under the advice of his friends', to forging a document—it seems to have been a document of agreement forged in order to protect his character in the bankruptcy case.

He was sentenced to death; this sentence was later commuted to fourteen years' transportation; and he spent time in the hulks awaiting transportation.

Greenway had been friendly with Admiral Arthur Phillip who was living in retirement at Bath, and Phillip wrote a letter to Governor Macquarie recommending Greenway to him.

Greenway arrived in Sydney, on the transport *General Hewitt* in February 1814; his wife and children followed on another ship.

He commenced work as a colonial architect by designing houses and additions to houses. Greenway first met Macquarie in July 1814 and Macquarie suggested he construct a town hall and courthouse and gave Greenway an instruction book to follow.

Greenway was so offended by this that he responded with a letter declaring his skills and suggesting his Excellency should utilise the opportunity for a better, more classical design. He stated, '. . . it is rather painful to my mind as a professional man to copy a building that has no claim to classical proportion and character.'

In 1816, Greenway was involved in an incident with Captain Sanderson. He had designed and decorated a series of Masonic aprons for members of the local military Masonic Lodge but had not finished Captain Sanderson's apron in time for a special event.

A letter of apology from Greenway angered the Captain who sent for Greenway and attacked him with a horsewhip. Greenway could not defend himself against an officer as he was a convict. He brought a case against Sanderson, won and was awarded damages of five pounds. The main problem was that Greenway was seen as an upstart felon who dared to engage on equal terms with officers. He was never very politically clever or diplomatic.

Between 1816 and 1818, while still a convict, Greenway was responsible for the design and construction of the Macquarie

Lighthouse near The Gap. It was later pulled down and the present replica was built in 1880.

After the success of this project, he was given his ticket of leave and began acting as Civil Architect and Assistant Engineer responsible to Captain Gill, Inspector of Public Works, on a salary of three shillings a day. He was given a house to live in—in George Street—and went on to build many significant buildings in the new colony.

Greenway's buildings included Hyde Park Barracks, Government House stables, the Parramatta Female Factory, St James' Church, St Matthew's, Windsor, and St Luke's, Liverpool. There are still forty-nine buildings in central Sydney attributed to Greenway's designs. He was given a full pardon by Governor Macquarie in 1819.

Greenway was an important citizen, but his arrogance made him misjudge his authority. He made many enemies and eventually fell out with Macquarie. He had financial worries and attempted to charge fees for the designs and for the work he had done while employed by Macquarie. He also asked for a land grant and cattle.

After he was dismissed by the next governor, Thomas Brisbane, in 1822, he continued to follow his profession with little success. Although he got his grant of land, at Maitland, he does not appear to have received the cattle.

In 1835, he advertised, 'Francis Howard Greenway, arising from circumstances of a singular nature is induced again to solicit the patronage of his friends and the public.' In other words, he was destitute.

His long-suffering wife, Mary, looked after him and their five children and ran a school for young ladies to make ends meet. Governor Macquarie described her as a pleasant and respectable lady.

After Mary died in 1826, Greenway attempted to sell the house he had been given to live in by Macquarie but the government took back the house saying he had no right to sell it.

Greenway died at his Maitland property, probably of typhoid in 1837, aged fifty-nine. The exact date of his death is not known.

He was buried in East Maitland cemetery on 25 September 1837, but his grave is unmarked. **JH**

JAMES HARDY VAUX

Who Was Transported Three Times

James Hardy Vaux was born in Surrey, England, in 1782, the son of a butler and house steward to George Holme Sumner MP, and was raised by his maternal grandparents who had retired to Shropshire after his grandfather had spent his life working in Fleet Prison as warden.

James Vaux was apprenticed twice, to a linen draper in Liverpool and a legal firm in Lincoln's Inn, but was dismissed both times for 'dissipation'.

In 1798, he joined the navy and served in the North Sea, but then he deserted and worked for a Covent Garden clothing firm until he became a professional thief and was sentenced at the Old Bailey to transportation for seven years for stealing a handkerchief, valued by the jury at elevenpence so that the accused might escape a capital sentence (one shilling and you were hanged).

Vaux reached Sydney in December 1801 and worked as a clerk at the Hawkesbury, in Sydney and in Parramatta. He served a term in the road gang for forging Governor King's signature but ingratiated himself with Samuel Marsden, the Parramatta chaplain and magistrate, who agreed to take him home in the *Buffalo* in 1807.

On the trip home Vaux was employed on board in writing King's log and in teaching his and Marsden's children but, when his sentence expired, he became insubordinate and was compelled to enlist as a seaman.

When the ship reached Portsmouth, Vaux deserted and resumed his old activities in London. On 21 July at St Paul's, Covent Garden, he married Mary Ann Thomas, a prostitute, in the hope that, if he were again transported, she might be allowed as his wife to join him in New South Wales.

In December, he narrowly escaped a further conviction, this time for stealing a snuffbox but, in February 1809, he was sentenced to death at the Old Bailey under the alias James Lowe for stealing from a jeweller's shop in Piccadilly.

This sentence was commuted to transportation for life and he reached Sydney in December 1810. Assigned to a Hawkesbury settler and then appointed deputy-overseer of the town gang in Sydney, he was sentenced in 1811 to twelve months' hard labour for receiving property stolen from Judge-Advocate Bent.

He was sent to the Newcastle penal settlement. In January 1814, after returning to Sydney, he was caught while trying to escape aboard the *Earl Spencer* and was flogged and returned to Newcastle.

During his previous spell there, Vaux had compiled a slang dictionary for the use of magistrates, and he was now encouraged to write the famous *Memoirs of the First Thirty-Two Years of the Life of James Hardy Vaux, a Swindler and Pickpocket; Now Transported for the Second Time, and for Life, to New South Wales.*

Published in London, Vaux received £33 18s 8d in royalties. The *Memoirs* were republished by John Hunt in 1827 and reprinted in 1829 and 1830. As the first full-length autobiography written in Australia, the book provides a fascinating picture of criminal life in London and of the penal system, while the *Vocabulary of the Flash Language*, probably the first dictionary compiled in Australia, gives a valuable glossary of London slang. In 1827, the *London Magazine* described the work as 'one of the most singular that ever issued from the press'.

On 3 August 1818 at Newcastle, Vaux married Frances Sharkey, a former Irish convict. The next month, he was allowed to return to Sydney as a clerk. In January 1820, he received a conditional pardon and soon became a clerk in the colonial secretary's office.

In April 1827, he married Eleanor Bateman, another Irish convict, although Frances Vaux was still alive. At the end of 1826, Governor Darling dismissed Vaux in accordance with his policy of not employing convicts and ex-convicts as clerks.

Vaux broke the terms of his conditional pardon and went to Ireland, where, in August 1830 at Dublin, he was convicted once more under the alias James Young, this time for passing forged bank notes.

He pleaded guilty and, with the cooperation of the bank concerned, his death sentence was commuted to transportation for seven years. On his arrival at Sydney in the *Waterloo* in May 1831, he was recognised, his previous life sentence was revived and he was sent to Port Macquarie penal settlement.

In 1837, he was allowed to return to Sydney and became clerk to a wine merchant. In May 1839, he was charged with criminal assault on a girl aged about eight. He was sentenced to two years' imprisonment, and, although Governor Gipps decided that his life sentence should be reapplied, he was released in 1841 on the recommendation of Chief Justice Dowling and disappeared from history.

He is the only convict known to have been transported three times to New South Wales. **JH**

CAPTAIN PIPER

Who Fathered Eighteen Children by Five Different Woman

Born in 1773 in Ayrshire, Scotland, the son of a doctor, John Piper's uncle got him a commission in the New South Wales Corps in 1791 and he arrived in Sydney in February 1792, when the settlement was still fighting for its life in the face of starvation.

He became friendly with John Macarthur, who secured him a land grant of 110 acres (45 hectares) at Parramatta, but in 1793 was sent on duty to Norfolk Island, possibly because of a sexual 'entanglement' from which friends were anxious to rescue him.

In 1795, Piper returned. He left for Scotland in 1797 and returned in 1800, promoted to captain. He acted as MacArthur's second in his duel with Colonel Patterson in 1801 and apologised and was acquitted at his court-martial in 1802.

From 1804 to 1810, he was acting commandant on Norfolk Island and so missed the Rum Rebellion. His rule was mild, and he 'had the good will and respect of everyone, for he had always conducted himself as a Christian and a gentleman'.

On Norfolk Island, however, he formed an attachment to Mary Ann Shears, the fifteen-year-old daughter of a convict and, when he sailed for Britain on leave in September 1811, he took along

Mary Ann, their two little boys and his daughter from an earlier liaison. His personal life caused problems with both his family and his career, but he evidently preferred Mary Ann and resigned from this commission and returned to Sydney in 1814 after being appointed the colony's naval officer in 1813.

As the collector of customs duties, excise on spirits and harbour dues, with a percentage on all monies collected, his income exceeded £4000 a year, and he bought the property now known as Vaucluse House. On 10 February 1816, he married Mary Ann by special licence. She had borne him two more sons while they were away and in due course they had nine more children.

Also in 1816, he was granted 190 acres (77 hectares) of land on Eliza Point, now Point Piper, for the site of his official residence. Here he built Henrietta Villa (also known as the Naval Pavilion) at a cost of £10,000. Extravagantly furnished, it was completed in 1822 and became the scene of many sumptuous entertainments.

Piper was a close friend of Governor Macquarie, who in 1819 made him a magistrate. In 1825, he was chairman of directors of the Bank of New South Wales, president of the Scots Church committee and, besides Point Piper, he had 475 acres (192 hectares) at Vaucluse, 1130 acres (457 hectares) at Woollahra and Rose Bay, a farm of 295 acres (119 hectares) at Petersham, 700 acres (283 hectares) at Neutral Bay, 80 acres (32 hectares) at Botany Bay, 2000 acres (809 hectares) at Bathurst, 300 acres (121 hectares) in Van Diemen's Land with various smaller farms, and an acre (0.4 hectares) of city land in George Street.

In 1825, the new Governor, Ralph Darling, ordered an enquiry into Piper's administration as naval officer and a deficiency of £12,000 was discovered. The collection of customs had been gravely mismanaged.

Piper tried to drown himself in the harbour but was rescued by his loyal servants who evidently saw him jump out of a small boat into the harbour and, knowing he could not swim, rushed out to save him.

In 1826, he mortgaged his property for £20,000 and eventually was forced to sell his Point Piper estate, Vaucluse and city properties, farms and shares in the midst of a financial recession. He sold the lot (a huge chunk of Sydney's now prestigious eastern suburbs) for only £5170 11s, but his debts to the government and others were paid in full.

Piper retired with his large family to his Bathurst property, Alloway Bank, where he raised cattle and sheep and started cheese production. He became a magistrate, worked for the Presbyterian Church and patronised horseracing.

The drought of 1838 forced him to sell Alloway Bank and move to Westbourne, a 202-hectare property beside the Macquarie River. There he died in 1851, and there Mrs Piper lived until her death twenty years later, with her numerous children.

John Piper, stalwart of the Presbyterian Church who, according to official records, had 'always conducted himself as a Christian and a gentleman', fathered eighteen children, thirteen by Mary Ann and five by four other women.   **JH**

BILLY BLUE

The Old Commodore

By 1810, a series of rowboat ferrymen had set up businesses to transport people around Sydney Harbour and from one side to the other. The most famous of these was Billy Blue, who was given the name 'The Old Commodore' by Governor Macquarie.

Billy was probably born in Jamaica and he claimed to have served with the British army in the American War of Independence. Quite possibly he was an African–American slave from colonial New York who had been granted his freedom.

In 1796, Billy was living at Deptford, London, loading ships at the docks and making and selling toffee and chocolate as a sideline. He was convicted of stealing sugar from the docks and sentenced to seven years' transportation. Described in convict records as 'a Jamaican Negro sailor aged 29', he spent four years in the hulks before he was sent to Sydney on the *Minorca*.

He had two years of his sentence left when he arrived in December 1801, and was soon working on the harbour with boats and selling oysters. His friendly, eccentric manner and humorous conversation made him popular and he became a 'character' in the colony.

Billy married English-born convict Elizabeth Williams in 1805 at St Philip's Church and they had six children. Appointed harbour watchman and constable in 1811, he was granted 80 acres (32 hectares) on the north side of the harbour from where he operated his ferry service. The area is still known as Blue's Point.

A colourful character in the true Australian meaning of the word, Billy spent a year in prison for smuggling rum in 1818 and lost his position as harbour watchman and constable. He was later also found guilty of harbouring escaped convicts and, on another occasion, manslaughter. A boy who was teasing Billy died after The Old Commodore threw a rock at him. Billy was not goaled for either offence.

Billy grew vegetables for the Sydney market and he ran his ferry dressed in a blue naval officer's coat and top hat. He died in 1834 at his North Sydney home. Although he would have been sixty-seven according to convict records, he claimed to be eighty in the 1828 census, which would make him eighty-six when he died. Five of his six children survived him and he has many descendants living in Sydney today.   **JH**

THE FLYING PIEMAN

The Eccentric and Athletic Entrepreneur

William King was aged twenty-two when he emigrated to Sydney as a free settler in 1829. It is thought he was sent out here by his family because he was quite eccentric.

King worked as a schoolteacher and baker before becoming our first true sporting entrepreneur. In an effort to sell his pies and pastries, he attempted odd sporting feats and advertised them, on the assumption that a curious crowd at such events would eventually get hungry and buy his wares. Outdoor sporting and entertainment events were rare in the colony in the early decades of the nineteenth century, apart from the odd race meeting and the public executions, which attracted enormous crowds.

In 1847, King walked 309 kilometres around Maitland racetrack non-stop—a feat that took him forty-six hours and thirty minutes. He walked from Campbelltown to Sydney carrying a dog in less than nine hours, and that is 53 kilometres!

As well as making a profit from the sale of the pies and cakes, he made a decent amount of money from taking bets on his bizarre feats. He bet that he could beat the mail coach from Sydney to Windsor, and succeeded. Then he beat the Brisbane to Ipswich mail coach by an hour carrying a pole weighing a hundred pounds (45 kilograms).

He once backed himself to run a mile (1.6 kilometres), walk a mile, wheel a barrow for a mile, pull a gig with a lady in it a half mile, walk backwards half a mile, pick up fifty stones and perform fifty jumps in under an hour.

So confident was the man who was now known in the colonies as 'The Flying Pieman', that he took rest breaks, which took up five minutes and fifteen seconds. It was a close call at the end of the hour, but he managed all those feats and won the bet with forty-five seconds to spare!

As his athletic abilities faded, he took to using his reputation to attract customers, selling his pies and pastries on the streets of Sydney wearing a top hat decorated with brightly coloured ribbons. Sadly, his eccentricity turned to mental instability and he was sent to the Liverpool asylum, where he died in 1873. **JH**

SIR HENRY DESPARD

His Inglorious Career

Henry Despard was an overbearing martinet whose place in Australian colonial military history was established by two major errors of judgement. He seems to have been the archetypal upper-class twit. His military tactics were decades out of date and his attitude towards the lower classes, other races and lower ranks was mind-bogglingly snobbish and reactionary, even by the standards of his time.

Born in 1784 in Devon, England, Despard was commissioned as an ensign in the 17th Regiment of Foot in 1799. He saw active service in several campaigns in India between 1808 and 1818, became a brigade major in 1817 and a lieutenant colonel in 1829, and was inspecting officer of the Bristol recruiting district from 1838 to 1842. In 1842 he took command of the 99th Regiment of Foot, stationed in Sydney.

On 1 June 1845, Despard and two companies of his regiment arrived in Auckland in response to an appeal for assistance by Governor Robert FitzRoy after attacks by Maoris led by Chief Hone Heke. Despard was given the temporary rank of colonel and took command of all British troops in New Zealand. On 8 June he sailed for the Bay of Islands with more than 600 men, the largest British force ever seen in New Zealand. They established a base at the Waimate mission station and began to bombard Ohaeawai, the first Maori *pa* designed to resist artillery fire. Its hundred-strong garrison was protected by a complex of bunkers and trenches.

On 1 July, the Maoris made a daring attack, which prompted Despard to attack that afternoon, although no real breach had been made in the stockade, using old-fashioned Napoleonic war tactics with his troops advancing shoulder to shoulder.

The attack of the British force made no impression on the virtually undamaged main stockade, and Despard was forced to order a recall. More than 120 of Despard's men were killed or wounded in this action. Despard at first blamed his men's failure to carry axes and other tools as he had ordered but he later conceded that his plan had had little chance of success.

Despard then attempted to negotiate a peaceful settlement but failed. Although he had a force of around 1300 British troops, several hundred Maori warriors and substantial artillery support, the northern war ended soon after without any British victories and Despard returned to New South Wales.

Despard's performance during the campaigns of 1845 was woeful. He was impatient and obstinate and had a contempt for the Maori, which led him to underestimate them. When Maori chief Waaka Nene offered his services to help the British, Despard replied that, when he 'required the assistance of savages', he would ask for it. Despard suffered from neuralgia and bad temper. His decision to attack Ohaeawai was one of the most incompetent and tragic in British military history—prompted more by a fit of temper than by any military considerations.

The position of commander of British troops during the northern war had been given to a man of sixty who had not seen active service for nearly thirty years and was unequal to the task. He was to soon be involved in the mutiny of an entire regiment. (see page 210) Yet, on 2 July 1846, Despard was knighted for his services and, in 1854, he was promoted to major general. He then retired from the army.

He died at Heavitree, Devon in 1859.   **JH**

JOHN KNATCHBULL

Who Pleaded Insanity

One of the biggest events in Sydney in the 1840s was the hanging of the nobly born criminal Captain John Knatchbull on 13 February 1844.

In January 1844, John Knatchbull went into the shop of a poor widow, Ellen Jamieson and, while she was serving him, he raised a tomahawk and 'clove the unfortunate woman's head in a savage manner'. She died after a few days, leaving two orphan children.

John Knatchbull was the son of country squire Sir Edward Knatchbull who married three times and had at least twenty children. John was sent to Winchester School, joined the navy in 1804, served with distinction and became a lieutenant and later a captain. He incurred bad debts in the navy and in 1824 was convicted of stealing with force and arms. He was sentenced to transportation for fourteen years.

Knatchbull's career was a series of ups and downs. Appointed as constable in the colony of New South Wales, he was given a ticket of leave in 1829 after apprehending eight runaways, but was then charged with forging Judge Dowling's signature to a cheque and sentenced to death. This was commuted to transportation for seven years to Norfolk Island, where he became partially crippled.

In 1834, he planned a mutiny and then turned informer and the twenty-nine other mutineers were sentenced to death. Judge Sir William Burton told the magistrate, who accepted Knatchbull's evidence, '. . . he was the chief of the mutineers . . . You have saved his life, or prolonged it. He never can do good.'

Knatchbull returned to Sydney in May 1839 to serve the remainder of his original fourteen years, received a ticket of leave in 1842 and, in January 1844, was arrested for the murder of Mrs Jamieson, having been found in the house with her body, with her purse and money in his hands.

An attempt was made to plead insanity, by Robert Lowe, Viscount Sherbrooke, a barrister who argued that insanity of the will could exist apart from insanity of the intellect; it was a novel defence for the time and the first time that moral insanity had been used as a defence. Lowe argued that Knatchbull had yielded to an irresistible impulse and could not be held responsible for his crime.

The court, however, found Knatchbull guilty. The Lowes subsequently adopted the murdered woman's two young children, Bobby and Polly Jamieson, and the murderer's brother, Sir Edward Knatchbull, sent out a handsome donation for the orphans.

In another weird turn of events, Knatchbull appealed unsuccessfully on the grounds that the judge had not directed that his body be dissected and anatomised, as required by law.

On 13 February 1844, 10,000 people witnessed the execution outside the gates of the three-year-old Darlinghurst Gaol. Captain John Knatchbull, aged fifty-six years, was led out into Forbes Street, at the gaol gates, and then 'ascended the fatal scaffold without trepidation or fear, and was launched into another world with a noble and fervent prayer trembling on his lips'.

The bell of St Phillip's tolled three times and John Knatchbull was dead.

JH

TEDDY DAVIS

Our Only Jewish Bushranger

Edward 'Jewboy' Davis (1816–41), was a convict who, in 1832 at the Old Bailey, under the name George Wilkinson, was sentenced to transportation for seven years for having attempted to steal a wooden till, valued at two shillings, and copper coins to the value of five shillings.

Davis arrived in Sydney in 1833 on the *Camden* and was put to work at Hyde Park Barracks. He escaped and was caught and sentenced to a further twelve months. In 1835, he escaped from a farm he was working on at Penrith and another twelve months was added to his term. He was assigned to a farmer at Hexham, but ran away a third time, and two more years were added to his sentence. He was caught, but in July 1838 he escaped a fourth time and formed a bushranger gang of runaway convicts.

For two years, his gang robbed settlers from Maitland down to Gosford. Davis sported curious tattoos and the gang wore colourful clothes and tied ribbons to their horses' bridles. Davis insisted his gang be courteous to women and he gave some of what he took from the richer squatters to their convict servants. His rule was 'no violence except to avoid capture'.

In December 1840, the inevitable happened. While the gang was robbing shops at Scone, a storekeeper's clerk fired a shot, and gang member John Shea killed him. Realising that now murder had been committed, the game was up, the gang fled to one of their hide-outs, Doughboy Hollow near Murrurundi.

A posse led by police magistrate Edward Day tracked them down and a gunfight took place. A bullet from Davis grazed Day's ear and Davis was wounded in the shoulder. Six of the gang were captured and taken to Sydney Gaol.

Shea was found guilty of murder, and the others were accused of aiding and abetting Shea. Davis' counsel tried to save his life by pointing out that he was not present at the murder, but the jury found all prisoners guilty and they were hanged.

There was much public sympathy for Davis, who was repentant and accepting of his fate, and many settlers appealed for a reprieve. On 16 March 1841, Davis was hanged, in the presence of a rabbi from Sydney Synagogue, at the rear of the old Sydney gaol on the corner of George Street and Sussex Street, together with his gang. He was buried in the Jewish portion of the Devonshire Street cemetery.

Davis seems to have been our only Jewish bushranger on record.

JH

FRANK GARDINER

King of the Road

Frank Gardiner's origins are shrouded in mystery. He was either born in Scotland in 1829 and migrated to Australia as a child with his parents in 1834, or he was born in the Boro Creek settlement near Goulburn in the early 1830s. His real name is thought to have been Francis Christie, though he often used one of several other aliases: Frank Clarke, Frank Christie, The Darkie, The Prince of Tobymen, General Gardiner and King of the Road.

He supposedly took the name Gardiner after a man who lived for some years with his family and who had taught him how to ride and break in horses. Although almost all legends state that his real name is Francis Christie, or Clarke, or even Girard, the famous outlaw himself signed his name 'Francis Gardiner, the Highwayman'. He even used the surname Gardiner while in America, and he remains perhaps the most mysterious Australian bushranger.

In 1862, he bailed up the Lachlan gold escort at Eugowra with Ben Hall and John Gilbert—the largest ever gold robbery in Australian history. The total value of the 2700 ounces of gold taken was estimated at two million dollars in today's terms. Almost half of the gold was recovered following a raid on Gardiner's hide-out in the Weddin Range near Forbes. The remainder was never found but it is rumoured that two Americans, who were thought to be Gardiner's sons, visited the Wheogo Station near the Weddins in 1911. Local legend says they had a map and shovels.

In early 1864, Gardiner was recognised working as a shopkeeper near Rockhampton, apprehended by New South Wales police operating outside their jurisdiction and sentenced to thirty-two years' hard labour. Gardiner served ten years and then successful appeals by his two sisters and public support saw him granted early release, conditional on his leaving the country.

The only Australian ever to have been exiled from his country, he left for Hong Kong in 1874 and ended up in San Francisco where he owned the Twilight Star Saloon. The circumstances of his death are not known due to the destruction caused during the 1906 earthquake. He may have died in 1904 of pneumonia.   **JH**

SAM POO

Australia's Only Chinese Bushranger

In 1865, Sam Poo was scratching over old worked-out claims on the Talbragar goldfields, near Mudgee, when he decided to try the less arduous, if more risky, profession of criminal. Having left the Chinese camp and living alone, he continuously practised shooting at an old stump near his camp.

One morning, diggers were alarmed by the news that a Chinaman had robbed and assaulted a woman on the Mudgee Road and was 'bailing up' travellers. Constable Ward of Coonabarabran hastened along to the Mudgee Road and met two men who had been held up by a Chinaman just an hour previously. After some hard riding, Ward saw a Chinaman on foot, carrying a gun, but the man also saw the constable and ran off the road into the bush.

Ward gave chase. He soon caught up and called out, 'Put down that gun.'

The Chinaman said, 'Me fire; you policeman.'

Ward jumped off his horse, drew his revolver and again told Sam to 'put down his gun'. Sam fired point blank at the constable, severely wounding him in the side. As he fell, Ward fired, but the Chinaman ran off into the bush. Ward would have bled to death but for the lucky arrival of a Mr Plunkett, who owned Talbragar Station, where the incident had taken place, and was out looking for stock. Ward was taken to the homestead and a man was sent on horseback for the nearest doctor, 80 kilometres away. When the doctor arrived next day, Ward was dead.

Meanwhile, the whole countryside was out looking for Sam Poo. Mounted police scoured the bush and an Aboriginal stockman named Harry Hughes tracked Sam down weeks later. A gunfight took place. Sam was shot through the neck and body with shotgun pellets and captured.

Next day he was taken to Mudgee, where his wounds were treated in the hospital. He was not expected to recover, but he did and was taken to Bathurst, where he was tried, convicted and hanged, nine months after his arrest at Mudgee.

So ended the brief career of the only Chinese bushranger ever known in Australia.   **JH**

BARNEY THE BUILDER

The Empire's 'Mr Fixit'

George Barney was the British Empire's 'Mr Fixit'. He was born in 1792 and his father was drawing master at the Royal Military Academy, Woolwich. George Barney joined the Royal Engineers in 1808 and served in the Peninsular War and in the West Indies, where he had several years experience of civil engineering.

Promoted to captain in 1813, Barney married Portia Henrietta Peale in Grenada, West Indies, in 1817. He built wharves and harbours in Britain and the West Indies. Wherever civil and military works were needed around the empire, they sent for Captain (later Colonel) Barney.

He arrived in Sydney with his wife and three children in December 1835 with a detachment of Royal Engineers. Governor Bourke put him in charge of 'fixing up Sydney'. His dream was to straighten out the streets of the town.

Among Barney's many achievements were the removal of obstructions to navigation in the Parramatta River and the building of the 'semi-circular quay' at Sydney Cove, forever after known by the ridiculous abbreviated name of Circular Quay. He also constructed a breakwater at Newcastle, the harbour at Wollongong, the beautiful and functional Victoria Barracks and he repaired roads and bridges throughout the colony.

In 1836, Barney reported that the defences of Sydney were 'in a very dilapidated state' and in 1839, after Sydney had woken up one morning to find five American ships anchored in the harbour, he reported that measures were needed to protect the ports of New South Wales against 'desultory attacks from foreign cruisers'.

Barney recommended that £5000 and two more engineer officers be provided for the construction of batteries and blockhouses for the defence of Sydney, Newcastle, Wollongong, Port Macquarie and Port Phillip.

The British government agreed to send out one additional officer, but would not adopt the plans for defence works. Governor Gipps, however, himself an officer of engineers, had already allotted Barney, now a major, 140 convict labourers, who were at work clearing sites for guns at Pinchgut Island and Bradley's Head in Sydney Harbour.

George Street barracks was disposed of and a new site allotted in Paddington, where in 1841 the building of new barracks (Victoria Barracks) was begun under Barney's supervision. They were occupied in 1848.

Pinchgut Island was quite a high and imposing island until Barney stripped the rock from it and levelled the island to build the famous fort. The new governor, Denison, reverted to Barney's plan for Pinchgut and the keystone in the base of the tower at Fort Denison was laid by Barney on 24 July 1856 and the fort completed in 1857. It cost over £15,000 to complete and the British treasury was furious. Fort Denison never fired a shot in anger and if the cannons had ever been fired anyone in the tower would have been deafened for life.

Barney died at St Leonards, Sydney, in 1862 and is buried in St Thomas' cemetery. His wife died twenty years later. They had one son and four daughters.

And the rock that was quarried from the island? Well, it was used to build the 'semi-circular quay'! He never did straighten out the streets of Sydney.   **JH**

J.F. ARCHIBALD

The Fake French Visionary

John Feltham Archibald (1856–1919) was the son of a Warrnambool policeman and historian. His mother died when he was young and this left him as a rather sad and dreamy child. He worked on a local paper then went to Melbourne and re-created himself as a Frenchman, Jules François, and revised his family history, making his mother both French and Jewish.

Archibald travelled to Cooktown on a steamer, lived in a hut with miners and with them survived a food shortage, snakebite and an outbreak of fever. The adventure lasted probably only a few months, but it was his one real experience of Australian frontier life.

Archibald drifted to Sydney, worked on a few newspapers and eventually founded *The Bulletin* with John Haynes in Sydney in 1880. After three years of working twenty hours a day to make the magazine a success, Archibald went to London where he met a young Jewish woman, Rosa Frankenstein. His time in London only strengthened his anti-British feelings and he was back in Sydney in 1885. Rosa followed him and they married in November 1885.

Archibald became a wealthy and influential man due to the success of the *Bulletin* and he and Rosa lived in a luxurious home in Darling Point. Rosa lost a baby and the marriage was never a happy one. She eventually drank herself to death and Archibald was in Callan Park Mental Hospital several times—but he recovered and died a wealthy man in 1919.

The Bulletin was anti-British and helped Australians to develop a sense of being Australian. Archibald helped to start the careers of just about *every* great Australian writer and cartoonist from 1880 to 1910. He was a strange mixture of dreamer, workaholic and visionary, and suffered depression all his life. His fortune was used to build the fountain in Hyde Park and endow the famous art prize and help journalists. He is buried at Waverley cemetery.

JH

LARRY FOLEY

The Father of Aussie Boxing

Larry Foley was the son of a schoolmaster. He was born in 1849 near Bathurst and at fourteen he went to Wollongong as a servant to a priest. He almost entered the priesthood himself, but changed his mind at seventeen, moved to Sydney and became a builder's labourer.

Any godly thoughts he'd had soon vanished. He joined a larrikin gang and soon became leader of The Green, a Catholic gang. He was taught to box by a Negro fighter called Black Perry and, on 18 March 1871, he fought Sandy Ross, champion of the Protestant gangs, on Georges River flat near the suburb of Como in Sydney. The fight lasted seventy-one rounds before police arrived, but most agreed Foley won.

Foley then had another change of heart, left the gang, became a building contractor and boxed in gloves in prize fights and exhibitions. He never lost a fight in that time.

At the height of the colonial rivalry between New South Wales and Victoria, Abe Hicken, the English-born Melbourne champion, challenged Foley to a bare-knuckle fight for the Australian championship.

In Victoria, after 1866, it was compulsory to wear gloves and follow Queensbury rules; bare-knuckle fights were illegal. Attempts to stage the fight in Victoria failed, so it was held near Echuca on the Murray River on 20 March 1879, on the New South Wales side of the river.

The fight was well publicised and men travelled from everywhere to see it. A special train brought 700 spectators from Melbourne to Echuca and they were then ferried across the river into New South Wales.

Foley won in sixteen rounds, and received a prize of £600.

A Ballarat newspaper reported, 'Victoria has lost the honourable distinction of being the proud dwelling place of the Australian champion, the glory of Melbourne has departed away, and we in the wilderness are in tears.'

The day before the fight, an old lady living alone in a cottage outside Echuca was asked by two 'well dressed and courteous young men' who were camped close to her house, if they might have a billy of boiling water to brew their tea, as they didn't want to light a fire in the dry bush. They had come to see the fight.

After the fight was over, one of the men shook Foley's hand and congratulated him, telling him that he himself had won the unofficial boxing championship of northern Victoria a few years before, in a fight against Isaiah 'Wild' Wright. It was Ned Kelly.

Kelly and Joe Byrne had ridden over to see the fight just six weeks after holding up the town of Jerilderie, 170 kilometres away.

Back in Sydney, a benefit concert and subscription fund were organised for Foley who became a publican, gave boxing lessons and trained many prominent boxers at early stages of their careers.

Foley died of heart disease in 1917, and is buried at Waverley cemetery—in the Catholic section. **JH**

FOLEY AND THE GREEN
ANONYMOUS

Now Paddy dear and did you hear the news that's going 'round,
That Sandy Ross has lost the fight at George's River ground?
No more his crowing will be heard, no more his colour seen,
I think he's had enough this time of Foley and the green.
The green the colour of the brave we raise high in the air,
And to our enemies we show the colour that we wear.
The orange flag has been pulled down, the battle fought out keen,
And Sandy Ross has lost the fight at George's River green.

The orange ties they mustered strong upon that Tuesday morn,
As Sandy he came up to scratch with head and beard all shorn.
His orange scarf around his waist was plainly to be seen,
As Foley stepped into the ring wearing Ireland's green.
'Sinn Fein, Sinn Fein!' he cried aloud to all his friends close by,
'I've come to fight for Ireland's cause and for that cause I'll die.

And to deny her colours, I ne'er would be so mean,
So in this ring I'll die or win for dear old Ireland's green.

'Here's to Him, lads, here's to Him, boys,' then Sandy Ross did say,
'I've come to fight for Old King Bill upon this glorious day.
The orange scarf around me waist will soon come into bud,
'Twill be dyed red upon this ground by this poor Fenian's blood!'
They both shook hands, you'd really think no feeling lay between
The colours bright that made this fight, the orange and the green.
For three long hours that fight did last till seconds came between,
And threw the sponge high in the air in favour of the green.

MEI QUONG TART

Mandarin of the Fifth Degree with a Scottish Accent

He spoke with a Scottish accent, wore a kilt and recited Robbie
Burns' poetry. He was a devout Anglican married to an English
woman. He was a Mason, a member of Royal Commissions, a
friend of the Governor and known for his charity work. He was
also Chinese, a tea and silk merchant, a Fourth Rank Mandarin
of the Blue Button, Chinese consul and interpreter for Chinese
prisoners in Sydney courts.

Mei Quong Tart was born in Canton Province, China, in 1850.
The son of Quong Tart, a dealer in ornamental wares, he arrived in
New South Wales aged nine with an uncle who took a shipload of
coolies for the Braidwood goldfields. He lived in Scotsman Thomas
Forsyth's store at Bell's Creek and learned English with a heavy
Scottish accent and was later 'adopted' by wealthy Robert Percy
Simpson and his wife Alice. They converted him to Christianity
and helped him to acquire shares in gold claims. He was wealthy
at eighteen.

After the Simpsons moved to Sydney, Quong built a cottage
at Bell's Creek and was prominent in the sporting, cultural and
religious affairs of Braidwood and Araluen. Friendly with both
Chinese and Europeans, he organised a series of popular Chinese
horse races. He was naturalised on 11 July 1871, joined a lodge of

Oddfellows and was appointed to the board of the public school at Bell's Creek in 1877. In 1885, he became a Freemason.

Quong visited his family in China in 1881 and on his return opened a tea and silk store in Sydney, followed by a tea shop which was intended to provide customers with samples of China tea, but proved so successful that it became tea house and restaurant and Quong began a chain of these establishments.

Quong campaigned to have opium imports banned and in 1883 was part of an investigation into the Chinese camps in southern New South Wales. The report revealed widespread opium addiction. Quong presented a petition to the colonial secretary, seeking the banning of opium imports. In Victoria, he tried to win support for his anti-opium crusade in Melbourne and Ballarat.

In 1886, Quong married a young Englishwoman, Margaret Scarlett. In 1887, he revived the anti-opium campaign with a second petition to parliament and published a pamphlet, *A Plea for the Abolition of the Importation of Opium*. With much anti-Chinese sentiment at that time, he spent much time defending his countrymen and acting as an interpreter. He was part of the New South Wales Royal Commission on Gambling and Bribery from 1891 to 1892.

Quong acted as consul for the imperial Chinese government. The Emperor made him an honorary Mandarin of the Fifth Degree in 1887 for his services to the overseas Chinese community and European–Chinese relations. On his third visit to China in 1894, he was advanced to the Fourth Degree—appointed Mandarin of the Blue Button and honoured by the Dragon Throne with the Peacock Feather.

Quong gave to many charities, and often provided dinners, gifts and entertainment to the Benevolent Society Home at Liverpool and the newsboys of Ashfield, Summer Hill, Croydon and Burwood. From 1885 to 1888 he provided a series of free feasts for the inmates of destitute asylums.

In 1889, Quong opened a classy restaurant in King Street and, in 1898, another in the new Queen Victoria Markets, which became *the* place to be seen in Sydney. In 1890, he opened a bazaar at Jesmond near Newcastle. His employees benefited from his enlightened policies, including time off for shopping and sick leave with pay.

Quong also supported the suffragettes who met in his tea rooms. He was in constant demand as a speaker at charitable and social functions; his Scottish songs and recitations mingled with quaint wit guaranteed full attendances.

In August 1902, he was savagely assaulted by an intruder in his office in the Queen Victoria Markets. After a partial recovery, he died from pleurisy at his home in Ashfield, in July 1903, and was buried at Rookwood. **JH**

BREAKER MORANT

'Shoot Straight, You Bastards . . .'

Breaker Morant claimed that he was born in Devon and was the illegitimate son of Admiral Morant, sent to Australia in disgrace as a 'remittance man' to be kept out of the way of the family after some sexual scandal. Both *The Northern Miner* and *The Bulletin* newspapers, however, identified him as Edwin Henry Murrant who had arrived at Townsville in Queensland on the SS *Waroonga* in 1883.

Murrant was the son of Edwin and Catherine Murrant, master and matron of the Union Workhouse at Bridgewater in Somerset and it seems that Edwin died in August 1864, four months before the birth of his son. His wife Catherine continued her employment as matron until her retirement in 1882.

When Catherine died in 1899, Harry Morant was in Adelaide. He had joined the South Australian Mounted Rifles as Harry Harbord Morant and was about to leave for South Africa, to fight the Boers.

Records show that an Edwin Henry Murrant, son of Edwin Murrant and his wife Catherine, née O'Reilly, married Daisy May O'Dwyer on 13 March 1884, at Charters Towers. Daisy May O'Dwyer would later become known as the famous anthropologist and champion of the Aborigines, Daisy Bates.

The two separated within months after Morant was arrested on a charge of stealing pigs and a saddle. He was acquitted and went to work further west at Winton. Later he began overlanding cattle south, through the channel country.

Daisy moved south and was employed as a governess at Berry, New South Wales. In February 1885, at Nowra, she married cattleman Jack Bates. When he went off droving, she travelled to Sydney where, on 10 June 1885, she was married again, to Ernest Baglehole.

Morant developed a legendary and romantic reputation as a hard-drinking horse breaker, bush poet and ladies' man. A fearless and expert horseman, he was one of the few horsemen who managed to ride the notorious buckjumper, Dargin's Grey, and once jumped his horse Cavalier over a 1.8-metre fence to win a bet.

Morant contributed bush ballads to *The Bulletin* and used the pen-name 'the Breaker'. When the South African War broke out in 1899 he enlisted in Adelaide in the 2nd Contingent, South Australian Mounted Rifles, as Harry Harbord Morant.

His skill as a horseman, and his education and manners, led to him becoming dispatch rider for General French. At the end of his one-year enlistment, he went to England and met Captain Percy Hunt, who had also served in South Africa. The two returned to South Africa in March 1901 and joined the Bush Veldt Carbineers, formed at Pietersburg to counter Boer guerillas. Morant was commissioned as lieutenant. Morant's war record shows him to be a brave and excellent soldier, but there were weak leaders and confused rules of war as the Boer War became more and more a guerrilla war.

Hunt was mortally wounded while on patrol on 4 August 1901. Some mutilation was done to the body, and clothing taken. Morant, now in command, became bent on vengeance. He led a patrol after the Boers and caught up with them late in the evening.

The order to attack was given too soon and all but one got away. Morant alleged that the wounded prisoner was wearing some of Hunt's clothing and shot him. Then eight Boers, supposedly coming to surrender, were met by a patrol led by Morant and Lieutenant Handcock and Morant had them shot. There was a court-martial and, on 27 February 1902, a firing squad of Cameron Highlanders executed Morant and Handcock.

Many British troops did what Morant did without being court-martialled for it. Banjo Paterson was appalled at the acts of brutality carried out by British troops against Boer civilians. Morant was a victim of British attempts to get the Boers to negotiate. Kitchener needed to appease the Boers and executing two 'war criminals' was one way to do it.

Kitchener even left headquarters so he couldn't receive the telegram asking for clemency that was sent by *all* members of the court-martial!

Morant himself wrote, the evening before he died—

It really ain't the place nor time
To reel off rhyming diction—
But yet we'll write a final rhyme
Whilst waiting cru-ci-fi-xion!

But we bequeath a parting tip
For sound advice of such men,
Who come across in transport ship
To polish off the Dutchmen!

If you encounter any Boers
You really must not loot 'em!
And if you wish to leave these shores,
For pity's sake, *don't shoot 'em!!*

And if you'd earn a DSO,
Why every British sinner
Should know the proper way to go is:
'Ask the Boer to dinner!'

His last words to the firing squad were, 'Shoot straight you bastards, don't make a mess of it.'   **JH**

A MEMORY OF BREAKER MORANT
A.B. (BANJO) PATERSON

The Breaker was one of the most colourful of all the larger-than-life characters from our past. Banjo Paterson knew Morant well and, being a solicitor, helped him with some legal matters from time to time. Here is one of Banjo's memories of The Breaker.

Amateur racing, for some reason or other, has always had some sort of encouragement from the Rosehill proprietary, and that club is the only metropolitan institution that caters for the 'lily-whites'. Their annual race at Rosehill is a sort of 'Custer's last stand'.

They used to also run an amateur steeplechase, and one of these was to some extent memorable, for among the riders was Harry Morant, whose tempestuous career was ended by a firing squad in the South African war.

Plucky to the point of recklessness, he suffered from a theatrical complex which made him pretend to be badly hurt when there was, really, not much up with him.

Morant was breaking in horses and mustering wild cattle somewhere up in the west, and he had been accustomed to ride after hounds in England.

Arriving in Sydney at the time of the amateur steeplechase, he set out to look for a mount.

Mr Pottie, of the veterinary family, had a mare that could both gallop and jump, but she was such an unmanageable brute that none of the local amateurs (and I was one of them) cared to take the mount.

Morant jumped at the chance, but as soon as they started the mare cleared out with him and fell into a drain, rolling her rider out as flat as a flounder.

He was carried in, supposed to be unconscious, and I was taken up to hear his last wishes.

The doctors could get nothing out of him, but after listening to his wanderings for a while I said, very loudly and clearly, 'What'll you have Morant?' and he said, equally clearly,

'Brandy and soda.'

BILLY HUGHES

The Little Digger

When Billy Hughes died in 1952, he had been a Member of Parliament for fifty-eight years! There are many stories of his humour and quick thinking. He was expelled from both the Labor Party and the conservative United Australia Party.

Born in London to Welsh parents in 1862, Hughes worked as a teacher in damp, stuffy classrooms before migrating to Australia in 1884. He was a small man and suffered from a chest weakness. He thought the sunshine would be good for his health.

He roamed the Queensland bush, worked on coastal boats and drifted to Sydney where he worked as an oven-maker, married his landlady's daughter and, in 1890, moved to Balmain where he opened a small mixed shop, took on odd jobs and mended umbrellas.

Hughes made his political début as a street-corner speaker for the Balmain Single Tax League and then, in 1892, he joined the Socialist League. He then joined the Labor Party, became a successful union leader, was elected to the New South Wales parliament in 1894 and wrote a column in the *Daily Telegraph*. He went into the federal parliament after Federation in 1901 and became Prime Minister in 1915.

Hughes' passionate support for conscription during World War I led to him being expelled from the Labor Party and earned him the undying respect of the AIF and the nickname The Little Digger.

Hughes formed a new party which merged with the conservative anti-Labor opposition and he was re-elected Prime Minister in 1917. He served as Attorney General and Deputy Coalition Leader in World War II until being expelled from the United Australia Party for joining the Labor-led War Advisory Council after Labor returned to government. He remained in parliament as an independent until his death in 1952.

As Prime Minister at the end of World War I, Hughes was our representative at the peace talks in Versailles. One day, soon after arriving in France, he was flying with an Australian pilot when the plane was forced down with engine trouble in the grounds of a military hospital. The pilot was worried as things were still unstable and the place was guarded and he had no permission to land there.

'Leave it to me,' said the man they called The Little Digger and, as the pilot tinkered with the engine, he strode purposefully towards the advancing and well-armed French soldiers.

'Ahh, you are expecting me, I see,' he beamed. 'Bonjour, I am the Prime Minister of Australia and I am here to inspect the facility!'

Hughes proceeded to inspect the hospital and the staff lined up to meet him while the puzzled military authorities looked at one another and wondered why they had not been told about the visit. When the engine was fixed, Hughes made a farewell speech and hopped back in the plane and the pilot took off.

Many years later, Hughes' secretary told of a conversation one morning at breakfast at Versailles. Hughes hated US President Woodrow Wilson, who wanted to make peace among nations by forming the League of Nations and was trying to stop the victorious nations from punishing the defeated nations by taking their territories. Hughes wanted the German possessions in New Guinea for Australia—and he eventually got them.

Wilson's Democratic Party had lost its majority in Congress in a mid-term election and the President had left the peace talks to rush back to the USA on the warship *Ulysses S. Grant.*

Hughes was reading the paper when his secretary arrived at the table and asked, 'What's the news, Prime Minster?'

'Terrible news,' replied Hughes, 'the *Ulysses S. Grant* is lost at sea with all hands.'

'That is terrible news!' replied his secretary.

Putting down the newspaper, Hughes said, 'And here's even worse news—it's not true!'   **JH**

PERCY GRAINGER

The Oddest Oddball of Them All

Percy Grainger took eccentricity to new heights. He was a genius of the highest order—and a mass of contradictions. He was a racist obsessed with Nordic purity but, as Dean of Music at New York University, he took up the cause of black musicians like Duke Ellington and invited them to lecture at the university.

He was a vegetarian who hated vegetables. He lived on nuts and wheat. He was a sadomasochist who flagellated himself and took photos and made notes on the bruises and scars, yet he composed the sweetest sugary melody, 'English Country Garden', which was a mega hit before World War II.

He donated two years' earnings to Melbourne University to establish a museum—about himself.

He designed his own clothes and also designed a bra for his Danish girlfriend—but he never ironed his clothes and was arrested mistakenly as a vagrant in New York when he was Dean of Music at New York University. He never drove a car but would run or cycle to each concert. On a South African tour he once ran 100 kilometres to his next concert.

He left the UK during World War I because he didn't believe in war and then joined up in the USA and played oboe and saxophone in an army band.

Grainger met the Swedish artist and poet Ella Viola Ström, and fell in love at first sight. He had her paged on a ship and decided to marry her. Their wedding took place on 9 August 1928 on the stage of the Hollywood Bowl in front of 20,000 people.

Perhaps it's easier to understand Percy if we look at his mother. Grainger was born in Melbourne in 1882 and his mother Rose was a very well-educated and cultured woman, who was also domineering and possessive. While pregnant, she allocated time each day to stare at a statue of a Greek god in the belief it would pass some of its qualities to her child.

Percy had blue eyes and brilliant orange hair and spent less than three months in school after refusing to attend because he was teased. He was home schooled by his mother who was a strict disciplinarian.

Grainger gave his first public piano recital at the age of twelve and critics hailed him as a new prodigy. He excelled in languages and his correspondence shows he was fluent in eleven foreign languages including Icelandic and Russian.

Grainger's friend, composer Edvard Grieg, considered Percy the greatest musical genius of his time. He was a pioneer folk song collector, brilliant concert pianist, and an inventor of machines which played atonal and non-sequential music.

He is buried in West Terrace cemetery, Adelaide, with his mother.

There is no doubt Percy's near madness stemmed from and revolved around his mother who had contracted syphilis from her husband early in their marriage. After Percy's birth, she refused to touch him until he was five years old, for fear of passing the disease on to him.

In 1890, Grainger's father took a sea voyage in order to improve his health and never lived with wife and child again. Rose wrote to Grainger warning him not to touch his father if they should meet. His father died in 1917 of tertiary syphilis.

Rose committed suicide in 1922 by jumping from the building where her son's manager, Antonia Sawyer, had an office. After his mother's death, Grainger found a letter that she had written to him the day before she took her life, explaining her suicide was caused by accusations of incest.

Grainger kept the letter for many years in a cylinder he wore around his neck. He later compiled an album containing photos of his mother (including several of her in her coffin), and had thousands of copies made and distributed to friends.

He donated many photos of himself being whipped and some whips and bloodstained shirts to the museum at Melbourne University and requested that his bones be used as a wind chime at the museum.

His mother's gravestone reads 'Wise, wonderful, devoted, angelic mother' and, in spite of all his weirdness, his friends and colleagues universally described him as 'the happiest of people'.   **JH**

ARTHUR STACE

Mr Eternity

Arthur Stace was born in Balmain, the child of alcoholics. In order to survive, he resorted to stealing bread and milk and searching for scraps of food in bins. By the age of twelve, Arthur, with virtually no formal schooling, had become a state ward. As a teenager, he became an alcoholic and was subsequently sent to jail at fifteen. Afterwards, he worked as a look-out for a two-up school. In his twenties, he was a scout for his sisters, who were prostitutes.

Arthur Stace was converted to Christianity on the night of 6 August 1930, after hearing an inspirational sermon by R.B.S. Hammond at St Barnabas Church on Broadway. Inspired by the words, he became enamoured with the notion of eternity. Two years later, on 14 November 1932, Arthur was inspired by a sermon by evangelist John G. Ridley on 'The Echoes of Eternity' from Isaiah 57:15: 'For thus saith the high and lofty One that inhabiteth Eternity, whose name is Holy; I dwell in the high and holy place, with him also that is of a contrite and humble spirit . . .'

John Ridley's words, 'Eternity, Eternity, I wish that I could sound or shout that word to everyone in the streets of Sydney. You've got to meet it, where will you spend Eternity?' would prove crucial in Stace's decision to tell others about his faith. In an interview, Arthur Stace said, 'Eternity went ringing through my brain and suddenly I began crying and felt a powerful call from the Lord to write Eternity.' Even though he was illiterate and could hardly write his own name legibly, the word 'Eternity', 'came out smoothly, in a beautiful copperplate script. 'I couldn't understand it,' he said, 'and I still can't.'

After eight or nine years, he tried to write something else, 'Obey God', and then, five years later, 'God or Sin', but he could not bring himself to stop writing 'Eternity'. Sydney Council brought him to the attention of the police as they had rules about the defacing of pavements, so much so that he narrowly avoided arrest around twenty-four times. Each time he was caught, he responded with, 'But I had permission from a higher source.'

Several mornings a week for the next thirty-five years, Arthur would leave his wife, Pearl, and their home in Bulwarra Road, Pyrmont, around five o'clock in the morning to go around the streets and chalk the word 'Eternity' on footpaths, train station entrances and anywhere else he could think of. It is estimated that he wrote the word around 500,000 times over the thirty-five years. Workers arriving in the city would see the word freshly written, but not the writer, and so, 'The man who writes "Eternity" ' became a legend in Sydney.

The mystery was solved when Reverend Lisle M. Thompson, who preached at the church where Arthur worked as a cleaner, saw him take a piece of chalk from his pocket and write the word on the footpath.

Arthur Stace died in a nursing home at the age of eighty-three on 30 July 1967. He bequeathed his body to Sydney University; subsequently, his remains were buried with those of his wife at Botany Cemetery around two years later.

One of Arthur Stace's iconic 'Eternity' signs, which he chalked on a piece of cardboard for a fellow parishioner is in the National Museum in Canberra. The museum also has an Eternity Gallery, inspired by Arthur Stace's story, which features fifty personal stories from ordinary and extraordinary Australians. The stories are tied together by emotional themes including joy, fear, separation, chance and loneliness, which are all elements of Stace's story.

In Sydney today, the word 'Eternity' can still be seen written in three places. It is on Stace's gravestone in Botany Cemetery and inside the bell in the GPO clock tower, which had been dismantled during World War II. When the clock tower was rebuilt in the 1960s, the bell was brought out of storage and, as the workmen were installing it, they noticed, inside the bell, the word 'Eternity' in Stace's chalk. This is the only surviving 'Eternity' in Stace's own hand in Sydney. (No one ever found out how Stace had been able to get to the bell, which had been sealed up.)

The third place you might see the word is in Town Hall Square. When the area was redeveloped in the 1970s, a wrought aluminium replica of the word in Stace's original copperplate handwriting was embedded in the footpath near a fountain as an eternal memorial to Arthur Stace.

As a tribute to Stace, the Harbour Bridge was lit up with the word 'Eternity' as part of the celebrations for the beginning of the year 2000.   **JH**

HUBERT WILKINS

The Aussie Who Was Scattered at the North Pole

Hubert Wilkins was born in 1888, the youngest in a family of thirteen children, on a sheep station at Netfield, 150 kilometres north of Adelaide.

When he was fifteen, the family moved to Adelaide and he enrolled in courses, which he never completed, at the School of Mines and the university. He moved to Sydney instead, and worked in Australia's pioneer film industry, then left for the UK to work making newsreels and filming events such as the Balkans War in 1912.

Wilkins made his first trip to the Arctic with a Canadian expedition in 1913 and photographed thousands of miles of previously unexplored territory. When he returned to Point Barrow, Alaska, in 1916, he was told the world had been at war for two years.

He was appointed official photographer for Australia's War Records Office and filmed the fighting on the Western Front. Although Wilkins refused to carry firearms, he was the only Australian photographer, in any war, to receive a combat decoration. He was awarded the Military Cross twice, firstly for rescuing wounded soldiers at the Battle of Ypres and secondly after he assumed command of a group of American soldiers whose officers had been killed, and directed them until support arrived. After the war, he made a photographic record of the battlefields of Gallipoli.

Wilkins then joined Dr John Cope on the Imperial Antarctic Expedition. After that, he was appointed as naturalist on Sir Ernest Shackleton's last expedition to the Antarctic and this led to the British Museum of Natural History offering him an expedition of his own to collect flora and fauna from outback Australia and the islands of Torres Strait. He did that for two years and then told the museum he wanted to work in the polar regions again.

With pilot Carl Ben Eielson, he was the first to fly across the Arctic Sea and the two men became international celebrities. The two of them then went on to explore Antarctica in 1928 and were the first men to fly a plane in Antarctica and map land that had never been seen before.

Wilkins was knighted and awarded the Patron's medal of the Royal Geographical Society of London and the Samuel Finley Breese Morse medal of the American Geographical Society and was on the world's largest airship, *Graf Zeppelin,* on the first around-the-world flight and was aboard the airship *Hindenburg* on its maiden voyage from Germany to America.

He then decided to take a submarine under the Arctic ice to the North Pole. Although the submarine, *Nautilus,* broke down and didn't quite make it, Wilkins proved it was possible to journey under the polar ice cap.

At the outbreak of World War II, Wilkins offered his services to the Australian war effort.

The Australian government could find no use for a polar explorer, now aged over fifty, but the US army employed him to teach survival skills to soldiers and, after the war, he remained as a consultant to the US army and navy, developing nuclear submarines for operations in the Arctic.

Wilkins died in 1958 and, on 17 March 1959, the nuclear submarine USS *Skate* became the first submarine to surface at the North Pole, where the crew held a memorial service and scattered the ashes of Sir Hubert Wilkins.   **JH**

ANNETTE KELLERMAN

The Perfect Woman

Swimmer, athlete, dancer, diver, actress, entertainer, author, designer, fitness expert, model, women's liberator, childhood cripple and movie star, Annette Kellerman was born in 1886. Her violinist father, Frederick, and her French-born mother, pianist and music teacher Alice, lived in the inner Sydney suburb of Marrickville.

Kellerman was crippled by rickets, a disease caused by vitamin deficiency, at the age of two and had to wear heavy leg braces until she was seven to prevent her legs from bowing. She started swimming on doctor's advice at Cavill's Baths at Lavender Bay. She liked swimming and her legs responded so well that at sixteen she was the women's 100 metres world record holder.

When the family moved to Melbourne, Kellerman gave swimming and diving exhibitions at the Melbourne baths, performed a mermaid act at an entertainment park and did two shows a day at the Exhibition Aquarium, where she swam in a glass tank full of fish.

In 1902, when Annette and her father went to England, she held all the world's records for women's swimming.

Kellerman soon began giving demonstrations. She swam 42 kilometres down the Thames in five hours, went to France and raced seventeen men down the Seine and finished third, and was the first woman to attempt to swim the English Channel. She tried three times but never made it. 'I had the endurance,' she said, 'but not the brute strength.'

Annette Kellerman almost single-handedly liberated women from stuffy Victorian dress codes. For her stage act and exhibitions, she made herself a one-piece swimsuit by stitching black stockings into a boy's costume, showing her legs above the knee.

In the USA in 1907, she was arrested on a Boston beach and charged with public indecency when she attempted to swim in an adapted men's swimsuit that showed her bare legs. The newspapers loved her and took up her cause and massive publicity followed.

She originated water ballet, which is now called synchronised swimming, and toured theatres across Europe and the United States, starring in a spectacular aquatic act as the 'Australian Mermaid and Diving Venus'.

She then became a movie star. Her first Hollywood film in 1914 was *Neptune's Daughter* and that was followed by *Venus of the South Seas, Daughter of the Gods* and *The Art of Diving*.

Kellerman did all her own stunts, including diving 30 metres into the sea and 18 metres into a pool full of crocodiles. A film of her life, *Million Dollar Mermaid*, made in 1952, starred swimmer turned movie star Esther Williams.

A teetotaller and a lifelong vegetarian, Kellerman promoted swimming for health and fitness and wrote several bestsellers, including *Physical Beauty and How to Keep It*. She toured America and Germany lecturing on health and fitness and ran a health-food store for many years at Long Beach in California.

Kellerman's childhood disease is often wrongly said to have been polio. Although she never suffered from polio, she did meet polio victim President Roosevelt and designed some exercises for him. During World War II she lived in Queensland where she assisted polio pioneer Sister Elizabeth Kenny. She also entertained US and Australian troops and worked for the Australian Red Cross.

In 1912, Kellerman married James Sullivan, who had managed her career from 1907 when her father became ill. They were together for over sixty years and, from 1970, they lived on the Gold Coast at Southport where Annette continued to swim daily until her death in 1974 at the age of eighty-nine.

After her arrest in Boston in 1907 and the resultant publicity, Harvard University Professor Dudley Sargent, who had been researching the female body for twenty-five years, measured every inch of her body and declared that she was the first woman in over 10,000 he had studied who had the same measurements as the Venus de Milo. He presented her on stage at Harvard in her bathing suit in front of his young male students and declared she was 'the perfect woman'.

Annette Kellerman modestly added, 'Maybe from the neck down.'   **JH**

ROY RENE

Mo

Roy Rene was a fascinating character. He was the toast of Australia, as far as comedy went, for the first half of the twentieth century, with his irreverent and uniquely Australian style of humour.

His professional name was Roy Rene and his real name was Harry Van Der Sluice. His stage name was Mo and his radio persona was Mo McCackie.

Mo was born in 1891, one of seven children of a Dutch cigar maker and an English mother, both Jews, who had migrated to Adelaide in the 1880s. Mo began his career singing at Adelaide Markets as a boy aged ten and later tried his luck in Melbourne before moving to Sydney and switching to comedy.

Mo's comedy persona was an odd blend of a Jewish caricature, a black and white face-painted clown and a sleazy slapstick Aussie larrikin. His brand of humour was delightfully Australian and very politically incorrect by today's standards.

His comedy ranged from lewd slapstick to quite surreal material, which was ahead of its time. One of my favourite bits of Mo's dark humour occurs in a skit about a visit to the psychiatrist. When the doctor suggests that Mo needs a hobby, he replies, 'I have a hobby, Doc, I keep goldfish.'

'Ah, that's nice, where do you keep them?' asks the doctor.

'In the fridge,' Mo replies.

'Good heavens,' says the shocked psychiatrist, 'they'll die in there!'

'Blimey, Doc,' says Mo with a pitying look and eyebrows raised, 'it's only a hobby!'

When the doctor gives Mo a Rorschach inkblot test and gets lewd responses to every inkblot, he diagnoses sexual obsession as Mo's problem.

'Blimey, Doc,' Mo complains, 'you're the one with all the dirty pictures!'

Although Mo received high praise as a comic genius from famous visitors such as Dame Sybil Thorndike, Jack Benny and

Fred Allen, he was never tempted to try his luck overseas. He said his humour was too Australian to work in the USA and often remarked, 'Look what they did to Les Darcy and Phar Lap!'

In his private life, he was a loving but strict father and quite narrow-minded, according to his wife. As far as his artistic temperament was concerned, he was, like many talented people, wary of other talented performers, dismissive of their talents and almost paranoid at times about being the top act on the show.

He fell out with his long-time stage partner Nat 'Stiffy' Phillips twice, once in 1925 and finally again after a brief reunion in 1928, and was renowned for being disparaging about other performers and quite ruthless and unfriendly at times, even to old friends.

The egos of many performers are part and parcel of their talent and often Mo's insecurity made him quite unconsciously funny.

When the harmonica virtuoso Larry Adler was receiving rave reviews in Australia, with sellout crowds and standing ovations, someone remarked to Mo what a great act Adler was.

'I don't see it at all,' replied the king of Australian variety dismissively, 'take away his mouth organ and he wouldn't be worth a zac.'   JH

BEA MILES

Delightfully Eccentric and Proudly Australian

Bohemian rebel Beatrice Miles was born on 17 September 1902 at Ashfield, Sydney, third surviving child of the five children of John Miles, a Sydney-born accountant, and his wife, Maria Louisa. The family moved to fashionable St Ives and Bea was educated at the famous private girls' school, Abbotsleigh.

An inheritance from her paternal grandmother allowed Bea to escape the violent scenes that characterised her relationship with her father. She enrolled in arts at the University of Sydney, but discontinued her studies after a year 'because they did not teach enough Australian stuff'. Soon after, she contracted encephalitis. Conflicts with her father continued, over her lifestyle and sexual 'freedom'. In 1923, he had her committed to the Hospital for the

Insane, Gladesville, where she remained until publicity in *Smith's Weekly* led to her release in 1925.

Thereafter, Miles became notable for her outrageous, disruptive conduct in public places, and her outspoken criticism of political and social authorities. Irresolvable differences over her behaviour and lifestyle occasioned the end of her long relationship with Brian Harper when she was thirty-eight. He wanted to marry, while she 'despised men who got married'.

Henceforth, Miles had 'no fixed address'.

Well-known in Sydney, she could be seen on city and suburban public transport wearing a green tennis shade, tennis shoes and a scruffy greatcoat. She had a number of ingenious methods of obtaining goods, services and daily support. One method was to give recitations from Shakespeare, with a threepence to three shillings price range.

She became notorious for refusing to pay fares, especially in taxis; cabbies often refused to pick her up. Sometimes, in retaliation, she would leap on their running boards, bumper bars or bonnet, or hurl herself against their sides, detaching doors from hinges. In 1955, however, she paid a female taxidriver £600 to drive her to Perth and back, which took nineteen days.

From the 1940s, her closest friend was a taxidriver called John Beynon, but this could not prevent the ire of unpaid drivers; she was assaulted several times in the 1950s.

Bea Miles was constantly harassed by police and she claimed to have been falsely convicted 195 times, and fairly convicted 100 times, though obituaries give lower estimates. She haunted the Public Library of New South Wales, reading many books each week, until she was banned from the building in the late 1950s.

The final years of her life were dogged by ill health, and in 1964 she entered the Little Sisters of the Poor Home for the Aged at Randwick. In old age, she reputedly claimed: 'I have no allergies that I know of, one complex, no delusions, two inhibitions, no neuroses, three phobias, no superstitions and no frustrations.' After renouncing her lifelong atheism and receiving Roman Catholic rites, she died of cancer on 3 December 1973.

As well as advocating free love, Miles was a fervent nationalist. At her request, Australian wildflowers were placed on her coffin, and a jazz band played 'Waltzing Matilda', 'Tie me Kangaroo Down, Sport' and 'Advance Australia Fair'.   JH

SMOKY DAWSON

The Aussie Cowboy

When Smoky Dawson died on 13 February 2008, my generation of Australians lost a hero and I lost a friend. For more than six decades, Smoky and Dot Dawson made a wonderful contribution to the Australian entertainment industry and to the community.

Herbert Henry Dawson was born in Collingwood, Melbourne, in 1913, and grew up in difficult circumstances. His dad had never recovered from World War I and was erratic and violent. Herbert spent time in an orphanage and later, as a teenager, he 'went bush' for a while, where a youthful and disastrous experiment with an old pipe gave him the nickname that became his famous trademark.

Smoky tried many things before music: farm work, rough riding, working in a tannery and even cycle racing. In 1932, he and his brother Ted became the Coral Island Boys and started looking for work on radio. In 1933, at a radio station audition, he met Florence Cheers, better known as Dot. She was a few years older than Smoky, a very clever woman who had a successful career in radio and understood how the new medium worked. They married in 1944, and together set about creating the legend that became 'Smoky Dawson'.

Smoky Dawson's *Pepsodent Rangers Show* was a hit on 3KZ and, by the early 1940s, Smoky was writing songs and recording and performing regularly in Melbourne and Sydney.

After serving and almost dying in World War II and spending a year in Concord Repatriation Hospital in Sydney, Smoky picked up where he left off, touring as a yodelling, whip-cracking, knife-throwing, singing cowboy.

He headed to the USA and, in 1952, signed a record deal with a label owned by Roy Acuff and Wesley Rose. From December

1952, back in Australia, Smoky starred in his own radio show, *The Adventures of Smoky Dawson*, which stayed on the air for ten years until 1962. Sponsored by Kellogg's, the show became the biggest networked radio program in Australia and later switched to television. Hundreds of thousands of Aussie kids became Smoky's deputies, received their deputy's certificates and pledged to be good and help Mum around the house.

Smoky told great yarns, and I remember him telling me about the night of his dreadful car accident in Sydney, driving home from the filming of *This Is Your Life* for his mate Slim Dusty.

Smoky's car had gone over a bridge and he was in a bad way. He was admitted to hospital and was waiting for the doctor to arrive. He'd been in his stage gear for the filming and the stage clothes were now piled on a chair in the hospital room.

Smoky was only a small bloke and looked frail and skinny without his famous western gear and hat. Now he was in a hospital gown, bruised and battered, resting in the bed.

The doctor came into the room and leaned over the bed. 'So, you're the famous Smoky Dawson,' he said.

'No,' the frail and bruised old man in the bed replied, 'I'm Herbert; Smoky's over there on that chair!'

I was lucky enough to record a duet with Smoky in 2004, when he was ninety-one. It was a song I wrote about him called 'Smoky on the Radio'.

Smoky and Dot were still living in their home at Lane Cove, with a bit of help from carers, and my wife and I called to pick him up to go to the studio. Robyn walked him to the car while I chatted to Dot at the back door.

'I don't know how long it will take, Dotty,' I said.

Now you must realise that they had lived together for sixty years and Smoky had a reputation for rarely, if ever, being quiet for more than a few minutes. He was already yarning away to Robyn about 'the old days' as they headed to the car.

Dot, who was ninety-seven at the time and sharp as a tack, looked at me and said slowly, 'Jim . . . keep him as long as you like!'

JH

SMOKY ON THE RADIO

Jim Haynes

Each day was an adventure, when we were young.
We were always playing cowboys, out having fun.
At night we'd turn the wireless on, the family gathered 'round,
And when those valves warmed up we'd hear that old familiar
  sound.

Smoky on the radio, it doesn't seem that long ago,
When you could tell right from wrong and go riding with a smile
  and a song.
To Jindawarrabel we'd go, with Smoky on the radio.

It was roping, riding romance in the great outback.
Righting wrongs and singing songs along a bushland track,
And a million little Aussies all came along for the ride,
And his old mate Flash would bring him back in time to say
  'goodnight'.

Smoky on the radio, it doesn't seem that long ago,
When you could tell right from wrong and go riding with a smile
  and a song.
To Jindawarrabel we'd go, with Smoky on the radio.

I found that broken wireless out in the shed a while ago
And I plan to get it working because you never know
If I can fix those valves and bits and get it working well
I might just find that station known as Jindawarrabel.

Smoky on the radio, it doesn't seem that long ago,
When you could tell right from wrong and go riding with a smile
  and a song.
To Jindawarrabel we'd go, with Smoky on the radio.

AUSSIE MYTHS AND MYSTERIES

Myths and legends are the yarns that enable members of a society or a nation or an ethnic group to have a common, shared folklore and understand their heritage. Children especially want to know how and why things are as they are and a system of legends and myths is how most societies make an effort to do that.

In Australia, Indigenous myths and legends vary substantially from place to place but there are some common elements and a belief system based on the Dreaming was common to all Aboriginal people. The Aboriginal legends and myths included here have been adapted from one of the first collections written by a European, the Welshman Jenkyn Thomas.

Some of our modern day Aussie 'monsters' are derived from Aboriginal stories of yowies and bunyips, and the legends that European settlers brought with them also had an influence on the types of myths and legends that developed among European communities, especially in the outback.

Stories like 'Crooked Mick of the Speewah' and 'The Oozlum Bird' owe a lot to the Celtic legends of giants, the Arabian Nights and the amazing adventures of Germanic folk heroes such as Till Eulenspiegel and Baron von Munchausen. Many so-called Aussie folk songs about heroes, fabled monsters and larger-than-life characters are adapted directly from Anglo–Celtic folklore and songs. To be honest, I lived in the bush a long time and heard a thousand yarns and stories told in pubs and around camp fires and I never heard one bushman yarn about the Speewah. Although writers like Julian Stuart and others have evidence that the yarns were told during the days of the shearers' strikes, I suspect that the Speewah was more a creation of city-based academics and writers than anything else.

We are all fascinated by mysteries and unexplained events and I have included two of my all-time favourite seafaring mysteries in this section. The true story of the SS *Waratah* and the fascinating dilemma of the Mahogany Ship are mysteries than may one day be solved—but I seriously doubt it!

MEN COME TO AUSTRALIA
TRADITIONAL/JENKYN THOMAS

Many years ago, when this old world was young, all the animals now living in Australia were men. At that time, they lived in a distant land across the ocean, and, having heard of the wonderful hunting grounds in Australia, they determined to leave their country and sail to this sunny land in a canoe.

They knew that the voyage would be a long and dangerous one; storms would sweep across the sea and lash the waves into a white fury; the wind would howl like the evil spirits of the forest, the lightning flash across the sky like writhing golden snakes, and death would hide in waiting for them beneath the brown sea kelp. It was therefore necessary for them to have a very strong canoe for the journey.

The whale, who was the biggest of all the men, had a great strong canoe that could weather the wildest storm. But he was a very selfish fellow and would not allow anybody the use of it. As it was necessary to have the canoe, his companions watched for a suitable opportunity to steal it and start on their long and lonely journey.

But the whale was a cunning creature. He always kept very strict guard over the canoe and would not leave it alone for a moment. The other people were at their wits' end to solve the problem of stealing the canoe, and they held a great council to consider the question. Many suggestions were put forward, but none was practical. It seemed an impossible task, until the starfish came forward to place his suggestion before the council.

Now, the starfish was a very intimate friend of the whale, so, when he spoke, everybody was very silent and attentive. He hesitated for a moment, and then said:

'Unless we get a very big canoe, it will be impossible to sail to the new hunting-grounds, where the fire of the sun never dies, the sea sand is soft and golden, and there is plenty of food. I shall get my friend, the whale, to leave his canoe and I shall keep him interested for a long time. When I give you the signal, steal silently away with it as fast as you can.'

The other men were so excited at the proposal that they all spoke at once and asked: 'How will you do it?'

But the starfish looked very wise and said, 'Your business is to steal the canoe and mine to keep the whale occupied while you do it.'

Some days later, the starfish paid a friendly visit to the whale, and, after talking for some time, he said, 'I have noticed what a great number of vermin you have in your hair. They must be very uncomfortable. Let me catch them for you.'

The whale, being greatly troubled with vermin on his head, readily agreed to the kind offer of his friend, the starfish. The whale moored his canoe in deep water and sat on a rock.

Starfish placed his friend's head in his lap and proceeded to hunt diligently for the vermin. While he was doing so, he told many funny stories and occupied the attention of the whale. The starfish then gave the signal to the men who were waiting, and they seized the canoe and sailed off.

But the whale was very suspicious. For a short time he would forget his canoe, but then he would suddenly remember it and say: 'Is my canoe all right?'

The starfish had cunningly provided himself with a piece of bark, and, tapping it on the rock in imitation of the boat bumping with the rise and fall of the sea, he would answer, 'Yes, this is it I am tapping with my hand. It is a very fine canoe.'

He continued to tell funny stories to the whale. At the same time, he scratched very hard around his ears in order to silence the sound of the oars splashing in the water as the other men rowed away with the canoe.

After some time, the whale grew tired of his friend's attention and storytelling, and decided to have a look at the canoe himself. When he looked around and found the canoe missing, he could hardly believe it. He rubbed his eyes and looked again. Away in the distance, he could see the vanishing shape of his canoe. Then the truth dawned upon him—he had been tricked.

The whale was very angry and beat the starfish unmercifully. Throwing him upon the rocks, he made great ragged cuts in the faithless creature. The starfish was so exhausted, that he rolled off the rocks and hid himself in the soft sand. It is on account of this cruel beating that, even to the present day, the starfish has a very ragged and torn appearance, and always hides himself in the sand.

After beating the friend who had betrayed him, the whale jumped into the water and chased the men in the canoe. Great white waves rose and fell, as he churned his way through the water, and, out of a wound in his head which the starfish had made, he spouted water high into the air.

The whale continued his relentless chase, and, when the men in the canoe saw him, they said, 'He is gaining on us, and, when he catches us, we shall all be drowned.'

But the koala, who was in charge of the oars, said, 'There is no need to be afraid; look at my arms. They are strong enough to row the canoe out of danger.'

This reassured his companions, and the chase continued.

The voyage lasted many days and nights. During the day, the hot sun beat down on the men in the canoe, and, at night, the cold winds chilled them. But there was no escape; they must go on. By day and night, they could see the whale spouting in his fury, and churning the sea into foam with the lashing of his tail.

At last land was sighted, and the men rowed very fast towards it. When they landed from the canoe, they were very weary, and sat down on the sand to rest. But the native companion, who was always a very lively fellow and fond of dancing, danced upon the bottom of the canoe until he made a hole in it. He then pushed it a short distance from the shore, where it settled down in the water and became an island, just off the coast.

When the whale arrived at the landing place, he saw the men on shore and his canoe wrecked. He travelled along the coast and spouted water with anger as he thought of the trick that had been played on him, and of the wreck of his beloved canoe.

Even to the present day, whales spout, the starfish is ragged and torn, the koala has very strong fore paws, and men still roam across the wild wastes of Australia.

THE COACHMAN'S YARN
E.J. BRADY

This is a tale that the coachman told,
As he flicked the flies from Marigold
And flattered and fondled Pharaoh.
The sun swung low in the western skies:
Out on a plain, just over a rise,
Stood Nimitybell, on Monaro;
Cold as charity, cold as hell.
Bleak, bare, barren Nimitybell—
Nimitybell on Monaro.

'Now this 'ere 'appended in 'eighty-three,
The coldest winter ever we see;
'Strewth, it was cold, as cold as could be,
Out 'ere on Monaro;
It froze the blankets, it froze the fleas,
It froze the sap in the blinkin' trees,
It made a grindstone out of cheese,
Right 'ere in Monaro.

'Freezin' an' snowin'—ask the old hands;
They seen, they knows, an' they understands,
The ploughs was froze, and the cattle brands,
Down 'ere in Monaro.
It froze our fingers and froze our toes;
I seen passenger's breath so froze
Icicles 'ung from 'is bloomin' nose
Long as the tail on Pharaoh.

'I ketched a curlew down by the creek;
His feet were froze to his blessed beak;
'E stayed like that for over a week—
That's cold on Monaro.
Why, even the air got froze that tight
You'd 'ear the awfullest sounds at night,

When things was put to a fire or light,
Out 'ere on Monaro.

'For the sounds was froze. At Haydon's Bog
A cove 'e cross-cut a big back-log,
An' carted 'er 'ome ('e wants to jog—
Stiddy, go stiddy there, Pharaoh!)
As soon as his log begins to thaw
They 'ears the sound of the cross-cut saw
A-thawin' out. Yes, his name was Law.
Old hands, them Laws, on Monaro.

'The second week of this 'ere cold snap
I'm drivin' the coach. A Sydney chap,
'E strikes this part o' the bloomin map,
A new hand 'ere on Monaro.
'Is name or game I never heard tell,
But 'e gets off at Nimitybell
Blowin' like Bluey, freezin' like 'ell
At Nimitybell on Monaro.

'The drinks was froze, o' course, in the bar;
They breaks a bottle of old Three Star,
An' the barman sez, "Now, there y' are,
You can't beat that for Monaro!"
The stranger bloke, 'e was tall an' thin,
Sez, "Strike me blue, but I think you win;
We'll 'ave another an' I'll turn in—
It's blitherin' cold on Monaro."

' 'E borrowed a book an' went to bed
To read awhile, so the missus said,
By the candle-light. 'E must ha' read
(These nights is long on Monaro)
Past closin' time, Then 'e starts an' blows
The candle out but the wick 'ad froze!
Leastways, that's what folks round 'ere suppose,
Old hands as lived on Monaro.

'So bein' tired, an' a stranger, new
To these mountain ways, they think he threw
'Is coat on the wick, an' maybe, too,
Any old clothes 'e'd to spare. Oh,
This ain't no fairy, an' don't you fret!
Next day came warmer an' set in wet,
There's some out 'ere as can mind it yet,
The real old 'ands on Monaro.

'The wick must ha' thawed. The fire began
At breakfast time. The neighbours all ran
To save the pub—an' forgot the man
(Stiddy, go stiddy there, mare-oh).
The pub was burned to the blanky ground;
'Is buttons was all they ever found.
The blinkin' cow 'e owed me a pound—
From Cooma his blinkin' fare, oh!

'That ain't no fairy, not what I've told;
I'm gettin' shaky an' growing old,
An' I hope I never again see cold,
Like that down 'ere on Monaro!'—
He drives his horses, he drives them well,
And this is the tale he loves to tell
Nearing the town of Nimitybell,
Nimitybell on Monaro.

THE FLOOD
TRADITIONAL/JENKYN THOMAS

In the Dreamtime, a terrible drought swept across the land. The leaves of the trees turned brown and fell from the branches, the flowers drooped their heads and died, and the green grass withered as though the spirit from the barren mountain had breathed upon it with a breath of fire. When the hot wind blew, the dead reeds rattled in the riverbed, and the burning sands shimmered like a silver lagoon.

All the water had left the rippling creeks and deep, still water-holes. In the clear blue sky, the sun was a mass of molten gold; the clouds no longer drifted across the hills, and the only darkness that fell across the land was the shadow of night and death.

After many had died of thirst, all the animals in the land met together in a great council to discover the cause of the drought. They travelled many miles. Some came from the bush, and others from the distant mountains.

The sea birds left their homes in the cliffs where the white surf thundered, and flew without resting many days and nights. When they all arrived at the chosen meeting place in Central Australia, they discovered that a frog of enormous size had swallowed all the water in the land, and thus caused the drought. After much serious discussion, it was decided that the only way to obtain the water again was to make the frog laugh. The question now arose as to which animal should begin the performance, and, after a heated argument, the pride of place was given to the kookaburra.

The animals then formed themselves into a huge circle with the frog in the centre. Red kangaroos, grey wallaroos, rock and swamp wallabies, kangaroo rats, bandicoots, koalas and ring-tailed possums all sat together. The emu and the native companion forgot their quarrel and the bellbird his chimes. Even a butcherbird looked pleasantly at a brown snake, and the echidna forgot to bristle. A truce had been called in the war of the bush.

Now, the kookaburra seated himself on the limb of a tree, and, with a wicked twinkle in his eye, looked straight at the big, bloated frog, ruffled his brown feathers, and began to laugh. At first, he made a low gurgling sound deep in his throat, as though he was smiling to himself, but gradually he raised his voice and laughed louder and louder until the bush re-echoed with the sound of his merriment. The other animals looked on with very serious faces, but the frog gave no sign. He just blinked his eyes and looked as stupid as only a frog can look.

The kookaburra continued to laugh until he nearly choked and fell off the tree, but all without success. The next competitor was a frill-necked lizard. It extended the frill around its throat, and, puffing out its jaws, capered up and down. But there was no humour in the frog; he did not even look at the lizard, and laughter was out of the question.

It was then suggested that the dancing of the native companion might tickle the fancy of the frog. So the native companion danced until she was tired, but all her graceful and grotesque figures failed to arouse the interest of the frog.

The position was very serious, and the council of animals was at its wits' end for a reasonable suggestion. In their anxiety to solve the difficulty, they all spoke at once, and the din was indescribable. Above the noise could be heard a frantic cry of distress. A carpet snake was endeavouring to swallow a echidna. The bristles had stuck in his throat, and a kookaburra, who had a firm grip of his tail, was making an effort to fly away with him.

Close by, two bandicoots were fighting over the possession of a sweet root, but, while they were busily engaged in scratching each other, a possum stole it. They then forgot their quarrel and chased the possum, who escaped danger by climbing a tree and swinging from a branch by his tail. In this peculiar position he ate the root at his leisure, much to the disgust of the bandicoots below.

After peace and quiet had been restored, the question of the drought was again considered. A big eel, who lived in a deep waterhole in the river, suggested that he should be given an opportunity to make the frog laugh. Many of the animals laughed at the idea, but, in despair, they agreed to give him a trial. The eel then began to wriggle in front of the frog. At first he wriggled slowly, then faster and faster until his head and tail met. Then he slowed down and wriggled like a snake with the shivers. After a few minutes, he changed his position, and flopped about like a well-bitten grub on an ant bed.

The frog opened his sleepy eyes, his big body quivered, his face relaxed, and, at last, he burst into a laugh that sounded like rolling thunder. The water poured from his mouth in a flood. It filled the deepest rivers and covered the land. Only the highest mountain peaks were visible, like islands in the sea. Many men and animals were drowned.

I'M THE MAN
FRANK DANIEL

My mate Frank Daniel never told a lie, so it was with some surprise that I learned he was actually the original Man From Snowy River . . . amazing!

I'm the one they talk about, the 'Man from Snowy River'.
The one who did those daring deeds that made old Clancy shiver.
It's true, I had a skinny horse, he wasn't all that hot,
In days gone by one had to do his best with what he'd got.
I came from Snowy River, up by Kosciusko's side.
As a lad I had no saddle and bareback learnt to ride.

I heard about the escapee, the 'colt from old Regret',
And always one for a bit of fun, I joined up for a bet.
I turned up at the Homestead with that wild and woolly lot,
And the old man said I'd never do, 'wouldn't keep up at a trot'.
But then my good friend Clancy stood up for me with a grin,
And the old man never argued, 'cause he knew he couldn't win.

We galloped off into the hills; my horse was pulling badly,
Whenever we had company, that horse would go so madly.
We found a mob of brumbies and the colt was with them, too,
And the old man gave his orders as into the scrub they flew.
The stockmen rode to wheel them, Clancy raced along their wing,
And my young heart beat so rapidly as I heard his stockwhip ring.

When we reached the mountain's summit, even Clancy pulled
    his steed,
But the yang that I was riding had no mouth and would not heed.
They say I swung my stockwhip round, they say I gave a cheer,
But I was struggling with my nag; those cheers were yells of fear.
It was only fear that saved me; fear had glued me to my seat,
And I never ever dared deny my confidence in that feat.

When I finally reached the bottom of that terrible descent,
I saw a wisp of dust to tell which way the brumbies went.

I found them in a dead-ender, in a gully walled with stone,
That's how I came to turn 'em back, and how I did it on my own.
Now I know I haven't got the right to stake my claim to fame,
So, having set the story straight, I'll just leave out my name.

THE MYSTERY OF THE MAHOGANY SHIP

*The riddle of the mahogany ship and the possible Portuguese discovery
of eastern Australia will remain unsolved until the long-lost wreck
is rediscovered. The 'Portuguese discovery' theory goes like this.*

*From 1511 till 1595, the Portuguese were the only European power
in what is today Malaysia and Indonesia. According to historian João
de Barros, Cristóvão de Mendonça set out on a planned expedition
with three large caravels from Malacca. He explored and charted the
coast of what was called 'Java La Grande' and what we call Australia.*

*Near Warrnambool, one of the caravels was either wrecked,
careened for repairs, ran aground accidentally or was abandoned
at sea and washed ashore. It is still there.*

*Mendonça returned to the Moluccas where he later became the
commander of the Portuguese fleet and, later still, a governor of
one of the provinces of the Spice Islands. Mendonça's original maps
were kept hidden from other foreign powers and were probably lost
in the Lisbon earthquake of 1755, but copies had been made and
they came into the hands of the French and British. Joseph Banks
certainly owned one of them, which is now in the British Museum.*

Here's the yarn.

In January 1836, three men left Port Fairy on a seal-hunting
expedition in a small sailing boat, which overturned near the
mouth of the Hopkins River. One man, Captain Smith, drowned
and the other two, Joseph Wilson and William Gibbs, walked back
to Port Fairy along the beach and discovered a wrecked ship in
the sand dunes.

On their arrival back at Port Fairy, they reported their find to
Captain John Mills who had established a base there for whaling

in 1826. Mills ran the port and whaling station and later became the official port master.

According to tales related later, Wilson told Mills that the wreck had good 'squared timber for the taking' and, having a need for timber at the settlement, Mills and Wilson took two whaleboats to investigate the wreck.

According to accounts given by 'Curly' Donnelly, many years later, they estimated the wreck as being about 100 feet (30.5 metres) long and 40 feet (12.2 metres) wide and half a mile (800 metres) from the low-water mark. It was made of very 'hard dark timber—like mahogany'.

A large group of Aborigines appeared and threatened them as they inspected the wreck. Shots were fired and, after some parlay and reconciliation, the men from Port Fairy left.

Donnelly gave over forty anecdotal accounts concerning the mahogany ship and claimed to have been in the original party led by John Mills to investigate the wreck.

There is indisputable evidence, however, that Donnelly arrived in Victoria with his wife and son as assisted migrants in 1841 and all his stories about the first sightings of the wreck were passed on to him by a lifelong friend, Tasmanian-born Jimmy Clarke, who was in Port Fairy in 1836.

In spite of this, there are almost a hundred references to the wreck in letters and writings throughout the nineteenth century, indicating that it was a common landmark and well-known to locals.

One of the most detailed accounts was given in 1876 by Captain John Mason:

> Riding along the beach from Port Fairy to Warrnambool in the summer of 1846, my attention was attracted to the hull of a vessel embedded high and dry in the Hummocks, far above the reach of any tide. It appeared to have been that of a vessel about 100 tons burden, and from its bleached and weather-beaten appearance, must have remained there many years. The spars and deck were gone, and the hull was full of drift sand. The timber of which

she was built had the appearance of cedar or mahogany. The fact of the vessel being in that position was well known to the whalers in 1836 when the first whaling station was formed in that neighbourhood, and the oldest natives, when questioned, stated their knowledge of it extended from their earliest recollections.

. . . The wreck lies about midway between Belfast and Warrnambool, and is probably by this time entirely covered with drift sand, as during a search made for it within the last few months it was not to be seen. [Port Fairy was known as Belfast from 1843 to 1887, it then reverted to its original European name.]

The Warrnambool Standard carried several articles on the wreck in June and July 1890. Alexander Rollo remembered it as being 'far above high water mark, her stern pointed towards Port Fairy and only her timbers were standing about three or four feet [about a metre] above the sand.'

In recent times, three symposia have been held to investigate the evidence: in 1980, 1987 and 2005. Many books have been written on the subject and, in 1992, the Victorian government offered a reward of $250,000 to anyone who could locate the wreck. Official searches using drilling equipment, in 1999 and 2004, found only small, unidentified fragments of timber.

Local historian Jim Henry spoke to elderly local residents who remembered the ship being seen on picnics to the beach.

Mrs Daisy Smith remembered her mother telling her she saw the ship in 1876:

Mother told us the timbers were very solid and smooth, and polished (she supposed) with the drift sand. The ship was well in the sand hills. It was seen a year or two later but only the top timbers, then it disappeared and has never been seen since.

Rob Simpson, author of *Warrnambool Shipwrecks*, used evidence gathered by Jim Henry, and aerial photography from Google Earth, and claimed to have located the wreck site, in 2010.

Even better, my friend Dennis O'Keeffe knows where the mahogany ship is, he even showed me!

Dennis lives on the outskirts of Warrnambool. He is the world's leading authority on the history of the song 'Waltzing Matilda'; he wrote a book about it.

I'd called in for a visit as I was passing through Warrnambool and happened to mention my interest in the sixteenth-century Portuguese exploration of Australia's coast.

'Oh,' said Dennis casually, 'I can show you where the mahogany ship is.'

I was stunned into silence for a full thirty seconds and sat, trying to consider the relevance of the statement. Why hadn't he claimed the reward offered by the Victorian government? Was he part of some secret local group intent on keeping the knowledge hidden?

'I'll show you where it is,' he added casually, standing up and heading into the kitchen.

I followed.

We stopped at the large picture window and gazed out across the miles of windswept dunes, along the coast to where Port Fairy sits at the end of the bay. Dennis waved his hand grandly across the horizon framed by the window . . . sweeping it slowly left to right over the coastal vista spread before us.

'It's out there . . . somewhere,' he said.

I should have known.

Maybe he's right. Is any of this true? We will never know unless the mystery ship appears again from below the sand.

Perhaps some things are better left a mystery.   **JH**

THE YOWIE

Anecdotal evidence for the existence of the yowie goes back to Aboriginal folklore, where it is referred to variously in different areas as yowie, yahoo-yahoo, doolagarl and goolagard.

In 1795, a group of European settlers on a hunting trip at what became Yowie Bay, near Sydney, reported sighting a man-sized hairy beast dashing away from them through the scrub. Places such as Yahoo Peak in Victoria and Yahoo Valley in New South

Wales are in areas named because they were places where yowies
were said to exist.

Their average height is estimated at 2.3 metres and they are
brown or black in colour, thickset and powerfully built. Their
heads are small in proportion to their bodies and they have no
neck. Their ears are not visible and their noses are flat. Yowie
arms are very long and hang down to knee level. They have
long fingernails and their little fingers act like a second thumb.
Normally bipedal, yowies may sometimes drop to all fours and
juveniles may climb trees.

Apparently they are omnivorous, as reports talk of them
enjoying kangaroo meat but also raiding vegetable patches and
stripping bark in search of grubs. Mostly solitary and nocturnal
by nature, they sometimes exude a foul odour and howl. They also
growl and occasionally beat their chests.

The strongest tradition is in the mountainous, forested areas
of the east coast, from south-east Queensland to north-east
Victoria. This is also supported by patterns of modern day sightings. Sightings of the creature have been reported by hundreds of
Europeans since the 1840s, especially in the 1970s, in Queensland
around Kilcoy and Springbrook, and Woodenbong in northern
New South Wales.

Prehistoric humans lived in Australia. Skeletons resembling
those of the species *Homo erectus* were found at Kow Swamp in
Victoria in 1967. During the digging of irrigation canals, about forty
very unusual skeletons were unearthed. The skeletons, between
9000 and 14,000 years old, were robust, large-toothed and radically
different from modern Aborigines. Their jaws were among the
largest human jaws ever found.

Reported sightings of the yowie are almost identical to those
of the 'bigfoot' or 'sasquwatch' of northern America. If they are
related, however, it's unlikely that they have had a family reunion
for quite some time.   **JH**

KOALA AND KANGAROO
TRADITIONAL/JENKYN THOMAS

The koala and the kangaroo were very friendly. They shared the same gunyah, and hunted together, and were very proud of their long tails.

At this time, a drought was over the land. Water was very scarce, and the two friends had camped by a shallow waterhole, which contained some stagnant water. After the clear springs of the mountains, such water made them sick, but it saved them from dying of thirst.

At sunset, banks of dark clouds would float low across the sky and give promise of heavy rain, but, at sunrise, the sky would be as bright and clear as before. At last, even the supply of stagnant water was exhausted, and the two friends were in a desperate plight.

After some time, the kangaroo spoke and said: 'I shall go to the river and see if I can dig and find water, for if we stay here we shall surely perish from thirst.'

The koala was delighted at the suggestion, and said: 'Yes! Let us both go down to the riverbed. I have very strong arms, and will help you.'

They made their way to the river, but, before reaching it, stumbled across some of their friends who had died of thirst. This made them very serious and determined.

When they reached the river, the sun was very hot and they were very tired. The koala suggested that the kangaroo should start digging, as he knew most about it.

The kangaroo went to work with a will, and dug a deep hole, but no signs of water were visible.

The kangaroo was exhausted with his work, and asked his friend to help him. The koala was very cunning, and said: 'I would help you, but I am feeling very ill; the sun is very hot, and I am afraid I am going to die.' The kangaroo was very sorry for his friend, and set to work again without complaining.

At last, his work was rewarded. A trickle of water appeared in the bottom of the hole, and gradually increased until it filled it to overflowing. The kangaroo went over to his friend, and, touching him gently on the shoulder, said: 'I have discovered water, and will bring some to you.'

Then the koala dashed straight to the waterhole without even replying to the surprised kangaroo. When the koala bent down to drink the water, his tail stuck out like a dry stick. The kangaroo, who could now see the despicable cunning of his friend, was very angry, and, seizing his boomerang, cut off the tail of the drinker as it projected above the waterhole.

To this day, the koala has no tail as evidence of his former laziness and cunning.

BUNYIPS

Bunyips are creatures that lurk in swamps, creeks, waterholes and riverbeds, emerging at night, often with terrifying cries and blood-curdling screams, devouring any animal or human venturing near their home. It is said that women are their favourite prey, most likely because they are more defenceless.

Descriptions of the bunyip vary greatly—from a gorilla-type animal, to half-human-half-animal, to similar to a fish, with scales. Some reports say the bunyip has fur or feathers, a long neck and tail or even claws and horns. Scientists suggest it may be a Diprotodon, which became extinct about 20,000 years ago.

The existence of bunyips was taken very seriously by the white settlers in colonial times. Out in the bushland at night, hearing strange, loud noises, they were sure that the bunyip was out there, waiting to attack them.

In Geelong, in 1845, the unfossilised knee joint of an enormous animal was found. A local Aborigine identified it as a bunyip bone and drew a picture of the bunyip. Around that time, a woman claimed that her mother was killed by a bunyip at Barwon Lakes, just a few miles from Geelong. There are reports of other women being killed at the Barwon River where the barge crossed to South Geelong.

Many Australians now do not believe in the bunyip and disregard it as being purely mythological. There are some though, who still believe the creature exists.

Certainly one of the troopers at the siege of Glenrowan believed in the monster. When Ned Kelly emerged from the mist dressed in armour and an overcoat, complete with his famous steel helmet, the reporters present later wrote that someone shouted, 'It's a ghost!' The troopers opened fire and the bullets bounced off Ned, and Senior Constable Kelly reportedly cried out, 'Look out, boys, it's the bunyip. He's bullet-proof!'   JH

THE BUNYIP
JAMES DEVANEY

Oh, came you up by the place of dread
(West red, and the moon low down)
where no winds blow and the birds have fled
and the gum stands dead and its arms gleam white,
and the tribe sneak by with a stealthy tread
in the ghostly light, in the ghostly light.
Brave Worraland went one grey nightfall
(A woi! woi!) where the grim rocks frown;
he came no more to the camps at all
(Skies dark, and the moon low down).

As we came up by the gully side
(Deep dusk, and the moon low down)
A Dingo whined and a Curlew cried
and the reeds replied as in hushed affright
where tall brave Worraland screamed and died
in the ghostly light, in the ghostly light.
For the Thing lurks there in the haunted place
(A woi! woi!) where the pool is brown,
where lost ones vanish and leave no trace
(Day dead, and the moon low down).

Oh, go not by near the bunyip's lair
(Stars dim, and the moon low down)
or tip-toe past and beware, beware
the dark pool snare and be set for flight,
for things of terror have happened there
in the ghostly light, in the ghostly light
and in the gunyas we crouch and hark
(A woi! woi!) where the dead men drown
the monster's bellow across the dark
(Stars gone, and the moon low down).

SEVEN SISTERS
TRADITIONAL/JENKYN THOMAS

In the Dreamtime, many ages ago, the cluster of stars, which we now know as the Pleiades, or the Seven Sisters, were seven beautiful ice maidens. Their parents were a great rugged mountain whose dark head was hidden in the clouds, and an ice-cold stream that flowed from the snow-clad hills.

The Seven Sisters wandered across the land, with their long hair flying behind them like storm clouds before the breeze. Their cheeks were flushed with the kiss of the sun, and in their eyes was hidden the soft, grey light of the dawn. So entrancing was their beauty, that all men loved them, but the maidens' affections were as cold as the stream which gave them birth, and they never turned aside in their wanderings to gladden the hearts of men.

One day a man named Wurrunnah, by a cunning device, captured two of the maidens, and forced them to live with him, while their five sisters travelled to their home in the sky. When Wurrunnah discovered that the sisters whom he had captured were ice maidens, whose beautiful tresses were like the icicles that drooped from the trees in wintertime, he was disappointed. So he took them to a camp fire, and endeavoured to melt the cold crystals from their beautiful limbs. But, as the ice melted, the water quenched the fire, and he succeeded only in dimming their icy brightness.

The two sisters were very lonely and sad in their captivity, and longed for their home in the clear blue sky. When the shadow of night was over the land, they could see their five sisters beckoning to them as they twinkled afar off. One day, Wurrunnah told them to gather pine-bark in the forest. After a short journey, they came to a great pine tree, and commenced to strip the bark from it. As they did so, the pine tree (which belonged to the same totem as the maidens) extended itself to the sky. The maidens took advantage of this friendly act, and climbed to the home of their sisters. But they never regained their original brightness, and that is the reason why there are five bright stars and two dim ones in the group of the Pleiades.

The Seven Sisters have not forgotten the earth folk. When the snow falls softly, they loose their wonderful tresses to the caress of the breeze, to remind us of their journey across our land.

When the Seven Sisters were on earth, of all the men who loved them, the Berai Berai, or two brothers, were the most faithful. When they hunted in the forest, or waited in the tall reeds for the wild ducks, they always brought the choicest morsels of the chase as an offering to the sisters. When the maidens wandered far across the mountains, the Berai Berai followed them, but their love was not favoured.

When the maidens set out on their long journey to the sky, the Berai Berai were grieved, and said: 'Long have we loved you and followed in your footsteps, O maidens of the dawn, and, when you have left us, we will hunt no more.' And they laid aside their weapons and mourned for the maidens until the dark shadow of death fell upon them. When they died, the spirits pitied them, and placed them in the sky, where they could hear the sisters singing. Thus were they happily rewarded for their constancy. On a starry night, you will see them listening to the song of the Seven Sisters. We call them Orion's Sword and Belt, but it is a happier thought to remember them as the faithful lovers who have listened to the song of the stars from the birth of time.

THE LEGEND OF FISHER'S GHOST

Four months after the mysterious disappearance of local farmer, Fred Fisher, in 1826, a respected and honest settler, John Farley, arrived at a local hotel in a state of shock.

In one version of the story it is said John claimed he had seen the ghost of Fred Fisher sitting on the rail of a bridge over a creek. The ghost pointed to a paddock down the creek then faded away. The body of Fred Fisher was later discovered in the paddock where the ghost had pointed.

The other version says Farley reported seeing a 'ghostly figure' sitting on the bridge railing. Investigations showed blood on the bridge at the point where Farley saw the spectre and a tracker was brought in and said he smelled 'white man fat' under the bridge. The body was found in a deep hole in the creek near the bridge.

Frederick George James Fisher was born in London in 1792. He was a shopkeeper and, either innocently or deliberately, obtained forged banknotes through his business. In 1815, Fred was sentenced to fourteen years' transportation to Australia. In 1822, he applied for a ticket of leave and secured a property at Campbelltown.

In 1825, Fred had an argument with a local carpenter and received a light prison sentence. Worried about his farm, Fred gave his neighbour, George Worrall, power of attorney during his sentence but, after his release in June 1826, Fred disappeared and George Worrall announced that he'd sailed for England. Three weeks later, George sold Fred's house and belongings. In September 1826, George Worrall was arrested on suspicion of Fred's murder. During the trial stories of the ghost emerged and George confessed—even though the tale of the ghostly sighting could not be told in court, as stories of the supernatural were not permitted in a court of law.

Worrall was hanged at The Rocks.   **JH**

THE BUNYIP AND THE WHISTLING KETTLE

JOHN MANIFOLD

I knew a most superior camper
Whose methods were absurdly wrong,
He did not live on tea and damper
But took a little stove along.

And every place he came to settle
He spread with gadgets saving toil,
He even had a whistling kettle
To warn him it was on the boil.

Beneath the waratahs and wattles,
Boronia and coolibah,
He scattered paper, cans and bottles,
And parked his nasty little car.

He camped, this sacrilegious stranger
(The moon was at the full that week),
Once in a spot that teemed with danger
Beside a bunyip-haunted creek.

He spread his junk but did not plunder,
Hoping to stay the weekend long;
He watched the bloodshot sun go under
Across the silent billabong.

He ate canned food without demurring,
He put the kettle on for tea.
He did not see the water stirring
Far out beside a sunken tree.

Then, for the day had made him swelter
And night was hot and tense to spring,
He donned a bathing-suit in shelter,
And left the firelight's friendly ring.

He felt the water kiss and tingle.
He heard the silence—none too soon!
A ripple broke against the shingle,
And dark with blood it met the moon.

Abandoned in the hush, the kettle
Screamed as it guessed its master's plight,
And loud it screamed, the lifeless metal,
Far into the malicious night.

WHY THE CROW IS BLACK
TRADITIONAL/JENKYN THOMAS

One day, a crow and a hawk hunted together in the bush. After travelling together for some time, they decided to hunt in opposite directions, and, at the close of the day, to share whatever game they had caught.

The crow travelled against the sun, and at noon arrived at a broad lagoon, which was the haunt of the wild ducks. The crow hid in the tall green reeds fringing the lagoon, and prepared to trap the ducks.

First, he got some white clay, and, having softened it with water, placed two pieces in his nostrils. He then took a long piece of hollow reed through which he could breathe under water, and finally tied a net bag around his waist in which to place the ducks.

On the still surface of the lagoon, the tall gum trees were reflected like a miniature forest. The ducks, with their bronze plumage glistening in the sun, were swimming among the clumps of reeds, and only paused to dive for a tasty morsel hidden deep in the waterweeds.

The crow placed the reed in his mouth, and, without making any sound, waded into the water. He quickly submerged himself, and the only indication of his presence in the lagoon was a piece of dry reed which projected above the surface of the water, and through which the crow was breathing. When he reached the centre of the waterhole he remained perfectly still. He did not have to wait long for the ducks to swim above his head. Then, without making any sound or movement, he seized one by the leg, quickly pulled it beneath the water, killed it, and placed it in the net bag.

By doing this, he did not frighten the other ducks, and, in a short time he had trapped a number of them. He then left the lagoon and continued on his way until he came to a river.

The crow was so pleased with his success at the waterhole that he determined to spear some fish before he returned to his camp. He left the bag of ducks on the bank of the river, and, taking his fish spear, he waded into the river until the water reached his waist. Then he stood very still, with the spear poised for throwing.

A short distance from the spot where he was standing, a slight ripple disturbed the calm surface of the water. With the keen eye of the hunter, he saw the presence of fish, and, with a swift movement of his arm, he hurled the spear, and his unerring aim was rewarded with a big fish. Many fish soon agitated the water, and the crow took advantage of this to spear many more. With this heavy load of game, he turned his face towards home.

The hawk was very unfortunate in his hunting. He stalked a kangaroo many miles, and then lost sight of it in the thickly wooded hills. He then decided to try the river for some fish, but the crow had made the water muddy and frightened the fish, so again he was unsuccessful.

At last the hawk decided to return to his gunyah with the hope that the crow would secure some food, which they had previously agreed to share. When the hawk arrived, he found that the crow had been there before him and had prepared and eaten his evening meal.

He at once noticed that the crow had failed to leave a share for him. This annoyed the hawk, so he approached the crow and said: 'I see you have had a good hunt today. I walked many miles but could not catch even a lizard. I am tired and would be glad to have my share of food, as we agreed this morning.'

'You are too lazy,' the crow replied. 'You must have slept in the sun instead of hunting for food. Anyhow, I've eaten mine and cannot give you any.'

This made the hawk very angry, and he attacked the crow. For a long time they struggled around the dying embers of the camp fire, until the hawk seized the crow and rolled him in the black ashes.

When the crow recovered from the fight, he found that he could not wash the ashes off, and, since that time, crows have always been black. The crow was also punished for hiding the food which he could not eat by being condemned to live on putrid flesh.

THE TANTANOOLA TIGER

The story goes that, in the early 1880s, a circus camped between Millicent and Mount Gambier, in south-east South Australia, discovered that a Bengal tiger had escaped; they reported this to the police. In the early 1890s, sheep began disappearing from the Tantanoola area and the tiger was blamed; one person saw an animal carrying a fully grown sheep in its mouth.

Tantanoola was besieged by tiger mania. Children were given shotgun escort to and from school. Guns were kept at the ready. In August 1895, Tom Donovan shot the Tantanoola Tiger 20 kilometres from town. A taxidermist in Mount Gambier identified it as an Assyrian or Russian wolf believed to have come from one of the three ships wrecked immediately off the coast between 1890 to 1893. You can see it in the pub at Tantanoola. It is quite harmless—it's stuffed!

Despite the shooting of the Tantanoola tiger, sheep continued being killed until Adelaide detective, Herbert Allchurch, arrested local trapper, Charlie Edmunson, who, at his trial in 1911, admitted to the theft of over 4000 sheep over twenty years. He had sold the skins and left the carcasses to rot. He got six years' hard labour in January 1911 and the Tantanoola tiger never struck again.

Australia has many large, mysterious cats, including the Jamberoo tiger, the Lithgow panther, the Cordering cougar and the Grampians puma. The beast of Buderim and the Cowra cougar are often said to be cougars which were brought over by American troops as mascots. There is no record of this ever happening.

Both the Jamberoo tiger, shot in 1932, and the Grampians puma, shot in 2005, turned out to be large feral cats.

I once asked northern New South Wales newspaper editor and local historian John Sommerlad what he thought the Emmaville panther was. The beast had been supposedly sighted at night on bush roads over the years and was variously described as a large, cat-like black beast with eyes like coals of fire.

John replied that he wasn't sure what it was, but it was very useful when there wasn't much news to put in the newspaper! **JH**

THE RAINBOW
TRADITIONAL/JENKYN THOMAS

Far to the west in the deep blue sea, there dwells a great serpent named Thugine. His scales are of many shimmering colours. When a rainbow appears in the sky, it is Thugine curving his back and the sun reflecting the colours of his scales.

Many years ago, a tribe camped close to a sea beach. One morning, they all went out to fish and hunt, with the exception of two boys, whom the old men left in charge of the camp. 'Wander not into the forest lest the wild dogs eat you, or to the beach, where Thugine the serpent is—waiting for children who wander alone.' This was the parting advice of the old men to the boys.

When the men had departed, the boys played about the camp for a while, but they soon grew tired of their games. The day was very hot, and, in the distance, the boys could hear the dull, deep booming of the surf. Both the boys were longing to go to the beach, but were afraid to speak their desire.

At last the elder boy spoke, and said: 'The fires of the sun are burning bright today, but on the breeze I can feel the cool breath of the sea. Let us go to the beach, and we shall return before the shadow of night has fallen. The men will not know.' The other boy hesitated and was afraid, but at last he yielded, and together they wandered hand in hand through the bush.

After walking for some time, they came to an opening in the trees, and, before their expectant gaze, a wonderful scene unfolded.

A golden beach stretched far away until it was lost to view in the dim distance. The cool waves rolled lazily in great green billows from the outer reef, and dashed in a haze of sparkling white foam on the hot sands of the palm-fringed beach. The song of the sea rose in a deep, loud booming, and gradually died away to a low, soft murmuring.

The boys were lost in wonder at the beauty of the scene. Never had they seen such an expanse of water sparkling in the sun like the blue sky. Over its rippled surface, the shadows of the clouds floated like sails across the sun.

Thugine, the serpent, had seen the boys coming from afar, and, while they played on the beach, he swam swiftly and silently to the shore and seized them. When the men arrived at the camp, they discovered the absence of the boys. They searched the bush all through the night, and at dawn came to the beach.

Far from the shore, they saw two black rocks jutting out of the sea. Then they knew that Thugine had taken the wandering boys and turned them into rocks. The men turned their faces again towards the camp; their hearts were heavy and their thoughts were sad.

To this day, the rocks remain between Double Island Point and Inship Point. When a rainbow appears in the sky, the old men of the tribe tell the story of the disobedience and punishment of the wandering boys.

THE GHOST OF THE PRINCESS THEATRE

Gounod's opera *Faust* was being performed at the Princess Theatre. The opera ends with Mephistopheles returning to the fires of Hell with his prize, Dr Faustus, who had sold his soul to the devil.

In March 1888, at the Princess Theatre in Melbourne, the role of Mephistopheles was being played by Frederick Baker, who used the more operatic sounding stage name of Federici.

The opera climaxes with a trapdoor opening and an invisible force taking Mephistopheles down to Hell. Federici vanished from the audience's view but evidently fell as he attempted to descend the ladder provided, and the fall brought on a fatal heart attack. He died moments later in his dressing room.

The rest of the cast were waiting in the wings to take their curtain calls and had no knowledge of the incident. The cast took its bows to the usual applause. When the cast was later told Federici had died and could not have returned to the stage, they replied in confusion: 'He's just been onstage and taken the bows with us.'

Over the years, a figure assumed to be the ghost of Federici was often seen by theatre staff sitting in an empty box observing various productions. New staff members would report that an audience member had somehow entered a closed section of the theatre but when they went to eject him he wasn't there. Long-time staff would reply, 'That's just Mr Federici, he's often here.'

Fast forward from 1888 to the early 1970s. George Miller (later well-known for his *Mad Max* movies and the Oscar-winning animated film *Happy Feet*) was filming a documentary at the Princess Theatre when a photograph was taken of the film set. The photograph revealed an ashen-faced, partly transparent observer in a cloak. No one had seen the figure on the set that day, and it only appeared in the photograph.   **JH**

EVENING STAR
TRADITIONAL/JENKYN THOMAS

Rolla-Mano was the old man of the sea. The blue ocean, with all its wonderful treasures of glistening pearls, white foam and pink coral, belonged to him. In the depths of the sea, he ruled a kingdom of shadows and strange forms, to which the light of the sun descended in green and grey beams.

The forests of this weird land were many trees of brown sea kelp, whose long arms waved slowly to and fro with the ebb and flow of the water. Here and there were patches of sea grass, fine and soft as a maiden's hair. In the shadow of the trees lurked a thousand terrors of the deep.

In a dark rocky cave, a giant octopus spread its long, writhing tentacles in search of its prey, and gazed the while through the water with large lustreless eyes. In and out of the kelp, a grey shark swam swiftly and without apparent motion, while bright-coloured fish darted out of the path of danger.

Across the rippled sand, a great crab ambled awkwardly to its hiding place behind a white-fluted clamshell. And over all waved the long, brown arms of the sea kelp forest. Such was the kingdom of Rolla-Mano, the old man of the sea.

One day, Rolla-Mano went to fish in a lonely mangrove swamp close to the seashore. He caught many fish, and cooked them at a fire. While eating his meal, he noticed two women approach him. Their beautiful bodies were as lithe and graceful as the wattle tree, and in their eyes was the soft light of the dusk. When they spoke, their voices were as sweet and low as the sighing of the night breeze through the reeds in the river. Rolla-Mano determined to capture them.

With this intention, he hid in the branches of the mangrove tree, and, when the women were close to him, he threw his net over them. One, however, escaped by diving into the water. He was so enraged at her escape that he jumped in after her with a burning fire stick in his hand. As soon as the fire stick touched the water, the sparks hissed and scattered to the sky, where they remain as golden stars to this day.

Rolla-Mano did not capture the woman who dived into the dark waters of the swamp. After a fruitless search, he returned to the shore and took the other woman to live with him forever in the sky. She is the evening star.

From her resting place, she gazes through the mists of eternity at the restless sea—the dark, mysterious kingdom of Rolla-Mano.

On a clear summer night, when the sky is studded with golden stars, you will remember that they are the sparks from the fire stick of Rolla-Mano, and the beautiful evening star is the woman he captured in the trees of the mangrove swamp.

THE DEMON SNOW-SHOES
A LEGEND OF KIANDRA
BARCROFT BOAKE

The snow lies deep on hill and dale,
In rocky gulch and grassy vale,
The tiny, trickling, tumbling falls
Are frozen 'twixt their rocky walls
That grey and brown look silent down
Upon Kiandra's shrouded town.

The Eucumbene itself lies dead,
Fast frozen in its narrow bed,
And distant sounds ring out quite near,
The crystal air is froze so clear,
While to and fro the people go
In silent swiftness o'er the snow.

And, like a mighty gallows-frame,
The derrick in the New Chum claim
Hangs over where, despite the cold,
Strong miners seek the hidden gold,
And stiff and blue, half-frozen through,
The fickle dame of Fortune woo.

Far out, along a snow capped range,
There rose a sound which echoed strange,
Where snow-emburthen'd branches hang,
And flashing icicles, there rang
A gay refrain, as towards the plain
Sped swiftly downward Carl the Dane.

His long, lithe snow-shoes sped along
In easy rhythm to his song;
Now slowly circling round the hill,
Now speeding downward with a will;
The crystals crash and blaze and flash
As o'er the frozen crust they dash.

Among the hills the first he shone
Of all who buckled snow-shoe on,
For though the mountain lads were fleet,
But one bold rival dare compete,
To veer and steer, devoid of fear,
Beside this strong-limbed mountaineer.

'Twas Davy Eccleston who dared
To cast the challenge: If Carl cared
On shoes to try their mutual pace,
Then let him enter for the race,
Which might be run by anyone—
A would-be champion. Carl said 'Done.'

But not alone in point of speed
They sought to gain an equal meed,
For in the narrow lists of love,
Dave Eccleston had cast the glove:
Though both had prayed, the blushing maid
As yet no preference betrayed.

But played them off, as women will,
One 'gainst the other one, until
A day when she was sorely pressed
To loving neither youth confessed,
But did exclaim—the wily dame,
'Who wins this race, I'll bear his name!'

These words were running through Carl's head
As o'er the frozen crust he sped,
But suddenly became aware
That not alone he travelled there,
He sudden spied, with swinging stride,
A stranger speeding by his side;

The breezes o'er each shoulder toss'd
His beard, bediamonded with frost,
His eyes flashed strangely, bushy browed,

His breath hung round him like a shroud.
He never spoke, nor silence broke,
But by the Dane sped stroke for stroke.

'Old man! I neither know your name,
Nor what you are, nor whence you came:
But this, if I but had your shoes
This championship I ne'er could lose.
To call them mine, those shoes divine,
I'll gladly pay should you incline.'

The stranger merely bowed his head—
'The shoes are yours,' he gruffly said;
'I change with you, though at a loss,
And in return I ask that cross
Which, while she sung, your mother hung
Around your neck when you were young.'

Carl hesitated when he heard
The price, but not for long demurred,
And gave the cross; the shoes were laced
Upon his feet in trembling haste,
So long and light, smooth polished, bright.
His heart beat gladly at the sight.

Now, on the morning of the race,
Expectancy on every face,
They come the programme to fulfil
Upon the slope of Township Hill;
With silent feet the people meet,
While youths and maidens laughing greet.

High-piled the flashing snowdrifts lie,
And laugh to scorn the sun's dull eye.
That, glistening feebly, seems to say—
'When Summer comes you'll melt away:
You'll change your song when I grow strong,
I think so, though I may be wrong.'

The pistol flashed, and off they went
Like lightning on the steep descent,
Resistlessly down-swooping, swift
O'er the smooth face of polished drift
The racers strain with might and main.
But in the lead flies Carl the Dane.

Behind him Davy did his best,
With hopeless eye and lip compressed:
Beat by a snow-shoe length at most,
They flash and pass the winning-post.
The maiden said, 'I'll gladly wed
The youth who in this race has led.'

But where was he? still speeding fast,
Over the frozen stream he pass'd,
They watched his flying form until
They lost it over Sawyer's Hill,
Nor saw it more, the people swore
The like they'd never seen before.

The way he scaled that steep ascent
Was quite against all precedent,
While others said he could but choose
To do it on those demon shoes;
They talked in vain, for Carl the Dane
Was never seen in flesh again.

***

But now the lonely diggers say
That sometimes at the close of day
They see a misty wraith flash by
With the faint echo of a cry,
It may be true; perhaps they do,
I doubt it much; but what say you?

THE MYSTERY OF THE SS *WARATAH*

Late one afternoon in July 1909, the steamship SS *Waratah*, Blue Anchor Line's newest addition to its fleet of twenty vessels, pulled away from the wharf in Durban, South Africa.

With Captain Joshua Ilbery watching from the foredeck, a tug steered the vessel safely out of port into deep water. Captain Ilbery waved the tug goodbye and the passengers lining the deck did likewise.

That was the last time any of the 211 passengers and crew of the SS *Waratah* were seen alive or dead. The ship and all aboard simply vanished without a trace.

The Blue Anchor Line's newest luxury passenger and cargo steamship, the SS *Waratah* had sailed on its maiden voyage from London to Australia on 5 November 1908 under the command of a sixty-nine-year-old Captain Ilbery, a man with thirty years' nautical experience.

At 150 metres long and weighing 9339 tons, the *Waratah* boasted eight state rooms, a hundred first-class cabins, a saloon and a luxurious music lounge. With its role in bringing emigrants to Australia from the Mother Country, the cargo holds could be converted into large dormitories capable of housing 700 steerage passengers. She had lifeboats for 921.

When not carrying passengers to new life Down Under, the *Waratah* could carry 15,000 tons of cargo and coal in her separate watertight compartments, which were similar to those built into the unsinkable *Titanic* a few years later. As an insurance risk, the *Waratah* was classified '+100 A1' at Lloyds—their top rating.

There were, however, some misgivings about the way she handled in rolling seas and Captain Ilbery took on more ballast to attempt to counter a list the ship developed in heavy weather.

On her first voyage, one passenger reported that, in heavy seas, she developed a list to starboard to such an extent that water would not run out of the baths, and she held this list for several hours before rolling upright. Another passenger, physicist Professor William Bragg, theorised that the ship's 'metacentre' was below her centre of gravity and when she slowly rolled over towards one side, she reached a point of equilibrium and would stay leaning over until a shift in the sea or wind pushed her upright.

One passenger on the vessel's second voyage from Australia to England was Claude Sawyer, a seasoned ocean traveller who also had some reservations about the seaworthiness of the *Waratah*. He noted that she seemed to behave oddly on big seas, leaving her nose down into every second wave and listing to starboard.

Other passengers and crew members later said the *Waratah* was perfectly stable, with a comfortable, easy roll.

One night at sea, during the return leg of her second voyage, Claude Sawyer dreamed he was standing on the ship's boat deck staring into the sea when a knight on a horse rose out of the waves swinging a medieval sword. A bloodstained flag was fluttering behind him. The apparition screamed out 'Waratah! Waratah!' then faded. Sawyer woke up screaming in his berth.

The following day, Claude Sawyer related his fears to several people and told them of his vision. One was Mrs Alexandra Hay, a lady from Coventry, who was going home with her daughter. While shocked by the story, she said she was not going to change ships.

Sawyer also pleaded with the man sharing his cabin, John Ebsworth, a solicitor on his way to defend a case in London, to get off the liner with him at Durban. Ebsworth was concerned enough to discuss the premonition with Father Fadle, a South African priest travelling on the ship, but the priest scoffed at the dream.

Claude Sawyer was the only London-bound passenger to leave the ship at Durban. He sent a telegram to his wife which read: 'Thought *Waratah* top-heavy, landed Durban.'

Sawyer explained his experiences in detail to the Board of Trade inquiry held in London in December 1910.

After leaving Durban, the *Waratah* headed south along the Transkei coast for Cape Town. With the sky clear and the headwinds increasing, Ilbery anticipated reaching Cape Town in four days.

The next morning, *Waratah* was spotted by the freighter *Clan McIntyre*, which had departed Durban the previous day. After learning via morse signals that the liner was the *Waratah*, the

Clan McIntyre asked about the weather they'd encountered coming from Australia.

'Strong southwesterly and southerly winds,' replied the *Waratah*.

'Thanks, goodbye. Pleasant voyage,' was the final message from *Clan McIntyre*.

Waratah replied, 'Thanks. Same to you. Goodbye.'

Captain C.G. Phillips of the *Clan McIntyre* stated at the inquiry that he kept sight of the *Waratah* for several hours after passing. The seas were now rolling, producing whitecaps, but visibility was improving.

He testified that the *Waratah* pulled about 10 miles (16 kilometres) ahead of the *Clan McIntyre*, and 'appeared to be perfectly upright and to be in no difficulty, steaming rapidly'.

At 9.20 a.m., the *Waratah* altered course, picked up speed and disappeared from sight into the mist. What happened after that remains a mystery to this day. The *Waratah* disappeared completely.

Captain Phillips told the inquiry something very odd.

'Some hours after I had sent the signal to the liner,' he stated, 'I was standing on the bridge when I sighted another ship, a sailing vessel. There was something strangely old-fashioned about her rig. I'm not a superstitious man, but I know my seafaring lore. The rig of the vessel immediately brought to mind the legend of the Flying Dutchman. The phantom ship held me spellbound. It disappeared in the direction taken by the *Waratah*, and I had a feeling it was a sign of disaster for the liner.'

Searches were conducted by three British navy cruisers and two different ships were hired by relatives and the shipping company to conduct exhaustive searches. The Blue Anchor Line chartered the Union Castle ship *Sabine* to conduct a search, which covered 22,500 kilometres, and relatives of the *Waratah* passengers chartered the *Wakefield* and conducted a search for three months in 1910.

All types of strange theories were put forward. Spiritualists in Australia and South Africa made announcements about the fate of the vessel based on messages supposedly given to them from those who died on her.

The inquiry was unable to come to any conclusions and, although it made negative comments about some of the company's practices, it did not attach any blame to the Blue Anchor Line.

Wrecks found and supposed to be the *Waratah* in 1925, 1977 and 2001 all proved upon investigation to be other ships. Emlyn Brown, who spent twenty-two years searching for the wreck, said in 2004, 'I've exhausted all the options. I now have no idea where to look.'

The most plausible theory is that the *Waratah* was hit by a giant, freak wave that rolled her over outright or stove-in her cargo hatches, filling the holds with water and pulling the ship down almost instantly. If the ship had capsized or rolled over completely, any buoyant debris would have been trapped under the wreck, explaining the total lack of any bodies or wreckage.

Waves of up to 20 metres in height occur in that part of the Southern Ocean and the cruiser HMS *Hermes*, while searching near the area of the last sighting of the *Waratah*, encountered waves so large and strong that she strained her hull and had to be placed in dry dock and repaired.

So, despite the long and thorough searches, and subsequent search expeditions over the years, the disappearance of the SS *Waratah* without a trace remains unexplained today. Nothing was ever found.

The Curse

The *Waratah* was named especially to please her prospective Australian customers. She was designed and built for the Britain to Australia run and several Australian newspapers enthused about the very Aussie name of this new 'state of the art' vessel when she was launched.

They may not have been so enthusiastic had they researched the name before writing so effusively about it.

In 1848, a sailing ship named *Waratah* bound for Sydney sank off Ushant, and thirteen lives were lost. In 1887, not one but two ships, each named *Waratah*, sank off Sydney within months of each other.

Two years later, following a cyclone, the newly built *Waratah* from the port of Fremantle, sank off Cape Preston in the Pilbara, with the loss of all crew and, just five years later, yet another trading vessel named *Waratah* was lost on the coast of northern Australia.

Lucky Jim

Mr James Hardy missed his berth on the doomed ship not once but twice. In London's *Daily Mail* he wrote:

> On the morning of June 26, 1909, I took a cab to the docks at Sydney, Australia, to catch the S.S. *Waratah*, due to sail to England. Bounding a corner a wheel came off and my vehicle collapsed. I missed the ship, which sailed with my heavy baggage, but I decided to catch her at Melbourne. The day before the *Waratah* left Melbourne I received an urgent telegram from a friend informing me he was leaving Sydney that night and he must see me before I sailed. When he arrived next morning his business proved so vital that once again I missed the *Waratah*.

JH

THE SPEEWAH
ANONYMOUS

The Speewah is a legendary sheep station which lies 'outback', 'beyond the black stump', 'back o' Bourke', 'west of sunset', 'in the land where the crow flies backward and the pelican builds her nest'. At any rate, the Speewah was so big that when the wood-and-water-joey went to close the gate to the house paddock, he had to take a week's rations, and the jackaroo who was sent to bring in the mustering horses that were hobbled in the horse paddock was often gone for three months.

When shearing was on, which it always was because the flock was so big it took a year to shear, the shearers' cook needed a good horse to get around the frying pan. The boundary riders had to change their watches when they passed through the different time

*zones. The flocks of galahs were so big that when they took fright
in a rainstorm no rain hit the ground for several hours.*

The station known as Speewah is three hundred miles across,
But every mile there's dams and huts where travellers can doss.
There's fifty sheep per acre and they're lambing all the year,
There's twenty million sheep on Speewah, or something very near.

We're off to the Speewah in the Never-Never Land,
Way across the Cooper and beyond the belt of sand,
We're sick of always travelling along the same old track,
So we'll make a break for Speewah in the land outback.

Although there's twenty million sheep that wear the Speewah brand,
You'll never find a dozen dead in all the Speewah land,
They always pay the union rate a pound-a-hundred pay,
And if the sheep are wet or not it's up to us to say.

We're off to the Speewah, see us step it out,
Off to the Speewah where there's never any drought,
Where the fleeces are fine and the sheep are tough,
We've stuck around the other stations for long enough.

There's plates of ice-cream in the shed, and on the hottest days,
Shandies with a foamin' head are handed round on trays.
So give us just a kiss or two and wish us luck ahead,
In six months we'll be safely through or else we'll all be dead.

We're off to the Speewah where the work's all right,
With a grand piano playing in the hut at night.
A pretty girl to play it, too, with golden hair,
We're off to the Speewah, where they treat you fair!

CROOKED MICK

Crooked Mick of the Speewah was larger than life—he grew so fast
as a kid his mother tried to slow his growth by ring-barking his
legs, which left him with a bad limp, but didn't stop him growing.

He could out ride, out shear and out swear any stockman, shearer or bullocky.

According to Alan Marshall, who documented the yarns and legends of this mythical Aussie, the legendary heroes of American folk tales, such as Paul Bunyan and Pecos Bill, are just sissies when compared to the men of the Speewah. Crooked Mick would sooner have a fight than a feed and, when he did eat, a normal meal was two sheep, or one and a half if they were the Border Leicester ration sheep used on the Speewah.

Mick's mother was a drover and a remarkable woman. One night, she was camped in her tent when she received a visit from a stranger. All she could recall, or would recall, in later years, was that he had a very thick bushy beard and a great sense of humour.

The stranger only stayed a few minutes and it was such a trivial event that she forgot all about it, which is quite understandable given that her work was so hard and her responsibilities so great, and there was a drought on. She only remembered the event suddenly and quite vividly nine months later when she was riding a bucking horse she was attempting to break in.

Crooked Mick was born on the back of that bucking horse and, although the brave woman was startled, she managed to stay on until the happy event was complete, and she was then thrown. Crooked Mick, however, stayed on the horse's back and completed the ride, bringing the beast to a standstill and then riding back to collect his mother.

When he was fully-grown, Mick's feet were so big that he had to go outside to turn around and it took a full bullock's hide to make him a pair of slippers. He was a heavy smoker from an early age and usually one jackeroo was employed full time in cutting tobacco and filling Mick's pipes.

In the shearing shed, no one could come near Mick's output. He worked so fast that his shears ran red hot and he used half a dozen pairs of shears at a time, with five pairs cooling in a pot of water while he used the sixth pair. He'd usually finish his tally by the end of the breakfast run. It took three wool pressers to handle his daily clip, and they had to work overtime at the end of the day to manage it.

When shearing was over, Mick would spend his time fencing with his dog for company. Firstly he would cut brigelow posts, which he did with an axe in each hand to save time. His dog would scout ahead and mark the best trees by tearing off patches of bark so Mick could easily recognise them, which meant he didn't have to stop walking as he used the two axes. Then the dog would run back and carry the posts to the fence line and drop them at the appropriate places.

Once the posts were cut and placed, Mick would start on the fencing. The dog would run ahead and calculate the correct places along the fence line for the posts, keeping the line absolutely straight and digging the first openings for each post. Then Mick would follow with a crowbar in one hand and a shovel in the other and complete the holes without breaking stride. The dog then doubled back and dropped the posts in and Mick would fill in and tamp down each post as he walked back to the station in the opposite direction going home.

Things are pretty big on the Speewah. Crooked Mick was once driving a mob of sheep through the bush on the Speewah when suddenly it became as dark as the inside of a black dog. For over a week, he kept moving those sheep through darkness so deep he couldn't even see them. His dog would do a round trip, circle the mob twice a day and come back and bark three times to tell Mick they were all accounted for.

Suddenly the light flickered and then came back on again. Mick was puzzled, and when he looked back he saw that he had been moving the mob of sheep through a hollow log.   JH

SHEARING ON THE SPEEWAH
ANONYMOUS

I had a relation on Speewah Station,
He told me what he'd seen there,

I won't deny it sounds a lie,
But then, I've never been there.

But I did hear it takes a year
To ride across the station,
It's quite a ride 'cause it's as wide
As a European nation.

The shearing shed, my relation said,
Was mostly made of stone.
It stretched a week along the creek,
It's length was never known.

Each catching pen for the shearing men
Was large beyond all reason.
He lost a pup once penning up,
And found its bones next season.

The boss of course had to ride a horse
Up and down the board,
And when he'd passed the rousies laughed
And cheered with one accord.

For well they knew, that cheeky crew,
He wouldn't be back for days.
They could laugh and play all through the day,
Or just sit back and laze.

It took a drought to make the shed cut out,
There were so many sheep there.
A million rams, twice as many lambs,
The musterers had to keep there.

This yarn is tall, no doubt at all,
But that place is pretty rough.
So, if you go, you ought to know,
Those blokes are really tough.

HEAT
LENNIE LOWER

Boastful remarks have recently come from the vicinity of Parkes. Eggs have been hatched in the heatwave, without the aid of the hen.

'A householder gathering eggs, found that one had rolled from the nest into the sunlight. It was perfectly fresh, but cooked.'

Stay those 'Oh, yeah!'s. We have been in places where it was so hot that men's moustaches burst into flame. Elderly gentlemen with beards were razed to the ground.

On our poultry farm new-laid incandescent eggs were always on deck. The fowls had to do their laying on the run. Every time we heard a cackle we had to rush out with a bucket of water to put the hen out.

You don't know anything about heat. Many's the time we had to crawl inside the stove to get a bit of coolth.

People going to the city would find themselves stranded in the middle of the bush, owing to the railway lines melting and running off down the embankment.

Then there was the girl who went out in a muslin frock, which burst into flames as soon as she got out of the shade. After that the whole male population of the town joined the fire brigade. We, yourself, walked about for a fortnight carrying a ladder, and always seemed to be in the wrong district.

We believe that things became much worse later on, but in the meantime, with the rest of the wealthier people, we had biffed off to the Sahara Desert for the winter sports.

Shortly after that we were frozen to death in Egypt. We always were unlucky.

THE LEGEND OF THE OOZLUM BIRD
W.T. GOODGE

It was on the Diamantina where the alligators grow,
And the native's allegations ain't particularly low.
He was old and he was ugly, he was dirty, he was low,
He could lie like Ananias, and they called him Ginger Joe.

He was 'wood-and-water joey' at the 'Jackeroos Retreat',
Where the swagmen and the shearers and the boundary riders
    meet,
And he 'pitched a lot of fairies' but the best I ever heard,
Was McPherson's trip to Sydney on the famous Oozlum Bird.

'You can talk about yer racehorse and the paces he can go,
But it jist amounts to crawlin', nothink else!' said Ginger Joe.
'And them cycle blokes with pacers, you can take my bloomin' word
They're a funeral procession to the blinded Oozlum Bird!

'Do yez know Marengo Station? It's a way beyond the peak,
Over sixty miles beyond it as you go to Cooper's Creek.
I was cook at Old Marengo when McTavish had the run
And his missus died and left him with a boy—the only one.

'Jock McPherson was his nephew, lately out from Scotland, too,
Been sent out to get "experience" as a kind of jackeroo.
Well this kid of old McTavish was a regular little brick,
And we all felt mighty sorry when we heard that he was sick.

'But, McTavish! Well, I reckon I am something on the swear,
But I never heard sich language as McTavish uttered there!
For he cursed the blessed country and the cattle and the sheep
And the station-hands and shearers till your blessed flesh would
    creep!

'It was something like a fever that the little chap had got,
And McTavish he remembered, when he'd cursed and sworn a lot,
That a chemist down in Sydney had a special kind of stuff
Which would cure the kiddy's fever in a jiffy, sure enough.

'So he sent me inter town upon the fastest horse we had
So that I can wire Sydney for the medsin for the lad.
They can send it by the railway and by special pack from Bourke;
It would take a week to do it and be mighty slipp'ry work.

'Well, off I gallops inter town and sends the wire all right;
And I looks around the township, meanin' stoppin' for the night.

I was waitin' in the bar-room, that same bar-room, for a drink,
When a wire from McPherson comes from Sydney! Strike me pink!

'I had left him at Marengo on the morning of that day!
He was talking to McTavish at the time I rode away!
And yet, here's a wire from Sydney! And it says, "Got here all right,
Got the medsin, am jist leavin', will be home again tonight!"

'Well, I thought I had the jim-jams, yes I did, for, spare me days!
How in thunder had McPherson got ter Sydney, anyways?
But he'd got there, that was certain, the wire was plain and clear!
I could never guess conundrums, so I had another beer.

'In the morning bright and early, I was out and saddled up,
And away to break the record of old Carbine in the Cup,
For I made that cuddy gallop as he never did before,
And, so-help-me-bob, McPherson was there waiting at the door!

'And the kid was right as ninepence, sleepin' peaceful in his bunk,
And McTavish so delighted he'd made everybody drunk!
And McPherson says, "Well, Ginger, you did pretty well I heard,
But you must admit I beat you—'cause I rode the Oozlum Bird!"

'He said he'd often studied science, long before he came out here,
And he'd struck upon a notion, which you'll think is mighty queer,
That the Earth rolls round to eastward, and that birds, by rising
    high,
Might just stop and travel westward, while the earth was rolling by!

'So he saddled up the Oozlum, rose some miles above the plain,
And let the Earth turn underneath him till he spotted The Domain!
Then he came down, walked up George Street, got the stuff and
    wired me,
Rose again and reached Marengo, just as easy as could be!

'"But," says I, "If you went westward, just as simple as you say,
How did you get back?" He answered, "Oh, I came the other way!"
So, in six-and-twenty hours, take the yarn for what it's worth,
Jock McPherson and the Oozlum had been right around the Earth!

'It's a curious bird, the Oozlum, and a bird that's mighty wise,
For it always flies tail-first to keep the dust out of its eyes.
And I heard that since McPherson did that famous record ride,
They won't let a man get near 'em, couldn't catch one if you tried!

'If you don't believe my story, and some people don't, yer know,
Why the blinded map will prove it, strike me fat!' said Ginger Joe.
'Look along the Queensland border, on the South Australian side,
There's this township, christened "Birdsville" to commemorate
    the ride!'

DRINKING YARNS

The Australian character seems to be inextricably linked to alcohol. 'Easy-going', 'tolerant' and 'fond-of-a-drink' are qualities, indeed clichés, that occur again and again when Australian stereotypes are being portrayed both at home and overseas. Did this develop as a result of the large percentage of Irish and Cockney migrants, who already had a drinking culture, in those early years of British settlement here? Or was it more to do with the male-dominated nature of Australian frontier society in the nineteenth century?

It is possible to argue quite simplistically that, with a population consisting entirely of convicts, soldiers, sailors and children born out of wedlock in prison hulks, the First Fleet set a national trend for drunkenness and tolerance of boozing that could never be entirely reversed.

It should be realised that the British settled this continent at a time when there was an extraordinarily widespread acceptance of alcohol throughout British society, especially in the navy. You have only to read accounts of British naval and merchant voyages in the eighteenth and nineteenth centuries to understand the huge role played by 'grog'—chiefly rum, or brandy for officers—in the daily life of a British vessel.

Of course, alcohol and drunkenness have been around almost as long as human beings. Appreciation of alcohol is one blessing, among many, passed down to other Western civilisations by the Ancient Greeks. The American writer and observer of human behaviour Ambrose Bierce (1842–1914) described Bacchus as 'a convenient deity invented by the ancients as an excuse for getting drunk'.

It was the British, largely accepting of alcoholic excess, who established colonies in Australia between 1788 and 1836 and it was the British navy and merchant fleet, with their easy acceptance of drunkenness as part of everyday life, that provided the only real link between Europe and those colonies.

So it's little wonder that many of our best yarns, in prose or verse, are about drinking.

RUM, BY GUM!

Although our national day is 26 January, the day the ships of the First Fleet moved from Botany Bay to Port Jackson, the male convicts were disembarked and the British flag was raised, perhaps we should spare a thought for 6 February 1788. On the evening of that day, following the disembarkation of the female convicts and extra rations of rum all round, there developed, in the words of historian Manning Clark, 'a drunken spree that ended only when the revellers were drenched by a violent rainstorm'.

Early in 1793, just after Arthur Phillip had returned to Britain and left Major Francis Grose temporarily in charge of the fledgling colony, an American ship with the ironic name of the *Hope* sailed into Sydney with a cargo that included 7500 gallons of rum. The captain, one Benjamin Page, refused to sell his cargo except in one lot, including the rum.

The colony had almost starved three years earlier and all supplies were scarce. In light of this and partly to prevent the captain from charging extortionate prices and holding the colony to ransom, the officers of the New South Wales Corps banded together with Grose's blessing to purchase the entire cargo. This gave them a monopoly on rum, which they exploited whenever a new ship arrived in the colony.

Until 1814, rum was the accepted currency in New South Wales. Soldiers were paid in rum, as were convicts who worked on officers' land. According to historian George Mackaness, in 1806, 'The population of Sydney . . . was divided into two classes, those who sold rum and those who drank it.'

This monopoly by the officers of what became known as the Rum Corps led eventually to the corruption that caused the so-called Rum Rebellion of 1808, when the Corps successfully rose up against the governor of the day, William Bligh.

In order to maintain a more usual style of authority, Bligh's successor Lachlan Macquarie arrived with his own regiment in 1810 and the Rum Corps was disbanded.

A canny Scot, Macquarie cleverly established a currency by purchasing a cargo of 10,000 Spanish dollars in 1814 and having the centre cut out of every coin. This had the double purpose of providing two coins of different denominations and rendering the coins useless outside the colony, so the currency remained in New South Wales. This strange coin, known as the 'holey dollar' (the bit in the middle, of much less value, was known as the 'dump') replaced rum as the official currency.

Macquarie was to write another chapter in the alcoholic history of New South Wales. In order to further control the rum trade, he gave the monopoly to import spirits to a group of businessmen. In exchange, they built Sydney's first hospital, which still exists. So, Sydney's first major public institution was built in exchange for rum, and was known for years as the Rum Hospital.   **JH**

JAMES SQUIRE

Who Stole Nine Chooks and Was Given a Cow

The name James Squire is a famous and popular one in Australia today as a brand name for a range of beers, but just who was James Squire?

He is remembered and revered by many Australians as the first man to grow hops and brew beer commercially in the colony of New South Wales. Apart from that, most Australians know nothing about his story, which is a shame because it is a remarkable and fascinating yarn.

Transported on the First Fleet to serve seven years for stealing, James Squire had an unusual background. He was from a family of gypsies; in fact, his parents were from the two Romany families involved in one of Britain's most scandalous court cases, the Canning Case, in which public outrage and prejudice against gypsies, or Romanies, or 'Egyptians', caused a major miscarriage of justice in 1754.

Squire's maternal grandmother, Susannah Wells, was convicted of abducting a young domestic servant, Elizabeth Canning, and keeping her imprisoned for a month. His other grandmother,

Mary Squire, was also accused of taking part in the assault and the theft of Elizabeth Canning's corsets which Mary Squire was alleged to have 'forcibly removed'.

Susannah Wells was found guilty, branded on the arm and imprisoned, but she was later exonerated when the maid, Elizabeth Canning, was convicted of perjury.

James Squire's uncle was sentenced to death for the alleged kidnapping, but later pardoned.

As a Romany, or gypsy, Squire grew up to a life of crime as a fringe dweller, smuggling and stealing. Romanies were feared and persecuted and denied civil rights in eighteenth-century Britain. They did, however, have good knowledge of hop cultivation as they provided the itinerant workforce for the hop planting and picking.

The transformation of James Squire from a despised criminal from the lowest social rank imaginable in England to a respectable and revered citizen of Sydney is an amazing story. It shows how the convict system could achieve amazing social reform by simply putting people in a place where their past was irrelevant to what they might achieve.

Squire was lucky to be alive to be sent to New South Wales. He had been found guilty previously of highway robbery after he ran from a house he had broken into and was arrested. The sentence, if he had been arrested inside the house, was death. He was sentenced to transportation to the American colonies but served the sentence in the army instead and was running a tavern at Kingston near London when he was found guilty of stealing nine chooks. The tavern he ran was, by all accounts, a den of thieves, smugglers, prostitutes and gypsies.

For stealing nine chooks, James Squire was transported on the First Fleet to what was to become a totally different life in New South Wales.

Old habits die hard. It took a while before James Squire, gypsy and thief, was able to transform himself into Mr James Squire, Esquire, respectable and successful business man, philanthropist and local constable.

In March 1789, Squire was sentenced to 150 lashes for the theft of medical supplies from Surgeon John White's store. It is not certain that the full sentence was ever carried out. He claimed at the time the herb he stole, 'horehound', was a tonic for his pregnant girlfriend, Mary Spencer. He admitted years later that he stole the herb because it was a substitute for hops in the brewing process. Squire had been making beer and selling it at fourpence a quart to the officers of the New South Wales Corps since the establishment of the colony.

His punishment was a slight one in the circumstances; normally such a theft was punished by hanging. No doubt the fact that he was already supplying beer to the officers had some effect on the leniency of the sentence. When Mary Spencer gave birth to a son, Francis, in 1791, James, aware that he could not support a child, enlisted him in the New South Wales Corps as an infant and he went on the payroll on his seventh birthday, as a drummer boy.

James Squire was a paradox as far as caring for his offspring was concerned. He left a wife and three children behind in England and fathered another eight in Sydney, seven with his second mistress, his convict servant Sarah Mason.

His cunning Romany ways were apparent in his land dealings. He added twelve other land grants to his own 30 acres (12 hectares) at Ryde and eventually had an estate of over 800 acres (40.5 hectares) along the Parramatta River. He cleverly complained to the Colonial Secretary about neighbouring land grants not being taken up and consequently purchased several of them for a shilling each.

James cultivated hops and grain and was the first successful brewer in Australia. He obtained a licence to sell liquor in partnership with another emancipist, Simeon Lord, in 1792, and set up the Malting Shovel Tavern on the river at Kissing Point, near Ryde. It was at the halfway point on the river between the two settlements of Sydney and Parramatta and proved a great success.

Oddly enough, the brewing of beer was seen as a good thing for a colony which was corrupted by the trade in rum. Rum had become the currency of the colony and led to a rebellion and massive military corruption.

It was considered a sobering influence to get the inhabitants of New South Wales to drink beer rather than rum, and Squire was much praised for his efforts in growing hops and grain and producing and selling a decent brew.

He was a very canny businessman with a gypsy's nose for horse-trading, but what I like about him is his egalitarian spirit and support of the underdog, which I have no doubt came from his Romany background. He set up a credit union for emancipated convicts and helped many less fortunate than himself. He was a friend to the Aborigines and especially to Bennelong, the Aborigine who was befriended by Governor Phillip and had been to Britain and back.

When Bennelong fell on hard times later in life, he spent much of his time on Squire's farm and he was buried there, with a memorial erected by James Squire.

The noted artist (and forger) Joseph Lycett said of him, 'Had he not been so generous, James Squire would have been a much wealthier man . . . his name will long be pronounced with veneration by the grateful objects of his liberality.'

Squire was an industrious and successful farmer. One hop vine he cultivated in 1806 covered 5 acres (2 hectares) by 1812 and produced 700 kilograms of hops. As a brewer he was similarly successful; by 1820 his brewery was producing 40 hogsheads (about 10,000 litres) of beer a week.

When he died in 1822, his funeral was the largest ever seen in the colony up to that time. His grandson, James Squire Farnell was premier of New South Wales from 1877 to 1878.

There are two delightful ironies in the story of James Squire.

The first is that he was one of only a few ex-convicts to be ever appointed a constable. After half a lifetime of thieving and stealing as a way of life, he applied to be made a constable for the district of Eastern Farms on the grounds that there was too much stealing and thieving going on in the area, especially from his properties!

When he managed to cultivate a hop vine in 1806, from plants he had been given a few years before, he took the first small crop to Governor King. The Governor's joy was unbounded at this sign of hope that the rum trade might one day be a thing of the past in New South Wales.

Governor King was so overjoyed at Squire's achievement, in fact, that he gave a directive that the gypsy, transported for stealing nine chooks, would have surely appreciated in more ways than one. The Governor 'directed that a cow to be given to Mr Squire from the Government herd'.   **JH**

BLUEY BRINK
ANONYMOUS

There once was a shearer, by name Bluey Brink,
A devil for work and a demon for drink;
He'd shear his two hundred a day without fear,
And drink without blinking four gallons of beer.

Now Jimmy the barman who served out the drink,
He hated the sight of this here Bluey Brink,
He stayed much too late, and he came much too soon,
At evening, at morning, at night and at noon.

One morning as Jimmy was cleaning the bar,
With sulphuric acid he kept in a jar,
In comes Old Bluey a'yelling with thirst:
'Whatever you've got Jim, just hand me the first!'

Now it ain't down in history, it ain't down in print,
But that shearer drank acid with never a wink,
Saying, 'That's the stuff, Jimmy! Well, strike me stone dead,
This'll make me the ringer of Stevenson's shed!'

Now all that long day as he served out the beer,
Poor Jimmy was sick with his trouble and fear;
Too worried to argue, too anxious to fight,
Seeing the shearer a corpse in his fright.

When early next morning, he opened the door,
Then along came the shearer, asking for more,

With his eyebrows all singed and his whiskers deranged,
And holes in his hide like a dog with the mange.

Says Jimmy, 'And how did you like the new stuff?'
Says Bluey, 'It's fine, but I ain't had enough!
It gives me great courage to shear and to fight,
But why does that stuff set my whiskers alight?

'I thought I knew drink, but I must have been wrong,
For that stuff you gave me was proper and strong;
It set me to coughing, you know I'm no liar,
And every cough set my whiskers on fire!'

A LETTER TO *THE BULLETIN*
HENRY LAWSON

Dear Bulletin,
I'm awfully surprised to find myself sober. And, being sober, I take up my pen to write a few lines, hoping they will find you as well as I am at present. I want to know a few things. In the first place: Why does a man get drunk? There seems to be no excuse for it. I get drunk because I'm in trouble, and I get drunk because I've got out of it. I get drunk because I am sick, or have corns, or the toothache: and I get drunk because I'm feeling well and grand. I got drunk because I was rejected; and I got awfully drunk the night I was accepted. And, mind you, I don't like to get drunk at all, because I don't enjoy it much, and suffer hell afterwards. I'm always far better and happier when I'm sober, and tea tastes better than beer. But I get drunk. I get drunk when I feel that I want a drink, and I get drunk when I don't. I get drunk because I had a row last night and made a fool of myself and it worries me, and when things are fixed up I get drunk to celebrate it. And, mind you, I've got no craving for drink. I get drunk because I'm frightened about things, and because I don't care a damn. Because I'm hard up and because I'm flush. And, somehow, I seem to have better luck when I'm drunk. I don't think the mystery of drunkenness will ever be

explained—until all things are explained, and that will be never.
A friend says that we don't drink to feel happier, but to feel less
miserable. But I don't feel miserable when I'm straight. Perhaps
I'm not perfectly sober just now, after all. I'll go and get a drink,
and write again later.

HOW O'LEARY BROKE THE DROUGHT
JACK SORENSEN

Men seek not for sandalwood at Dargaminder Bay,
The shanty stands forsaken and the jetty's swept away.
Beyond the far, foam-crested reef, outlined against the sky,
Regardless of 'the passageway', the ships of trade go by.

Grim drought had cast its shadow over Dargaminder Bay,
Where close beside the jetty Tim O'Leary's shanty lay.
Sad men who sought the sandalwood were moping down the creek,
For the shanty hadn't functioned as a shanty for a week.

For harassed by a hurricane the steamer had gone by,
Upon its way to Derby with the shanty's month's supply.
So O'Leary sent McSweeney with his lugger further down,
To bring a small consignment from the nearest coastal town.

The man who kept the shanty was himself a trifle dry,
As he gazed beyond the jetty where the ocean met the sky.
And, as the sun was setting, to the settlement's relief,
They saw the lugger coming in the passage through the reef.

The thirsty population of the drought afflicted place
Were gathered at the landing with a smile on every face,
While McSweeney berthed his lugger, but they looked a little glum
When he told them he could only raise one keg of Queensland rum.

'Tisn't much,' said Tim O'Leary, but 'twill do to break the drought,
So I'll hump it to the shanty and proceed to serve it out.'
But, as he strode down the plankway with the barrel in his grip,
The lurching of the lugger caused his hobnail boot to slip.

Then shouting to McSweeney, 'Kindly throw a rope to me,'
O'Leary and the barrel took a header in the sea.
The water closed above him, but he swiftly rose again,
Repeating his instructions in a voice imbued with pain.

They hustled and they bustled as he shouted from below,
'Throw a rope ye lazy beggars, or I'll let the barrel go!'
They found a rope and threw, and the end he fastened tight
In a loop around the barrel, then, exhausted, sank from sight.

Ships call no more for sandalwood at Dargaminder Bay,
The jetty piles lie shattered on the coastline grim and grey,
But they who sought the sandalwood still spread the tale about
Of how Tim, the blessed martyr, gave his life to break the drought.

NAME YOUR POISON

Although Australians were to become known as great beer drinkers
in the twentieth century, beer was not the main alcoholic choice
until late in the century; ale was merely one form of 'grog'.

In 1860, a rather frustrated temperance crusader, Nathaniel
Pidgeon, noted that, 'By a rough calculation, it would appear
that one gallon of beer, 1½ pints of brandy, 1¼ pints of gin, and
a quart of rum has arrived for every man, woman and child in
the colony! It is surely high time for the friends of humanity to
bestir themselves!'

Friends of humanity, however, were not particularly thick upon
the ground in most areas of the continent at the time. Indeed,
thanks partly to the gold rushes, the kind of friendship that was
developing was known as 'mateship', and part of mateship was a
very strong dependence on drinking alcohol together as a male
bonding experience.

This anonymous rhyme sums up Australian drinking habits
of the time:

Now Louis likes his native wine and Otto likes his beer,
The Pommy goes for 'half and half' because it gives him cheer.

Angus likes his whisky neat and Paddy likes his tot,
The Aussie has no drink at all—he likes the bloody lot!

With widespread refrigeration and ice production in the 1880s and 1890s, beer became the standard drink for most Australian men, which is, I suppose, not surprising given the climate and the general outdoor style of work at the time.

While twentieth-century Australia remained a basically beer-drinking nation, all the alcoholic trends that developed in other Western nations were also experienced here. Cocktail drinking became trendy and popular in the 1920s and 1930s, and awareness of more sophisticated food and wine consumption developed slowly after World War II. New 'boutique' beers and fruit drinks became fads in the 1980s, and their popularity has continued to grow.

Rum remained a popular drink, perhaps partly because of tradition and partly because of the sugar industry that developed in Queensland from the 1860s. Brandy, whisky and gin were also popular, particularly among the middle classes, and there was sherry for the ladies. While toleration of alcoholic excess was the norm among men, it was, after those early riotous years of the colony, rarely extended to women.

Wine was one of the first crops grown in the colony and regions like the Hunter Valley in New South Wales have a long and praiseworthy history of producing great wines from the earliest days of settlement. In South Australia, German migrants and other pioneer families had established a tradition of great wine production by the late nineteenth century in areas like the Barossa, Clare Valley, McLaren Vale and Langhorne Creek.

But general appreciation of wine did not really come to Australia until the 1970s, when the wine industry took off. Its spectacular growth coincided with a changing attitude to drinking generally. Australia has slipped well down the table of beer drinkers, for example, from number one in the world for consumption per head of population in the 1950s to a miserable tenth in 1999.

Changes in licensing laws greatly affected drinking habits in Australia. Pubs were forced to close at six o'clock during the 1940s and 1950s. The idea was that this would improve family life and encourage temperance. What resulted, of course, was the notorious 'six o'clock swill'. Early closing simply led to men drinking as much as they could as fast as they could from the time they finished work until six every evening. Even after its demise, early closing had established a tradition of a regular 'drinking session' in the evenings after work.

Today, Australia is a complex society with different drinking cultures. Many changes have occurred in recent times. We tend to drink more often with meals than before or after them, as in the past. We drink more wine and less beer. We are perhaps more temperate due to strict drink-driving laws and a growing awareness of the harmful effects of alcohol on our health and our society. On the other hand, many Australians are drinking at a younger age, and binge drinking and alcohol abuse are more discussed and worried over than ever.

Attitudes to drinking in our society will naturally vary from total acceptance to extreme intolerance. Opinions about Australian drinking have always differed. Visitors to our shores have had mixed reactions to our drinking habits. In 1873, English author Anthony Trollope found our drunkenness to be a reflection of some of our better characteristics: 'Australian drunkenness,' he said, 'so far as it exists, is not of the English type. It is more reckless, more extravagant, more riotous, to the imagination of man infinitely more magnificent; but it is less enduring, and certainly upon the whole less debasing.'

A century later, however, in 1975, Danish journalist Poul Nielsen was moved to comment, 'I have felt scared since I arrived in Sydney, in fact I feel more relaxed in New York than here. There is something desperate about the way people drink here.' If he thought that of Sydney, I wonder what he would have made of Darwin.

Perhaps the disparity in opinion here has something to with the nationality of the observer. Or perhaps it has more to do with the company Trollope and Nielsen kept while visiting our shores, or social changes over the intervening century.

Contradictory opinions exist also on the home front. In the year 1974, for instance, an article appeared in the Australian Church Record describing the evils of drink inflicted on eleven year olds in state schools:

> The girls had their first cooking lesson. The tasty morsel to be cooked was rum balls. Whether rum essence or the real jungle juice scarcely matters. Small girls were to be introduced to this highly desirable alcoholic flavour. Perhaps it is part of the modern approach to cooking, which is to saturate almost everything in some form of alcohol and give it a French name.

In the same year, advertising agency executive John Singleton commented quite matter-of-factly that, 'The advertising industry lives a very cyclical sort of life. December is the month for getting pissed.'

How does the average Australian handle these contradictory views of disapproval and acceptance? How do we cope with attempts to restrict and control our drinking and yet remain true to the Aussie belief in a 'fair go'?

Perhaps some insight can be gained from this item which appeared a few years ago in *The Sydney Morning Herald*'s 'Column 8':

> By chance a colleague booked into a north Queensland motel before learning that its dining-room was not licensed. 'Think nothing of it,' said the waitress. 'If you want a bottle of beer with your steak just say Steak and Laundry. It doesn't show on the records.'   **JH**

McCARTHY'S BREW
GEORGE ESSEX EVANS

The team of Black McCarthy crawled down the Norman Road,
The ground was bare, the bullocks spare, and grievous was the
     load,
The brown hawks wheeled above them and the heatwaves
     throbbed and glowed.

With lolling tongues and bloodshot eyes and sinews all astrain,
McCarthy's bullocks staggered on across the sun-cracked plain,
The wagon lumbered after with the drivers raising Cain.

Three mournful figures sat around the camp fire's fitful glare,
McKinlay Jim and 'Spotty' and McCarthy's self were there,
But their spirits were so dismal that they couldn't raise a swear!

'Twas not the long, dry stage ahead that made those bold hearts
    shrink,
The drought-cursed ground, the dying stock, the water thick as ink,
But, the drinking curse was on them and they had no grog to
    drink!

Then with a bound up from the ground McCarthy jumped and
    cried:
''Tis vain! 'Tis vain! I go insane. These pangs in my inside!
Some sort of grog, for love of God, invent, concoct, provide!'

McKinlay Jim straight answered him: 'Those lotions, sauce and
    things
Should surely make a brew to slake these thirstful sufferings,
A brew that slakes, a brew that wakes and burns and bucks and
    stings.'

Down came the cases from the load—they wrenched them wide
    with force.
They poured and mixed and stirred a brew that would have
    killed a horse,
Cayenne, painkiller, pickles, embrocation, Worcester sauce!

Oh, wild and high and fierce and free the orgy rose that night;
The songs they sang, the deeds they did, no poet could indite;
To see them pass that billy round, it was a fearsome sight.

The dingo heard them and with tail between his legs he fled!
The curlew saw them and he ceased his wailing for the dead!
Each frightened bullock on the plain went straightway off his
    head!

Alas! and there are those who say that at the dawn of day
Three perforated carriers round a smouldering camp fire lay:
They did not think McCarthy's brew would take them in that
　　way!

McCarthy's teams at Normanton no more the Gulf men see.
McCarthy's bullocks roam the wilds exuberant and free;
McCarthy lies, an instance of preserved anatomee!

Go, take the moral of this rhyme, which in deep grief I write:
Don't ever drink McCarthy's brew. Be warned in case you might—
Gulf whisky kills at twenty yards, but this stuff kills at sight!

A BUSH PUBLICAN'S LAMENT
HENRY LAWSON

I wish I was spifflicated before I ever seen a pub!

You see, it's this way. Suppose a cove comes along on a blazin'
hot day in the drought—an' you ought to know how hell-hot it
can be out here—an' he dumps his swag in the corner of the bar;
an' he turns round an' he ses ter me, 'Look here, boss, I ain't got a
lonely steever on me, an' God knows when I'll git one. I've tramped
ten mile this mornin', an' I'll have ter tramp another ten afore
tonight. I'm expectin' ter git on shearin' with ol' Baldy Thompson
at West-o'-Sunday nex' week. I got a thirst on me like a sunstruck
bone, an' for God sake put up a couple o' beers for me an' my
mate, an' I'll fix it up with yer when I come back after shearin'.'

An' what's a feller ter do? I bin there meself, an', I put it to you!
I've known what it is to have a thirst on me.

An' suppose a poor devil comes along in the jim-jams, with
every inch on him jumpin' an' a look in his eyes like a man bein'
murdered an' sent ter hell, an' a whine in his voice like a whipped
cur, an' the snakes a-chasing of him; an' he hooks me with his
finger ter the far end o' the bar, as if he was goin' ter tell me that
the world was ended, an' he hangs over the bar an' chews me lug,
an' tries to speak, an' breaks off inter a sort o' low shriek, like a
terrified woman, an' he says, 'For Mother o' Christ's sake, giv' me

a drink!' An' what am I to do? I bin there meself. I knows what the horrors is. He mighter blued his cheque at the last shanty. But what am I ter do? I put it ter you. If I let him go he might hang hisself ter the nex' leanin' tree.

What's a drink? Yer might arst, I don't mind a drink or two; but when it comes to half a dozen in a day it mounts up, I can tell yer. Drinks is sixpence here, I have to pay for it, an' pay carriage on it. It's all up ter me in the end. I used sometimes ter think it was lucky I wasn't west o' the sixpenny line, where I'd lose a shillin' on every drink I give away.

An' a straight chap that knows me gets a job to take a flock o' sheep or a mob o' cattle ter the bloomin' Gulf, or South Australia, or somewheers, an' loses one of his horses goin' out ter take charge, an' borrers eight quid from me ter buy another. He'll turn up agen in a year or two an' most likely want ter make me take twenty quid for that eight, an' make everybody about the place blind drunk, but I've got ter wait, an' the wine an' sperit merchants an' the brewery won't. They know I can't do without liquor in the place.

An' lars' rain Jimmy Nowlett, the bullick driver, gets bogged over his axle trees back there on the Blacksoil Plains between two flooded billerbongs, an' prays till the country steams an' his soul's busted, an' his throat like a lime kiln. He taps a keg o' rum or beer ter keep his throat in workin' order. I don't mind that at all, but him an' his mates git floodbound for near a week, an' broach more kegs, an' go on a howlin' spree in ther mud, an' spill mor'n they swipe, an' leave a tarpaulin off a load, an' the flour gets wet, an' the sugar runs out of the bags like syrup, an', what's a feller ter do? Do yer expect me to set the law onter Jimmy? I've knowned him all my life, an' he knowed my father afore I was born. He's been on the roads this forty year till he's as thin as a rat, and as poor as a myall black; an' he's got a family ter keep back there in Bourke. No, I have ter pay for it in the end, an' it all mounts up, I can tell yer.

An' suppose some poor devil of a new chum black sheep comes along, staggerin' from one side of the track to the other, and spoutin' poetry; dyin' o' heat or fever, or heartbreak an' homesickness, or a life o' disserpation he'd led in England, an' without a sprat on him, an' no claim on the Bush; an' I ketches him in me arms as he stumbles inter the bar, an' he wants me ter hold him up while he turns English inter Greek for me.

An' I put him ter bed, an' he gits worse, an' I have ter send the buggy twenty mile for a doctor—an' pay him. An' the jackaroo gits worse, an' has ter be watched an' nursed an' held down sometimes; an' he raves about his home an' mother in England, an' the blarsted university that he was eddicated at, an' a woman, an' somethin' that sounds like poetry in French; an' he upsets my missus a lot, an' makes her blubber.

An' he dies, an' I have ter pay a man ter bury him (an' knock up a sort o' fence round the grave arterwards ter keep the stock out), an' send the buggy agen for a parson, an', well, what's a man ter do?

I couldn't let him wander away an' die like a dog in the scrub, an' be shoved underground like a dog, too, if his body was ever found. The government might pay ter bury him, but there ain't never been a pauper funeral from my house yet, an' there won't be one if I can help it, except it be meself.

An' then there's the bother goin' through his papers to try an' find out who he was an' where his friends is. An' I have ter get the missus to write a letter to his people, an' we have ter make up lies about how he died ter make it easier for 'em. An' goin' through his letters, the missus comes across a portrait an' a locket of hair, an' letters from his mother an' sisters an' girl; an' they upset her, an' she blubbers agin, an' gits sentimental, like she useter long ago when we was first married.

There was one bit of poetry, I forgit it now, that that there jackaroo kep' sayin' over an' over agen till it buzzed in me head; an', weeks after, I'd ketch the missus metterin' it to herself in the kitchen till I thought she was goin' ratty.

An' we gets a letter from the jackaroo's friends that puts us to a lot more bother. I hate havin' anythin' to do with letters. An' someone's sure to say he was lambed down an' cleaned out an' poisoned with bad bush liquor at my place. It's almost enough ter make a man wish there was a recordin' angel.

An' what's the end of it? I got the blazin' bailiff in the place now! I can't shot him out because he's a decent, hard-up, poor devil from Bourke, with consumption or somethin', an' he's been talking to the missus about his missus an' kids; an' I see no chance of gittin' rid of him, unless the shearers come along with their cheques from West-o'-Sunday nex' week and act straight by me.

Like as not I'll have ter roll up me swag an' take the track meself in the end.

They say publicans are damned, an' I think so, too; an' I wish I'd bin operated on before ever I seen a pub.

THE GUILE OF DAD McGINNIS
W.T. GOODGE

When McGinnis struck the mining camp at Jamberoora Creek
His behaviour was appreciated highly;
For, although he was a quiet man, in manner mild and meek,
Not like ordinary swagmen with a monumental cheek,
He became the admiration of the camp along the creek
'Cause he showed a point to Kangaroobie Riley!

Both the pubs at Jamberoora had some grog that stood the test
(Not to speak of what was manufactured slyly!)
And the hostel of O'Gorman, which was called The Diggers' Rest,
Was, O'Gorman said, the finest house of any in the west;
But it was a burning question if it really was the best,
Or the Miners'—kept by Kangaroobie Riley.

Dad McGinnis called at Riley's. Said he 'felt a trifle queer',
And with something like a wan and weary smile, he
Said he 'thought he'd try a whisky'. Pushed it back and said, 'I fear
I had better take a brandy.' Passed that back and said: 'Look here,
Take the brandy; after all, I think I'll have a pint of beer!'
And he drank the health of Kangaroobie Riley!

'Where's the money?' asked the publican; 'you'll have to pay, begad!'
'Gave the brandy for the beer!' said Dad the wily,

'And I handed you the whisky when I took the brandy, lad!'
'But you paid not for the whisky!' answered Riley. 'No,' said Dad,
'And you don't expect a man to pay for what he never had!'
—'Twas the logic flattened Kangaroobie Riley!

'See,' said Kangaroobie Riley, 'you have had me, that is clear!
But I never mind a joke,' he added dryly.
'Just you work it on O'Gorman, and I'll shout another beer.'
'I'd be happy to oblige yer,' said McGinnis with a leer,
'But the fact about the matter is—O'Gorman sent me here!—
So, good morning, Mr Kangaroobie Riley!'

THE OLDEST PUB IN AUSTRALIA

You might think that finding the oldest pub in Australia would be a simple enough thing. Think again! It's a minefield of different criteria. Do you mean the oldest building? The oldest licence? The oldest pub name? Or, maybe, the oldest continuously trading establishment? We are only talking about licensed pubs here. There may well be older pubs that began trading without a licence and then obtained one at a later date.

The oldest licence still trading belongs to the Woolpack in Parramatta, which began trading in April 1796. This pub has changed its name several times, however, and at one stage moved across the road into a different building.

The oldest continuously trading pub in New South Wales is the Surveyor General in Berrima, which received a licence in 1834, but the pub in the oldest building is the Macquarie Arms at Windsor. The building which houses this hotel was built in May 1815 after Governor Macquarie, in 1811, had given Richard Fitzgerald a 'large allotment in the square on the expressed condition of his building immediately thereon a handsome commodious inn of brick or stone and to be at least two stories high'.

Naturally, the owner was delighted at the vice-regal patronage and called the pub the Macquarie Arms. Not long after the pub began trading in May 1815, the Governor graced the hotel with his presence and the *Sydney Gazette* reported:

> That spacious and commodious new Inn at Windsor, called The Macquarie Arms, was opened by the GOVERNOR, on Wednesday the 26th instant, when HIS EXCELLENCY entertained at dinner the Magistrates and other principal Gentlemen residing at Windsor, and in that neighbourhood. Mr. Ransom, who has taken on himself the duties of Innkeeper, is, from his experience in the avocation, thoroughly competent to the undertaking, which we are convinced will be conducted on a liberal footing. Its necessity has long been manifest as there was no house of public reception at Windsor capable of accommodating large and genteel companies, whereas the Macquarie Arms from its extent, plan of building, and adequate number of apartments will be doubtless found worthy of the most liberal patronage and support.

The licence of the Macquarie Arms has not, however, been continuous as the pub ceased trading for long periods of the building's history.

The Macquarie Arms often claims to be the oldest pub 'on the mainland' because the oldest continually licensed hotel operating on the same site and in the same building in Australia is actually the Bush Inn in New Norfolk, Tasmania, which operates in a building as old as the Macquarie Arms, being also constructed in 1815. The licence was granted to this pub on 29 September 1825.

New Norfolk was so named because it was the place to which the residents of Norfolk Island were taken when the island was closed as a penal settlement in 1814. Until then the island settlement had operated in conjunction with the one at Sydney. The island was to lie abandoned until 1825 when another convict settlement was begun there.

Apparently the relocated residents of Norfolk Island drank illegally in their new home from 1814 until the local pub was granted a licence in 1825. **JH**

MULLIGAN'S SHANTY
W.T. GOODGE

Things is just the same as ever,
On the outer Never-Never,
And you look to find the stock of liquor scanty,
But we found things worse than ord'nry,
In fact, a bit extraord'nry,
When meself and Bill the Pinker struck his shanty.
'Shanty?' says you, 'what shanty?'
'Why, Mulligan's shanty.'

I says, 'Whisky'; Bill says 'Brandy';
But there wasn't either handy,
For the boss was out of liquor in that line.
'We'll try a rum,' says Billy.
'Got no rum,' he answers chilly,
'But I'd recommend a decent drop o' tine.'
'Tine?' says Bill, 'what tine?'
'Why, turpentine!'

'Blow me blue!' says Bill the Pinker,
'Can't you give us a deep-sinker?
Ain't yer got a cask o' beer behind the screen?'
Bill was getting pretty cranky,
But there wasn't any swanky.
Says the landlord, 'Why not try a drop o' sene?'
'Sene?' says Bill, 'what sene?'
'Why, kerosene!'

Well, we wouldn't spend a tanner,
But the boss's pleasant manner
All our cursing couldn't easily demolish.
Says he, 'Strike me perpendic'lar
But you beggars are partic'lar.
Why, the squatter's in the parlour drinking polish.'
'Polish?' says Bill, 'what polish?'
'Why, furniture polish!'

THE OLDEST PUB IN SYDNEY?

Now, which is the oldest pub in Sydney really is a matter for conjecture or, rather, a matter for making up your own set of criteria and then putting in a claim!

The Lord Nelson in Kent Street is a heavyweight contender. On 29 June 1831, Richard Phillips obtained a liquor licence for the Shipwright Arms on the north-east corner of Kent and Argyle streets. The next year, because of the support of the seafarers and the workers on Observatory Hill, he changed the name to The Sailor's Return.

In 1838, Phillips sold the pub to a plasterer, William Wells, who lived on the opposite corner in a two storey colonial home he'd built in 1836 using sandstone blocks quarried from the area at the base of Observatory Hill. Wells continued to operate the pub opposite his home firstly as The Sailors Return, and in 1840 as The Quarryman's Arms.

In 1841, he sold the pub and, on 1 May 1841, he obtained a liquor licence for his home, which he then called the Lord Nelson.

The hotel has now been restored with the aid of an 1852 photograph and is often cited as Sydney's oldest pub, although the licence was not only transferred, it was also not, perhaps, the original licence granted on which the pub now operates. To make things even more confusing, the licence was also restored or renewed, or lapsed and was re-granted at some other point in the pub's history.

Confused? Don't worry, just go and have a drink there, the Lord Nelson is a beaut pub!

The Fortunes of War in George Street was licensed in 1828 and the 1830 certificate of the licence renewal is still on the wall. The pub you visit on the site may well be the oldest continuously licensed public hotel in Sydney, but it is not the original building. The current pub was built in 1922 in art nouveau style after a fire destroyed the original.

The Hero of Waterloo in Lower Fort Street can lay claim to being the oldest continuously operating pub in the same building in Sydney.

The Hero was built by convict labour in 1843 for stonemason George Paton and was licensed in 1845. If you look at the walls you can still see the gouges in the rock from when they were heaved out of the ground so long ago. If you look really hard, you can see that the gouges are a consistent pattern on particular stones, but vary from stone to stone. That's because each convict had to meet a certain quota of stones, and the particular cut on the stone allowed the convict to identify his stones at the end of the day.

The best thing about the Hero, probably because of the stone, is that it is still in the same basic condition it was in 155 years ago. While most so-called 'old pubs' only have a piece or two of the original old pub left in them, the Hero is the real thing. It was a favourite with the various 'Red Coat' regiments of the British army that were posted to Sydney throughout the nineteenth century.

There is a delightful irony in the fact that the Hero is now called an Irish pub, and employs many Irish staff. Although it was the soldiers sent to keep order, rather than the freed convicts, who frequented this pub after transportation ceased in 1840, there is still some tenuous historic connection between the pub's name and its current Irishness. After all—one third of the convicts sent here were Irish, and the British soldiers sent to keep them in order needed a drink!   **JH**

A CURIOUS REMINISCENCE
ALEXANDER MONTGOMERY

Of all the bloomin' awful things, the awfullest I've knowed
In the five-and-sixty years I've bin alive,
Took place at Paddy Doolan's on the old Jerilda road,
Way back in sixty-four or sixty-five.

Old Doolan was a handy man, a useful sort of chap,
But a real, right-down tiger for his rum;

And one day, being tipsy, why he tumbles from a trap,
An' cracks his skull, an' goes to kingdom come.

Well, they sends an' tells the trooper, an' the trooper rides across,
'An',' says he, 'I'll have to let the "Crowner" hear;'
So they stretches out old Jerry in the place he used to doss,
A tumbledown old shanty at the rear.

I was trampin' down from Bulga and had just run out of grub;
Rainin' too, till every rag on me was soaked;
So, you bet, I wasn't sorry to pull up at Doolan's pub
On the evenin' of the day that Jerry croaked.

Well, I'd had me bite o' tucker and a glass or two o' beer
And was sitting' there a-fillin' of me pipe,
When in comes Mad McCarthy and Long Jim from Bundaleer,
An' my word! But they was well upon the swipe.

Two strappin' big six-footers an' as strong as bullocks, both;
An' ripe for any devilment as well;
The man that interfered with them, you might just take your oath,
Stood a pretty lively chance o' catchin' hell.

Well, they dank an' laughed an' shouted, an' they swaggered an'
   they swore,
Till McCarthy took a notion in his head
That they'd make old Jerry drunker than he'd ever been before;
'Yez can't do that,' says Doolan, 'Jerry's dead!'

'Dead drunk, you mean!' says Jimmy. 'No,' says Doolan, 'no, begob!
He's as dead as he can be, without a lie!
For he tumbled out of Thompson's trap, right fair upon his nob.'
Says McCarthy, 'Come, old man, that's all my eye!'

'Bedad,' says Pat, 'then take a light an' go yerselves to see,
Sure he's lyin' in the shed forninst the gate.'
So the fellers get a candle an' they tips a wink to me,
An' out they goes to see if it were straight.

Well, sir, back they comes directly an' a laughin' fit to split,
An' behind them Mother Doolan cryin', 'Shame!'
An' well she might, for there, between the pair of 'em, was it,
The clay that used to answer Jerry's name!

With its head a-hangin' forward, and its legs a-draggin' loose,
You can bet it was a dreadful sight to see!
An' I started up to stop 'em, but says Doolan, 'What's the use?
They could smash a dozen chaps like you an' me.'

So they humped their fearsome burden to a corner o' the bar,
An' they propped it on a cask agin the wall;
'What will Jerry drink?' says Jimmy, an' McCarthy says, 'Three Star!
For we won't be mean with Jerry, damn it all!'

Well, sir, Doolan fills three nobblers an' McCarthy collars one,
An' slaps it down before the senseless clay;
Then they bobs their heads to Jerry, an' they says, 'Old man,
    here's fun!'
An' they punishes their liquors right away.

Then 'twas, 'Fill 'em up again, Pat, fill 'em right up to the brim!'
Till they'd swallered half a dozen drinks a head.
Then McCarthy stares at Jerry's glass, an' then he stares at Jim,
'By the Lord!' he says, 'Old Jerry must be dead!

'For it's five-an'-twenty minutes he has had his poison there,
An' he's never tried to touch a bloomin' drop!
So you're right for once, old Doolan! Have a drink an' let us square,
For it's nearly getting' time for us to hop.'

So they humped poor Jerry back again to where he was before,
Mother Doolan still a-scoldin' them in vain;
Then they staggers to their horses that was standin' at the door,
An' they gallops off like madmen through the rain.

THE ENTERPRISE OF PETER DEGRAVES

While you cannot, perhaps, give a clear and definitive answer to the question, 'What's our oldest pub?', there is no such doubt about the oldest brewery in Australia. The oldest brewery is the famous Cascade Brewery in South Hobart.

There is nothing contentious or doubtful about Cascade's claim to being the oldest brewery in Australia.

A true pedant might argue that it hasn't been in Tasmania all that time—as Tasmania was known as Van Diemen's Land until 1856 when the name was changed in an attempt to rid the colony of all traces of its horrific past history.

An amazing character, Englishman Peter Degraves, received permission to build the brewery in 1824 but, as we will see, the brewery wasn't established until 1831.

Peter Degraves was born in 1778 into a well-respected family of French descent, in Dover. His father was a doctor and Peter studied engineering. He was a risk-taker who was imprisoned for theft and was bankrupt for several years before deciding to emigrate to Van Diemen's Land in 1821 with his family and his brother-in-law and business partner Major Hugh McIntosh.

They purchased a ship called the *Hope* and raised money for the venture by selling passages to migrants.

Degraves was arrested for overcrowding the ship and then imprisoned for debt, but finally arrived in Hobart with his wife and eight children in 1824. He and McIntosh were granted land at the Cascades in 1824 and started a sawmilling business as well as providing water to Hobart from a dam they built.

In 1826, his creditors in Britain renewed charges against Degraves and he was imprisoned and faced bankruptcy again when a British judge decided the discharge of the previous debt was not valid in law.

Degraves was in custody until 1831 when Governor Arthur had him released. While in Hobart Prison, he designed new plans for remodelling it.

The court took the sawmill and his house, but after Degraves' release he and McIntosh soon started a second sawmill, a flour-mill and several bake houses, as well as the brewery, which they completed in 1832.

It was reputed that the beer, timber, flour, bread and biscuits they produced brought in about £100,000 a year.

Water rights for the brewery were a problem and, when the government built a dam above Degraves' water source in the 1840s, he attempted to sue the Public Works Department. When the editor of the *Hobart Town Guardian* criticised him, Degraves threatened him and was prosecuted and briefly imprisoned again in 1848.

He eventually lost his battle over water rights.

After McIntosh died in 1835, Degraves started a shipbuilding business and built many large ships, including the barque *Tasman*, the largest ship built in Van Diemen's Land at the time, at 563 tons.

In 1834, he formed a syndicate that designed and built the Theatre Royal in Hobart, renowned as the best theatre in Australia. After a disagreement with the other syndicate members, Degraves became the sole proprietor in 1841.

When the gold rush began in Victoria, he loaded his ships with timber, which was used to build thousands of houses in the rapidly growing town of Melbourne.

Degraves died at Hobart on 31 December 1852.

The Theatre Royal still stands today, almost as it was built, the oldest theatre in Australia, and famous Cascade beer, 'from the clear waters of Tasmania', is still just about the best drop you can drink!   JH

HOW AUSSIE IS FOSTER'S?

In the 1970s and 1980s, you may well have heard the phrase 'as Aussie as Foster's lager' in Britain and the USA especially, where Foster's was marketed as the beer Australians made and loved to drink. The slogan for Foster's was 'It's Australian for beer'.

Well, it may have been marketed as 'Australian for beer', but what is the answer to the question 'How Aussie is Foster's?'

If you take the nationality of the founders of Foster's famous beer into account, it's not Australian at all—it's American!

The Foster brothers, William and Ralph, arrived in Melbourne in 1887 and they were not primarily interested in beer or brewing. They were pioneers in the refrigeration industry and they arrived with the latest in refrigeration equipment.

They set up their brewery and, in 1888, successfully brewed the very first local lager-style beer in Australia, a beer that needed to be kept cold to be enjoyed properly.

Having done what they had planned to do, Ralph and William promptly sold their entire operation to some locals in 1889 and went back to the USA. No one seems to know what the two enterprising Americans did after that.

In 1908, there was a massive amalgamation of breweries in Melbourne. Carlton, McCracken's City, Castlemaine, Shamrock and Foster's breweries all combined to form Carlton United. The Foster's brewery in Rokeby Street was closed and the Foster's name was almost lost. Carlton United only continued to brew a beer branded as Foster's because there was some demand for the label in Queensland and Western Australia.

In 1971, Foster's was introduced to England through Barry Humphries' highly successful cartoon strip in the magazine *Private Eye*. The strip was used as the basis for two very successful movies, *The Adventures of Barry McKenzie* and *Bazza Holds His Own*.

The hero of the cartoon strip and movies was rarely seen without a can of Foster's in his hand and Foster's took off in Britain, where lager-style, cold beer was just taking over the beer market from the more traditional styles of beer and ale.

Foster's then launched into the USA in 1972 where it was marketed along with sport. Foster's sponsored the 1972 America's Cup challenge and tennis championships and was the official Olympic beer for Australia at the 1984 Los Angeles Olympics.

For over a decade from 1985, the Melbourne Cup was known as the Foster's Melbourne Cup.

John Newcombe claimed in advertisements that he drank five cans after each tennis match and Paul Hogan was brought in to the advertising campaign. Hoge's first Foster's commercial script was this:

> G'day. They've asked me over from Oz to introduce youse all to Foster's Draught, here it is. Cripes! I'd better start with the basics. It's a light, golden liquid, like, except for the white bit on top, the head, and it's brewed from malt, yeast and hops. Technical term is *lager*. That's L-A-G-E-R. But everyone calls it Foster's. Ahhhh, ripper! Tastes like an angel cryin' on yer tongue. Foster's.

Of course, the famous Aussie Foster's lager marketed to Poms and Yanks is also brewed locally—not here in Australia. Foster's is brewed in eight countries, including China, Spain and Sweden. It is sold in 135 countries.

Australians living in the USA and Britain in the 1980s spent a lot of their time telling the locals they didn't drink Foster's! After all, it's an American invention!   **JH**

CARLTON UNITED AND CASTLEMAINE

Carlton United Breweries was formed in 1908 when the Melbourne brewers Carlton, McCracken's, Castlemaine, Shamrock and Foster's combined to create a massive company with economies of scale unmatched by any other brewer in Australia.

Their famous ad was an old bushie at a bar saying, 'I allus has wan at eleven'—but the full verse was:

> I allus has wan at eleven
> It's a duty that has to be done
> If I don't have wan at eleven
> I must have eleven at wan!

Castlemaine Brewery had been founded by two Irish Fitzgerald brothers. They migrated from Galway in 1859 and began their brewing business at Castlemaine in Victoria. In 1875, they established a brewery in South Melbourne and, in 1877, they also set up in Brisbane where, from 1878, they brewed the famous Castlemaine

Ale that became associated with Queensland—although it was named after a town in Victoria!

The beer became Castlemaine XXXX in 1916 and ever since that time the joke has been that it's called XXXX because Queenslanders can't spell 'beer'.

If you are wondering what 4X was called before 1916—cease wondering. From 1878 to 1916 it was known as Castlemaine XXX Sparkling Ale in other words—3X!   **JH**

CRAWLIWIGS
TRADITIONAL/JIM HAYNES

Reginald Cadwallider, scientifically inclined,
Always had taxidermy firmly on his mind.
Crawliwigs and crows and creepers, gathered far and wide,
Reggie stuffed and mounted 'em, and others, too, beside.

Far afield he found fine fishes, finches, frogs and fleas,
Killed and skinned and stuffed and mounted birds and bugs and
    bees.
One day afield he met a swaggie, trudging down the track,
His old black billy swinging and his swag upon his back.

'Pardon me,' said Reggie, 'If you live round about
Can you help me find the kind of fauna I am seeking out?
See, I'm a taxidermist and I'm seeking creatures rare,
Reptiles, creepicrawlies, have you seen some anywhere?'

'I have,' replied the swaggie, 'reptiles, snakes and lizards, too!
I can tell you where there's heaps of 'em! A squirming, bloomin' zoo!
Pink and blue and spotted ones, I've seen thousands, mate!
Crimson rats and yeller frogs, I'll give it to you straight!

'Red-haired beetles chasin' spotted spiders all about,
Blue-nosed toads with purple stripes and waistcoats inside-out!'
'Heavens, man!' cried Reggie, 'Where are they? In the scrub?'
'No!' the swaggie told him, 'Down the track, at Casey's Pub!

'Underneath the v'randah, sometimes crawling through the floor!
If you can spare a bloke two-bob—I'll go and see some more!'
Reginald Cadwallider, scientifically inclined,
Sadly headed home and left the 'specimens' behind!

PUB NAMES

In Australia, pubs originally were often named patriotically—after
royalty, like the King's Head or The Crown. This was very much
in the British tradition; The Crown is the most common pub
name in Britain.

Sadly, the quirkier British pub names rarely appeared here.

Among my favourites from Pommyland are the very common
Drum and Monkey which probably derives from early Victorian
times when pubs used 'drumming monkeys' from the colonies
as novelties to attract customers, and the Swan with Two Necks,
which is a corruption of 'the swan with two nicks'.

Due to an old, odd tradition, all swans in Britain were owned
by noble families or by various ancient guilds of merchants.
Ownership was distinguished by a pattern of cuts in the beak of
each bird. Most swans were owned (and still are) by the king or
queen, who could claim all unmarked adult birds.

The swans owned by the guild of wine and beer merchants were
marked with two nicks in the beak, thus the name was associated
with pubs.

The very odd Elephant and Castle, which is a suburb of South
London as well as a common pub name, has had some weird and
wonderful stories invented to explain its origin.

Among the more ridiculous of these is the story that it was the
cockney version of 'Infanta de Castille' (little princess of Castille),
the Spanish princess who became Henry VIII's first wife, Catherine,
mother of Mary Tudor. Sadly, the story breaks down when you
realise that Catherine was a Princess of Aragon, not the nearby
province of Castille.

The elephant and castle was in fact the symbol of the cutlery
factory that originally occupied the site of the first pub called

Elephant and Castle. Because the factory made cutlery with ivory handles, it used the image of an elephant with a 'howdah' or covered shelter, vaguely reminiscent in shape of a castle tower, on its back. This image was used on the sign hanging outside the pub that replaced the factory.

But, back to Aussie pub history.

As time went by in colonial Australia, the pubs were named rather more prosaically than their British counterparts, though many copied British pub names that can still be found here, like the White Horse, the Black Lion, and the Rose, Shamrock and Thistle. Others, like the Macquarie Arms and Surveyor General, seem to have been named in thanks to those who granted the land or the licence.

Some were simply named after their owners, like the famous Young and Jacksons in Melbourne, but many more were named from their clientele.

The Sailors Arms, Ship Inn, and First and Last are all found near the wharves. The Woolpack was a common name, and those pubs would be found where teamsters rested their horses and bullocks, usually near a ford or bridge. The Commercial was often the middle-class pub in any country town and had accommodation and smoking rooms designed for commercial travellers.

The Railway, or sometimes the Locomotive, which was always near the station and catered to passengers and railway workers, often became the 'blood house' or rough pub, while the more up-market pubs, like the Imperial, The Royal and The Squatters Arms, catered to the landed gentry and more conservative drinkers.

Labor voters were more likely to be found drinking at The Australian, The Southern Cross, the Workers Arms or the Railway, while the Tattersall's, Sportsman Arms, Bat and Ball and Cricketers Arms catered for sportsmen and gamblers.

Many pubs simply took the name of the closest landmark and were known by such dull names as The Pier, The Bridge and The Lakes.

There are a few pubs that used history to brand themselves as patriotic. Most of these date from colonial times and celebrate British History, such as The Hero of Waterloo, The Wellington and The Iron Duke—all named after the same bloke!

Sydney also has The Trafalgar and the Lord Nelson but there are some local heroes too, if you want to count the Captain Cook, the Joseph Banks and the Endeavour as representing Aussie history, rather than British.

Pub names come and go and often lose touch with their original clientele and history. The historic suburb of Botany, in Sydney, is a perfect case in point.

Botany has a mix of historic and matter-of-fact pub names. It has the rather obvious Botany Bay and Pier, although the actual pier 'disa-pier-ed' decades ago. Botany also has the local historic connection with the patriotic Joseph Banks and Captain Cook.

Until recently, Botany also had the Endeavour, but that pub has recently been renovated and reverted to its original name, the Waterworks. It was the pub where the workers from the Botany waterworks and pumping station drank when the nearby Millpond, previously known as the Botany Swamp, was Sydney's water supply from 1860 to 1888.

It's nice to see some accurate history restored. The crew of the Endeavour certainly never drank there. They were too busy drinking Captain Cook's potent fruit punch to prevent scurvy!　　　**JH**

BOOZE AND SPORT

Drinking and sport have been linked in our history since the earliest colonial times.

Early sporting events were often organised by publicans in order to boost sales of alcohol. Horseracing, foot racing and various novelty events were used to attract crowds to the field beside the pub. Or at the very least, the finish line was at the pub!

Sydney's first official race meeting in Hyde Park in 1810 caused widespread drinking and became a three-day holiday for the entire colony.

On 15 October 1810, officers of the 73rd Regiment organised a three-day race meeting in Hyde Park. Of course, there had been unofficial meetings before that—often at pubs in outlying areas.

The records tell us that Captain Ritchie's grey gelding, Chase, won the very first race. The horses raced clockwise as the course design suited that direction due to the position of the afternoon sun. The finishing line was where Market Street meets Elizabeth Street today.

The three-day meeting caused massive drinking and rowdiness and a stray dog brought down D'Arcy Wentworth's good horse, Gig, during a race on the final day. The jockey, incidentally, was D'Arcy's nineteen-year-old son William Charles Wentworth.

Luckily uninjured, W.C. Wentworth went on to become one of our greatest and most famous political activists and statesmen.

All in all, the 1810 meeting was deemed to be a huge success and it became a part of the Sydney social calendar until 1814 when the 73rd Regiment was transferred to Ceylon and the colony lost its race committee.

Racing lapsed into unofficial match races and was banned for a time by Governor Macquarie until a brief revival at Hyde Park was followed by a further ban under Governor Brisbane.

In 1825, the Sydney Turf Club was formed and began racing at Captain Piper's racecourse at Bellevue Hill under the patronage of Governor Brisbane, who was happy to see some sort of organised racing replace the mayhem and drunkenness of unofficial meetings around the old dilapidated course at Hyde Park.

Alcohol-fuelled riots were not unusual at football matches in Melbourne throughout the latter half of the nineteenth century, and foot racing, boxing, cycling and wresting were commonly held at pubs, as was cock fighting.

Champagne and rum drinking were common at race meetings, and still are to a certain degree, but, since refrigeration came along in the late 1880s, beer and most sports just seem to go together quite naturally in Australia.

The gentle game of cricket, which stopped for lunch and tea breaks, is now perhaps the worst example of sport and booze being mixed unwisely by large groups of spectators. Journalist Rory

Gibson once wrote of a match he remembered from the 1970s, when cans were still allowed at major grounds like the Gabba.

Apparently a poor Pom paraded on the hill with a huge Union Jack draped around his shoulders. Of course, all the Aussies immediately began using him for target practice and hundreds of beer cans rained down from further up the hill. He attempted to run but that was only further incentive for the locals to pick up the thousands of empties lying around and pelt them at him.

When he eventually crouched down and covered his head with his hands, a very unsympathetic Aussie fan picked up one of the forty-four-gallon drum garbage tins full of empties and poured the lot over him. The crowd cheered as the police arrived and the poor Pom was arrested for 'inciting the crowd'.

Evidently he was smiling and everyone was happy—just another day at the cricket.

Sponsorship is a serious business and the famous competition between Foster's and Lion Nathan for Spring Carnival sponsorship rights in Melbourne is just one example of the importance of booze in the world of sport.

It's a serious matter for players, too. Rory Gibson reminds us that former North Queensland Cowboys rugby league player Ian Russell was twice fined by his club, once $5000 and then $10,000 for being seen by team officials publically drinking a can of VB, when the team was sponsored by XXXX. That's an expensive can of beer!

Wendy Green, the Darwin schoolteacher whose horse, Rogan Josh, won the 1999 Melbourne Cup, tells a great yarn about driving back to Darwin after the Cup and stopping at Tennant Creek to celebrate with some of the locals who were having a party. She was recognised and soon joined the festivities, which became a celebration of her Cup win.

Towards the end of the celebration, a local mum asked her to christen her new baby boy. Wendy explained that she wasn't qualified and had no holy water handy, but suggested the captain of the tourist bus which had pulled in to join the fun might be qualified in the same way as a ship's captain.

The bus driver was reluctant but agreed to do the job, no doubt realising he'd be a thousand miles away in two days' time.

When the mum said the name was to be 'Rogan Josh' and offered a can of VB to be used instead of holy water, Wendy protested. She pointed out that Foster's was the official sponsor of the Melbourne Cup and it didn't seem right. So, she offered the French champagne she had in her car and everyone was happy with that.

When Wendy asked the mother if she was sure about the name, she was told that it was fine, in fact it was almost traditional as there was another distant relative who'd been christened Phar Lap Dixon.   **JH**

A FRIENDLY GAME OF FOOTBALL
EDWARD DYSON

We were challenged by the Dingoes, they're the pride of Squatter's
    Gap,
To a friendly game of football on the flat by Devil's Trap,
So, we went along on horses, sworn to triumph in the game,
For the honour of Gyp's Digging, and the glory of the same.

And we took the challenge with us, it was beautiful to see,
With its lovely, curly letters and its pretty filigree.
It was very gently worded and it made us all feel good,
For it breathed the sweetest sentiments of peace and brotherhood.

We had Chang and Trucker Hogan, and the man who licked
    The Plug,
Also Heggarty, and Houlahan, and Peter Scott, the pug;
And we wore our knuckle-dusters and we took a keg on tap
To our friendly game of football with the Dingoes at The Gap.

All the fellows came to meet us and we spoke like brothers dear,
They'd a tip-dray full of tucker and a wagon load of beer,
And some lint done up in bundles, so we reckoned there'd be fun
'ere our friendly game of football with the Dingo Club was done.

Their umpire was a homely man, a stranger to the push,
With a sweet, deceitful calmness, and the flavour of the bush.
He declared he didn't know the game, but promised, on his oath,
To see fair and square between the teams, or paralyse them both.

Then we bounced the ball and started, and for twenty minutes quite
We observed a proper courtesy and a heavenly sense of right,
But Fitzpatrick tipped McDougal in a handy patch of mud,
And the hero rose up chewing dirt and famishing for blood.

The umpire dragged them from the ruck, pegged out a little patch.
And let them settle it politely with a proper boxing match.
You could hardly wish to come across a fairer-minded chap,
For a friendly game of football, than that umpire at The Gap.

Then young Magee took on a local chap named Bent,
And four others started fighting to avoid an argument.
Tim Hogan hit the umpire and was promptly put to bed
'Neath the ammunition wagon, with a bolus on his head.

Sixty seconds later, twenty couples held the floor
And the air was full of whiskers and the grass was tinged with gore,
And the umpire kept good order in the interests of peace,
While spectators, to oblige him, sat severely on the p'lice.

Well, we fought the friendly game out, but I couldn't say who won;
We were all flat out on stretchers when the glorious day was done.
Both the constables had vanished, one was carried off to bunk,
And the umpire was exhausted and the populace was drunk.

So, we've written out a paper, with good Father Feeley's aid,
Breathing brotherly affection, and a challenge is conveyed
To the Dingo Club at Squatter's, and another friendly game
Will eventuate at this end, on the flat below the claim.

COURT DAY AT BILLYBILLY
ANONYMOUS

This yarn, printed in The Bulletin *in 1896, is supposedly a court report from a country town which exposes the hypocrisy of the judicial system and the endemic nature of alcoholism in the colonies, common themes in Aussie yarns about booze. The Irish immigrants are often singled out as the biggest and worst boozers.*

The old joke about seeing double has been around for centuries, it first occurs in Ancient Greek and Roman stories.

The court house interior was almost bare of furniture, the walls were unlined and the weatherboards gaped here and there, so that the grasshoppers jumped in and out at their pleasure. Their worships the magistrates (two of them) sat on a small form behind a pine table, the prisoner hung over a deal railing about eighteen inches from the wall, and Constable O'Toole stood near, reciting the villainies of the accused in a thick, monotonous, unintelligible brogue.

The shrill, ringing whirr of the locusts filled the air for miles around, a bird chipped its beak sharply on the iron roof, and a tall, attenuated goat stood in the doorway, supinely observing the proceedings of the court, and emitting an occasional contemptuous 'bah'.

But the court seemed oblivious to everything but the dreadful heat and its own sorrows. One magistrate, open-mouthed, followed the meanderings of a lame bull ant on the table, between intervals of sleep, and occasionally stirred the insect up with a straw to add to the excitement. The other, with his head thrown back and his occiput resting on the chair rail, gazed meditatively at the roof, daydreaming of strong drinks and occasionally relapsing into a gurgling snore suggestive of a frog croaking in a ship's hold, and then pulling himself together with an effort and trying to look wise.

And all the time Constable O'Toole droned along about 'this yere mahn' who had been discovered the night previous, howling on the road 'afore widder Johnson's', with nothing on, 'barrin' th' dust, yer worships, which he'd buried hisself in'.

Prisoner was charged with drunkenness and disorderly conduct, and was a woebegone object, the Sahara incarnate. His tongue could be heard grating against his palate and he looked piteously thirsty. When the policeman had done, he put in a word or two in extenuation of his weakness, reminding their worships of the weather they had been having, and concluding with a touching and wholly ineffectual effort to expectorate.

The court felt itself called upon, and one magistrate arose, and, steadying himself by leaning over the table, assumed a look of inhuman gravity, and said: 'Prisoner, such conducksh wholly indefenshible—disgrash tyer manhood. Your are fined sheven daysh or twenty-four hoursh.'

Then he sat down, with the air of a man who has done his duty by his country, and the other arose, and, after blinking for a few moments at the prisoner, with an assumption of owl-like wisdom, added: 'Sheven daysh 'r twenty-foursh hoursh, both of you!'

'Yesh,' corroborated the first, rising again, 'both of you!'

Then the court adjourned.

DIPSO AND THE TWINS
JIM HAYNES

Here's my version of the old joke, featuring Dipso Dan, the town drunk of my home town, Weelabarabak, which is on the border of New South Wales and Western Australia if you're looking for it on the map.

Dipso Dan has made us suffer
For his alcoholic sins,
But strike me pink he made us laugh
The day he met the twins!

They were college mates of Dougie's son
Stayin' over for some function,
The B and S Ball perhaps it was,
Or the game against Cooper's Junction.

And 'struth were they identical,
Talk about Bib and Bub—
So we thought we'd have a bit of fun
With Dipso down the pub.

The twins of course were in on it.
We made 'em dress the same
And practise identical movements,
And answering to one name.

All the regulars were in on it.
We waited till late in the night—
The plan was we'd ignore the twins
And give Dipso Dan a real fright.

And when we gave the nod to Dougie
He says, 'Dipso, you've had enough,
You'll be bloody seeing double
If you drink any more of the stuff.'

That's the cue for the twins to enter,
Perfectly synchronised,
They walked right up beside Dan and stopped
And you should have seen his eyes.

And when they ordered a beer in unison
His hair began to stand,
And when they lifted their glasses and drained 'em as one,
His glass slipped from his hand.

'Thanks,' said the twins together,
And then they left the bar.
Dipso Dan was as white as a ghost,
We thought we'd gone too far.

'Are you alright, Dan?' asked Nugget,
'D-D-D- . . . Did you see that?' says Dan,
'It's enough to make me quit the grog.
It's enough to reform a man!'

Well, Doug can't stand it any more,
He wants no damage done.
'Calm down Dan—it was just a joke,
They're identical mates of me son.

'We were having you on—c'mon, relax,
You won't see any more of 'em.'
'Well, ya had me fooled,' said Dipso Dan,
'Identical, eh, all bloody four of 'em!'

ANZAC NIGHT IN THE GARDENS
LENNIE LOWER

Lennie Lower was one of the most inventive wordsmiths and yarn spinners Australia ever produced. His cleverness at telling a story and turning a phrase still takes my breath away. He deserted twice from the armed forces but was still more than willing to keep up the Anzac Day tradition of drinking to excess. Here he is talking to the statues in the Botanic Gardens, with no real idea how he got there!

Lost in the wilds of the Botanic Gardens! Heavens, shall we ever forget it! The last human face we saw was that of Matthew Flinders, the great explorer.

We got in with a few Anzacs last night, and we forget how we got into the Gardens, but believe us, it's terrible. Instructive, but terrible.

Nothing to drink but goldfish.

Bottle-trees dotted about the place, and we had no opener. Naked men and women standing on square whitewashed rocks. All dumb!

We wandered up to a signboard, thinking to read, 'Ten miles to . . . ,' and saw there, 'Please do not walk on the grass borders.'

Starving, practically, we climbed a coconut tree for food and found it was a date tree without any dates on it.

We came to a tree marked 'Dysoxolum'. We thought, we knew how sox were dyed, but what shall it profit a man if he lose himself in the Gardens?

We came to where the tortoise slept, and knocked on his shell. Like all the rest of our friends, he was in, but he didn't answer.

Dawn found us clawing at the front of the Herbarium, shrieking hysterically for just a little thyme.

The keeper who found us said that everything was all right and this was the way out. We don't know what became of the others.

Probably their bodies will be found in the bandstand and identified by their pawn tickets. The Anzacs certainly were, and still are, a tough crowd. We will never go into the Gardens again without wearing all our medals and two identification discs. It's always best to carry a spare on Anzac night.

DRINKS WITH A KICK IN THEM
LENNIE LOWER

The President of the Housewives' Association says that she does not believe in cocktail drinking and could, if necessary, produce a drink with a 'kick' in it, from fruit.

Anticipating, we have evolved a few recipes to suit all tastes.

Banana Flutter: Take one banana, slice, and put into glass. Take half a coconut and beat it into a stiff froth. Mix briskly and serve. The 'kick' is obtained by standing on one foot on the skin of the banana and leaning forward while pouring the drink down the back of the neck.

Then we have the Flying Mule: Take half a dozen raspberries, being careful to remove the seeds, also the sound. Mash lightly with hammer. Mix with a little ice-water, and add seeds slowly, one at a time, until you are so thirsty that you'd drink anything. Now take a red-hot nail, and dip it smartly into the mixture, removing it almost immediately. Drink nail.

The Watermelon Whoopee: Take one large watermelon, cut in half. Hollow out one half and place contents in washbasin. Save seeds from other half. Place in washbasin one small cup of gramophone needles, half-pint of sulphuric acid. Drink before bottom falls out of washbasin.

A similar mixture is the Hangover Blues: The watermelon is put into the washbasin as before, but covered with crushed ice. The hollowed-out portion is then quarter-filled with crushed ice and placed over the head, taking care to pull it well down over the forehead. The face is then laid gently in the washbasin.

It will be seen from the above recipes that the uses of fruit as a drink are practically unlimited. Furthermore, most fruit is full of vitamins. These need not worry the hostess, however, as they can easily be detected by the small holes in the outside of the skin, and this part can be cut out.

And don't forget, all these drinks have a kick.

The careful hostess should warn her guests of this danger.

HOW SEXY REX CLEARED THE BAR

Sexy Rex was a shearers' cook, or had been . . . or said he had been.

When I knew him he spent most of his time telling people about being a shearers' cook—from a corner of the bar at the Tatts, or the Royal—or at odd times when his liver was having a bad day, from a table near the window in the Paragon Café. Maybe he'd never been a shearers' cook at all. I never met anyone who remembered him being one. There were plenty of people, however, who remembered him telling them about being one.

Being a shearers' cook doesn't seem much to boast about, or spend most of your time reminiscing about. Most blokes I know who had been shearers' cooks kept pretty quiet about it and found other things to talk about. They certainly found other things to boast about. But Sexy Rex liked to boast about being a shearers' cook.

He was probably called 'Sexy Rex' because he was the least sexy person imaginable, or simply because it was the first rhyme that sprang to mind—or perhaps a bit of both.

Anyway, Sexy Rex walked with a pronounced limp, when he walked at all. He didn't walk much, for two reasons. Firstly because of his pronounced limp and secondly because his main claim to fame, his real skill in life, was cadging lifts from one pub to the other, because he walked with a pronounced limp.

No one ever questioned that Rex's limp was a result of 'the war'. But the funny thing was that he never talked about 'the war' or claimed to have fought in World War II. He'd arrived in the district after the war, complete with his pronounced limp, so I guess everyone just assumed that he acquired the limp in the war.

He didn't wear an RSL badge and he didn't march in the Anzac Day parade because of his limp. He did do his share of 'anzacing' at the pub after the march, but his reminiscences, even on Anzac Day, were invariably about being a shearers' cook.

It was actually Spanner Toole who cleared the bar at the Royal, and that was because he was fed up with Boof Simpson and Billy O'Shea reminding him about the belting they'd given him the night before outside the town's other pub, the Tatts.

Now the hiding Spanner had copped the night before outside the Tatts was pretty much Spanner's fault. He could be fairly annoying when he tied one on and he had this bad habit of digging up a little 'local history' and broadcasting it around the bar, airing other people's dirty laundry in public.

Let's be honest, Spanner was a nasty piece of work when he'd had a few. There weren't many drinkers at the Tatts who had any time for him when he was in that condition. On Friday night at the Tatts, he was getting no encouragement from the other drinkers, but he expounded his theories nonetheless and anyone who was in the bar couldn't help but hear them.

On this particular occasion, his theory concerned the alleged results of an alleged relationship between his own father, now deceased, and Nola Simpson.

Nola Simpson was not deceased but very much alive and kicking. What's more, she was Boof's mother and Billy's aunt. Boof and Billy were quite willing to do the kicking necessary to defend her honour, especially when the person getting kicked was Spanner Toole.

By all accounts, Nola's son and nephew had done a pretty good job of defending her honour in her absence outside the Tatts that night.

The resulting fight outside the Tatts had, by all accounts, not been a pretty sight and Spanner was an even less pretty sight than usual when he arrived at the Royal for a recuperative drink the next day.

Boof and Billy were already drinking at the Royal when Spanner arrived; they had naturally been barred from the Tatts for giving Spanner a hiding.

Boof and Billy held no particular grudge against Dougie, the Tatts' publican, about being barred from the Tatts by Dougie, even though they had not started the fight. They pretty much accepted that, if you got involved in a Friday night 'incident' and then gave someone a hiding outside a pub, you would be barred from that pub for a time. So Boof and Billy were drinking at 'the other pub' and having a few bets with Fancy Youngman, the SP bookie, when Spanner arrived.

In charge of the bar that day was Harold Davis, known as Happy Harold to the desperate drinkers who frequented the Royal, because he never smiled. He lived alone in a bit of a shanty on the edge of town, in a bend of the river known to locals as Happy Valley.

Happy Harold was a 'Jimmy Woodser', a solitary drinker who was always sober when he was at work behind the bar at the Royal, and never sober any other time. He had a dry wit, told a good story and got drunk as soon as he finished a shift.

It wasn't Spanner Toole alone who cleared the bar at the Royal that Saturday afternoon, it was a combination of Spanner and the old side-by-side double-barrelled shotgun he got out from under the seat of his ute and carried back into the bar. He did this because he was fed up with Boof Simpson and Billy O'Shea insulting him and reminding him about the belting they had given him the night before outside the Tatts.

'When Spanner and the shotgun entered the bar,' Harold said later, 'the bar cleared pretty quickly.'

A lot of blokes disappeared into the toilets at the end of the bar. Gender was suddenly not an issue according to Harold, the Ladies being just as popular as the Gents at that particular moment. A lot of the bar cleared into the lounge and taproom at the further end. The bar did not, oddly enough, clear into the street, perhaps because the area in the general vicinity of that door was more or less occupied by Spanner and the shotgun.

Harold was left alone in the relative safety of the area behind the bar, with the glasses piled high along it. He had simply to duck down to remove the immediate threat of being in the firing line of Spanner and his shotgun.

Which brings us to the crux of the story really. It was at that point, as he ducked down, that Harold realised he was no longer alone behind the bar. He had been joined there by Sexy Rex.

Harold says that Sexy Rex, in spite of his limp and alleged bad leg must have cleared the bar and the glasses stacked on it to join him in relative safety behind it.

Were we to believe Happy Harold would tell lies? Or did we choose to believe that our local crippled ex-serviceman could clear a four-foot bar, stacked with glasses, in a split second with no apparent side effects?

It was a dilemma which would concern the town longer than the current crisis. Because Spanner stopped yelling abuse at the whole town in general, and Boof and Billy in particular, when the sergeant arrived a few minutes later to relieve him of the shotgun.

While Spanner climbed quietly into the paddy wagon to be taken to the lockup, the sergeant did something quite uncharacteristic. He had Spanner's collar in one hand and the shotgun in the other and, knowing Spanner as well as he did, he assumed that Spanner would never actually load a shotgun and take it into the bar of the Royal. So he pointed the gun, which was cocked, at the outside brick wall of the pub, and pulled the trigger.

The marks of the pellets are still there in the brickwork today. They serve as a constant and historic reminder of Harold's amazing claim that Sexy Rex cleared the bar the day that Spanner Toole cleared the bar with the loaded shotgun.

But even Harold was forced to admit he didn't actually see Sexy Rex clear the bar. Perhaps Sexy Rex got behind the bar another way. None of us can imagine how, but we prefer to leave the episode in the unsolved file rather than believe that Sexy Rex was not the genuine article.   **JH**

YARNS FROM OUR PAST

The best bits of history are always the personal stories and those quirky, coincidental and seemingly unlikely occurrences.

As the 'Australiana Guy' on the long running Radio 2UE weekend program, *George and Paul on the Weekend*, it's my job to find a fascinating story from the past every week in order to get listeners calling in with their own reminiscences and answering the questions we ask about some of the lesser known aspects of our past.

Of course, the things I talk about need to be interesting enough to keep people listening.

Doing this for over ten years has helped confirm what I always thought about our history. It was always the odd coincidences and human stories that I found fascinating, rather than the momentous military and political events.

As a teacher of history, among other subjects, for almost twenty years, it seemed to me that most kids, especially those who were not really the top students or big fans of formal learning, reacted more positively if I made history lessons into yarns and stories about interesting characters. I was accused of taking this too far by one department head who said, 'Jim, I don't mind you telling the kids in that Year Nine class about the Punic Wars as if it was an adventure serial at the Saturday movie matinee, but it's a bit rich when they can tell me the names of all Hannibal's elephants!'

In spite of any past such embellishments on my behalf when teaching, all the yarns I have included here are factually correct—honest. After all, you just could not invent some of the true stories from our past.

Allan Peters, who runs a website for the South Australian Police Historical Society, has found some gems among the police archives. During elections in South Australia in the early 1900s, for example, Police Inspector John Kelly received an urgent message to say that the keys of the polling booth at Sliding Rock had been sent to Blinman by mistake.

Kelly set off into a blinding dust storm and rode 65 kilometres to deliver the keys. He arrived exhausted at the polling booth at

six o'clock in the morning on Election Day and opened the booth
. . . and not a single person turned up to vote.

Then there is the story of sixty-year-old Claude McNamara
who was shot while waiting for a tram in Redfern, Sydney, when
a bullet, fired into the head of a dying dog by a policeman 150
metres away, passed through the animal's skull, bounced off a
pipe and hit poor old Claude in the leg.

My favourite is the one about the policeman sent to Iron
Range on remote Cape York Peninsula to investigate the theft of
the temporarily closed police station and its entire contents. The
building had been sawn from its stumps and carted away.

When the officer investigating threatened dire consequences
for the town if nothing was returned, one of the thieves sneaked
back at night and left a police badge on one of the stumps.

You just can't make up yarns like that.

THE DOGGED CAPTAIN COOK

Captain Cook encouraged the making and consumption of fruit-
based home brew (a jungle juice that might or might not have
helped ward off scurvy) and his crew was very often more drunk
than sober.

The London-based Polish–Prussian botanist Johann Forster,
who went on Cook's second voyage, was not a big fan of Captain
Cook and his methods. He described the crew of the *Resolution* as
'solicitous to get very drunk, though they are commonly solicitous
about nothing else'.

James Cook was not too fond of Forster, either. He had jumped
on board the expedition with his son and pet dog when Sir Joseph
Banks pulled out. Forster was a friend of the geographer Alexander
Dalrymple, who was Cook's greatest critic. Forster had good
connections at court and, travelling on the voyage as a botanist,
was paid more than five times what Cook received in wages.

Not only did the fastidious Prussian disapprove of the crew's
alcohol consumption, he also argued with Cook about where the
ship should be going and became dreadfully agitated when Cook

sailed deep into the Antarctic to finally prove once and for all that there was no habitable continent south of Terra Australis.

Forster spent much of the voyage complaining and threatening to report various officers to the king on his return. Cook found him so annoying that he soon ignored him completely, as did most of the crew.

Captain Cook had the last laugh, however.

Cook took the *Resolution* further south than any man had ever been and only turned back when the ice prevented any further southward progress. On his way back from the Antarctic, Cook became seriously ill. There was no fresh food on board, so the second officer ordered that Forster's pet dog be killed and cooked. Captain Cook ate it in a nice stew and soon recovered his health.

JH

FORGERY ON THE HIGH SEAS
JOHN WHITE

My favourite account of the voyage of the First Fleet is that written by the surgeon, John White. Here he is telling the remarkable yarn about some convicts forging coins to buy goods when the fleet reached the Portuguese port of Rio de Janiero, in Brazil.

5th August 1777. Still calm. This morning a boat came alongside, in which were three Portuguese and six slaves, from whom we purchased some oranges, plantains, and bread.

In trafficking with these people, we discovered that one Thomas Barret, a convict, had, with great ingenuity and address, passed some quarter dollars which he, assisted by two others, had made out of old buckles, buttons belonging to the marines, and pewter spoons, during their passage from Teneriffe.

The impression, milling, character, in a word, the whole was so inimitably executed that had their metal been a little better the fraud, I am convinced, would have passed undetected. A strict and careful search was made for the apparatus wherewith this was done, but in vain; not the smallest trace or vestige of any thing of the kind was to be found among them.

How they managed this business without discovery, or how they could effect it at all, is a matter of inexpressible surprise to me, as they never were suffered to come near a fire and a sentinel was constantly placed over their hatchway, which, one would imagine, rendered it impossible for either fire or fused metal to be conveyed into their apartments. Besides, hardly ten minutes ever elapsed, without an officer of some degree or other going down among them.

The adroitness, therefore, with which they must have managed, in order to complete a business that required so complicated a process, gave me a high opinion of their ingenuity, cunning, caution, and address; and I could not help wishing that these qualities had been employed to more laudable purposes.

The officers of marines, the master of the ship, and myself fully explained to the injured Portuguese what villains they were who had imposed upon them. We were not without apprehensions that they might entertain an unfavourable opinion of Englishmen in general from the conduct of these rascals; we therefore thought it necessary to acquaint them that the perpetrators of the fraud were felons doomed to transportation, by the laws of their country, for having committed similar offences there.

HMS *SIRIUS* SAILS ROUND THE WORLD - A MAN GOES MAD

By September 1788, things were looking grim in the little colony at Port Jackson. The cattle had wandered away and been lost in June when their keeper, a convict named Corbett, had absconded and attempted to live in the bush with the Aborigines. He eventually returned and was hanged for losing the cattle.

Governor Phillip realised that the colony was in danger of starving. Few crops had grown from the seed carried on the First Fleet, much of which had spoiled on the voyage. Crops, which were planted out of season in late summer, produced only enough grain for seed.

With the crop failure, the Governor could see famine in the not-too-distant future and, by September 1788, the situation was desperate, rations were cut and theft of food was a constant problem. Phillip decided to send the *Sirius* to Cape Town: '. . . in order to procure grain and . . . what quantities of flour and provisions she can receive.'

The stoic Scot, Captain John Hunter, realised that his vessel was in poor shape; 'much neglected' was his term. Hunter had already noted that the ship had been poorly prepared and refitted in Britain and had problems with rotten fittings and leaks. He also knew his crew had been on salted rations for over a year and would be prone to scurvy.

Hunter was a loyal friend to Arthur Phillip and followed his instructions to the letter. He had the ever-reliable Lieutenant Bradley, a teacher from the Royal Naval Academy who had signed on as first mate on the *Sirius* to further his scientific knowledge.

Hunter was not a man to question orders.

Eight guns, with cannon balls and powder, were taken off the *Sirius* and, reluctantly, her longboat was also left behind. It was decided to follow the southern gales eastward and so, on 2 October 1788, the *Sirius*, already leaking badly and without a longboat, headed out of Port Jackson and sailed south towards the Antarctic.

Ten days later, she passed the southern tip of New Zealand and within days scurvy had appeared among the crew and the ship was leaking badly. Passing under Cape Horn, the ship sailed through masses of icebergs and experienced gale force winds, snow, sleet and hail.

Hunter's meticulous notes give some idea of the stoic nonchalance of the brave Scottish mariner:

> We now very frequently fell in with high islands of ice. On the 24th, we had fresh gales with hazy and cold weather, and met so many ice islands, that we were frequently obliged to alter

our course to avoid them. On the 25th, we had strong gales with very heavy and frequent squalls: as we were now drawing near Cape Horn . . . we passed one of the largest ice-islands we had seen; we judged it not less than three miles [5 kilometres] in length, and its perpendicular height we supposed to be 350 feet [107 metres].

The strangeness and danger of such a voyage would prove too much for one man. Third Lieutenant Maxwell became insane as the ship passed under Cape Horn and, while on watch, began cramming on all sail in a gale. Apparently, as ascertained from his ravings, he had decided that he wanted to see if the ship would sail underwater and emerge from hell 'with the same set of damned rascals she was carrying'.

Hunter came on deck in his shirt and reefed the sails himself while Maxwell was restrained and confined to his cabin. He never regained his sanity.

Watkin Tench summarised in his journal on their return that:

The *Sirius* had made her passage to the Cape of Good Hope, by the route of Cape Horn, in exactly thirteen weeks. Her highest latitude was 57 degrees 10 minutes south, where the weather proved intolerably cold. Ice, in great quantity, was seen for many days; and in the middle of December water froze in open casks upon deck.

The first death from scurvy occurred just after Cape Horn and another four men died before Cape Town was reached. By then forty men were too sick to move and another ten worked their watch without the use of at least one limb due to scurvy.

On sighting Table Mountain, Hunter was anxious to make port as quickly as possible to save as many of the crew as he could:

The weakly condition of that part of the ship's company, who were able to do duty upon deck, and the very dejected state of those who were confined to their beds, determined me, if possible, to bring the ship to an anchor before night; as the very idea of being in port, sometimes has an exceeding good effect upon the spirits of people who are reduced low by the scurvy; which was the case with a great many of our ship's company; and indeed, a considerable number were in the last stage of it.

On arrival at the Cape, Hunter needed to repair both his ship and his crew. A hospital was set up on shore and the men rested and ate fresh fruit and vegetables for a month until all were well again.

The trip back was a nightmare. The crew pumped constantly as the overladen ship leaked steadily and a gale arose with mountainous seas, which threatened to blow them onto a lee shore and wreck the ship on the wild west coast or southern tip of Van Diemen's Land. The sun disappeared for days at a time and the ship was awash as fierce winds and heavy seas bore away her topmasts and even the figurehead of Lord Berwick.

Hunter was well aware that the ship was in grave danger of striking the shore as he could not rely on his best efforts at calculating their position. His dour, understated journal entry belies the reality of the danger:

It may not be improper here to observe, that three days had now elapsed without a sight of the sun during the day, or a star during the night, from which we could exactly determine our latitude . . .

Hunter then casually relates how the ship was caught on a dead lee shore and her destruction seemed imminent:

. . . we saw the land again, through the haze close under our lee bow, and the sea breaking with prodigious force upon it, it was impossible to weather it . . . the sea running mountain high . . . we knew not what bay, or part of the coast we were upon, nor what dangerous ledges of rocks might be detached some distance from the shore; we had every moment reason to fear that the next might, by the ship striking, launch the whole of us into eternity . . . The ship was at this time half buried in the sea by the press of sail, since she was going through it (for she could not be said to be going over it) at the rate of four knots.

Lieutenant Bradley noted that the surf breaking on the rocks 'could not be distinguished from that of the sea which was all breakers to the horizon'.

All through the storm, with the constant fear of being run aground, the ship continued to leak badly: 'In this trying situation, the ship being leaky, our pumps during such a night were a distressing tax upon us; as they were kept constantly at work.'

In his dour fatalistic style, Hunter put their survival down to divine providence, with a little help from skilled navigation and seamanship:

> I do not recollect to have heard of a more wonderful escape. Every thing, which depended upon us, I believe, was done; but it would be the highest presumption and ingratitude to Divine Providence, were we to attribute our preservation wholly to our best endeavours . . .

On 8 May 1789, the *Sirius*, having circumnavigated the globe in an unseaworthy condition, limped back into Port Jackson, minus her topmasts and figurehead, with seed grain and four months' supply of food. It was 219 days since she had left the colony.

Phillip was relieved and grateful. He invited the ship's officers to dinner to express his gratitude. Rations were still in force and food scarce, so scarce in fact that the officers were told to bring their own bread rolls to the Governor's dinner.

One officer not invited was poor mad Lieutenant Maxwell who was confined in the hospital on his return to Sydney Cove and was later discovered to have buried the seventy guineas his family sent for his care somewhere in the hospital garden, in order that his fortune might grow with a good crop of guineas the next year.

JH

MARY BRYANT GOES HOME

While some of the more simple-minded convicts from the First Fleet attempted to escape overland and met their death in the bush from starvation or fatal encounters with the various Aboriginal tribes, the only sane and practical way to escape was obviously by sea.

Escape of any kind was highly unlikely to succeed, but life was grim for the first batch of convicts whether they stayed or ran. After all, the whole point of sending convicts to Botany Bay was that the Lord Commissioners of the Treasury knew it was a place 'from whence it is hardly possible for persons to return without permission'.

'Hardly possible' perhaps, but not entirely impossible.

Against all odds, the convict Mary Bryant escaped in 1790 and successfully returned to her home in Cornwall; what's more, she received a pardon and financial aid from no less a personage than James Boswell, the biographer of Dr Samuel Johnson.

Unlike the spontaneous or opportunistic escapes that occurred from time to time, the escape of Emanuel William and Mary Bryant, their two children and seven convict companions, was carefully planned and well prepared.

William was well qualified for the escape attempt. He was a Cornish fisherman sentenced to death, commuted to seven years' transportation to America, for a smuggling offence ('resisting revenue officers') in 1784 at the age of twenty-seven. As the American option had already been lost to Britain when the American War of Independence ended a year earlier, William spent the first half of his sentence on the hulks, where he met Mary Braund, daughter of a mariner and also from Cornwall.

Mary was described as being 'marked with smallpox with one knee bent but not lame'. She was 1.6 metres in height with grey eyes, brown hair and a sallow complexion. Her family were associated with the sea and were also noted sheep stealers. Mary was sentenced to death, commuted to transportation, for assaulting and robbing a spinster in company with two other young women when she was aged twenty.

William and Mary both travelled on the *Charlotte* with the First Fleet. William was trusted with the supervision of food distribution and Mary gave birth to a daughter during the voyage. She gave her daughter the name of the ship on which she was born, Charlotte.

William's privileged position continued in Port Jackson where he was given a hut apart from the other convicts and was made the fisherman for the colony. He was also put in charge of the colony's small boats.

One reason for the hut being apart from the other convicts on the eastern side of the Tank Stream was to prevent an easy trade in black market fish developing. However, on 4 February 1789, William was caught selling some of his catch. He was dismissed from his post as fisherman, lost his hut, and received 100 lashes. Mary was forced to deliver their second child, a son, in the convict camp at The Rocks.

William continued in a lesser role, maintaining the colony's small boats and helping with the fishing, as he was the most skilled and capable man for the job. He took extra care to maintain the government cutter, as he had a plan for escape, but he waited until there were no ships in the colony capable of pursuit.

The escape was extremely well planned. After the boat was overturned in a squall, Bryant restored it to first-class order with new sails, new masts and a complete refit, all at government expense. He and Mary stashed away 45 kilograms of rice, the same of flour and also salt pork, water, tents and tools.

The *Sirius* was wrecked at Norfolk Island and the *Supply* was on its way to Norfolk Island when the Dutch supply ship *Waaksamheyd* sailed from Port Jackson on 28 March 1791.

The *Waaksamheyd* was a 'snaw brig', a two-masted merchant ship, which had been chartered from Batavia by Captain Ball who had sailed there in the *Supply* in April 1790. She arrived in December 1790 with much needed supplies, having lost most of her crew to fever on the way. After difficult negotiations between Phillip and her captain, Detmer Smit, she was then chartered to take the crew of *Sirius* back to Britain for the statutory court-martial after her loss on the reef on Norfolk Island.

William Bryant knew he was technically a free man, he had served his time, but Governor Phillip was waiting for the convict indents to arrive; he had no record of which convicts had served their time and which had not.

Bryant approached Captain Smit for help and outlined his escape plans to the Dutchman. Sailing and rowing a small open boat to Timor meant a voyage of 5230 kilometres. Smit told Bryant that Captain Bligh had made the journey from Tahiti to Timor in a similar boat and supplied him with a compass, quadrant, two guns, ammunition and detailed charts of the Great Barrier Reef.

At midnight on the same day that the *Waaksamheyd* sailed, William and Mary Bryant and their two infant children and seven other convicts rowed out through the heads and turned north.

They survived storms in which they were lost in 'mountainous seas' and encounters with hostile Aborigines who chased them out to sea in large canoes. They navigated the Great Barrier Reef, coming ashore for water and supplies and shelter many times. They crossed the Arafura Sea and finally all made it safely to Koepang, on Timor, after seventy days at sea.

The Dutch governor treated them well and believed their story about being castaways from a shipwreck until September when Captain Edwards arrived at Koepang with survivors of his crew from the wrecked *Pandora* and of his captured mutineers from the *Bounty*. Edwards questioned the fugitives, who confessed. They were taken to the fever-ridden port of Batavia, where both Emanuel and William Bryant died. Three of the others died at sea, but Mary, Charlotte and four surviving convicts were taken to the Cape and transferred to the HMS *Gorgon* for the final voyage to Britain, on which Charlotte died.

The press took up the story and James Boswell appealed to the Home Office for clemency. The five were ordered 'to remain on their former sentences until they should expire' but Mary Bryant was finally pardoned in May 1793, six weeks after her original sentence had expired. The four other male convicts were released the following November and it is believed one of them later enlisted in the New South Wales Corps and returned to the colony.

The last that history knows of the resilient Mary Bryant is a letter of thanks received by James Boswell in November 1794 from her home in Cornwall.   **JH**

OUR FIRST FREE SETTLERS

In 1792, the first organised group of free settlers left Britain to be settled at what was appropriately called Liberty Plains—the area around modern-day Strathfield.

Lieutenant Governor Grose decided to settle the farmers at Strathfield for the 'convenience and safety of the travelling public' moving between the two settlements of Sydney and Parramatta.

The original group of settlers was made up of three farmers, a baker, a blacksmith, a gardener, a millwright, two women and four children. They arrived as passengers on the *Bellona* in January 1793 and land grants were formalised in May of the same year. Edward Powell, aged thirty, described as a farmer and fisherman from Lancaster, was given 80 acres, as were Thomas Webb, a gardener, and his wife. Thomas Rose, aged forty, a farmer who arrived with his wife Jane, their four children and another female teenage relative, was given 120 acres.

Those who were not farmers were given 60 acres, and all the settlers had their passages paid and received tools and implements from the public stores plus two years' provisions, clothing and the services of assigned convicts as labour. They cleared the land and grew wheat, potatoes and corn. The settlers gave their farms names like Charlotte Farm, Webb's Endeavour and Dorset Green.

The settlement at Liberty Plains was soon followed by another immediately to the north and north-west (near modern-day Concord and Homebush) where 25 acres per man was allotted to the officers and non-commissioned officers of the New South Wales Corps and several other citizens.

Many of these soldiers sold their lots as soon as they were granted, or within the next few years. Many never even saw the land but, eventually, there were about sixty settlers and soldiers farming in the two adjacent areas of Liberty Plains and Concord, most not particularly successfully.

The name Liberty Plains was obvious; the settlers there had their liberty. Lieutenant Governor Francis Grose named the other settlement Concord after the first battle fought in the American War of Independence in 1794, in which he had fought.

When Samuel Crane was killed while felling a tree, which fell on him, his 25-acre farm was advertised for sale as having 'a comfortable hut, four acres planted to corn and half an acre to potatoes'.

The next governor, John Hunter, was evidently not a fan of the free settlers farming scheme. In 1796, he wrote that, in his four years as governor, only eleven men had migrated as free settlers, eight with families. He described them as 'not of a high calibre'.

Hunter complained, in a letter to the Duke of Portland, that the English free settlers arrived in the colony with high expectations based on false reports of permanent government assistance and with no real understanding of the work required to develop the land. His main complaint was that when they were given animals for the purposes of breeding in order to build up flocks and herds, they immediately slaughtered and ate them.

The Reverend Samuel Marsden visited the area in 1798 and reported dire poverty and very little food being produced. The farmers had run out of seed wheat, which suggests that all efforts to grow a crop had failed or that they had eaten the wheat provided for seed.

Marsden commented that the settlers had no money to buy any food or goods at all. 'Should a ship arrive with any articles of consumption,' he wrote, 'they can't raise a single pound in the two districts.'

The enterprising Blaxland brothers, who migrated to the colony 'seeking their fortunes' as free settlers in 1805 bought cheaply many of the land grants that had been given to the officers of the New South Wales Corps and used them to establish the famous Newington estate.

Liberty Plains was renamed Strathfield in 1885 after the large local property of John Hardie, who called his place Strathfield after the estate given by the king to the Duke of Wellington in 1817.

JH

THE MAN THEY COULDN'T HANG

When I was kid, my uncle used to say when he saw me, 'Here he is—the man they couldn't hang—couldn't find his neck for dirt!'

I had no idea there really was a 'man they couldn't hang'.

Right up until 1985, you could still be executed for three crimes in New South Wales—treason, setting fire to a naval dockyard and piracy.

In colonial times, hangings were quite commonplace and provided entertainment for the public. Apart from race meetings and privately organised sporting events, there was not much in the way of outdoor entertainment for the population of Sydney in those days.

The gallows in Sydney was originally on Pinchgut Island, which was quite a high rock until levelled in the 1850s. Then hangings took place at Parramatta and also at a high spot near the Argyle Cut.

Later the scaffold was on the corner of Castlereagh and Park Streets, and a hotel next door offered lunch and a good view of the hangings from a balcony. When Darlinghurst Gaol was completed in 1841, it became the venue for hangings until it was closed as a prison in 1907. The last few prisoners hanged in New South Wales were executed at Long Bay Prison.

In 1803, Joseph Samuel, 'the man they couldn't hang', was sentenced to death for petty theft and aiding in the murder of the constable who chased the four robbers.

Samuel was a Jewish convict, transported for robbery in 1801. He and three others escaped and robbed the home of a wealthy widow and the constable who chased after them was murdered.

The gang was soon caught and Samuel confessed to stealing the goods but denied being part of the murder. The others were not convicted but the woman recognised Joseph and he was sentenced to death.

With another criminal, he was taken in a cart to Parramatta where hundreds gathered to watch the hanging.

After prayers were said and the nooses were fastened securely around their necks, the cart drove off. This was the common method of hanging at that time, and caused death by slow strangulation.

The ropes used were made of five-hempen cords designed to hold 450 kilograms for up to five minutes without breaking.

While the other criminal died by strangulation, Samuel's rope snapped and he dropped to his feet, sprained an ankle and collapsed. The executioner found another rope and repeated the process. Samuel fell from the cart a second time, but the noose slipped and his feet touched the ground.

As the executioner stood Samuel up to try again, the crowd turned nasty and called for Samuel to be freed. The executioner fastened another five-hempen rope around Samuel's neck and ordered the cart driven away. The rope snapped, and Joseph Samuel dropped to the ground and fell over as he tried to avoid landing on his sprained ankle.

Now the crowd was in an uproar. The executioner called a halt to the hanging and the Provost Marshall rode to find Governor King who decided it was a sign from God and granted Joseph Samuel a full reprieve saying, 'May the grateful remembrance of these events direct his future course.'

A doctor attended to Joseph's sprained ankle and he was sent to work in the Hunter coalmines. People said he was never quite 'right in the attic' after being hanged three times and, in 1806, he ran away with seven other convicts and stole a boat.

Joseph Samuel and the other escaped convicts headed out to sea and disappeared in a storm, never to be seen again.   **JH**

WHO CROSSED THE BLUE MOUNTAINS?

I believe there is good evidence to show that an Irish ex-convict, James Byrne, was the first European to cross the Blue Mountains west of Sydney, though there is also evidence that John Wilson, another ex-convict, crossed the mountains further south well before Byrne and well before the famous trio Blaxland, Lawson and Wentworth, who get all the credit.

It is also possible that Lieutenant William Dawes crossed the mountains quite early in the colony's history, with the help of his Aboriginal friends.

The official records of the Blaxland, Lawson and Wentworth expedition, including the diaries of the explorers, made no mention of the names of the 'four servants' who accompanied them.

The Sydney Gazette only mentioned the expedition briefly at the time and it was not until a hundred years later that the three 'gentlemen' are made heroes in history books for school children.

So, that bit of our 'history' seems to have been invented at a time when the historians were looking for heroes, around the time of Australia's Federation. Convicts were unsuitable as role models, it seems, so the long forgotten expedition by the 'three gentlemen' was dusted off and became a feat of great endeavour to inspire school children.

Five convicts were remunerated for their services in the first two expeditions across the mountains, the one with the 'three gentlemen' and the next with surveyor Evans.

It is possible that ex-convict, James Byrne, was the first man to cross the mountains west of Sydney and later led the three famous 'explorers' across. Byrne was born in 1769 in Wicklow, Ireland, and was transported as an 'Irish rebel' on the *Anne*, arriving in Port Jackson on 21 February 1801. Byrne is never mentioned by name in Blaxland's journal, being referred to only as 'a man who was used to shooting kangaroos in that country' and 'a servant'.

A document dated February 1814 shows Byrne was paid from the Police Fund for services as a guide to the party who crossed the Blue Mountains and again 'for services in making discoveries west of the Blue Mountains', in a document dated 30 April 1814.

Five other convicts or ex-convicts were paid from the Police Fund for services in 'making discoveries west of the Blue Mountains', in a document dated 30 April 1814. They received grants of land in December 1814 for 'crossing the Blue Mountains'.

The earlier date of 5 February 1814 for James Byrne, as well as other research, indicates that he was part of the first 'official' expedition over the Blue Mountains.

All five convicts accompanied George Evans on the second expedition.

James Byrne was granted land at Appin and later moved south with his family to settle at Collector, where he died in 1849.   **JH**

THE AMAZING CAPTAIN SWALLOW

Hollywood, and even the Australian film industry, have a tendency to repeat the same adventure stories over and over. Robin Hood, Tarzan, stories of the Bounty *and Ned Kelly have been told and retold many times. And yet there are true stories from our past that make these seem tame and lame by comparison. Take the story of William Walker, for example, though I am sure Hollywood would prefer a title like 'The Amazing Captain Swallow'.*

William Walker (also known by the surnames of Brown, Shields, Swallow and Waldron) was born in 1792, in North Shields near Sunderland. He worked on coal boats from the age of fifteen and was press-ganged into the navy at eighteen. He served two years and then fell victim to the Depression and unemployment that followed the Napoleonic Wars. In 1820, he was sentenced at Durham Assizes to seven years' transportation for stealing a quilt and goods valued at eightpence.

In those days, the jury decided the value of the stolen goods. This was important, as you could hang for stealing anything valued at one shilling or more. If the jury thought a prisoner didn't deserve to die, they simply valued the stolen goods at less than a shilling.

On the way to London to be put aboard the hulks, Walker convinced another prisoner to jump overboard with him. The poor fellow did so, before Walker, and drowned. Then Walker used the diversion to slip over the other side himself and stay afloat using some cork he had found on board. He was picked up by a passing ship and put ashore in London, claiming he was a sailor who had fallen from the rigging.

After earning some money working as a rigger on the docks, he grew a beard, called himself Brown and returned to Sunderland as a crewman on a collier. He was recognised and arrested, convicted of absconding, sent to the hulks and transported to Van Diemen's Land on the *Malabar* in 1821.

In early 1822, Walker and several other convicts stole a schooner from the Derwent River and escaped. Walker was found living in Sydney as John Shields, posing as a seaman apprenticed to a merchant ship.

He was placed on board a ship called the *Deveron*, which was almost wrecked in a huge storm on the way back to Hobart. Walker saved the day by climbing the mast in mountainous seas to cut away the topmast which was broken and fouling the rigging of the ship.

For attempting to escape, he was sentenced to 150 lashes and transportation to the more brutal penal settlement of Sarah Island, in Macquarie Harbour on the wild west coast of Van Diemen's Land. The transfer to Sarah Island was cancelled, however, due to his heroism.

In 1823, Walker somehow stowed away on the *Deveron* and escaped again, eventually returning to England via Rio de Janeiro. He called himself William Swallow and lived with his wife and two children for six years until his arrest for housebreaking led to a life sentence and return to Van Diemen's Land, as William Swallow, on the *Georgiana*.

William Swallow was put to work on boats for a month and then was part of the crew loading the *Georgiana*, which had been chartered to take wheat, onions and potatoes to Sydney after unloading the convicts. He was found hiding among the cargo after the ship's departure was delayed and sentenced to fifty lashes and transportation to Sarah Island, yet again, for 'absconding from the public works with the intention of escaping'. Walker was flogged but again escaped being sent to Sarah Island by claiming he fell asleep in the hold while loading the ship.

His luck was about to run out, however, as about this time someone realised who he was and he and another convict were locked in the cells for 'being runaways and returned under second sentence of transportation'.

William Walker should have been hanged; it was the mandatory sentence for the crime. Instead, he was put aboard the brig *Cyprus* to be sent, yet again, to Sarah Island. But it would be two years before he arrived there. While the *Cyprus* was anchored up in Recherche Bay, the guards were overwhelmed and a chicken coop was used to block the hatchway and keep the other soldiers below decks while the prisoners were freed. The soldiers fired up through the decks but water was poured down on them to make their muskets useless and the convicts secured the ship and told the soldiers they would not be harmed if they surrendered their weapons.

All passengers and crew, along with convicts unwilling to take part in the plan, were conveyed to the shore with a few rations, which took five trips. Apart from two guards who were knocked on the head at the start, no one was hurt and the *Cyprus* sailed off with eighteen men aboard, leaving forty-four people on the beach at Recherche Bay.

William Walker sailed the *Cyprus* to New Zealand and then past Tahiti to Keppel's Island, where seven convicts left the ship. One man was lost overboard and three others went ashore on islands in the China Sea before the remaining seven finally reached the coast of China.

There the *Cyprus* was scuttled and the convicts used the longboat to reach shore where they spun a concocted story that they were survivors of a shipwreck of a ship called the *Edward*.

Walker, using the alias Captain Waldron, and three others returned to London after signing on as crew on the *Charles Grant*. The other three sailed to America on a Danish ship and were never heard of again. Meanwhile, the three who left the *Cyprus* earlier arrived in Canton and told different versions of the alibi story. Then news arrived from Sydney of the mutiny and one of the survivors confessed.

The *Kellie Castle*, a faster ship than the *Charles Grant*, sailed to London with one of the convicts as a prisoner and arrived six days before the *Charles Grant*. Three of the others were arrested when the *Charles Grant* arrived. Swallow escaped on the docks but was later found and stood trial with them.

Two of the convicts, Davis and Watt, were hanged at Execution Dock (and were probably the last men hanged for piracy in Britain).

Another of the men who left the ship in the Pacific was later found and hanged in Hobart.

Swallow somehow convinced the court that he was forced to do as the others ordered and was only an unwilling member of the mutiny. He and the other two were sent back to Hobart and finally arrived at Sarah Island prison in Macquarie Harbour just as the authorities were closing it down.

William Walker spent a year at Sarah Island and was then sent to Port Arthur where he died of tuberculosis in May 1834. Amazingly, his official convict record noted that he was 'a very good man'.

The forty-four people left at Recherche Bay finally made a miraculous return to Hobart after many trials and tribulations, which included a Welsh convict building a coracle to cross the dangerous straits to seek help, and a gruelling cross country expedition by some of the group across rivers and through hostile territory where they were attacked by Aborigines. But that's another story!   **JH**

THE *CYPRUS* BRIG
FRANK McNAMARA (FRANK THE POET)

Come all you sons of Freedom, a chorus join with me,
I'll sing a song of heroes and glorious liberty.
Of lads condemned from England upon Van Diemen's Shore,
Their Country, friends and parents, to never see them more.

Starved and flogged and punished, deprived of all redress,
The Bush our only refuge, with death to end distress.
Hundreds of us all shot down, for daring to be free,

Numbers caught and banished to life-long slavery.

But Swallow, Watt and Davis, were in our noble band,
Determined at the first chance to quit Van Diemen's Land.
In heavy chains and guarded, on the *Cyprus* Brig conveyed,
The topsails being hoisted, the anchor being weighed.

The wind it blew Sou'Westerly and on we went straightway,
And found ourselves all wind-bound, in gloomy Recherche Bay.
'Twas August eighteen twenty-nine, with thirty one on board,
Lieutenant Carew left the Brig, and soon we passed the word.

While some lads turned faint-hearted and begged to go ashore,
Eighteen boys rushed daring, and took the Brig and store.
We brought the sailors from below, and rowed them to the land
Likewise the wife and children of Carew in command.

The Morn broke bright, the Wind was fair; we headed out to sea
With one more cheer for those on shore and glorious liberty.
For our elected captain, Bill Swallow was the man,
Who laid a course out neatly to take us to Japan.

Then sound your golden trumpets; play on your tuneful notes,
The *Cyprus* Brig is sailing, how proudly now she floats.
May fortune help the Noble lads, and keep them ever free
From Gags, and Cats, and Chains, and Traps, and Cruel Tyranny.

THE 99TH REGIMENT ARE REVOLTING!

Not long after his miserable performance in the Maori wars (see page 150), Colonel Henry Despard returned to Sydney where he was to provoke the infamous mutiny of the 99th Regiment.

The mutiny by the 99th Regiment in 1846 was ostensibly caused by the abolition of the daily grog allowance—on the order of Colonel Despard. It lasted for approximately four weeks and ended when the rebels learnt that 400 troops from Hobart were onboard the ship *Tasmania* standing off Sydney Heads.

The mutiny was a protest against Colonel Despard's decision to discontinue the daily allowance of grog normally supplied to troops on foreign service. But, in fact, it was also a protest against his over officious style of leadership and his attempts to separate the troops from the townspeople.

Evidently Despard was of the opinion that the troops might have to be used against the unruly part-convict population, and he was dead against them being seen to be a part of the general community. He was of the opinion that the 'foreign service' grog ration encouraged the troops to be far too like the people they were there to control.

Despard also gave an order that prohibited citizens from walking on any part of the grass-covered area in front of the barracks when listening to the band play. This had been the town's chief entertainment for many years but Despard thought it unmilitary and likely to lead to dangerous fraternising.

The old military quarters in Sydney were known as the George's Square Barracks. They covered an area including Wynyard Square on the western side of George Street and eastern side of Clarence Street, from Barrack Street to Margaret Street. The entrance gate was on the western side of George Street at the junction of York and Barrack Streets.

The 99th were so annoyed when the wowserish Despard stopped their grog ration that they 'forgot their obligations to their Queen and country, by refusing to obey the lawful commands of their Officers, or to perform any further duty'.

Despard reported to General Sir Maurice O'Connell, overall commander of troops in the Australian colonies, and he went to the barracks and threatened to arm the convicts at Cockatoo Island and march them against the mutineers.

The 99th then took up their arms and returned to Barrack Square, compelling the General and his officers to leave the barracks.

The General forwarded a dispatch to Colonel Bloomfield of the 11th Regiment in Hobart directing him to proceed to Sydney without delay, with as many men as could be spared, to disarm the mutineers of the 99th Regiment.

The barque *Tasmania* was chartered and 400 men and officers embarked for Sydney. Three days later they were in sight of Sydney Heads, but an offshore gale kept the vessel from entering the Heads for seven days.

The 99th Regiment somehow found out that a vessel full of troops was outside the Heads and offered to return to duty.

The 11th Regiment arrived in Sydney on 8 January 1846 and marched four deep, with fixed bayonets, along George Street with the band playing 'Paddy Will You Now' till they halted at the barracks' main gate.

They entered the Barrack Square to a most hearty welcome and cheers from the 99th Regiment and their women and children, together with as many citizens as could fit into the barrack grounds.

Thus ended the mutiny of the 99th Regiment.

The 11th Regiment gave a sumptuous dinner to the citizens of Sydney and their wives and children with entertainment consisting of old English sports, games and other amusements.

The grog ration was restored to the 99th Regiment and Sydney's citizens were again allowed to walk on the grass in front of Barrack Square, and listen to the band play on Thursday afternoons.   **JH**

THE THREE COOLANGATTAS

In our brief European history of 225 years, with a small and scattered population, our coastal sea lanes have been home to over 5000 ships operated by over 300 Australian-based shipping companies. Australia relied on coastal trade from the earliest days of the colonies until the 1960s. There were no interstate roads to speak of until the twentieth century, air travel was only a novelty until World War II and the rail gauges were all different.

The town of Coolangatta is named after a ship wrecked off the point way back in 1846. The wreck was an attraction for visitors for forty years, but then was buried in sand until 1974 when cyclonic seas washed away the sand and the wreck floated ashore.

It was a cyclone that helped to wreck the ship 130 years earlier—in fact, it was the first low-pressure system ever recorded by official weather-watchers on the east coast.

The topsail schooner *Coolangatta* was named after its owners' property at Shoalhaven in southern New South Wales, which in turn was named after a nearby mountain. Coolangatta, in the local Aboriginal dialect, means 'splendid view'.

The ship's main task was to collect red cedar from the Tweed estuary on what is now the north coast of New South Wales. The logs were dragged overland from Terranora Inlet and rafted from the beach to cargo vessels like the *Coolangatta*, which took them to Brisbane or other settlements along the coast. On the *Coolangatta*, in addition to the crew, were two prisoners—one of them in irons—who were being taken south from Brisbane (which was part of New South Wales until 1859).

The captain and some of the crew were ashore getting water, when a gale sprung up while the ship was at anchor being loaded with timber. She was driven ashore a short distance northward of the River Tweed. The prisoners were released from the below-decks lockup when the ship foundered and Captain Steele and the crew unloaded her and walked overland to Amity Point, a distance of 112 kilometres, where they very luckily fell in with the steamer *Tamar*, from Moreton Bay, bound for Sydney.

The south coast NSW Coolangatta is a resort and winery today and you stay in the original convict-built buildings which were erected for the first white man to settle on the south coast, Alexander Berry.

Of course, you can find plenty of places to stay in the 'other' Coolangatta; it's a holiday destination just over the New South Wales border, on Queensland's Gold Coast.   JH

THE COLONY THAT NEVER WAS

The story of the remarkable Captain Barney appears elsewhere in this collection (page159). Born in 1792, he arrived in Sydney in 1835 with a detachment of Royal Engineers and set about 'fixing up Sydney'. His dream was to straighten out the streets of the town.

Among his many achievements were the building of the 'semi-circular quay' at Sydney Cove, Victoria Barracks and Fort Denison.

Governor Gipps retained Barney in the position of colonial engineer until May 1844 when he returned to England. In 1846, he again arrived in Sydney, having been commissioned by the Secretary of State for the colonies, William Gladstone, to be superintendent of the new convict colony of North Australia.

Barney sailed north and chose Port Curtis as the centre for the new settlement. On 8 January 1847, the *Lord Auckland* sailed for Port Curtis with eighty-eight persons including Barney and his family, seven other officials and a detachment of one officer and twenty-two men of the 99th Regiment. By late February, more stores and fifty more troops, and some more civilians, had arrived.

It was mid-summer. It rained heavily. The temperature in the tents reached 110 degrees Fahrenheit day after day. The colonists were tormented by mosquitoes. The Aborigines were hostile.

Barney was a good engineer but he was a poor and indecisive leader. *The Sydney Morning Herald* denounced the convict settlement, saying 'hordes of marauding and blood-thirsty reprobates' would pour southward if it went ahead.

A party was sent overland with more stores but was caught in floods, ate the stores and returned to Sydney.

In July 1846, Earl Grey had succeeded Gladstone as Secretary of State and he wrote to tell Governor FitzRoy that Britain had decided to abandon the settlement at Port Curtis. Barney and his colony were recalled. The failed venture had cost the British government £15,402.

Barney was appointed Chief Commissioner of Crown Lands and, in 1855, he was appointed Surveyor-General to succeed Major Mitchell.

He never did straighten out the streets of Sydney and the place where he failed to establish a new colony was later named after the man who sent him to do it, and had become British Prime Minister, William Gladstone. **JH**

HANGED IN UNIFORM

Michael Flanagan, a native of Ireland and a member of that country's constabulary, migrated to Australia in 1859 where he joined the Victorian Police Force two years later. Stationed in Victoria's Western District, he was charged with drunkenness, losing his horse, telling lies and being found at the racetrack without permission while on duty. When transferred to Hamilton, Station Sergeant Thomas Hull kept reporting Flanagan, who was finally dismissed from the force for persistent drunkenness.

Flanagan blamed his colleagues for the loss of his job. Naturally, Sergeant Hull had to inspect Flanagan's equipment and to issue a receipt for its return.

At about half past two in the afternoon of Friday 20 November 1868, Sergeant Hull came upon Flanagan arguing with Constable Martin Conway outside the police barracks at Hamilton.

Flanagan was arguing about being thrown out of the force and claimed Hull and Conway were to blame.

Hull spoke to Flanagan for a short time and told him that his pistol was dirty and had to be cleaned before being returned. The disgruntled constable stormed off to his quarters, then returned almost immediately with his service revolver. He raised the weapon and shot Sergeant Hull twice. Conway, who had been standing nearby, grappled with Flanagan and was able to subdue him with the assistance of another constable. Hull died half an hour later and Flanagan was charged with his murder.

He was convicted the following March, sentenced to death, and was hanged at Melbourne Gaol on the morning of 31 March 1869. Having been granted special permission to do so, Flanagan strode boldly onto the gallows at the Melbourne Gaol and was duly executed, wearing his old mounted police constable's uniform.

JH

BOOMERANG PAYBACK

It was 1868, ten years before an official Australian cricket team toured Britain, and fourteen years before the Ashes series began, when a team of Aborigines from Victoria's Western District went to England on tour, led by Charles Lawrence, a former Surrey professional cricketer, who was their manager and coach.

They played forty-seven matches against some of the best sides in Britain. They won fourteen, lost fourteen and drew nineteen. They played against W.G. Grace, who commented on their 'conspicuous skill at the game'. They were great fielders and very fast. There were no boundaries in those days, and one player named Twopenny 'made a drive for nine (no overthrows)', while helping the team to a 154-run victory.

The team had been assembled in 1866 from players who had played on stations in the western district. They played in Melbourne and Sydney before finally heading off to Britain after financial backing had been found. Evidently the tour was a financial success; 20,000 turned out to see them play at Lords.

The team produced one legendary player, a young man called Munarrinim. Known on tour as Johnny Mullagh, he scored 1698 runs and claimed 245 English wickets in 45 games.

The Times was not impressed and called the team 'the conquered natives of a convict colony'. But there were moments when the 'conquered natives' had some revenge against the Poms, and not only on the cricket pitch. At the completion of each game, the team gave an exhibition of 'native sports', including boomerang and spear throwing. The results of these exhibitions were, oddly, recorded in the official scorebook. On one occasion, the scorer noted, 'Mullagh was throwing the boomerang when, the wind taking it among the crowd, it struck and severely injured a gentleman on the head.'

Johnny Mullagh went on to play as a professional for the Melbourne Cricket Club and had another chance to get some 'pay back' against the Poms when he represented Victoria in a match against the English in 1879—and top scored in the second innings.

JH

'BEN HALL PERMITTING'

Ben Hall was born in the Hunter Valley on 9 May 1837. His parents were both convicts. On 15 June 1862, Frank Gardiner led a gang of ten men, including Hall, and robbed the gold escort coach of banknotes and 2700 ounces of gold worth more than £14,000 pounds.

Hall and several others were arrested in July, but police were unable to gain enough evidence to formally charge him. Mounting legal costs and police harassment forced him to sell his farm and he gradually drifted further into a life of crime.

Hall and his gang bailed up Robinson's Hotel in Canowindra and held all the people of the town captive for three days. The hostages were not mistreated, and were provided with entertainment. The local policeman was subjected to some humiliation by being locked in his own cell. The gang insisted on paying the hotelier and giving the townspeople 'expenses'.

During an attempted robbery of the gold coach near Araluen by Hall and his gang, John Gilbert killed Sergeant Parry; and then Constable Nelson was killed by John Dunn at Collector.

In early 1865, the authorities determined on radical legislation to bring an end to the careers of Ben Hall, Dunn and Gilbert. The Felons Apprehension Act was pushed through for the specific purpose of declaring Hall and his comrades outlaws. This meant that they could be killed by anyone at any time without warning.

From 1863 to 1865, a hundred robberies are attributed to Hall's gang, including hold-ups in twenty-one towns and the theft of twenty-three racehorses. Cobb & Co schedules at the time read: 'Ben Hall permitting'.

At dawn on 5 May 1865, Ben Hall was ambushed by eight policemen and shot in the back as he ran away, eventually being shot thirty times. Ben Hall was buried in Forbes Cemetery and a headstone was erected in the 1920s. His grave is well maintained and attracts many visitors.

In 2007, Peter Bradley, a descendent of Ben Hall's younger brother Henry, announced he was calling for the inquest into the bushranger's death to be reopened. Bradley believes that, as the

Felon Apprehension Act had not yet come into force when Hall
was killed, his execution was illegal.   JH

BRAVE BEN HALL
ANONYMOUS

Listen all Australian sons
A hero has been slain,
Yes, he was butchered in his sleep
Upon the Lachlan Plain.

Pray do not stay your seemly grief,
But let a tear-drop fall;
For manly hearts will always mourn
The fate of Bold Ben Hall.

No brand of Cain e'er stamped his brow,
No widow's curse did fall;
When tales are read, the squatters dread
The name of Bold Ben Hall.

He never robbed a needy man—
His records best will show—
Staunch and loyal to his mates,
And manly to the foe.

They found his place of ambush,
And cautiously they crept,
And savagely they murdered him
While their victim slept.

No more he'll mount his gallant steed,
Nor range the mountains high.
The widow's friend in poverty,
Bold Ben Hall! Good-bye!

A 'TOUCH OF HOME'

Rabbits in Australia

Many Australians believe that there were no rabbits in Australia until Thomas Austin released twenty-four of them in 1859.

Not true.

There were rabbits in Australia from the First Fleet onward. They were bred as food animals, mostly in cages. In the first decades of the colony's existence, they do not appear to have been numerous, judging from their absence from archaeological collections of early colonial food remains.

In Tasmania, however, a newspaper article of 1829 noted '. . . the common rabbit is becoming so numerous throughout the colony, that they are running about on some large estates by thousands. We understand, that there are no rabbits whatever in the elder colony [New South Wales]'.

This was clearly untrue. The famous botanist and explorer Allan Cunningham came from England to live in Parramatta in 1818. Writing in the 1820s, he says '. . . rabbits are bred around houses, but we have yet no wild ones in enclosures . . .'

What Cunningham meant was that rabbits were bred and kept in cages, rather than larger enclosures as they were in Britain.

The Colonial Secretary, Alexander Macleay, built Elizabeth Bay House in the late 1830s and the extensive gardens included 'a preserve or rabbit-warren, surrounded by a substantial stone wall, and well stocked with that choice game'.

By the 1840s, court records show evidence of the theft of rabbits from houses around Sydney, and recipes from that time include quite a lot of rabbit.

It is true, however, that the famous rabbit infestation appears to coincide with the release of twenty-four rabbits at Barwon Park, near Winchelsea, Victoria, in October 1859 by Thomas Austin.

Austin had been an avid hunter back in the 'Old Country', regularly dedicating his weekends to rabbit shooting. Upon arriving in Australia, which had no native rabbit population, Austin asked his nephew William Austin, in England, to send him twenty-four grey rabbits, five hares, seventy-two partridges and some sparrows so that he could continue his hobby in Australia by creating a local population of the species. At the time he had stated, 'The introduction of a few rabbits could do little harm and might provide a touch of home, in addition to a spot of hunting.'

William could not source enough grey rabbits to meet his uncle's order, however. So he topped it up by buying domestic rabbits. One theory as to why the Barwon Park rabbits adapted so well to Australia is that the hybrid rabbits that resulted from the interbreeding of the two distinct types, were particularly hardy and virile. Many other farms released their rabbits into the wild after Austin.

The rabbits were extremely prolific breeders and spread rapidly across the southern parts of the country. Australian conditions were perfect for them; the climate allowed them to breed all year.

The spread of farming and clearing of forests created ideal habitat for rabbits. It is said that they crossed the Murray River into western New South Wales from Victoria within two years of Austin's infamous 'first release'.

By 1869, just ten years later, two million were being shot or trapped annually without any effect on the rabbit population. It was the fastest growth and infestation of a mammal population ever recorded.

The rabbit caused more ecological damage to Australia than any other creature (including humans). Native species became extinct and massive erosion ruined farmland and destroyed the natural ecology.

On the up side, rabbit became a staple food in two Depressions (during the 1890s and 1930s) and rabbit trapping was a great way for children on farms and properties to make pocket money.

There were 'chillers' (refrigeration units) throughout the bush which were usually manned by a trapper who also bought rabbits from others.The fur was used to make the iconic Aussie hat, the Akubra, in an industry that kept the town of Kempsey prosperous for almost a century.

In Western Australia, a rabbit-proof fence was built between

Cape Keraudren and Esperance to stop the spread of the rabbit into Western Australian farming areas. It didn't work.

In 1950, myxomatosis was released and the rabbit population dropped from 600 million to 100 million. Genetic resistance to the virus saw the rabbit population recover to an estimated 200 to 300 million by 1995 when a new virus, the calici virus, was developed on Wardung Island off the coast of South Australia.

When the virus somehow escaped from the island and began killing rabbits as far away as the northern areas of South Australia, a general release was put into operation and rabbit numbers quickly fell across eastern Australia.

In 2012, the ABC reported that immunity to the calici virus was growing throughout the state of Victoria—and so was the rabbit population!

Rabbit farming was banned for many years in Australia and these days most rabbit sold in Australia comes from New Zealand.

JH

RABBIT
ANONYMOUS

Rabbits big and rabbits small
Rabbits short and rabbits tall
Rabbits black and rabbits white
Rabbits in the morning and rabbits at night
Rabbits by the dozen and rabbits by the score
Rabbits by the hundred knocking at the door.

Rabbit hot and rabbit cold
Rabbit young and rabbit old
Rabbit fat and rabbit lean
Rabbit dirty and rabbit clean
Rabbit stewed and rabbit roast
Rabbit in gravy and rabbit on toast
Rabbit tender and rabbit tough
Spare us from rabbit—Lord, we've had enough!

AUSTRALIA'S BELFAST

Port Fairy is a coastal town in western Victoria 28 kilometres west of 'The Bool' (Warrnambool) and 290 kilometres west of Melbourne on the Moyne River. The towns of Portland and Port Fairy were the first European settlements on the south coast of Australia.

In the early nineteenth century, sealers and whalers came to this region. The bay was named by the crew of the whaler the *Fairy* in 1828. John Griffiths established a whaling station in 1835 and a store was opened in 1839.

In August 1840, the Colonial Land and Emigration Commissioners of the British Government decided to allow the purchase of land anywhere in the 'Port Phillip District of NSW' by Special Surveys that could be requested to enable the purchase of 5120 acres (2070 hectares), or 8 square miles, for £1 per acre. This price was significantly below the value of the land at that time.

Sydney solicitor James Atkinson purchased land in the town by special survey in 1843. He drained the swamps, subdivided and leased the land, and built a harbour on the Moyne River. He renamed the town Belfast on 1 January 1854.

Agriculture developed quickly in the region, and Belfast became an important transport hub. By 1857, the town had a population of 2190. In the mid-to-late nineteenth century, Belfast was one of Australia's largest ports, catering to the whaling industry. In 1887, the town went back to the original name Port Fairy, as a result of an Act of Parliament.

Port Fairy district was settled by Irish immigrants and later was the site of soldier settlements after World War I. The nearby town of Koroit calls itself 'the most Irish town in Australia'.

Today, Port Fairy has a population of 2500 and it is the home port for one of Victoria's largest fishing fleets. Port Fairy contains fifty buildings protected by the National Trust. The Stag Inn, currently the Seacombe House hotel, was built in 1847 by Captain John Sanders.

Nearby beaches, which are part of a national park, are home to an enormous breeding colony of mutton-birds and viewing platforms enable visitors to experience the mass return of the parent birds at dusk from fishing in the Great Southern Ocean. This occurs during the period when chicks are being raised and is a truly unique and unforgettable event.

Port Fairy is also the home of Australia's most successful annual folk music festival, which started there in 1977. The festival is a true community event and profits are used to provide the town with many excellent amenities.

The Port Fairy community is a wonderful example of cooperation and community spirit being used to preserve our heritage in many ways. This book was inspired by the annual yarn-spinning and story-telling event held every year at the festival—instituted by, and now held in memory of, Pat Glover, a great yarn-spinner and a beaut bloke, who passed away in 2005. **JH**

THE FLYING CHINAMAN

The story of the paddle-steamer *Providence* was told to me when I was a young schoolteacher living at Menindee, on the Darling River. I lived there for six years and had a great time working as an honorary ranger in Kinchega National Park in my spare time and visiting properties along the river.

The version of the *Providence* story I was told as 'gospel' included the fact that the crew had all spent far too long at the famous Maiden's Hotel before they set off down the river.

Maiden's Hotel was where the Burke and Wills expedition had base camp. I even know some people who claimed that the pub played a part in the disaster that befell those intrepid, if somewhat inept, explorers. If those left at Menindee had not enjoyed the hospitality at the pub, some people say, the search parties might have been sent earlier and been more successful.

I myself have been waylaid at Maiden's on more than one occasion

But, back to the tragedy of the paddle-steamer *Providence*.

Providence was built at Goolwa, South Australia, in 1865. She was 24 metres long and weighed 16 tons. Powered by a thirty horsepower steam engine, the vessel had a cast-iron roundish 'scotch-type' boiler, which was 2.4 metres long and 2.7 metres in diameter. The boiler was fed by two furnaces.

The official report says that the *Providence* was 'wrecked on account of explosion of boiler cause unknown, accident occurred about 1½ miles above Kinchega Station, River Darling NSW. 5 lives lost'.

The *Providence* had been stranded near Kinchega Station for twelve months due to low river levels. When the river rose again, a crew was sent and the vessel and barge she was towing were loaded with wool from Kinchega Station.

The laden boat was moored at Maiden's Hotel wharf and the crew imbibed freely before setting out. Captain John Davis had steered the vessel some 14.5 kilometres downriver from Menindee when he noticed an engine problem, steered into the bank to investigate and stopped the steam. The vessel then blew up.

Providence was split in two by the explosion and sank. The boiler flew out of the vessel 'striking a tree on the side of the bank and then rolling into the river'. One large piece of the boiler, which was split off by the explosion, was found a hundred yards away deeply buried in the bank.

The crew of another steamer working up the river visited the scene later and reported that:

> the banks were strewn with boards and debris of all kinds; while high up on neighbouring trees were lodged pieces of timber, bedding and rugs, firewood, etc. A bag of flour was thrown over the tops of the trees and landed about 70 yards from the banks of the river, while a sledge hammer and several heavy pieces of casting were carried an incredible distance.

Thomas Gun, the vessel's Chinese cook, was blown 'thirty feet into a gum tree and had to be winched down. His injuries were treated but he died a short time later'.

Various theories were put forward. The reporter for the *Adelaide Observer* thought low water levels in the boiler caused a build up of gasses that were ignited by the heat. The *Pastoral Times* attributed the accident to the engineer 'putting cold water into the boiler while it was empty and much heated'.

The story I was always told was that the crew members were all drunk and had forgotten to refill the boiler with water. Five men died, including Captain Davis, but the local story always ended with 'they found the Chinese cook in the top of a gum tree'.

Those killed were buried in the Kinchega Homestead cemetery.

The boiler from the *Providence* sits on top of the bank of the Darling River in the Kinchega National Park; a plaque marks the site.

The boat's engine was salvaged and used to power a new paddle-steamer called the *Queen*.   **JH**

WHERE'S THE RIVER?

A yarn you often hear out west is the one about the paddle-steamer sitting many miles from any river in the middle of the plain. The story usually goes that the greedy captain tried to get up a flooded creek to load wool from a station and was trapped when the water level suddenly fell.

Guess what?

It's true . . . more or less.

The 15-ton paddle-steamer *Wave* was built at Echuca in 1886 and operated on the Darling River as a general carrier between Bourke and Brewarrina. She was then used to carry wood and supplies to the Bourke pumping station.

In 1921, there were very high water levels in the river and the *Wave* was using a short cut across flooded paddocks north of the town rather than traversing the many bends and meanders of the Darling River. One day she snagged and failed to make it back into the main river channel as the water level fell.

Her owner, Lloyd Surrey of Bourke, decided to make the best of the situation and continued living in the stranded vessel until his death in 1926, aged seventy-seven years. Due to the large number of children and various animals that were always around the boat, the locals called it 'Noah's Ark'!

The remains of the *Wave* are still there, in a paddock full of eucalypts, on the northern side of the Darling River, opposite the north-east end of the old Bourke wharf.   JH

A NAUTICAL YARN
KEIGHLY GOODCHILD

I sing of a captain who's well-known to fame;
A naval commander, Bill Jinks is his name.
Who sailed where the Murray's clear waters do flow,
Did this freshwater shellback, with his 'Yo heave a yo'.

To the port of Wahgunyah his vessel was bound,
When night came upon him and darkness around;
Not a star on the waters its clear light did throw;
But the vessel sped onward, with a 'Yo heave a yo'.

'Oh, captain! Oh, captain! Let's make for the shore,
For the winds they do rage and the waves they do roar!'
'Nay, nay!' said the captain, 'though the fierce winds may blow,
I will stick to my vessel, with a "Yo heave a yo".'

'Oh, captain! Oh, captain! The waves sweep the deck;
Oh, captain! Oh, captain! We'll soon be a wreck—
To the river's deep bosom each seaman will go!'
But the captain laughed loudly, with his 'Yo heave a yo'.

'Farewell to the maiden—the girl I adore;
Farewell to my friends—I shall see them no more!'
The crew shrieked with terror, the captain he swore—
They had stuck on a sandbank, so they all walked ashore.

THE NIGHT THEY BURNT THE *RODNEY*

The *Rodney* was built at Echuca in 1875 by Thomas McDonald and was owned by rural agents Permewan, Wright & Co. She was one of the most powerful steamers on the river.

On Friday 26 August 1894, Captain Dickson was in command of the *Rodney* as she came upriver, carrying forty-five non-union labourers to work in the woolsheds at Tolarno Station.

Although the 1894 strike was shorter and less hostile than the famous 1891 strike at Barcaldine, which led to the formation of the Australian Labor Party, it did result in the only recorded destruction of a riverboat, coastal or ocean-going vessel in the context of any industrial dispute in Australia.

Captain Dickson had earlier been warned by the captain of the steamer *Trafalgar* to expect attacks by union shearers along the river, but he believed he was well prepared for such an event.

On Sunday 28 August, the steamer reached a woodpile two miles above Moorara Station and it was there the attack occurred. Armed men crept aboard and the crew awoke too late. They tried to reverse away from the bank but they hadn't unhitched the mooring rope.

About 150 striking shearers took control. They moved the passengers ashore and used kerosene and set the boat alight. The *Rodney* was soon ablaze and was left to drift down the river as the triumphant shearers sang the latest popular tune of the day, 'After the Ball Is Over'. Eventually, the vessel burnt to the water line and sank.

The incident was described in the *Mildura Cultivator* as 'the very worst outrage that has yet been perpetrated by shearers in these colonies' and a reward was offered for the capture of those involved—but no one was ever convicted.

On 20 August 1994, a centenary re-enactment event was organised and more than 700 people came from far and wide to witness a replica being doused in kerosene and set alight, and to celebrate in song with a woolshed dance.

My mate Dennis O'Keefe was there that night and he wrote a new set of lyrics to 'After the Ball is Over', in honour of the occasion. **JH**

THE RODNEY
DENNIS O'KEEFFE

Once a young rouseabout, boiled a billy of tea,
He asked an old shearer, a story tell me please,
I'll tell you a story, but you must tell no-one,
Something my mates and I, in days gone by have done,
Once there was a captain, of a river boat,
With forty-five free labourers, on the Darling they did float,
The year was 1894, the strikes had just begun,
And shearers blood was being spilt, far worse than '91.

Chorus:
After we burnt the *Rodney*, We danced on the river-bank,
There we played an old tune, until the Rodney sank,
Many a heart was happy, if you could only see,
We had a bloody great bonfire,
The night we burnt the *Rodney*.

We did not like this captain, of him we had no fear,
To stations he'd been taking scabs, upon the river for years,
We'll take his boat the men yelled, we'll teach Captain Dickson,
So, wire stretched across the river, to the trees we started fixing.
But the Captain heard of our little game, and tied up miles below,
Through the marshes on the river-bank, running we did go,
Then swimming through the water, the men all followed me,
And in the darkness of the night, we climbed aboard the *Rodney*.

The Captain could not believe his eyes, to see us standing there,
With raddle painted faces, and mud smeared into our hair,
The crew we did not harm at all, but let them row away,
The scabs we left on an island, a small price they did have to pay.
Then we soaked the decks with kerosene, from stem to stern,
Then all us lads went ashore, and cheered as the *Rodney* burned,
No-one recognised us, they knew not who to blame,
So young man, you must tell no-one, Joe Cummins is my name.

THE 'FAILURE' THAT SUCCEEDED

Mildura Irrigation Colony

Mildura, on the Murray River in the Sunraysia District, is an area with a fascinating and unique history.

In the early 1880s, the Victorian government began examining the idea of irrigation colonies on the Murray River. In 1884, Victorian Premier Alfred Deakin led a delegation to the USA and met the Canadian brothers George and Ben Chaffey, who had established irrigation colonies in Ontario and California.

George Chaffey visited Victoria in 1886 and, having decided on the Mildura Run as a suitable location for an irrigation colony, the Chaffeys sold their Californian interests at a loss in order to invest in this new venture.

The Mildura Run was in liquidation. It had a river frontage of 64 kilometres and reached 32 kilometres back with flats subject to frequent flooding. One squatter called it 'the most wretched and hopeless of all the Mallee regions' and another 'a Sahara of blasting hot winds and red driving sands, a howling, carrion-polluted wilderness'.

In 1886, after months of negotiations, the Chaffey brothers signed an agreement, which was rejected by the Victorian parliament. The property was put up for public tender, but the Chaffeys decided not to tender. Instead, they negotiated with the South Australian government and, on 14 February 1887, they signed an agreement securing 250,000 acres at Bookmark Plains which went on to become the town Renmark.

The Victorian government received no suitable tenders and finally 'The Chaffey Brothers Agreement' was passed in May 1887. An indenture was signed for 250,000 acres of the old Mildura Run, which the Chaffeys took possession of in August. 50,000 of them were at £5 per acre to be subdivided into cleared 10-acre blocks between irrigation channels and a further 200,000 acres at £1 plus water rights to the equivalent of a 24-inch rainfall.

This amounted to 1699 cubic metres per minute, approximately one third of the Murray's lowest rate of discharge in drought.

Prospective settlers or investors could purchase irrigated blocks for £20 per acre (0.4 hectares) and Chaffey Brothers Ltd managed blocks for absentee owners for a fee of £5 per annum. George Chaffey, who was an engineer, had pumps capable of delivering up to 40,000 gallons per minute to main channels built and installed and the Chaffeys invested in brickworks, an engineering company, a timber mill and, in 1888, the River Murray Navigation Company.

In the early years, favourable conditions meant Mildura could rely mostly on river transport with freight and passengers going downstream for a railway connection to Adelaide, and upstream to Swan Hill and Echuca for connections to Melbourne.

Pests such as locusts damaged crops and there were continual problems with the irrigation. When water rates of fifteen shillings per acre (0.4 hectare) were introduced in 1891, settlers who had suffered three years of failed crops could not afford to pay and the Chaffeys shut down the pumps, labourers struck for better wages and conditions and were sacked and many men working for blockholders were never paid.

When Alfred Deakin and members of a Royal Commission arrived at the Company Wharf aboard the *Pearl*, so many settlers with complaints rushed on board that the vessel almost capsized. They were ordered to make their complaints in writing.

The problem of getting produce to markets in good condition remained until the arrival of the railway in 1903.

Added to the technical difficulties encountered in getting water to the crops, was the inter-colonial bickering over the rights to the Murray's water. New South Wales Premier, Sir Henry Parkes, called the Chaffeys 'trespassers', as the New South Wales Constitution Act of 1855 stated 'that the whole of the watercourse of the River Murray is and shall be in the territory of New South Wales'.

After one flood, the mayor of the Victorian town of Echuca telegraphed the then premier of New South Wales requesting that the New South Wales water be removed from his town!

On allotments that were owned or managed by the Chaffeys, plantings were generally successful. They employed 500 men and 500 horses and, with intensive labour, good horticultural practices and an adequate supply of water, crops would thrive, if variable seasonal conditions—frosts, hail, pests and diseases—were allowed for.

But, in December 1895, the company went into liquidation and, in 1896, the Victorian government held a Royal Commission into its affairs.

Block holders were given tenure over their land with a five-year period to meet their dues and the Mildura Irrigation Trust was created to 'conduct and control the supply of water for irrigation purposes'. Six commissioners elected by the growers ran it.

George Chaffey returned to the USA after the enquiry, but his brother Ben remained in Mildura as a fruit grower until his death in 1926.

Today Mildura is a thriving and prosperous city—one of the nicest towns in inland Australia!   JH

THE GROG COMES TO MILDURA
MONTY GROVER

The Chaffeys were teetotallers and the Mildura Colony was initially a 'temperance colony', modelled on their Canadian and Californian ones, devoid of any liquor outlets. There was a sly grog trade I am sure, but working men had nowhere to legally drink.

The good side of the lack of alcohol in the irrigation colony was that the colony's crime rate was so low there was only one policeman for the 2300 population.

In 1895, the famous Working Man's Club was established. It went on to become one of the largest liquor outlets in Australia and boasted the 'longest bar in the Southern Hemisphere'. The first shipment of alcohol for the club arrived on the paddle-steamer Nile, *which was reported to be carrying 40 tons of liquor.*

The following verse was printed in The Argus, *a Melbourne newspaper, on the day the club opened; it was written by Monty*

Grover, a great newspaperman, character and poet who has sadly been almost forgotten today. (Note: The most popular beer back then was Hennessy's Three Star.)

The sky burned like brass above, and the land was fevered with
    drought,
As we wandered with blistering gullets, and tongues that were
    hanging out.
With the *water* of the Murray to tempt us, at the edge of the
    sun-dry flat.
But no, we were men of Mildura—we hadn't come down to that.

In a moment of human weakness, I stepped to the river's brink,
It was flowing before me, *water*, would I be condemned to drink!?
Then we heard the beat of paddles, the rescuing steamboat *Nile*.
Louder and ever louder, coming nearer all the while.

'Courage!' the skipper shouted, as he moored to the blighted scrub,
'There's forty tons of liquor aboard, consigned to the local club.'
And the band burst into music, while the temperance banners
    waved,
And we saw Three Stars in the evening sky, and we knew Mildura
    was saved.

HOW SYDNEY WAS REMODELLED BY THE PLAGUE

Many people think that the plague ended way back in the sixteenth or seventeenth century—not so.

On 19 January 1900, Arthur Paine, a thirty-three-year-old deliveryman who carted goods from the Sydney wharves, suddenly fell ill. Dr Sinclair Gillies, honorary physician at Royal Prince Alfred Hospital, saw him and realised that the bubonic plague had hit Sydney.

It had appeared in Adelaide four days earlier.

In Sydney, which was much worse hit than the City of Churches, 303 cases were reported and 103 people died.

There were twelve major plague outbreaks in Australia between 1900 and 1925.

Government health archives record 1371 cases diagnosed and 535 deaths, nationwide. Sydney was hit hardest, but also hit were North Queensland, Melbourne, Adelaide and Fremantle.

The Chief Government Medical Officer, John Ashburton Thompson, put bacteriologist Frank Tidswell in charge of research and appointed William Armstrong and Robert Dick as 'Medical Officers to the City of Sydney'. Thompson, Dick and Tidswell went on to produce outstanding research on plague and are credited with developing twentieth-century scientific understandings of the disease.

Quarantine areas were established in the Rocks and at East Sydney, Glebe, Woolloomooloo, Redfern and Manly. Around 2000 people were forced from their homes in Sydney and quarantined at North Head. Many homes and outbuildings were demolished, whole streets and parts of suburbs disappeared. Some districts of Sydney were cordoned off by sanitary inspectors and invaded by an army of 'cleansing teams'.

Cleansing and disinfecting operations in the quarantine areas lasted from 24 March to 17 July 1900 and included the demolition of 'slum' buildings. Wharves and docks were cleared of silt and sewage. Chloride of lime, carbolic and sulphuric acid were used. Rat catchers were employed and the rats burned in a special rat incinerator. Over 44,000 rats were officially killed.

One of the sadder results of the 'cleansing' was that many picturesque parts of The Rocks were completely lost.

Whole streets leading down to the harbour were demolished and artist Sidney Long spent the brief time before they were destroyed painting and recording the steep winding lanes and quaint streets. His paintings are a nostalgic record of a bygone age of Sydney's oldest suburb, much more of which was also later demolished to build the approaches to the Sydney Harbour Bridge.

As a direct result of the plague, an attempt was made to rethink housing for Sydney's poorer population and schemes like the suburbs of Daceyville and Pagewood were established to provide public housing and cheaper housing for Sydney's working class residents.   **JH**

ROSS SMITH AND THE GREAT RACE

Captain Ross MacPherson Smith, Knight Commander of the Order of the British Empire, Air Force Cross (twice), Military Cross (twice), Distinguished Flying Cross (three times), was born in Adelaide, in 1892.

A gifted athlete and horseman, he enlisted as a trooper in the 3rd Australian Light Horse at the outbreak of war in 1914. All eleven members of the school cricket team, which Smith had captained, enlisted. Five were killed, including his younger brother Colin, and another five were wounded.

Smith's elder brother, Keith, was rejected by the AIF because he had varicose veins, so he had them surgically removed, made his way to Britain and joined the Royal Flying Corps.

Ross Smith served at Gallipoli. He was promoted to Regimental Sergeant Major in August 1915 and commissioned as a second lieutenant in September, just as he was evacuated from Gallipoli with enteric fever.

He spent six months recovering, then was given command of a machine-gun section in Egypt in early 1916, fought at the decisive Battle of Romani, and decided to join the Australian Flying Corps.

He began training in Cairo in October 1916, received his observer's wings in January 1917 and his pilot's wings in July 1917.

Despite starting so late and spending most of his time with No 1 Squadron, which was a bomber and reconnaissance unit, he finished the war as Australia's tenth top pilot for confirmed 'kills' in air combat and was decorated for gallantry five times between January 1917 and November 1918.

Smith flew Lawrence of Arabia on secret missions into the desert and gained expertise with all kinds of aircraft including *Bristol* Fighters, various prototypes called 'British Experimentals' (christened 'Bloody Emergencies' because of their unreliability), and the lumbering *HP100* heavy bomber, made by Handley Page. His experience with the *HP100*, which could carry a ton of bombs over long distances, was to change his life and turn him into a legend.

After the Armistice, Ross Smith made the first ever flight from Cairo to Calcutta in the *HP100*, with Brigadier Borton and Sergeants Wally Shiers and Jim Bennett. They intended to fly on to Australia and travelled as far as Timor by ship to check for landing places and talk to the Dutch colonial authorities. Meanwhile their *HP100* was flown to the north-west frontier to deal with an Afghan uprising and crashed in a storm.

They had abandoned the idea of flying to Australia when a chance acquaintance showed them the first Australian newspaper they had seen in five years. On the front page was an offer from Prime Minister Billy Hughes of £10,000 to the first Australian air crew to fly a British aircraft from England to Australia in less than thirty days.

Hundreds of Australians attempted to enter the race and the Australian government recruited the Royal Aero Club as arbiters and organisers. The rules were strict in order to avoid the government being criticised for putting lives in danger.

The aircraft entered had to be airworthy. This meant, in effect, that only an aircraft entered by a manufacturer was acceptable. Most would-be entrants could not afford new machines.

Each crew had to have a navigator, which eliminated the entry put up by Charles Kingsford-Smith, and solo entries were forbidden by the regulations, so Lieutenant Bert Hinkler's entry in a *Sopwith Dove* was also eliminated.

Ross Smith knew somebody who really could navigate and who could also share the burden of flying the machine—his own brother, Keith, an RFC and RAF flying instructor who was still based in Britain and available to take part in the venture.

Altogether, six Australian crews, five of them backed by the cream of the British aircraft industry—*Sopwith, Vickers, Blackburn, Alliance and Martinsyde*—took part in the race. The sixth crew, Lieutenants Ray Parer and John McIntosh, after months of setbacks and failed schemes, were backed by Scottish whisky magnate Peter Dawson and entered a war surplus *De Havilland DH.9*.

There was also an unofficial 'seventh' entry. French flyer, Etienne Poulet and his mechanic, Jean Benoist, flying a tiny *Caudron* biplane, set off from Paris on 14 October 1919. Not being Australian, they were ineligible for the cash prize, but they were determined to win the race, and the glory, for France. They were to lead the race for over half the distance.

Of the seven entrants, only two would reach Australia.

The two Smith brothers, with Sergeants Shiers and Bennett acting as mechanics, took off in their *Vickers Vimy* from Hounslow Heath at 9.05 a.m. on 12 November 1919. They flew up to ten hours each day, then Shiers and Bennett would work on the Rolls-Royce engines while Ross and Keith refueled, straining petrol through a chamois leather filter. They followed this routine for twenty-seven days.

Of the other entrants, two crashed fatally: the *Alliance Endeavour*, flown by Roger Douglas and Leslie Ross , just after taking off from Hounslow, and the *Martinsyde*, flown by fighter ace Cedric Howell and George Fraser, when it ditched off Corfu in the Adriatic Sea after a navigation error during the night.

The *Blackburn Kangaroo* of Captain Sir Hubert Wilkins was forced to turn back to Crete with engine trouble and crashed on landing, while George Matthews and Tom Kay in the *Sopwith Wallaby* nearly made it but crashed in a banana plantation in Bali.

Etienne Poulet in his tiny *Caudron* G4 biplane just kept plugging away and led the field as far as Rangoon before he too was eliminated with engine trouble.

The astonishingly determined Ray Parer and John McIntosh limped from one near-disaster to another in their single-engined DH.9, eventually arriving in Darwin eight months after leaving London. Their flight was the first to Australia in a single-engined plane.

The biggest problem for the competitors was that there were no landing grounds between India and Darwin. There wasn't even a landing ground at Darwin.

The Dutch had set up a couple of flying schools in Indonesia and constructed rudimentary airstrips during 1919, but elsewhere most 'airfields' consisted of racecourses like those at Rangoon and Singapore, or clearings in the jungle with a stockpile of fuel.

The *Vickers Vimy* touched down on the specially built Fanny Bay airstrip near Darwin at 3.40 p.m. on 10 December. Her tanks were almost empty. 'We almost fell into Darwin,' Wally Shiers recalled many years later. The journey had taken twenty-seven days and twenty hours.

Waiting to greet them were a customs officer and quarantine official and Ross Smith's old friend from the 1st Squadron Australian Flying Corps, Hudson Fysh, who had built the airfield at Darwin and surveyed the air route from Darwin to Brisbane in case anyone got that far. It was this survey that convinced Fysh that air travel was the answer to Australia's vast distances and led directly to the formation of Qantas.

Brigadier Borton called the flight 'the most magnificent pioneer undertaking of the age' and I think he was right!   **JH**

RADIO 2UE

2UE is the oldest surviving commercial radio station in Australia.

The first radio 'broadcast' in Australia was organised by George Fisk of Amalgamated Wirelesss Australia (AWA) on 19 August 1919. The national anthem was broadcast from one building to another as part of a lecture he'd given on the new technology to the Royal Society.

AWA continued to give demonstration broadcasts privately each week from 1921. Fisk's idea was to sell customers a radio set that only received from the station owned by the company that sold you the set.

Licences along these lines, called 'A' licences, were issued to several stations in capital cities to be financed by listeners' licence fees imposed and collected by the government. In January 1924, 2FC and 2SB (later 2BL), in Sydney, and 3AR and 3LO, in Melbourne, began broadcasting.

Only 1400 people took out licences for the 'fixed station' system in the initial phase and, if you could build a radio receiver, you could avoid paying. The system wasn't a success and these stations were later taken over to become the beginnings of the ABC in 1932.

A new 'open system' was introduced and 'B' class licences were offered to anyone who wanted to have a go. The 'B' stations would have to generate their own revenue through advertising.

Mr C.J. 'Pa' Stevenson owned an electrical business in George Street, Sydney, known as Electrical Utilities, from where he sold radio sets and electrical wares. He also carried out experiments in wireless transmission from his shop and from his home in Maroubra.

He obtained a 'B' class licence, which enabled him to broadcast programs publicly. This could be financed by any means at his disposal. He took as his call sign 2EU, which represented the initials of his business. He soon changed the call sign to 2UE when he realised that 2EU sounded like a birdcall when spoken on air!

The first broadcast from 2UE, on Australia Day 1925, consisted of two hours of recorded music from 8 p.m. until 10 p.m.. Many of Stevenson's broadcasts utilised his pianola. Once a pianola roll had been played, Stevenson would leave the microphone 'live' as he removed the roll and replaced it with another, whistling while he completed the task.

In order to relieve the silences and long pauses in the program, Stevenson obtained advertising. The first contract was with the butcher Harry Woods, from George Street, who paid one shilling for each advertisement.

There was one 'B' class station that began before 2UE. This was 2BE; it began in November 1924, but it soon shut down, which makes 2UE the oldest operating commercial radio station in Australia.

JH

THE PLEASURE FERRY *RODNEY*

Strangely, there are two famous nautical calamities concerning a vessel named *Rodney* in Australia's history.

On 13 February 1938, the police band was performing on Sydney Harbour, on the police launch *Cambrai* to farewell the visiting warship, the USS *Louisville*.

Hundreds of ferries and other craft were on the harbour, including the month-old pleasure ferry, *Rodney*, crowded with 150 people waving goodbye to American sailors.

As the *Louisville* passed Bradleys Head, the *Rodney* went across the wake and, as it did, the passengers moved from one side to the other. Normally, this would not have been a problem, except that the majority of the *Rodney*'s passengers were on the top deck of the ferry. This sudden shift in weight tilted the ferry dangerously to starboard. It poised for a few seconds, then it overturned completely.

The *Cambrai*, on the other side of the *Louisville*, was hailed by an American officer and arrived on the scene in seconds. Eleven bandsmen dived in and rescued many stricken passengers, while others remained on board, resuscitating and calming survivors.

In all, nineteen passengers drowned, but without the work of the police bandsmen, the number would have been higher. Band members were later awarded a special certificate by the Royal Life-Saving Society for their part in the rescue.   **JH**

THE ENEMY BELOW

Real estate prices plummeted in Bondi, Rose Bay, Woollahra, Vaucluse and Bellevue Hill on 8 June 1942. After midnight, the Japanese submarine I-24, positioned about 6 kilometres offshore, fired ten rounds that landed in those suburbs. Four exploded, doing minor damage to buildings. In the general panic, house prices fell in the eastern suburbs and rose in the Blue Mountains.

Twenty-seven Japanese submarines were known to have been operational along the east coast of Australia during 1942, 1943 and 1944, attacking around fifty merchant vessels. Twenty sinkings are confirmed to be from Japanese submarine attacks, another nine are officially unconfirmed but probably were. In the unprotected shipping lane where the hospital ship *Centaur* was sunk, the vessels *Kalingo*, *Lydia M. Childs*, *Wollongbar*, *Fingal* and *Limerick* had all been sunk by Japanese submarines in the previous six months.

The attacks by Japanese submarines were part of a plan to destroy supply convoys to New Guinea, cut off supply lines to the war zones to the north and drive a wedge between Australia and the USA and prevent them operating freely in the Pacific.

The three 'midget' submarines which made their way into Sydney Harbour weighed 50 tons and were over 24 metres long. They were carried on the decks of the large subs, which were huge vessels almost 122 metres long with crews of ninety-five men.

A fleet of five 'mother' submarines was off the coast of Sydney; the two that didn't carry midget subs carried seaplanes for reconnaissance. When the midget subs failed to return, the large submarines attacked at least seven merchant vessels between them and sank the *Iron Chieftain* on 3 June, the *Iron Crown* on 4 June and the *Guatemala* on 12 June. As a result, fifty lives were lost and escorted convoys introduced.

None of the mother submarines that attacked Sydney Harbour survived World War II. The US navy ships sank four of them and one was sunk by two British destroyers off the Maldives.

The two main targets of the midget submarine attacks in Sydney Harbour also failed to see out the war. The USS *Chicago* sank following the battle of Rennell Island in January 1943 and the HMAS *Canberra* was lost near Savo Island in August 1942.

JH

BUSH YARNS AND TALL TALES

B ush yarns always seem to verge on the incredible. Far be it
from me, however, to argue over the veracity of stories told
to me by some of my good mates, like Paddy Ryan, Paul B. Kidd
and Frank Daniel, let alone those spun by great Aussie poets like
Banjo Paterson and Thomas E. Spencer!

All of these things could have happened . . . couldn't they?
I have researched these yarns carefully, even interviewed some
of the authors in depth, and I can assure you, dear reader, that
these are mostly 'tall but true' tales, with a few 'tall but untrue
tales' thrown in.

After all, strange things happen all the time in the bush and
I am sure that all the stories here could possibly have happened
just as they are told . . . if every coincidence fell into place, if the
planets aligned just right . . . if Murphy's Law was in operation
. . . if pigs flew!

THE QUEENSLAND BORDER

The scene is a tiny one-teacher school in the middle of the mulga.
School is in session and one kid rides up bareback, ties up his pony
and dashes into the building, clutching his satchel.

He is obviously quite late for school and the teacher asks him why.

'I had to make my own lunch, Miss,' he replies.

'Well, sit down and get out your book, and don't let it happen
again,' snaps the teacher.

Next day, it's the same thing. School is well under way when
the kid gallops up bareback, ties up his pony and rushes into the
building, his satchel bouncing along behind him.

'You're late again!' the teacher says in exasperated tones, 'What's
your excuse today?'

'Sorry, Miss,' says the kid, puffing as he sits down, 'but I had
to make my own lunch.'

'This can't keep on happening,' says the teacher severely. 'If
you keep doing this you will miss valuable lessons and I'll have
to punish you!'

Next day, it's the same thing, except the kid is even later and the class is halfway through a geography lesson, with the teacher pointing out the various features on the map of Australia.

The kid gallops up full pelt, jumps off the pony, races into the class and dives into his seat, dragging his satchel along the floor.

The teacher stops the lesson and calls the boy to the front of the class.

'Why are you so late?' she demands.

'Sorry, Miss,' says the kid, staring down at his boots, 'but I had to make my own lunch.'

'I can't believe that you're late again!' the teacher says angrily. 'You have missed a good part of the geography lesson and if you can't answer this geography question you will have to be punished!'

She hands the boy her pointer and asks him, in an icy voice, 'Where is the Queensland border?'

'In bed with Mum, Miss,' replies the kid, 'that's why I have to make me own lunch!'   JH

MULGA BILL'S BICYCLE
A.B. (BANJO) PATERSON

'Twas Mulga Bill, from Eaglehawk, that caught the cycling craze;
He turned away the good old horse that served him many days;
He dressed himself in cycling clothes, resplendent to be seen;
He hurried off to town and bought a shining new machine.

And as he wheeled it through the door, with air of lordly pride,
The grinning shop assistant said, 'Excuse me, can you ride?'
'See here, young man,' said Mulga Bill, 'from Walgett to the sea,
From Conroy's Gap to Castlereagh, there's none can ride like me.

'I'm good all round at everything, as everybody knows,
Although I'm not the one to talk—I hate a man that blows.
But riding is my special gift, my chiefest, sole delight;
Just ask a wild duck can it swim, a wildcat can it fight.

'There's nothing clothed in hair or hide, or built of flesh or steel,
There's nothing walks or jumps, or runs, on axle, hoof, or wheel,
But what I'll sit, while hide will hold and girths and straps are tight:
I'll ride this here two-wheeled concern right straight away at sight.'

'Twas Mulga Bill, from Eaglehawk, that sought his own abode,
Perched beside the Dead Man's Creek, beside the mountain road.
He turned the cycle down the hill and mounted for the fray,
But ere he'd gone a hundred yards it bolted clean away.

It left the track, and through the trees, just like a silver streak,
It whistled down the awful slope towards the Dead Man's Creek.
It shaved a stump by half an inch, it dodged a big white box:
The very wallaroos in fright went scrambling up the rocks.

The wombats hiding in their caves dug deeper underground,
As Mulga Bill, as white as chalk, sat tight to every bound.
It struck a stone and gave a spring that cleared a fallen tree,
It raced beside a precipice as close as close could be;
And then, as Mulga Bill let out one last despairing shriek,
It made a leap of twenty feet into the Dead Man's Creek.

'Twas Mulga Bill, from Eaglehawk, that slowly swam ashore:
He said, 'I've had some narrer shaves and lively rides before;
I've rode a wild bull round the yard to win a five pound bet,
But this was the most awful ride that I've encountered yet.

'I'll give that two-wheeled outlaw best; it's shaken all my nerve
To feel it whistle through the air and plunge and buck and swerve.'
It's safe at rest in Dead Man's Creek, we'll leave it lying still;
A horse's back is good enough henceforth for Mulga Bill.'

BULLOCKY BILL IS MISSING

It was during the big floods of the post World War I era that many
parts of the Darling River basin were near impassable for weeks
after the Darling had flooded.

When the Darling floods, you wait weeks for the water to come down and then weeks for the inundation to subside. You get plenty of warning that the flood is coming, but if you miscalculate, you can be stranded for weeks on high ground.

There are two types of soil out on the Darling. Where the river doesn't flood, you get the typical inland red soil. Where it does flood, you get the famous Darling River black mud: gluey, sticky stuff that sticks to everything and will leave a vehicle stranded with its wheels coated. It's thick, grey, slippery goo that simply means no traction is possible.

You bog down in red soil, but with black soil you can be bogged sitting on the surface—going nowhere.

The other thing about black soil is that it develops holes just under the surface. If you break through black soil at certain places you simply disappear into irregular shaped potholes and crevices that change shape once more water comes along.

So, the story is told that, after the flood subsided, it was realised that no one had seen Bullocky Bill and his team for weeks. Bill had been taking a load of wool from an outlying station to the river at Menindee, where the riverboats could take over the task of getting the wool down to Mildura and then on to Melbourne or Geelong.

Bullocky Bill, his team and load are missing in the floods, so the men from the nearby stations all ride out looking for poor old Bill and his team, following the route he should have taken.

Bullock teams move slowly. Maybe Bill could not outrun the slowly advancing floodwaters. There were grave fears for the safety of the old bullock driver.

The men look for days, across the red soil plains and then down into the river basin where the black soil is still treacherous and wet and sticky. Finally, someone in one of the search parties spies an object in the distance, conspicuous on a flat, black-soil claypan.

The party rides over to investigate and the object is identified at a distance as Bullocky Bill's hat, sitting there on the flat claypan. The men ride up and dismount. One man lifts the hat reverentially and—lo and behold, there's Bill stuck deep in the mud with just his head showing!

' 'Struth, Bill, are you okay?" asks the bloke who lifted the hat.

'Yeah, I'm fine,' Bill replies stoically and matter-of-factly, 'but I think the team's in pretty deep!'   JH

HOW WE CASHED THE PIG
JACK SORENSEN

We shore for a farmer at Wallaby Bend,
Myself and my mate, Dan McLean;
And while we were toiling, an old bushman friend,
Wrote saying the farmer was mean.

We finished his shearing (the flock was not big),
And imagine our wrath and dismay,
When he went to a sty and returned with a pig,
And said, 'This is all I can pay.'

We set off next morn down the long dusty track,
In the blackest of humours I fear.
I carried our pig in a bag on my back,
While McLean trudged along with our gear.

I talked as we journeyed—it lightened my load—
And was pointing out how we'd been robbed,
When we came to a shanty that stood by the road,
And I turned out my pockets and sobbed.

'Cheer up,' cried McLean, 'we will drink and forget
That old blighter back at the Bend.'
I said in soft accents imbued with regret,
'Alas! we have nothing to spend.'

My comrade replied, 'What a dullard you are,
We'll drink and make merry in style.'
Then seizing our pig he walked into the bar,
And ordered our drinks with a smile.

Our host filled 'em up and went off with the pig,
As though the affair was not strange;
We scarcely had time our refreshments to swig,
When he came back with ten piglets change.

We stayed at the shanty that night and next day
(Good liquor was much cheaper then),
And gladly rejoicing we went on our way,
With a basket of eggs and a hen.

BUFFALO FLY, GO AWAY
LENNIE LOWER

Ever seen a buffalo fly?

Now, don't lie to us! On Friday nights, for instance?

Buffalo flies are causing a lot of damage in North Queensland. We have made a close study of buffalo flies, starting from the birth of the insect and working up through the calf-fly stages until we managed to secure fully-grown specimens of the buffalo fly itself with horns measuring 8 feet across.

The flies live entirely on buffaloes. They fly to about the height of a buffalo's back and then hover in the air, waiting for a buffalo to walk underneath.

The method of egg-laying is of great scientific interest. You are, of course, aware that when a buffalo is pleased, it wags its tail.

Taking advantage of this, the fly grasps the animal's tail firmly between its two front paws and waves the tail gently from side to side.

The buffalo thinks he is pleased, and smiles. The fly then lays its eggs in the wrinkles. As regards ridding the north of buffalo flies, we think it would be better to get rid of the buffaloes. You can swipe a buffalo fly, but it takes a good man to swot a buffalo.

However, if the extinction of the flies is insisted upon, we suggest that a lot of empty tomato sauce bottles be scattered about where the insects are most prevalent, they being very fond of tomato sauce.

On finding the bottles empty, the flies would become enraged and smash the bottles.

They would then cut their feet walking on the fragments, dirt would get into the cuts, and they would all die of tetanus.

THE SHEARER'S NIGHTMARE
ANONYMOUS

Old Bill the shearer had been phoned to catch the train next day,
He had a job at Mungindi, an early start for May.
So he packed his port and rolled his swag and hurried off to bed,
But sleep? He couldn't steal a wink to soothe his aching head.

He heard the missus snoring hard; he heard the ticking clock,
He heard the midnight train blow in, he heard the crowing cock.
At last Bill in a stupor lay, a-dreaming now was he,
Of sheep and pens and belly-wool he shore in number three.

He grabbed the missus in her sleep and shore her like a ewe.
The fine performance started as up the neck he flew,
Then he turned her for the long-blow, down the whipping side he tore,
With his knee upon her back and a firm grip round her jaw.

Then he rolled her over, like a demon now he shore,
(She dared not kick or struggle, she had seen him shear before).
He was leading 'Jack the Ringer', he was matching 'Mick the Brute',
When he called for tar and dumped her, like a hogget, down the chute!

Then he reached to stop the shear machine and put it out of gear,
And turned the electric light on so all was bright and clear.
He was gazing out the window, now awakened from his sleep,
And down there on the footpath lay his missus in a heap!

He said, 'Blimey, I've had nightmares after boozin' up a treat,
And I've walked without me trousers to the pub across the street,
But this sure takes some beatin', and it's one I'll have to keep.
I dare not tell me mates I shore the missus in me sleep!'

THE LOADED CROC
PAUL B. KIDD

Although this story may be a few years old now, it is Sydney eastern suburbs folklore, and while the variations of it are many, this is the 'fair dinkum' version. Though conspicuous by their absence in recent years, the main characters are real and the story never came to light until long after the incident—one day they had a monumental altercation at the Royal Oak Hotel and one blurted out just how stupid his mate was and gave this story as an example.

We christened him Haemorrhoids because he hung out in dark places. We broke it down to Piles for short. One of those dark places he hung out in was the old front bar of the Royal Oak Hotel in Double Bay in Sydney's eastern suburbs, where he was a member of the legendary Royal Oak Fishing Club.

He was a bald, short, unshaven revoltingly fat heap with a Charles Bronson drooping moustache who wore stubbies and a football jumper every day, guzzled vast quantities of beer and wore out two pairs of thongs a month. The locals reckoned that one day when he was lying on Bondi Beach, the Greenpeace truck came to a halt and six guys rushed out and tried to force him back into the water.

The only person who could cop him was a bloke we'd nicknamed Morphine on account of the fact that he was a slow working dope. Morph was as long and lean as Piles was short and rotund, wore a Sydney Swans beanie, checked long-sleeved flannelette shirts, flared trousers and ugg boots all year round. Standing at the bar they looked like Abbott and Costello who had been outfitted by Saint Vincent de Paul.

Piles and Morph were inseparable; quaffing down schooners night after night over the pool table at the Oak. And when they weren't playing pool or figuring out how to get away with more sickies from their jobs as road workers on the local council, they filled out their weekly Lotto coupon, methodically double and triple checking to make sure that they got their lucky numbers—which, incidentally, were the same every week—exactly right.

They figured they had the winning combination by using the numbers that meant the most to them. Their birth dates: 16 and 24; their ages: 37 and 39; their IQs from the council's aptitude test: 28 and 28; their past lovers: 0 and 0; and their friends: 1 and 1, being each other.

So that was the combination: 16, 24, 37, 39, 28, 0 and 1 as the supplementary. Week in and week out, they took the same numbers and every Monday night at half past eight, the Oak would come to a standstill as the beautiful Alex Wileman called the numbers with the three lotteries officials looking on.

But they never won a crumpet. In fact, the best they ever got was two numbers. But their faith in their system was unfailing.

This particular Monday, Morph had taken a sickie off work, got on the turps and was horribly flyblown when he took it upon himself to fill in the Lotto numbers before having a dozen or so more schooners at the Oak while waiting for his mate to come in after work.

When Morph produced their ticket at Lotto time, Piles nearly had a stroke.

'You idiot,' he exploded. 'You've written out the wrong numbers. I couldn't trust you to take a piss by yourself. You can bet your life that they'll go off tonight and we won't be on 'em.'

With that he grabbed a snooker cue in one hand and Morph by the throat with the other and was just about to fracture his dopey mate's skull with it when Alex Wileman called out the first number—17.

'Hey, that's one of your bodgie numbers,' Piles noted, lowering the cue and taking interest. 'Number 4,' the sensational Alex Wileman gushed as Piles noted that that number was also on the ticket.

And so was the next one, and the next one after that and the one after that. They had the first five numbers in and the Oak was hushed in anticipation and then went berserk as Alex called the sixth number and it matched the ticket.

The Dickbrain Brothers had won Lotto by default, but Morph wasn't letting on that it was a fluke.

'It's me new scientific system of gettin' the numbers,' he told anyone stupid enough to listen. 'I'd had seventeen schooners when I bought the ticket; me nephew's four next birthday . . .' etc, etc. Of course no one with an eighth of a brain took any notice.

There turned out to be three other winners, and by the time the four split the $1.5 million Lotto first prize, Piles and Morph had enough to buy the best Toyota 4WD, camping gear and a trailerable boat that money could buy and they decided to go on an extended fishing vacation into northern Australia, much to our eternal gratitude.

'That'll teach youse pricks to take the piss out of us,' Piles announced down at the Oak on the eve of their departure when they begrudgingly threw a lousy $20 on the bar for their final and only shout. 'Me and me genius mate 'ere, Morph, is gunna shoot through to the Northern Territory and get stuck into the barramundis and none of youse billygoats is welcome.'

And thank Christ for that. Peace from the boneheads at last. Even if it was only temporary.

It took Piles and Morphine six days to reach Darwin, where they loaded up with cases of beer and supplies and headed for the Mary River. They found a great big barra-filled lagoon and set up camp.

What a treat. No bastard for miles, stacks of ice in the freezer for the beer, no sheilas to drive 'em mad and a hole full of fish. Heaven on earth. Well, not quite.

There was just one minor problem—the old croc who'd made the huge billabong his home for the past thirty years. The cranky old bastard was far from impressed with his new neighbours and expressed his disapproval by nicking every decent-sized fish they hooked.

'There's that rotten mobile suitcase at it again,' Morphine would blubber to his mate as the croc sat waiting for a jumping barra to land in its giant, foul-smelling gob hole.

'I wish he'd piss off and leave us alone,' moaned Piles as he lost yet another barra, a $15 lure and lots of line to the croc.

But they were reluctant to move on, because the fishing—minus the croc—was about as good as it gets. Besides, there would most likely be a resident croc wherever they wound up. One or the other had to go and sooner or later something had to give. It did.

'Have you noticed how he shoots through every night around six,' noted Piles, his skills of observation working overtime. 'I reckon he goes back to the missus in the lair, chunders up some of the fish he's pinched from us all day and feeds 'em to 'er 'cos he's on a promise and then packs it in for the night.'

'The dirty bastard—I'd like to blow him and his ugly missus up while they're right in the middle of dinner.'

They laughed hilariously at the thought of two crocodiles sitting down to a candlelit dinner, and wondered how they got along romantically what with the putrid breath and all those teeth.

Neither of them was renowned for his powers of deduction, so while the thought of a prehistoric animal living to a timetable would be absurd to most of us, it certainly wasn't to Piles and his dopey mate. Instead, it gave one of them an idea.

'Speakin' of blowin' the bastard and his missus up, you've given me a real good idea,' Piles chuckled to his mate. 'Let's go into town tomorrow and I'll get somethin' that might just sort our problem right out. He'll be a caveless croc come dusk.'

In town the following morning, they loaded up with supplies, then ducked into the hardware store. They bought a case of dynamite and all of the other ingredients which they needed to blow up fish-stealing, prehistoric reptiles.

'Do you really think it'll work?' Morph asked his mate, plainly in awe of the brilliant scheme.

' 'Course it will,' said Piles. 'We wait until the bastard comes up for his last fish of the arvo and we'll chuck him a couple of nicely iced-off barra out of the big Esky under the 4WD.

'Only this time, they'll have enough dynamite attached to blow up Ayers Rock. Once the greedy bastard's swallowed the lot, we'll let him swim off with the fuse wire trailing out of his gob and when he stops we'll wait till we reckon he's on the job and then we'll light it, and give his missus the biggest bang she's ever had.'

They laughed outrageously at their scheme and went about fishing from the bank well down the river from their camp site and preparing themselves for the afternoon's events. And, as if on cue, the croc did his bit by turning up and pinching their fish all day long.

'Go on, make the most of it, ya turd of a thing,' Morph abused the old croc from the bank. 'Ya might as well, seein' as today's ya last day on this planet. In a coupla hours your head's gunna be in Darwin and ya tail's gunna be in Alice Springs.'

Mid-afternoon they returned to the camp, grabbed a couple of nice cold barramundi from the Esky under the Land Cruiser and taped four sticks of dynamite to them with electrician's tape.

Just on six, they hooked a beaut fish that brought the crocodile within feeding range, and, as it gulped the leaping barra down, Piles threw the dynamited fish at him and he gulped those down, too.

'The silly prick's fallen for it,' laughed Morphine. 'You're a bloody genius, Piles. Now, let's wait for a while and we'll teach the bastard to pinch our fish.'

So they sat on the bank and watched as the waterproofed fuse wire steadily disappeared from the giant coil into the water as the croc headed off upstream.

They'd brought plenty of beer and it was only a five-minute trip by boat back to the camp. They yarned the time away as the croc kept on the move.

'It'll be interestin' just to see where the explosion goes off,' said Piles. 'Christ, he must have 1000 metres of fuse wire out by now. One thing's for certain—the big bang won't be close to us.'

Then the croc stopped. They waited for a couple of minutes, then lit the fuse and watched the smoke snake down the bank and into the water.

'I hope he's on the job when it goes off,' roared Piles. 'That'll make the earth move for Mrs Croc in a manner she wasn't counting on!'

Then it happened. The bank shook as a huge explosion rocked the earth all around and a mushroom-shaped ball of smoke belched high into the sky from downriver—in the direction of the camp.

They took off in the boat at breakneck speed amid falling debris, mostly flesh and blood.

'Jesus, that was a big bit,' Piles gulped at a huge splash near them. 'And it didn't look like a blown-up croc or stump to me. It looked more like a gearbox. A Toyota gearbox.'

Morphine ducked just in time to miss decapitation by a flying steering wheel. And as they raced toward camp they realised that their worst nightmare had come to pass.

'You idiot!' screamed Morph at Piles.

'You gave that croc the taste for cold barramundi and the bastard's crawled up to the Esky for more and you've blown our bloody truck into the Kimberley. Now how are we gunna get home?'

As it turned out, it was the least of their worries. That evening they were arrested for violations of the Protection of Crocodiles Act and their return to Double Bay was interrupted by a stay in the Darwin Gaol.

Morphine and Haemorrhoids are barred from the Northern Territory for life.

SCOTTY'S WILD STUFF STEW
FRANCIS HUMPHRIS-BROWN

Yarns about shearers' cooks are legendary—and, naturally, they are all true. This one, from the 1890s, is a favourite of mine.

The cause of all the trouble
Was McCabe, the jackaroo,
Who had ordered what, facetiously,
He'd christened 'Wild Stuff Stoo'.
He had shot a brace of pigeons
And had brought them home unplucked;
It was not the first occasion,
And no wonder Scotty bucked
As aside he threw the pigeons
And addressed the jackaroo:
'Ye'll pluck those blinded pigeons,
Or ye'll get no blinded stoo.'

But the jackaroo objected,
And objected strongly, too.
Said he, 'I'm not a slushy;
You can keep your blinded stoo.'
But Scotty didn't argue much,
He winked across at Blue
And, turning to the slushy, said,
'I'll give him "Wild Stuff Stoo".'
The next day it was Sunday, and,
Not having much to do,
We all assisted Scotty
In the making of a stoo

We raked along the woolsheds,
In the pens and round about—
It was marvellous, all the wild things
That us rousies fossicked out;
There was Ginger found a lizard,
Which they reckoned was a Jew—
It was rather rough to handle,
But it softened in the stew.
Then Snowy found some hairy things
Inside a musterer's tent;
And Splinter found a lady frog—
And in the lady went.

From McGregor, who'd been foxing,
We obtained a skin or two,
It should have gone to bootlace
But it went into the stoo.
Then someone found a 'Kelly'
That the boundary-rider shot—
It was more or less fermented,
Still, it went inside the pot;
And Scotty found some insects
With an overpowering scent,

And the slushy trapped a mother mouse—
And in poor mother went.

There was some hesitation
'Bout a spider in a tin:
We didn't like the small red spot,
But Scotty dumped it in.
There were a host of other things—
I can't recall the lot—
That were cast into eternity
Per medium of the pot.
And when the jackaroo arrived
A happy man was he
To find that Scotty, after all,
Had cooked a stoo for tea.

He rolled his eyes, and snuffed the fumes,
'Twas dinkum stuff he swore;
He complimented Scotty, and
He passed his plate for more.
And when we'd let him have his fill,
We took him round to view
A list of what had left this world
To enter Scotty's stew.
I grant you there were wild things
Connected with that stoo,
But there was nothing wilder
Than McCabe the jackaroo.

He got the dries and then the shakes,
And we felt shaky, too;
We were thinking of the spider
With the red spot in the stoo.
We rushed him to the homestead,
They told him there 'twas flu,
But us rousies, we knew better—
It was Scotty's 'Wild Stuff Stoo'.

But Scotty isn't cooking now,
For Scotty long is dead;
They say he turned it in through booze
At Thurlagoona shed;
And away across the border
There's a certain jackaroo,
Who for years has never tasted
What he christened 'Wild Stuff Stoo'.

'ARD TAC
ANONYMOUS

This yarn could be in the Drinking Yarns section. It's a very typical example of 'old style' Aussie humour. When you consider that a small mob of two hundred sheep can be shorn in a day by some shearers (and Jackie Howe managed 321 in a day and 1437 in a week!) it makes the phrase 'and so six weeks went by' very amusing—to me anyway. I also love the vernacular style of this yarn in verse.

I'm a shearer, yes I am, and I've shorn 'em sheep and lamb,
From the Wimmera to the Darling Downs and back,
And I've rung a shed or two when the fleece was tough as glue,
But I'll tell you where I struck the 'ardest tac.

I was down round Yenda way killin' time from day to day,
Till the big sheds started movin' further out;
When I struck a bloke by chance that I summed up in a glance
As a cocky from a vineyard round about.

Now it seems he picked me, too; well, it wasn't 'ard to do,
'Cos I had some shears, a-hangin' at the hip.
'I got a mob,' he said, 'about two hundred head,
And I'd give a ten pound note to get the clip.'

I says: 'Right—I'll take the stand'; it meant gettin' in me hand;
And by nine o'clock we'd rounded up the mob

In a shed sunk in the ground—yeah, with wine casks all around.
And that was where I started on me job.

I goes easy for a bit while me hand was gettin' fit,
And by dinner time I'd done some half a score,
With the cocky pickin' up, and handing me a cup,
Of vino after every sheep I shore.

The cocky had to go away—about the seventh day,
After showin' me the kind of casks to use;
Then I'd do the pickin' up, and manipulate the cup,
Strollin' round them casks to pick and choose.

Then I'd stagger to the pen, grab a sheep and start again,
With a noise between a hiccup and a sob,
And sometimes I'd fall asleep with me arms around the sheep,
Worn and weary from me over-arduous job.

And so, six weeks went by, until one day with a sigh,
I pushed the two hundredth through the door,
Gathered in the cocky's pay, then staggered on me way,
From the hardest bloody shed I ever shore!

WHAT ARE THEIR NAMES?

A yarn in a similar vein to the previous one concerns the hobby farmer, a retired accountant who has moved to a small country town in the central west and keeps a small flock of sheep on his ten acre block.

The sheep need shearing and all the local blokes are off with the big shearing teams and the bloke is desperate. Being a city bloke, he has no idea how to do the job himself.

He is telling his problem to the local produce merchant and the bloke feels sorry for him and says, 'Look, mate, Stewie Carmichael's team have just finished shearing at Thurlow Downs and Stewie's in the pub having a few before they move on to do a big run out near Hay. He might do you a favour and knock over your few sheep before he leaves town. Go and ask him.'

So the city bloke heads to the pub and finds Stewie having a beer and yarning with some of his team of shearers.

'Excuse me,' says the hobby farmer politely, 'but I have a mob of sheep that need shearing badly, could you help me out?'

'Well,' says Stewie, 'if we'd known sooner we might have fitted 'em in. We have to be out near Hay on Monday to start doing a mob of 20,000. How many do you have?'

'Only fourteen,' the bloke replies.

'Geez, mate,' says Stewie, 'fourteen thousand is gonna take us a few days, but if I rearrange a few things and keep a few blokes sober we might manage it!' He puts his beer down on the bar and gets serious, 'I better make a few phone calls.'

'No,' says the hobby farmer sheepishly, ' not fourteen thousand—just fourteen.'

Stewie stops in his tracks, then picks up his beer again and relaxes, leaning on the bar. He smiles at the hobby farmer and pushes back his hat.

'I might be able to manage that,' he says, 'what are their names?'

JH

THE SPIDER FROM THE GWYDIR
ANONYMOUS

By the sluggish River Gwydir
Lived a vicious redback spider,
He was just about as vicious as could be,
And the place that he was camped in
Was a rusty Jones's Jam tin,
In a paddock by the showground at Moree.

Near him lay a shearer snoozing,
He'd been on the grog and boozing
All the night and half the previous day,
And the 'kooking' of the kookas
And the spruiking of the spruikers
Failed to wake him from the trance in which he lay.

Then a crafty looking spieler
With a dainty little sheila
Came along collecting wood to make a fire.
Said the spieler, 'Here's a boozer,
And he's gonna be a loser,
If he isn't you can christen me a liar!

'Stay here and keep nit, Honey,
While I fan the mug for money,
And we'll have some little luxuries for tea.'
Said the sheila, 'Don't be silly!
You go home and boil the billy,
You can safely leave this mug to little me.'

So she circled ever nearer
Till she reached the dopey shearer
With his pockets bulging, still asleep and snug,
But she never saw the spider
That was creepin' up beside her,
'Cos her mind was on the money and the mug.

Now the spider needed dinner,
He was daily growin' thinner
He'd been fasting and was empty as an urn,
As she eyed the bulging pocket,
He darted like a rocket,
And he bit the spieler's sheila on the stern.

Well, the sheila raced off squealin'
And her dress began unpeelin'.
As she sprinted she was feelin' quite forlorn.
On the bite one hand was pressing
While the other was undressing
And she reached the camp the same as she was born.

Now the shearer, pale and haggard
Woke and back to town he staggered,
Where he caught the train and gave the booze a rest,

And he never knew that spider
That was camped there by the Gwydir,
Had saved him sixty smackers of the best!

LATE FOR SCHOOL

Little Johnny is late for school in the little one-teacher schoolhouse in the mixed farm district.

'Why are you so late, Johnny?' the prim and proper young school teacher asks.

'I had to take the house cow down to McGregor's farm to be mated to their bull, Miss,' comes the reply. 'It's that time of the year when she needs to be serviced.'

'Well, can't your father do that?' she asks sternly.

'No, Miss,' Johnny replies, 'it has to be the bull.   **JH**

SERVICE
ANONYMOUS

When I was a kid on my daddy's farm,
He sometimes used to say,
'Take the house cow down to "service"
To the farm along the way.'

Each time I took the cow down there
The farmer he would say,
'Just leave the cow with me, me boy,
Come back another day.'

Now, it really had me puzzled,
What did this 'service' mean?
So, one day I decided,
This 'service' must be seen.

Through a knot-hole in the barn door,
With me youthful naked eye,
I seen what they was talking about,

In all those times gone by.

Now a lot of politicians say,
'I serve my country true.'
I don't know what they mean by that,
I'll leave it up to you.

'We're hear to serve the people.
Elect us just once more.
For years we've tried to serve you
And we'd love to serve you more.'

So, at the next election,
When you put your name on the dot,
Make sure you vote for the right one . . .
Or we'll get what the house cow got!

STRAIGHT FROM THE HORSE'S MOUTH
LENNIE LOWER

We judged the horses yesterday at the show. From what we could see from the grandstand, they seemed to be all right.

Each one seemed to have the correct number of legs and looked to be wide enough to sit on without undue discomfort.

Though how they get their tails knotted up like that beats us. Temperament, we suppose.

On the other hand, after spending most of our lives among horses (we lived for twelve years with the one horse) we can state definitely that Nature provided horses with tails, not to show which end went into the cart first, but to whisk flies off.

The knotted tail would, of course, not only whisk them, but so stun them that by the time they came to, the horse would be somewhere else.

Clydesdales may be picked out by the uninitiated quite easily. Their feet—well, only a few of them are allowed into the ring at the same time. They have beards on their ankles. Mostly used for dragging brewer's wagons, they are known as draught horses. The bottled horses are in a different section, the prices for the latter being exorbitant.

We can say nothing authoritative about Suffolk Punches at the moment, as we haven't tasted them.

The withers of exhibited horses this year are a great improvement on last year.

Probably this is accounted for by the excellent withering conditions now prevalent in our country districts.

About the other breeds of horses in the fetlock and wither class, we are unable to go into details.

It came on to rain, as a matter of fact, and we can't bear to see horses standing in the rain, so we went to see Whatsitsname, 'half man and half woman. She will disrobe for you!'

Which is more than you can say for a horse.

HOW McDOUGAL TOPPED THE SCORE
THOMAS E. SPENCER

This is the most famous Aussie sporting 'tall tale' in verse.

A peaceful spot is Piper's Flat. The folk that live around—
They keep themselves by keeping sheep and turning up the ground;
But the climate is erratic, and the consequences are
The struggle with the elements is everlasting war.
We plough, and sow, and harrow—then sit down and pray for rain;
And then we all get flooded out and have to start again.
But the folk are now rejoicing as they ne'er rejoiced before,
For we've played Molongo cricket, and McDougal topped the score!

Molongo had a head on it, and challenged us to play
A single-innings match for lunch—the losing team to pay.
We were not great guns at cricket, but we couldn't well say no,
So we all began to practise, and we let the reaping go.
We scoured the Flat for ten miles round to muster up our men,

But when the list was totalled we could only number ten.
Then up spoke big Tim Brady: he was always slow to speak,
And he said—'What price McDougal who lives down at Cooper's
   Creek?'

So we sent for old McDougal, and he stated in reply
That he'd never played at cricket, but he'd half a mind to try.
He couldn't come to practise—he was getting in his hay,
But he guessed he'd show the beggars from Molongo how to play.
Now, McDougal was a Scotchman, and a canny one at that,
So he started in to practise with a paling for a bat.
He got Mrs Mac to bowl to him, but she couldn't run at all,
So he trained his sheep-dog, Pincher, how to scout and fetch the ball.

Now, Pincher was no puppy; he was old, and worn, and grey;
But he understood McDougal, and—accustomed to obey—
When McDougal cried out 'Fetch it!' he would fetch it in a trice,
But, until the word was 'Drop it!' he would grip it like a vice.
And each succeeding night they played until the light grew dim:
Sometimes McDougal struck the ball—sometimes the ball struck him.
Each time he struck, the ball would plough a furrow in the ground;
And when he missed, the impetus would turn him three times round.

The fatal day at last arrived—the day that was to see
Molongo bite the dust, or Piper's Flat knocked up a tree!
Molongo's captain won the toss, and sent his men to bat,
And they gave some leather-hunting to the men of Piper's Flat.
When the ball sped where McDougal stood, firm planted in his track,
He shut his eyes, and turned him round, and stopped it—with
   his back!
The highest score was twenty-two, the total sixty-six,
When Brady sent a yorker down that scattered Johnson's sticks.

Then Piper's Flat went in to bat, for glory and renown,
But, like the grass before the scythe, our wickets tumbled down.
'Nine wickets down, for seventeen, with fifty more to win!'
Our captain heaved a heavy sigh, and sent McDougal in.
'Ten pounds to one you'll lose it!' cried a barracker from town;

But McDougal said, 'I'll tak' it, mon!' and plonked the money down.
Then he girded up his moleskins in a self-reliant style,
Threw off his hat and boots and faced the bowler with a smile.

He held the bat the wrong side out, and Johnson with a grin
Stepped lightly to the bowling crease, and sent a 'wobbler' in;
McDougal spooned it softly back, and Johnson waited there,
But McDougal, crying 'Fetch it!', started running like a hare.
Molongo shouted 'Victory! He's out as sure as eggs,'
When Pincher started through the crowd, and ran through
    Johnson's legs.
He seized the ball like lightning; then he ran behind a log.
And McDougal kept on running, while Molongo chased the dog!

They chased him up, they chased him down, they chased him
    round and then
He darted through the slip-rail as the scorer shouted 'Ten!'
McDougal puffed; Molongo swore; excitement was intense;
As the scorer marked down twenty, Pincher cleared a barbed-
    wire fence.
'Let us head him!' shrieked Molongo. 'Brain the mongrel with a bat!'
'Run it out! Good old McDougal!' yelled the men of Piper's Flat.
And McDougal kept on jogging, and then Pincher doubled back,
And the scorer counted 'Forty' as they raced across the track.

McDougal's legs were going fast, Molongo's breath was gone—
But still Molongo chased the dog—McDougal struggled on.
When the scorer shouted 'Fifty' then they knew the chase could cease;
And McDougal gasped out 'Drop it!' as he dropped within his crease.
Then Pincher dropped the ball, and as instinctively he knew
Discretion was the wiser plan, he disappeared from view;
And as Molongo's beaten men exhausted lay around
We raised McDougal shoulder-high, and bore him from the ground.

We bore him to McGinniss's where lunch was ready laid,
And filled him up with whisky-punch, for which Molongo paid.
We drank his health in bumpers and we cheered him three
    times three,

And when Molongo got its breath, Molongo joined the spree.
And the critics say they never saw a cricket match like that,
When McDougal broke the record in the game at Piper's Flat;
And the folks were jubilating as they never did before;
For we played Molongo cricket—and McDougal topped the score!

HOW WE LOST HOPKINS
FRANK DANIEL

About a hundred years ago now, or thereabouts, give or take a
few (years, not hundreds), the Daniel brothers were busy in their
sawmill working long hours to fill a big order for delivery by horse
teams to Queanbeyan—located 47 miles away—that is to say, 75.6
kilometres to the west.

With all the rush and bother that was going on, a young
employee by the name of Hopkins was working the docking saw
when he tripped and fell across the blade, severing his left arm
below the elbow.

Not having time to waste on such a trivial matter, the older
brother, Charlie, dressed the wounded stump with an old flannelette shirt and some padding made up of an old singlet and a
couple of socks, then wrapped it all in hessian and tied it tightly
with binder twine while another brother shook the sawdust off
the severed arm and wrapped it in some newspaper and a towel
and shoved it into a sugar bag to keep the flies away while he
waited about an hour and a half for the mail truck to arrive from
Captains Flat.

The mail contractor was asked to deliver the patient to the
Queanbeyan hospital—located 47 miles away—that is to say, 75.6
kilometres to the west.

Many weeks later, the mail truck, on one of its bi-weekly runs,
pulled up at the front gate and young Hopkins alighted. He walked
up to the mill from the roadway with the mail in his hands and
some parcels under his arm. If you discounted the roughness and
red scarring left by the repair, he looked as good as new and, after
a short welcome back, Charlie put him straight back to work on

the docking saw, replacing another useless, inexperienced bloke from up the bush.

It was always safer to use experienced labour in a sawmill.

Charlie was pleased to have Hopkins back as the work load had increased and the pressure for urgent deliveries was still on in earnest.

Shortly after his return, young Hopkins had the misfortune to fall into the whirring saw blade again, this time losing his right arm. It was a clean cut and so the men got to work bandaging the poor bloke in readiness for the mail truck which was due within the hour.

Hopkins was extremely lucky to have these accidents on mail days, especially when the nearest hospital was located 47 miles away—that is to say, 75.6 kilometres to the west.

The same story again. Hopkins returned several weeks later with the repair job looking as good as gold but still with some redness and slight swelling after such a major operation.

For safety's sake, Charley moved him from the docking saw and set him to work on the breaking down bench where a huge blade, six-feet in diameter broke the big logs down to a more manageable size.

He must have been a clumsy bugger, because within a week he tripped in some deep sawdust, fell across the bench and the massive blade cut his head off—as clean as a whistle.

By now Charlie was sick of this useless young fellow and swore that he would give him the sack when he came back, and so, doing the best they could, they packed the stump where his head came from with another old shirt, another sugar bag and two pillow cases from Mrs Daniel's clothesline, and sat a brick on top to keep it all in place.

Charlie's brothers took the head, shook the sawdust off and wrapped it in calico, and placed the parcel in one of those new fangled plastic shopping bags to keep it clean.

Because they reckoned the mailman may have thought they were becoming a nuisance, they drove Hopkins in their T-model Ford truck to the Queanbeyan Hospital located 47 miles away—that is to say, 75.6 kilometres to the west.

Not having time to hang about, they left him and his head at the front door of the hospital in the charge of a very young trainee nurse and bolted back to the sawmill located 47 miles away—that is to say, 75.6 kilometres to the east.

Three months went by with plenty of work coming in and never a thought of Hopkins, no messages about his condition, no word at all; so with no real concern for such trivialities, they waited another couple or three weeks before ringing the hospital to make enquiries about his condition.

The matron responded rather haughtily that 'whoever delivered the poor chap left no forwarding address, not even his name, and, to make matters worse,' she was very sorry to say, 'some silly oaf put his head in an air-tight plastic bag and he suffocated.'

HOLUS BOLUS
E.G. MURPHY

Anyone who works with camels deserves all the sympathy we can muster, and there are many good camel yarns. Now, I have it on very good authority that this old yarn is true. How do I know? Well, I've heard so many different versions of it that one of 'em must be true!

He lay in the hospital, pallid and weak,
The wreck of a once healthy man;
His breathing was wheezy, his voice was a squeak,
As his story of woe he began.

''Twas Danny O'Hara,' he murmured in pain,
'Who told me his camel was bad,
A bulky young bull, with the strength of a crane,
But a temperament quiet and sad.

'The camel was sick, up at Cassidy's Hill,
And he'd think me an angel from heaven
If I'd help him to give it a "pick-me-up" pill,
To keep it from "throwing a seven".

'A pipe was procured, three feet of bamboo,
Then Danny, myself and the pill,
Went bravely this medical office to do
For the patient at Cassidy's Hill.

'"When the pill's in the pipe and the pipe's in his jaws,
Which I'll open," O'Hara observed,
"You place the free end of the blow-pipe in yours,
And puff when 'is gullet's uncurved,

'"I'd blow it myself, but me bellows are weak,
And I haven't the strength in my lungs,
Since I had that bad accident up at The Peak,
My puffing machinery's bung.

'"The pill is composed," he further explained,
"Of axle-grease, sulphur and tar;
And a piquant and suitable flavour is gained
By a dip in the kerosene jar.

'"To aid his digestion there's gravel and shot,
And I've seasoned it strongly with snuff;
And I want in his system to scatter the lot,
So take a deep breath and then puff."

'With the pipe to my lips a long breath I drew,
Till my diaphragm threatened to burst,
Then, bang! Down my gullet the flaming pill flew!
For the blithering camel blew first!'

GUILTY AS CHARGED

During the Great Depression, two mates, Nugget and Blue, decided
to quit the big smoke and try their hand at prospecting around
some of the old gold mining areas west of Sydney.

   If nothing else, they could live off the land, rabbits and a few
rations, maybe do a spot of rabbit trapping and of 'roo shooting

to earn a quid and, who knows, poking around the old goldfields, they might get lucky.

So off they went to Sofala and such like places, trying their luck and living off the land.

One day, they were tramping over some old diggings near Mile End. They thought some of the old mine shafts might produce a few ounces if they were safe to enter and could be shored up so that a man could work at the bottom safely.

But they needed to know how deep the shafts were.

They were walking through the mullock heaps and barren rocky outcrops of that strange, lunar landscape when they came upon a big, seemingly quite sound, but very deep, shaft. It still had a tin and timber entrance with a sort of safety rail about a metre high, which was enclosed in old tin sheets, and it looked quite promising.

Nugget picked up a rock, tossed it into the hole and stood listening for the rock to hit bottom. Nothing.

He turned to Blue and said, 'That must be a deep shaft—let's throw a bigger rock in there and listen for it to hit bottom.'

The two men found a bigger rock, picked it up and lugged it to the shaft, balanced it on the old safety fence and then dropped it in.

They listened for some time—again, nothing.

It was odd. They discussed the situation and agreed that either there was a very muddy bottom that muffled the sound of the rocks landing, or this must be one very deep shaft, indeed.

They decided that the only way to find out for sure was to throw something much bigger into the shaft, ideally something with a different shape to a stone.

They scanned the area around about and saw an old railway sleeper lying not far from the shaft—perfect!

They took an end each and picked up the sleeper. Grunting and groaning in the heat with their backs bent they struggled the few metres to the shaft and threw it in.

They were bent over the head of the shaft, listening intently, when they heard a clatter in the distance and a high-pitched squeal behind them. They turned to see a big nanny goat racing towards them from between the mullock heaps.

Naturally their first thought was that the goat had been stalking them and, seeing her opportunity to attack, had made her charge towards their backsides, as they temptingly bent over the rail of the mineshaft entrance.

They leapt aside as the goat charged and she came flying towards them flat out, head down, squealing.

Blue hoped the goat would turn in the direction of Nugget and Nugget hoped the goat would follow Blue.

Strangely, however, the charging beast flew past both men, hurdled the metre-high fence protecting the mineshaft entrance and dived straight down into the shaft. Then there was silence.

Puzzled and astounded, and not a little shaken from the experience, Nugget and Blue made their way back towards where they had set up a temporary camp near the road.

They were walking through the stretch of scrub near the edge of the mullock heaps when they were hailed by a voice cooeeing and saw an old man waving to them from a small hut on the edge of the mullock heaps.

The old man had a camp fire going and invited the two mates to have a cuppa with him. He said he fossicked the area and made a few bob now and then from the few specks he found. He had a quite comfortable little shack and had a few vegies growing and a few animals and chooks. He wasn't exactly a hermit but he didn't see many visitors and was keen for a chat.

After the usual niceties and chat, the two mates asked the old bloke if he had a goat among his flock.

'Yes, I have as a matter of fact,' replied the old bloke, 'why?'

Blue looked at Nugget and Nugget looked at Blue.

'Errr, is your goat sort of mad and dangerous?' asked Nugget.

'Not particularly,' the old bloke replied, ' she's as nasty as any old nanny goat, but she still gives a bit of milk and hasn't gone mad yet, why?'

'I'm sorry to say she might have gone mad on you,' said Blue and the two mates told the story of the incredible incident they had just witnessed. How a goat had attacked them as they looked down a shaft, and then dived headlong into oblivion, down the very same shaft.

'That's quite a story,' said the old bloke. 'I never heard the like of that before. Anyway, it couldn't have been my goat, she's grazing up in the mullock heaps tied by a really long piece of rope to a big old railway sleeper.'   JH

SOMEONE PINCHED OUR FIREWOOD
JIM HAYNES

Someone pinched our firewood, what a mongrel act!
It's about as low as you can go—but it's a bloody fact!
We spent a whole day cutting it—bashing round the scrub,
I bet the bloke who pinched it spent the whole day in the pub.

We nearly got the trailer bogged—flat tyre on the ute,
So when we finally got it home, we thought, 'You bloody beaut!
No more cutting firewood, at least until the spring.'
We unloaded it and split it up to size and everything.

Stacked it really neatly, a ute and trailer load,
Trouble was we stacked it too close to the road!
And some miserable mongrel started sneaking 'cross the park,
Every night or two, to pinch some—after dark.

Now, as luck would have it, we'd gunpowder in the shed,
We hollowed out one log and packed that in instead.
Then back up on the pile it went—next night he took the bait,
We'd soon know who the bugger was, we settled back to wait.

He was a contract shearer, only new in town,
I never got to meet him 'cos he didn't stick around.
The house was only rented; the whole town heard the pop,
They say the Aga Cooker split right across the top.

'Tho justice is its own reward, I wish I'd heard that cove,
Explaining to the landlord the condition of his stove.
Folk in our town mostly are a warm and friendly lot,
Until you pinch our firewood—and then we're bloody not!

THE BIG LOAD
FRANK DANIEL

In 1968, I was transporting grain from the Riverina District into Sydney via the Hume Highway. The most popular meal stop on the highway at that time was Bimbo's Roadhouse at Bargo, midway between Mittagong and Campbelltown.

I was having breakfast at Bimbo's Roadhouse one morning with another truck driver, a good mate of mine, when I related a story I'd read in the *Daily Telegraph* a few days before.

The story was about the manufacture of a very large vault door, by an engineering firm in Newtown.

This door was so large that, when finished, it posed a problem in transferring it from the workshop to the semitrailer, which was waiting to carry it to a new bank building in the city.

A Coles crane was brought in to lift the heavy door and that's where the trouble started. The crane wouldn't fit through the door and, to make matters worse, the vault door, inside the factory, was larger than the shed entrance.

This didn't pose a problem for the engineers. They simply removed the front wall of the corrugated iron shed and a portion of the gabled roof and one of the roof trusses. This enabled the crane driver to make a direct lift from above the workshop; a few minor adjustments and the door was lifted skyward out of the shed and slewed onto the waiting truck and trailer.

My mate didn't appear to have much faith in my story and the harder I tried to convince him that I wasn't telling him a yarn, the less he believed me.

I told him that there was an actual photograph in the paper, and that I would prove it to him. I burrowed through a pile of old newspapers in the dining room, but blow me down, there was not a single copy of that particular issue of the *Tele* to win my argument.

Three or four days later, I was having a meal at Bimbos when my mate walked in and joined me at the table.

'I saw the biggest load that I've ever seen in my life yesterday,' he began. 'It was massive.'

'There was two big fat coppers driving two of them new Mini-Cooper S pursuit cars, one on each side of the centre line, with lights flashing on the roof of each car and their hazard lights winking and blinking.

'Coming behind them,' he went on, 'was a bloody great big Brambles Mack R-700 carrying a 15 ton concrete block of ballast. It had a stiff-arm hooked to the bullbar of another big Bulldog Mack which was hooked up to a four-axle dolly which in turn was towing an eight-axle wide-spread low-loader.'

I was more than impressed.

He went on.

'Another whopping great Mack R-700 with a 15 ton block of ballast was coming behind with a similar stiff-arm set-up and was pushing as hard as it could to help the two prime movers up the front.

'On each side of this big turnout were three more motor cycle cops with lights flashing and keeping the traffic at a safe distance off the road.'

This yarn was getting the better of me as he continued.

'Now! Coming up behind this whole shebang was two more big fat coppers in Mini-Coopers, with lights flashing, one each side of the centre line.'

Here he paused for a few seconds and then said, 'It was the biggest load I ever saw in my life!'

I was amazed. It didn't take me too long to bite!

'What were they carrying on the low-loader?'

He gave me a good hard look and replied slowly, 'The combination for that safe you saw the other day!'

MICKETY MULGA
T. RANKEN

He worked wid us at Wantigong—
Old Mickety Mulga Jim.
We'd all a-gone blue mouldy if
It 'adn't bin for him.

He'd keep us yarnin' at the fire,
An' laughin' be the hour
At 'is amusin' anecdotes,
Be George, he 'ad a power.

'E told us up in Queensland, where
'E'd never go again,
He come to some dry water-'ole
Upon a ten-mile plain.

The tank was dry, and Jim was dry,
But be a 'appy thought,
He wrung 'is empty water-bag
An' got about a quart;

But couldn't find a stick o' wood
To bile his billy by,
So stuck a match into the grass,
Which then was pretty dry.

He 'eld the billy to the flame
Wid a bit of fencing-wire,
But 'ad to go to foller it,
So rapid run the fire.

Five miles acrost that flamin' plain
He raced that fire, did he,
But when at last the billy boiled,
He 'ad forgot the tea!

DALEY'S DORG WATTLE
W. T. GOODGE

'You can talk about yer sheep dorgs,' said the man from Allan's
    Creek,
'But I know a dorg that simply knocked 'em bandy!—
Do whatever you would show him, and you'd hardly need to speak;
Owned by Daley, drover cove in Jackandandy.

'We was talkin' in the parlour, me and Daley, quiet like,
When a blowfly starts a-buzzin' round the ceilin',
Up gets Daley, and he says to me, "You wait a minute, Mike,
And I'll show you what a dorg he is at heelin'."

'And an empty pickle bottle was a-standin' on the shelf,
Daley takes it down and puts it on the table,
And he bets me drinks that blinded dorg would do it by himself—
And I didn't think as how as he was able!

'Well, he shows the dorg the bottle, and he points up to the fly,
And he shuts the door, and says to him—"Now, Wattle!"
And in less than fifteen seconds, spare me days, it ain't a lie,
That there dorg had got that insect in the bottle.'

THE BULLOCKY'S TALE
ANONYMOUS

I've got the finest bullock team was ever lapped in hide,
And if you'd care to listen to my tale,
Of how they broke a record on the Woolumundry side,
Just light your pipe an climb up on this rail.

It was back in 1895, when we had heavy rains,
I was coming down the river with the team,
There were miles of slush and water on the stock routes and the plains,
And every little gutter was a stream.

I had wool from Bogandillon and I piled the load so high
That the boss and pressers reckoned I was mad;
It would have been a record pull if roads were hard and dry,
You can guess what it was like when they were bad.

Well, we got out to the crossing and the current made me think,
But I pushed the leaders at it with a rush,
And the wagon reached the middle, then the wheels began to sink,
While the bullocks were all scrambling in the slush.

Yes, she 'set' there pretty solid, and the crowd strolled from the shed,
They were hoping they would have a bit of fun,
And Paddy Foley barracked me until I punched his head,
And told the boss I'd kick him off the run.

Now, I reckoned that the bullocks needed half an hour's spell,
So I takes 'em off an drives 'em up the lane,
And the crowd think that I'm beaten and let out a nasty yell,
But I tells 'em that we'll tackle it again.

Then I hitched the team back on again, the bullocks know my plan,
They were ready when I swung the whip around,
I yelled, 'Gee up! Test the jewellery! Tear a quill out if you can!'
And they stuck their toes a foot into the ground.

They were straining 'gainst the yokes and I was chopping chunks
     of skin,
And using all the language that I knew,
And after twenty minutes, when I thought of giving in,
I saw the wagon started to come through.

I suppose it was a minute 'fore they'd move a dozen feet,
But I would that greenhide lash about their flanks,
And at last the team got going, just to see 'em was a treat,
And then I said—well—many fervent thanks.

In a little while I stopped, and I looked behind and saw
Just what they'd done! It hit me like a shell!
For they dragged that loaded table-top a hundred yards or more—
And they'd dragged the bloody creek along as well!

CRUEL TACTICS OF THE EMU
LENNIE LOWER

Sad news comes from Wangrabelle.

It seems that emus chase the sheep and kill them by repeatedly
jumping on their backs. They do the same thing to pigs.

It is supposed that the emus do this out of a spirit of sportive destructiveness as they do not further mutilate the animals after killing them.

Anyone who knows anything at all about emus must know that it's not the fault of the emus. They have nothing else to do. They are merely emusing themselves.

As an emuologist who has made a close study of emus for many years, we say without fear of contradiction that if the sheep or pig, as the case may be, would only keep steady, the emu would not have to keep jumping on and off.

Experiments have proved beyond all doubt that a pig or sheep once jumped on begins to wobble.

The Emu Research Society, of which we are the founder, in combination with the Be-Kind-To-Emus League, has jumped on the backs of 3425 pigs and a similar number of sheep in the course of experiment, the animals being kindly lent by owners of piggeries and sheeperies.

In every case the result was fatal; this may be accounted for by the fact that there is a total of 132 in the experimental party, and even though the investigators jumped one at a time, the animal selected soon weakened and was ultimately flattened out.

Emus cannot be curbed. An emu which was born in our own home and fed by our own hand, returned to its wild state at the end, and after laying an egg in the jardiniere, kicked the back out of the fireplace.

The solution lies in breeding stronger sheep. More powerful pigs. Given the right physique, look what a saving in freights would be effected if farm produce could swim to the London market.

There's something wrong with the backs of our sheep. The knees of our pigs are not all that they should be. We ought to look into the backs and knees of our sheep and pigs. In the meantime, you leave our emus alone.

TALL TIMBER
C.J. DENNIS

A snake that fastened on a man's leg in Burnie, Tasmania, was much disgusted to find that the leg was a wooden one.

That sort o' reminds me of the old days (said Bill)
In the bush at Toolangi, at Switherton's mill—
A sor-mill, you know—an' the sawyer we 'ad
Was old 'Oppy McClintock, a wooden-legged lad.

'E was walkin' one day for to tighten a peg,
When a tiger snake grabs at 'is old timber leg;
An' there it 'angs on, till I fetched it a crack,
But old 'Oppy jist grins as 'e starts to walk back.

An' then somethink 'appens. We seen 'Oppy stop,
As 'e stumbles a bit, an' looks down at 'is prop
With a dead funny look. Then 'e lets out a yell:
'Ere, boys! Take it off me! It's startin' to swell!

Well, we unstraps 'is leg, an' it swole an' it swole.
Snake pisen? Too right! 'Twas a twenny-foot pole
In less than five minutes! Believe it or not.
An' as thick—it's as true as I stand on this spot!

We was 'eavin it out, when the boss starts to roar:
'Ere! Why waste good wood? Shove it on to the sor!
So we sors it in two, down the middle, an' then,
Them there slabs swole an' swole; so we sors 'em agen.

An' we sors, an' we sors; an' it swole, an' it swole,
Till the end of the day, when the tally, all tole,
Was two thousan' foot super. You doubt it? (said Bill)
You ask any ole 'and up at Switherton's mill!

I'M NOT LOST

My favourite yarn in the Dad and Dave genre is the one about the city motorist whose shiny car pulls up on a back road where Dave is leaning on the gatepost gazing across the paddocks.

'Hey, mate,' say the car driver, 'where can I get petrol around here?'

'I'm not sure,' says Dave.

'Well, does this road lead to Toowoomba?'

'I dunno,' says Dave slowly.

'Well, what town does this road lead to?'

'I can't say,' says Dave, 'I don't really know.'

'Well, if I go back to that fork in the road down the hill, and take the other road, where will that take me?' asks the frustrated city slicker.

'I dunno,' says Dave after a pause.

'You don't know much, do you?' says the frustrated driver, sarcastically.

'No, I don't,' agrees Dave, 'but I'm not lost!'   JH

THE BOASTER AND THE OUTLAW
ANONYMOUS

He had come to Numerella in the drought of '98,
When the plains were but a lonely sea of sand,
And the philanthropic super, taking pity on his state,
Had given him a start as 'extra hand'.

Jimmy really was a wonder; all night long he'd sit and boast
Of all the marvellous feats he'd seen and done:
How he'd won the axeman's trophy at the show at Bundaberg,
And killed an Indian hawker just for fun;

How he'd rung the board at Blackall, beating Howe by thirty sheep,
How he'd broken outlaw horses in the night,
And in seven rounds at Gympie put O'Sullivan to sleep
With a blow on which he had the patent right.

Now we had a horse, an outlaw born on Numerella run,
No fiercer horse had ever stretched the reins.
He'd thrown every man who'd tried him and the station breaker,
    Dunn,
Said he was the toughest outlaw on the plains.

The boss came strolling down one day, we'd planned the joke of
    course;
'I've letters here must catch the mail,' he said,
'You better take 'em, Jimmy, you can ride the chestnut horse,
But mind him or he'll have you on your head.'

So Jim threw on the saddle, and the colt stood like a sheep,
For a moment there we thought our joke would fail.
But Jim was scarcely seated when the chestnut gave a leap
Like a demon and he cleared the upper rail.

Down the track went horse and rider, and we opened wide our eyes,
For Jim just seemed to be content to sit,
And he hit him with his stockwhip every time that he would rise,
And dig his heels in every time he hit!

We rushed for horse and bridle; down the track we followed fast,
For to see our outlaw thrashed was something new,
But when we neared the timberline where we had seen them last,
Both man and horse had disappeared from view.

So we searched for horse and rider, but our searching was in vain,
Though we searched that outback country everywhere,
From the cattle camps on Kyder to the farms on Little Plain,
But all our searches ended in despair.

The days turned into weeks but still no tidings came to hand,
We had given Jimmy up and thought him lost,
Till a traveller going eastward found some hoof prints in the sand,
Showing plainly where a horse had lately crossed.

On a piece of rugged country, way out back of Ondaloo,
Hemmed in by rugged hills and gorges deep,

We found that outlaw bucking still for all he ever knew,
And Jimmy there astride him—sound asleep!

A SNAKE YARN
W.T. GOODGE

'You talk of snakes,' said Jack the Rat,
'But, blow me, one hot summer,
I seen a thing that knocked me flat—
Fourteen foot long, or more than that,
It was a reg'lar hummer!
Lay right along a sort of bog,
Just like a log!

'The ugly thing was lyin' there
And not a sign o' movin',
Give any man a nasty scare;
Seen nothin' like it anywhere
Since I first started drovin'.
And yet it didn't scare my dog.
Looked like a log!

'I had to cross that bog, yer see,
And bluey I was humpin';
But wonderin' what that thing could be
A-layin' there in front o' me
I didn't feel like jumpin'.
Yet, though I shivered like a frog,
It seemed a log!

'I takes a leap and lands right on
The back of that there whopper!'
He stopped. We waited. Then Big Mac
Remarked, 'Well, then, what happened, Jack?'
'Not much,' said Jack, and drained his grog.
'It was a log!'

AUSSIE ICONS

Here is a bunch of yarns about some of our iconic Aussie events, buildings, sayings and phrases . . . and characters, both real and imaginary.

A few of these yarns explain how some of our typical Aussie phrases came about, like 'Blind Freddy could see that' and 'beyond the black stump'. The truth about these things is more interesting than anything you could make up.

The stories behind some of our Aussie institutions, like Qantas, Cobb & Co and the Melbourne Cup are fascinating and very often not at all what you would expect.

The yarns that were most fun to write in this section, and the ones that tend to interest me the most, are those that concern some of our legendary real Aussies. I find that when a person becomes 'larger than life' the public image tends to overshadow the real person.

We all think of Banjo Paterson as the great poet who wrote our most famous song, but very few Australians would know he enlisted in World War I at the age of fifty-one, or that he played in the first ever New South Wales polo team. For that matter, few Australians would know that Charles Kingsford-Smith was the first person ever rescued from the surf using a life-saving reel—at Bondi, when he was just ten years old.

The standard history of these icons is well-known, so I have tried to find interesting or little-known aspects of their stories that are 'good yarns'. We all love insights into the real people behind the legends and I have tried to make the yarns about characters like Melba, Banjo, Slim Dusty, Kingsford-Smith and others reveal something of their real lives, which are often more extraordinary than you could possibly imagine.

CAPTAIN JAMES COOK

Great Navigator, Poor Yarn Spinner

James Cook was a very good captain and a great navigator but generally his storytelling left a lot to be desired.

Admittedly, he was mostly writing a ship's log or official letters, not trying to entertain anybody. Still, his matter-of-fact expression always leaves me feeling he was a rather cold-blooded type with a very stiff upper lip.

Cook rarely lets us see any emotion. There is hardly any figurative language in his narratives; the ship's log is mostly about weather and position.

Sir Joseph Banks is even worse. His journals are quite dull reading and full of scientific references and facts.

The only person on the *Endeavour* who made any attempt to record his feelings was the artist Sydney Parkinson, who sadly died after the ship left Batavia and never made it home.

I'll show you what I mean. Let's look at a typical day, almost 250 years ago, through the eyes of the captain, the naturalist and the artist.

It's 2 October 1769 and the *Endeavour* is in the Pacific approaching New Zealand.

Cook says,

Little wind. At 3 PM hoisted out a Boat to try the current but found none, saw several Grampusses. AM. Had a Boat in the water, and Mr Banks shot an Albetross which measur'd 10 feet 8 inches from the tip of one wing to the other; he likewise shot two Birds that were very much like ducks . . . we first saw these Birds in the Latitude of 48 degrees South.

Joseph Banks writes,

Calm: I go in the boat and take up *Dagysa rostrata, Serena, polyedra, Beroe incrassata, coarctata, medusa vitrea, Phyllodoce velella*, with several other things which are all put in spirits. See a seal but cannot come near him to shoot. Shoot *Diomedea exulans, Procellaria velox, pallipes, Latirostris, longipes* and *Nectris fuliginosa.*

The artist Sydney Parkinson observes in his diary,

> On the 2nd, the sea was as smooth as the Thames, and the weather fair and clear. Mr. Banks went out in a little boat, and diverted himself in shooting of Shear-waters, with one white Albatross, that measured, from the tip of one wing to the other, ten feet, seven inches; and also picked up a great many weeds of various kinds.

At least Sydney Parkinson had some flair in his writing, even if the marine plants were all just 'weeds' to him, 'weeds' that he had to draw and paint.

When you get different versions of any yarn, the exact truth is hard to find; Cook and Parkinson don't even agree on how big the dead albatross was!

I hate to pick on such a famous and iconic figure as James Cook, but just look at how mundane are his accounts of two momentous and historically significant events—finding the east coast of Australia and arriving at Botany Bay:

> THURSDAY, 19th April 1770.

> Fresh Gales at South-South-West and Cloudy Squally weather, with a large Southerly Sea; at 1 AM brought too and sounded, but had no ground with 130 fathoms of line. At 5, set the Topsails close reef'd, and at 6, saw land extending from North-East to West, distance 5 or 6 Leagues, having 80 fathoms, fine sandy bottom.

'Saw land . . . fine sandy bottom'! This is the birth of our *nation!* There is no pride, no sense of achievement or triumph, not even any patriotic platitudes or thanks to the Almighty. He simply gives the latitude and longitude of the first landmark sighted and then says, 'I have named it Point Hicks; because Lieutenant Hicks was the first who discover'd this Land.'

It's hardly riveting stuff is it? He has just discovered the east coast of the Great South Land and the best he can manage is 'saw land'. It's the same when he arrives at Botany Bay. After trying to land at Jervis Bay and being stopped from doing so by adverse winds, he again tried to land near Bulli but the surf was too strong, so he returned to the ship:

> At this time it fell Calm, and we were not above a Mile and a half from the Shore, in 11 fathoms, and within some breakers that lay to the Southward of us; but luckily a light breeze came off from the Land, which carried us out of danger, and with which we stood to the Northward. At daylight in the morning we discover'd a Bay, which appeared to be tollerably well shelter'd from all winds, into which I resolved to go with the Ship, and with this View sent the Master in the Pinnace to sound the Entrance.

> Sunday, 29th. In the P.M. wind Southerly and Clear weather, with which we stood into the bay and Anchored under the South shore about 2 miles within the Entrance in 5 fathoms.

When they set foot on shore Cook doesn't mention it, he's too busy observing the Aborigines and worrying about their weapons. He had already fired a warning shot at a group on shore who made threatening gestures with spears.

> One of them took up a stone and threw at us, which caused my firing a Second Musquet, loaded with small Shott . . . Immediately after this we landed, which we had no sooner done than they throw'd 2 darts at us; this obliged me to fire a third shott . . .

So, in that magic moment, the first British foot on Australian soil (well *eastern* Australian soil, anyway), all the famous captain was thinking about was firing his musket at the locals.

Joseph Banks' account is even less exciting. He describes the momentous event like this: 'In the mean time we had landed on the rock.'

There is a much better version of Cook's party first landing on Australian soil. It's one I was told as a kid at school and again by my mum when we visited the place at Kurnell where it all happened.

It's a well-known story that involves Isaac Smith, who was the son of Cook's wife Elizabeth's cousin Charles.

Isaac was a midshipman on the *Endeavour* and was in the first boat ashore at Botany Bay. According to the family legend, Cook said, 'Jump out, Isaac,' and thus the boy became the first European to set foot on the Great South Land's east coast. But the story does not appear in any of the journals written at the time. Indeed, Cook himself never mentions it.

Given that he was busy taking pot shots at seemingly aggressive natives on the shore it would seem that telling a member of your wife's family, 'You go first!' might not be the sort of thing you would want the in-laws to know!

Isaac sailed with Cook again on his second voyage and was the first man to make charts of the southern parts of South America. He was commander of the 36-gun frigate HMS *Perseverance* at the Battle of Tellicherry against the French in 1791 and retired, due to having contracted hepatitis, as Rear-Admiral in 1807. Isaac was obviously like a younger brother to Cook's widow Elizabeth and, as all her six children died young, they shared a house when he retired. Isaac died in 1831 at the age of seventy-eight and Elizabeth Cook died four years later in 1835, aged ninety-three.

The story of Isaac being the first European to set foot on eastern Australia was related years after Elizabeth's death by her second cousin Canon Frederick Bennett, who said the story was a 'family legend'.

It's not like a respectable clergyman to pass on mere hearsay, surely!

Anyway, it's a lot better than, 'In the mean time we had landed on the rock.'   **JH**

CAPTAIN COOK
JIM HAYNES

There once was a captain named Cook,
Sailed south just to have a quick look,
There he found a land,
Stuck a flag in the sand—
That's how native title got took.

MATTHEW FLINDERS - THE MAN WHO NAMED AUSTRALIA

Matthew Flinders should have been a country doctor—a physician like his father, grandfather and great-grandfather, in and around the village of Donington, Lincolnshire, where he was born in 1774.

Educated at Donington Parish School and Horbling Grammar School, he learned Latin, Greek, Classics and Mathematics; but he dreamed of joining the navy.

His cousin was governess to the daughter of Captain Thomas Pasley of the Royal Navy and, at just fourteen years of age, Flinders persuaded his cousin to introduce him to the captain.

Flinders joined the navy as an officer's servant at fifteen and served on Captain Pasley's vessels, HMS *Scipio* and *Bellerophon*. In 1791, aged seventeen, he joined the *Providence* as a midshipman on William Bligh's second voyage of exploration and sailed to the Pacific Ocean, Asia and the West Indies.

Three years later, Flinders was back on the *Bellerophon*, this time as an aide-de-camp to Pasley, who had been promoted to rear admiral. On 1 June 1794, the warship, known to her less-than-classically-educated crew as the *Billy Ruffian*, was involved in the famous Battle of Ushant, afterwards known as 'the Glorious First of June'.

Young twenty-year-old Matthew Flinders sat calmly on the deck of the *Bellerophon* throughout the battle, observing and making notes. As chaos reigned around him and the *Bellerophon* took broadside after broadside from the French warships *Eole* and

America in a pitched gunnery battle, he prepared what was to become the most accurate account of the famous battle, a report that ran to forty foolscap pages.

Rear-Admiral Pasley lost a leg to a cannonball in the battle, as his protégé sat on deck making notes. This left Flinders free to move on to another stage of his naval career. He joined the HMS *Reliance* and sailed to New South Wales with ship's surgeon George Bass and John Hunter, who was returning to the colony to be the new governor. Bass and Flinders explored the coasts and rivers of New South Wales and circumnavigated Tasmania. Flinders also explored the coast of Queensland and was eventually commissioned to chart the coast of Australia.

He was given a ship, HMS *Investigator*, which was a converted shallow draught collier, refitted with extra cabins and storage for scientists. She was not in good condition, but she was all that could be spared by a navy preparing for war. Flinders married Ann Chappell, a girl from his hometown, and sailed away several weeks later.

He charted the southern, eastern and northern coasts of the continent for two years before the fact that the ship was leaking badly forced him to abort his mission in 1803.

In August 1803, he sailed as a passenger from Port Jackson on HMS *Porpoise*, hoping to secure a more suitable ship in England to complete the task of mapping the continent. A week out of Sydney, sailing at night in convoy with the passenger ships *Cato* and *Bridgewater*, *Porpoise* hit an uncharted reef in heavy seas 450 kilometres east-north-east of the modern-day town of Gladstone.

Both the *Porpoise* and the *Cato* sank on the reef and the *Bridgewater* sailed off in the dark, leaving them to their fate. Flinders organised the rescue operation and managed to get ninety-four survivors safely onto a small sandy island within the reef. Determined to preserve discipline, he read aloud the articles of war and had one seaman publicly flogged for disorderly conduct.

The survivors had tents and food and Flinders saved almost all of his charts, papers and scientific drawings from the wreck. He then took one of the *Porpoise*'s two six-oared longboats, with an officer and crew, and made his way back to Port Jackson, where he arranged the rescue of all the survivors on the reef.

Flinders then left for England in the locally built 29-ton schooner *Cumberland*, which proved almost impossible to sail on the open sea. He therefore decided to seek assistance at Ile-de-France (Mauritius). War had again broken out between England and France, however, and he was imprisoned on the island for over six years. He finally returned to the woman he had married just before sailing in the *Investigator* nine years and three months after his departure.

Flinders never did complete the charting of our continent. His health was poor and he was an old man by the age of forty, probably dying of cancer. He spent several years finishing and editing his wonderful and important work, *A Voyage to Terra Australis*. The first copies were delivered to his home on 18 July 1814. His wife Ann laid the volumes on his bed while he slept and he woke the following day only to touch the books and whisper his last words, 'My papers', before he closed his eyes and died.

Flinders' wife and daughter lived in poverty on a small pension until 1852 when the governments of the colonies of New South Wales and Victoria, learning of their situation, each voted that a pension of £100 be paid to them. Flinders' widow died before this took place, but his daughter, Mrs Ann Petrie, wrote:

> it would indeed have cheered her last days to know that my father's long-neglected services were at length appreciated . . . and the handsome amount of the pension granted will enable me to educate my young son in a manner worthy of the name he bears.

Her son would become Sir William Matthew Flinders Petrie. Born the year the pensions were granted, he was the most celebrated and respected archaeologist of his era and the first professor to hold a chair of Egyptology in the United Kingdom. He died in 1942.

We owe Matthew Flinders the honour of naming our nation. The name 'Australia' was popularised by Flinders, who wrote in 1804, 'I call the whole island Australia' and he wished to use the name in his published works, but was talked out of it by Sir Joseph Banks.

Governor Macquarie read Flinders' comment about the name. He liked the idea and began using the term. By 1901, the name 'Australia' was in such common use that there was little debate about the name that should be used when the colonies federated to form our nation.   JH

THE BLACK STUMP

Is there a genuine 'black stump'?

Well, there are, or have been, Black Stump hotels or inns at Coolah, Merriwagga and Trunkey Creek. Is one of those locations the site of the 'real' black stump?

The answer is no—not really, there were many 'black stumps'; they were used to mark survey lines in the nineteenth century. Anywhere beyond the boundaries of the original nineteen counties declared by Governor Ralph Darling and surveyed by John Oxley and Major Thomas Mitchell was technically 'beyond the black stump'.

The Manning River was the northern boundary of the nineteen counties, the Liverpool Range was the western boundary and the Clyde River at Bateman's Bay was the southern boundary. So the nineteen counties were within an area from Kempsey to Bateman's Bay and the western boundary went as far as the town of Wellington.

Any town or settlement on the perimeter of the surveyed area could be 'the black stump'.

Governor Darling declared that land 'beyond' the surveyed nineteen counties was not for settlement. Those who broke the law and settled there were 'squatters'.

Governor Bourke allowed land outside the nineteen counties to be taken up after 1836. An inn called The Black Stump Inn was built in the 1860s at the junction of the roads leading to Gunnedah and Coonabarabran, at Coolah.

The inn later became the Black Stump Wine Saloon and was destroyed by fire in 1908. It was a staging post and stopover point for Cobb & Co and it became a marker by which people gauged their journeys. This helped sustain the term 'beyond the black stump', but the term originated with the survey of the nineteen counties.

In 1887, a group of surveyors arrived on Astro Station near Blackall in Queensland, 1000 kilometres west of Brisbane, and used a stump of blackened petrified wood as a base for their theodolites. The surveyors were there to take longitudinal and latitudinal observations, to be used as part of the accurate mapping of inland Australia.

So, the country to the west of Blackall was also 'beyond the black stump'. The stump of petrified wood is now found at a monument near Blackall State School.

There is also a Black Stump Hotel at Trunkey Creek in New South Wales and a Black Stump lookout and rest stop at Mundubbera in Queensland.   **JH**

FREEMAN COBB

The Man Who Stayed Three Years

Freeman Cobb was born in 1830 in Brewster, Massachusetts, USA and, at eighteen, contracted rheumatic fever, which left him permanently lame. This led him to seek employment in an industry that did not require strenuous physical activity or the ability to walk great distances.

Cobb worked for Adams & Co coaching lines, an outfit which was established during the Californian gold rush.

In May 1853, aged twenty-three and with an excellent knowledge of the coach and cargo business, he arrived in Melbourne with his associate George Mowton, supposedly to establish a branch of Adams & Co.

Mowton and Cobb had met some other Americans on the voyage out to the young colony of Victoria. They had all heard that gold had been discovered and opportunities for the coaching business were growing fast. Their new friends all worked for the famous Wells Fargo coach company and were travelling to Victoria with very similar ideas to those of Freeman Cobb.

So, instead of establishing a new branch of Adams & Co Coaching, Cobb and Mowton joined Swanton, Lamber and Peck, from Wells Fargo, to form Cobb & Co.

Their average age was only twenty-two, but their enthusiasm and experience counted for a great deal. The company started out only carrying freight, but changed to passenger coaches in January 1854 and began operating daily each way between Bendigo, Castlemaine and Melbourne, except on Sundays.

Cobb & Co became a part of Australian history, as iconic as Ned Kelly or Don Bradman or Qantas. The coaches of Cobb & Co carried freight and passengers all around Australia until well into the twentieth century.

But what happened to the founder, the man who gave his name to what became an Aussie institution?

Well, it seems that Mr Cobb was an opportunist in true American fashion. In May 1856, almost exactly three years after he arrived on Australian soil, Freeman Cobb announced that the business had been sold and he left for America. He returned to Brewster, married his cousin Annette Cobb and they had two children.

From 1864 to 1865 he was a senator for Barnstaple County in the Massachusetts State Legislature. In 1871, however, he took his family to South Africa where he formed Cobb & Co Ltd and operated a coach service between Port Elizabeth and the diamond fields at Kimberley.

The firm failed after several years and Cobb was declared insolvent and died in 1878 at his home in Port Elizabeth.   **JH**

THE LIGHTS OF COBB AND CO
HENRY LAWSON

Fire lighted; on the table a meal for sleepy men;
A lantern in the stable; a jingle now and then;
The mail-coach looming darkly by light of moon and star;

The growl of sleepy voices; a candle in the bar;
A stumble in the passage of folk with wits abroad;
A swear word from a bedroom, the shout of 'All aboard!'
'Tchk-tchk! Git up!' 'Hold fast, there!' and down the range we go;
Five hundred miles of scattered camps will watch for Cobb and Co.

Old coaching towns already decaying for their sins;
Uncounted 'Half-Way Houses', and scores of 'Ten-Mile Inns';
The riders from the stations by lonely granite peaks;
The black-boy for the shepherds on sheep and cattle creeks;
The roaring camps of Gulgong, and many a 'Digger's Rest';
The diggers on the Lachlan; the huts of Farthest West;
Some twenty thousand exiles who sailed for weal or woe
The bravest hearts of twenty lands will wait for Cobb and Co.

The morning star has vanished, the frost and fog are gone,
In one of those grand mornings which but on mountains dawn;
A flask of friendly whisky—each other's hopes we share—
And throw our top-coats open to drink the mountain air.
The roads are rare to travel, and life seems all complete;
The grind of wheels on gravel, the trot of horses' feet,
The trot, trot, trot and canter, as down the spur we go
The green sweeps to horizons blue that call for Cobb and Co.

We take a bright girl actress through western dusts and damps,
To bear the home-world message, and sing for sinful camps,
To stir our hearts and break them, wild hearts that hope and ache
(Ah! when she thinks of those days her own must nearly break!)
Five miles this side the goldfield, a loud, triumphant shout:
Five hundred cheering diggers have snatched the horses out:
With 'Auld Lang Syne' in chorus, through roaring camps they go
That cheer for her, and cheer for Home, and cheer for Cobb and Co.

Three lamps above the ridges and gorges dark and deep,
A flash on sandstone cuttings where sheer the sidings sweep,
A flash on shrouded wagons, on water ghastly white;
Weird bush and scattered remnants of 'rushes in the night';
Across the swollen river a flash beyond the ford:

Ride hard to warn the driver! He's drunk or mad, good Lord!
But on the bank to westward a broad and cheerful glow
New camps extend across the plains, new routes for Cobb and Co.

Swift scramble up the siding where teams climb inch by inch;
Pause, bird-like, on the summit—then breakneck down the pinch;
By clear ridge-country rivers, and gaps where tracks run high,
Where waits the lonely horseman, cut clear against the sky;
Past haunted half-way houses—where convicts made the bricks—
Scrub-yards and new bark shanties, we dash with five and six;
Through stringybark and blue-gum, and box and pine we go—
A hundred miles shall see tonight the lights of Cobb and Co!

SYDNEY'S FAMOUS FERRIES

Sydney's harbour is famous for its ferries and shipyards, but
building sturdy seagoing vessels in the colony of New South Wales
was a risky business in the convict era. Early governors and colonial
administrators were faced with a dilemma as far as shipbuilding
was concerned.

Ships and boats were the only viable means of transport, not
only to and from the colony, but also around the colony. Due to
the British East India Company's government-approved monopoly,
however, no vessel capable of trading with Asia or the South Seas
could be built in the colony. The British East India Company
insisted that no Asian trading be undertaken by the new colony.
The company feared that the new penal settlement, which was not
under their control, would become another British trading post
and threaten their very cosy relationship with the Crown (and the
Dutch East India Company).

At first, the two government ships, HMS *Sirius* and *Supply*,
were used along with the whaleboats, cutters and other small
vessels which arrived with the First Fleet. When the last of the
First Fleet transports departed in July 1788, the harbour had very
few boats of any kind to do the carrying, exploring and guarding
necessary for the colony's existence. This became more apparent

eighteen months after arriving, when Governor Phillip decided
to set up a second settlement on better farming land at a place
he considered more easily defensible than the wide expanses of
the harbour. Originally called Rose Hill, this place was generally
known from the start as Parramatta.

This was the main reason that the first substantial vessel was
built in the colony. In October 1789, a 12-ton vessel was launched
named the *Rose Hill Packet*. She was designed to use sails, oars or
poles to carry stores between the two settlements at Sydney and
Parramatta. Round trips took a week to complete.

The *Rose Hill Packet* was convict-built and was a rather clumsy
barge-like vessel universally known as 'the Lump'. Her brief life
was over by 1800 as, by then, other government vessels had been
acquired or built and small private ferries were operating around
the harbour and the river, charging fares for passengers and freight.

Colonial authorities were constantly anxious about escape
attempts and sought ways to prevent the possibility of convicts
escaping; so in 1791, after the successful escape of the Bryant
family and seven other convicts in the government fishing boat,
a regulation was introduced prohibiting the building of vessels
more than 14 feet (4.3 metres) in length.

By 1800, quite a few enterprising ferrymen were operating
around the harbour. The best known of them was the Negro
ex-convict Billy Blue, who wore a naval officer's coat and hat and
was given the name 'The Old Commodore' by Governor Macquarie.

Small ferry companies continued to operate around the harbour
until 1861, when the North Shore Ferry Company became Sydney's
first large commercial ferry service. Although less than 1000 people
lived on the north shore, the company prospered and, in 1878, it
was renamed the North Shore Steam Ferry Company.

Few Australians realise that, along with the much vaunted
Australian inventions we always hear about—rotary clotheslines,
motor mowers, cask wine—the double-ended ferry is also an
Australian invention.

It was the North Shore Ferry Co that invented the double-ended
propeller-driven ferry in 1868. The company's captains were

tired of turning ferries around in small coves and bays and the increasing use of the harbour for recreation was making the task more dangerous. Someone suggested building two front sections of a steam ferry and joining them together so that only one end operated at a time. The ferries had propellers and a steering deck at either end and the captain merely walked along the deck, changed ends and the ferry never had to turn around.

Many of Sydney's early ferries were paddle-steamers, but the double-ended propeller-driven ferries took over the harbour in the late nineteenth and early twentieth century. The ferries were made at shipyards around the harbour, such as Mort's Dock where the classic Manly ferries like the *Barragoola* were built.

In 1899, most of Sydney's ferry services amalgamated to form Sydney Ferries Limited, which had become the world's largest ferry operator by 1932.

In 1928, the famous Scottish-built ferries *Dee Why* and *Curl Curl* arrived. Although they were identical, the *Curl Curl* was always slightly faster than her twin sister, in fact she was the fastest ferry ever to operate on the harbour. The grandest ferry of them all, the mighty *South Steyne*, arrived from Scotland in 1938.

Seventy metres in length, *South Steyne* was the world's largest operational steam ferry. She steamed the 22,000 kilometres from Leith, where she was built, to Australia in 1938 and crossed between Circular Quay and Manly over 100,000 times over her thirty-six-year career, carrying close to 100 million passengers. Unlike most of the great ferries of my childhood, which have been stripped and scuttled to provide homes for fish and adventures for recreational divers, she still exists, as a floating restaurant in Sydney.

The opening of the Sydney Harbour Bridge saw ferry travel drop from 30 million to 13 million passengers a year. The great era of the ferries was over.

The company struggled on for another twenty years but, but by the time World War II ended, cars were becoming a huge threat to the ferries' viability and, with the operators facing financial ruin, the New South Wales government intervened and agreed to take over Sydney Ferries Limited in 1951.

The Port Jackson & Manly Steamship Co was born and services were revised and revamped.

The famous advertisements encouraging the public to take the ferry to Manly for a day out were a great success. For many years from 1940, government buses all carried ads for the service, telling passengers that Manly was 'seven miles from Sydney, and a thousand miles from care'.

Manly had an amusement pier and two swimming beaches, one with a shark-proof net inside the harbour and the famous surf beach just a short stroll away down the Corso. Ferries also serviced Taronga Park Zoo and Luna Park. A ride on a ferry became part of a fun day out.

While recreational services were all well and good, commuters needed a faster service, so the company introduced hydrofoils in 1965.

An opportunity to compete with the increasingly congested roadways of Sydney saw RiverCat vessels arrive in 1992; they provided services to Parramatta and added over one million passengers to the ferry service annually. Purists, of course, argued that these new vessels were not 'real ferries'.

Sadly, the last nine ships added to the 'real' ferry fleet are not double-ended. The nine First Fleet Class ferries are single-ended and double-hulled, which means they are catamarans. Introduced in 1985, they are much smaller than the grand old ferries we knew as kids, but more manoeuvrable, perfect for fast short runs around the harbour with fewer passengers. They are all named after ships of the First Fleet.   **JH**

SYDNEY-SIDE
HENRY LAWSON

Lawson wrote this poem about taking a berth back to Sydney from Western Australia.

Where's the steward?—Bar-room steward? Berth? Oh, any berth
    will do—
I have left a three-pound billet just to come along with you.
Brighter shines the Star of Rovers on a world that's growing wide,
But I think I'd give a kingdom for a glimpse of Sydney-Side.

Run of rocky shelves at sunrise, with their base on ocean's bed;
Homes of Coogee, homes of Bondi, and the lighthouse on South
    Head;
For in loneliness and hardship—and with just a touch of pride—
Has my heart been taught to whisper, 'You belong to Sydney-Side.'

Oh, there never dawned a morning, in the long and lonely days,
But I thought I saw the ferries streaming out across the bays—
And as fresh and fair in fancy did the picture rise again
As the sunrise flushed the city from Woollahra to Balmain:

And the sunny water frothing round the liners black and red,
And the coastal schooners working by the loom of Bradley's Head;
And the whistles and the sirens that re-echo far and wide—
All the life and light and beauty that belong to Sydney-Side.

And the dreary cloud line never veiled the end of one day more,
But the city set in jewels rose before me from 'The Shore'.
Round the sea-world shine the beacons of a thousand ports o' call,
But the harbour-lights of Sydney are the grandest of them all!

THE MELBOURNE CUP

How Rivalry Created an Aussie Icon

The Melbourne Cup was the brainchild of Captain Standish, Chief
Commissioner of Police in Melbourne and Victoria Turf Club
Chairman at the time.

There was intense rivalry between Melbourne's two racing clubs,
the Victoria Turf Club and the Victoria Jockey Club. Up until the
1850s, the Melbourne races were run annually in the autumn but,
with the gold rushes bringing money into the city and a booming

economy, Melbourne became the largest and most prosperous city in Australia. Then the Victoria Turf Club decided to make its mark and hold a spring meeting—it was a masterstroke!

The Cup was first run in November 1861 at Flemington. The new race attracted top colonial horses from the parent colony of New South Wales, including the winner, Archer. This established a great Cup tradition of interstate rivalry, or inter-colonial rivalry as it was back then.

One of the main reasons for the Cup being established was to assert Melbourne's superiority over Sydney both as a city and sporting capital. Victorians were keen to establish Melbourne as the sporting capital, as well as the financial capital, of all the colonies.

So the Victoria Turf Club announced the running of a great new race. It was to be an egalitarian affair with the best horses carrying extra weight to make the race more equal. The trophy was a gold watch and the prize money of £710 was the most ever put up for a race in the colonies.

A horse from parent colony New South Wales winning the great new race was exactly what was *not* supposed to happen. When the unthinkable *did* happen a wonderful tradition of myths, legends and larger-than-life history developed around the Cup right from the start.

The story of Archer's two victories in the first two Cups is the stuff of legend. He is supposed to have walked from his home near Nowra to Melbourne twice, but the truth is that Archer went by steamship from Sydney to Melbourne three times to compete in Victorian Spring races, in 1861, 1862 and 1863.

Etienne de Mestre's horses usually boarded the steamer at Adam's Wharf near his property at Terara, on the Shoalhaven River. Floods in 1860 altered the course of the river channels and made navigation dangerous. So, from 1860 to 1863, horses were walked to the wharf at Greenwell Point 13 kilometres to the east. This may be the origin of the 'walking to Melbourne' myth. There is no doubt Archer went by steamship to Melbourne or Sydney or Newcastle to race; all racehorses did the same.

Etienne de Mestre was to upset the Melbourne owners and bookmakers just as his horse upset the local champion and race favourite, Mormon.

Archer won the first Cup convincingly by six lengths from Mormon. Seventeen horses started and a dreadful fall resulted in two being killed. A crowd of some 5000 saw the race and de Mestre, who had prepared his horse for the race away from prying eyes at St Kilda, backed Archer from ten to one into six to one and made a killing, taking untold amounts of Victorian 'gold' back to New South Wales.

The irony of a New South Wales horse winning a race organised to display Victorian superiority was reinforced when Archer started favourite and won again the following year, this time defeating Mormon by eight lengths in spite of carrying 64.4 kilograms.

A further irony, which modern race goers may not realise, is that there was no prize at all for running second back then.

The story of how Archer missed running in a third Melbourne Cup is also part of the Cup legend. Although Archer was given the massive weight of 71.6 kilograms by the handicapper in 1863, de Mestre accepted by telegram on the due date. While that particular day was a normal working day in New South Wales, however, it was a holiday in the colony of Victoria and the telegram was not delivered until the following day and the entry was not accepted. All the interstate entrants pulled out in protest and only seven local horses ran.

It is another delightful irony that the public holiday that enabled this act of unbridled inter-colonial perfidy to be perpetrated was Separation Day, the day that Victoria celebrated its official separation from New South Wales in 1851.

The debacle of the third Melbourne Cup had positive results. The two Melbourne racing clubs, realising that parochialism was not the best policy, merged to form the Victorian Racing Club and the Cup recovered its prestige and went on to become our number one sporting event.   **JH**

THE MELBOURNE CUP
LESBIA HARFORD

I like the riders
Clad in rose and blue;
Their colours glitter
And their horses, too.
Swift go the riders
On incarnate speed.
My thought can scarcely
Follow where they lead.
Delicate, strong, long
Lines of colour flow,
And all the people
Tremble as they go.

BLIND FREDDY

There are two main theories about the derivation of the Aussie
term 'Blind Freddy'.

In Aussie slang, Blind Freddy is someone who is rather stupid
and simple-minded. When a thing is glaringly obvious to one
and all, we say, 'Even Blind Freddy could see that!' The 'blindness' implied by the phrase is more the metaphorical kind, about
understanding rather than physical blindness.

One story is that Blind Freddy was a blind street hawker in
Sydney in the 1920s—but there is absolutely no documented
evidence of that being true.

Blind Freddy was, in fact, an upper class, titled Englishman, just
the kind of bloke that Aussies like to sneer at and use as the butt
of jokes. He was the archetypal Pommy twit whose incompetence
was so famous that bushrangers and members of the public named
him Blind Freddy.

Sir Frederick William Pottinger was born in 1831 in India,
second son of Lieutenant-General Sir Henry Pottinger of the East
India Co. Educated privately and at Eton, Pottinger purchased

a commission in the Grenadier Guards in 1850 and served in England until 1854. He lost much of his adoring mother's wealth on the racecourse, succeeded his father as second baronet in 1856 and soon squandered his inheritance.

Forced by debt to leave England, he migrated to Sydney. After failing on the goldfields, he joined the New South Wales police force as a mounted trooper. A superb horseman, he spent the next few years on the gold escort between Gundagai and Goulburn.

Pottinger kept his title secret, but in 1860 it was discovered by the inspector-general of police and promotion came rapidly to clerk of petty sessions at Dubbo and then assistant superintendent of the Southern Mounted Patrol. Under the 1862 Police Regulation Act, Pottinger was appointed an inspector of police for the Western District. In April 1862, he arrested Ben Hall on a charge of highway robbery, but Hall was acquitted.

Soon afterwards, Hall and Frank Gardiner and their gang robbed the Lachlan escort of some £14,000. Pottinger remained on the trail for a month and arrested two of the bushrangers, but they escaped several days later in a gun battle. In August, Pottinger and a party of police surrounded the house of Gardiner's mistress, Kate Brown, but the bushranger escaped when Pottinger's pistol misfired.

Pottinger arrested a young boy on suspicion of being an accomplice and allowed him to remain in the lockup without food and water. He died in custody in March 1863 from gaol fever. Pottinger and Constable Hollister also burned down Ben Hall's homestead.

Ben Hall blamed Pottinger for turning him into a criminal through his sheer incompetence and failure to catch the bushranger Frank Gardiner.

Hall said,

> Pottinger arrested me on Forbes racecourse last year and I was held for a month in gaol, an innocent man . . . Then I was arrested for the mail coach robbery and held another month before I was let out on bail. When I came home, I found my house burned down and cattle perished of thirst, left locked in yards. Pottinger

has threatened and bullied everybody in this district just because he can't catch Gardiner.

Early in January 1865, hoping to lure Ben Hall and John Dunn into the open, Pottinger rode in the Wowingragong races in breach of police regulations and was dismissed from the police force on 16 February 1865. On 5 March 1865, at Wascoe's Inn in the Blue Mountains on his way to Sydney to seek redress through official channels, Pottinger accidentally shot himself in the upper abdomen while boarding a moving coach. He died on 9 April 1865. He was buried at St Jude's Anglican Church, Randwick.

So there is the true derivation of the term 'Blind Freddy', it was Sir Frederick William Pottinger—Blind Freddy could see that!

JH

BURKE AND WILLS

The 'Dig' Saga

On 20 August 1860, Robert O'Hara Burke led an expedition of sixteen men out of Melbourne in an attempt to be first to cross the continent from south to north.

The idea was to open up a route by which the new-fangled invention of the telegraph line could be connected via Java to Europe, to explore the possibility that there was an inland sea, and to discover a possible route for a railway.

An added incentive was a £2000 reward for being the first to survey a route north; Charles Sturt and John Stuart were already planning similar journeys from Adelaide.

Burke was to lead the expedition with George James Landells, who had brought the camels and drivers to Australia from India, as second in command and William John Wills as surveyor. They took a two-year supply of food, as well as beds, hats, buckets and eighty pairs of shoes.

Landells quit the expedition at Menindee and Wills became second in command. Menindee became the headquarters for the expedition.

At the Darling River, William Wright and Charles Gray joined the crew and led them to Coopers Creek where, on 11 November, they set up base camp. It was at this point things began to go wrong.

After a long wait at the base camp for the others to reach them with additional supplies, an impatient Burke decided to leave with Wills, King and Gray anyway and worry about the additional supplies when they returned.

They finally reached the mangroves and could hear the ocean in the distance, so they turned back.

Arduous conditions, intense summer heat, and problems with dysentery and health delayed their return from the Gulf, which they reached in February 1861, and the party waiting at the base camp left just nine hours before they arrived back, leaving buried supplies under a tree beside the creek after carving 'DIG' into it.

The tree at Coopers Creek with its inscription is now a national monument.

Gray had died of dysentery on the return journey from the Gulf and Burke, Wills and King survived for two months at the site before deciding to attempt to reach Mount Hopeless Station 250 kilometres to the west.

They left a note explaining what they were doing in the hole where the supplies had been, but didn't alter the message carved on the tree.

When the relief party came back no one thought to look and see if the supplies were gone and the note was not found. Burke and Wills died in the desert and King was finally found and helped by Aborigines. He was later found by a search party and returned to Melbourne where he died in January 1872 aged thirty-one. His grave is in the Melbourne Cemetery.

There is a monument to Burke at Castlemaine in the goldfields area of Victoria where he was a superintendent of police up until the time he led the expedition.

There is also a large monument to the explorers in Melbourne.

Robert O'Hara Burke was born in 1821 and educated in Galway, Ireland; he served as a captain in the Austrian Army until 1848 when he joined the Irish Police Force. He came to Tasmania in

1853 and later worked in Beechworth and Castlemaine in Victoria as a policeman and superintendent until the 1860 expedition. He was forty when he died.

William John Wills was a doctor and surveyor. Born in Devon, England, he and his brother Thomas left for Australia in 1852, arriving in Melbourne on 3 January 1853. He began work as a surveyor with the Surveyor of Crown Lands. He accompanied Burke as the official surveyor for the ill-fated expedition, which cost him his life, aged twenty-seven.   **JH**

NED KELLY

Villain or Hero?

There are two versions of the Ned Kelly story.

While at school, Ned saved a seven-year-old boy from drowning and received a silk sash for his courage. At the age of twelve, he was forced to quit school to become the family breadwinner after the death of his father, but despite this he educated himself and was known for his good use of language and fine sense of humour. He was a great horseman and won the unofficial boxing championship of Northern Victoria by defeating Isaiah 'Wild' Wright in twenty rounds at Beechworth.

Ned claimed the law was unfair and picked on the poor; he and his relatives began to pay back the local wealthy landowners by rustling their cattle. Constable Alexander Fitzpatrick sexually assaulted Kate Kelly and was wounded by a gunshot to the wrist. Fitzpatrick swore he'd pay the Kelly family back and his false report about the incident led to Kelly's mother being jailed for three years. Ned wrote his famous Jerilderie letter to make known his side of the story.

Historian Malcolm Ellis, however, described Ned Kelly as 'one of the most cold-blooded, egotistical, and utterly self-centred criminals who ever decorated the end of a rope'.

In 1869, Ned was arrested for an alleged assault on a Chinese pig and fowl trader, with the delightful name of Ah Fook, and held for ten days on remand. The next year, he was arrested and held in custody for seven weeks as a suspected accomplice of Harry Power, the bushranger.

In 1870, Kelly was convicted of summary offences and imprisoned for six months. Soon after release, he was sentenced to three years' imprisonment for receiving a mare knowing it to have been stolen. In 1874, he was discharged from prison. His mother married George King and Ned joined his stepfather in stealing horses.

The Kellys were rarely out of trouble with the law. Ned's younger brother, James, was sentenced to five years' imprisonment for cattle stealing in 1873; released in 1877, he went to Wagga Wagga where he was sentenced to ten years' imprisonment for stealing horses. The third brother, Dan, had been sentenced to three months' imprisonment in 1877 for damaging property and, soon after his release in 1878, a warrant was issued for his arrest for stealing horses.

Sergeant Kennedy and Constables Lonigan, Scanlon and McIntyre set out to capture Ned and Dan. They camped at Stringybark Creek where Ned saw them. The Kelly Gang surprised the camp and, when Lonigan drew his revolver, Ned shot him dead. McIntyre surrendered. When Kennedy and Scanlon returned, they did not surrender when called on, and, in an exchange of shots, Ned killed Scanlon and mortally wounded Kennedy. Ned later shot him in the heart, claiming it was an act of mercy. McIntyre escaped to Mansfield and reported the killings.

There are also two ways of seeing the Jerilderie letter.

The letter was written before the Kellys' raid on the Riverina town of Jerilderie in February 1879, and one reason for the raid was to deliver the letter to the newspapers. After robbing the bank, Kelly sought out the town's newspaper editor, who was nowhere to be found. The bank's accountant, Edwin Living, offered to accept the letter and pass it on. Kelly gave it to him saying, 'Mind you get it printed, or you'll have me to reckon with next time we meet.'

Undeterred, Living ignored the order and the letter was sent to Melbourne. It was returned to Edwin Living after Kelly's execution. The letter remained in private hands until it was donated to the Victorian State Library in 2000.

Approximately 8000 words long, the letter is Ned Kelly's 'manifesto' and passionately articulates his pleas of innocence and desire for justice for the poor Irish selectors of Victoria's north-east. The letter outlines Ned Kelly's troubled relations with the police and offers his version of the events at Stringybark Creek, where three policemen were killed in October 1878.

Much of the letter is an articulate and reasonable refutation of the police evidence against Ned—but it also has a ring of Irish 'terrorist' about it and an illogical hatred of any authority:

> A Policeman is a disgrace to his country, not alone to the mother that suckled him . . . he is a rogue in his heart, but too cowardly to follow it up without having the Force to disguise it. Next, he is a traitor to his country, ancestors and religion, as they were all Catholics before the Saxons. Since then they were persecuted, massacred, thrown into martyrdom and tortured beyond the ideas of the present generation.

There are even two versions of Ned's last words. Some claim he said 'So, it has come to this.' Most of us prefer the other reported last words, the more poignant and philosophical 'Such is life.'

Ned Kelly's bones were positively identified in 2012 using DNA from his sister's great grandson. The skull claimed to be his proved to be someone else's. He was buried privately by his family in 2013 after the bones were returned to them.   JH

NED KELLY
ANONYMOUS

Ned Kelly was born in a ramshackle hut,
He'd battled since he was a kid:
He grew up with bad men and duffers and thieves,
And learnt all the bad things they did.

Now down at Glenrowan they held up the pub,
And were having a drink and a song,

When the troopers rolled up and surrounded the place:
The Kellys had waited too long.

Some say he's a hero and gave to the poor.
While others, 'A killer,' they say;
But to me it just proves the old saying is true,
The saying that crime doesn't pay.

Yet, when I look round at some people I know.
And the prices of things that we buy;
I just think to myself, well perhaps, after all,
Old Ned wasn't such a bad guy.

THE ASHES

The first test was played in 1877 between the touring Englishmen and a Combined Australian XI . . . what is significant about that?

Well, there was no 'Australia' in 1877. Cricket gave us an Aussie identity twenty-four years before we were a nation and it had a huge effect on national spirit, even though only three states were represented in the team: New South Wales, Victoria and Tasmania.

British teams had toured here from the 1850s, but had always played against teams of seventeen or fifteen players from each separate colony; in 1866, an Aboriginal team toured the UK, and did quite well.

New South Welshman Charles Bannerman set two records in the first test ever played and one will never be beaten, although the other might be. He scored the first run in test history and scored sixty-seven per cent of the runs in an innings—he made 165, retired hurt.

There was controversy right from the beginning. Due to the bitter inter-colonial rivalry that existed at the time, the two best bowlers in the country refused to play. Victorian Frank Allen decided to go to the Warrnambool Show instead and New South Wales bowler Fred Spofforth would not bowl to the Victorian wicketkeeper Jack Blackham and refused to play.

There's also an irony in our first test team's make up—seven of the Australian team were born in Britain, including Bannerman!

The next year, a combined team, including Spofforth, paid their own way to the UK and destroyed W.G. Grace's MCC side at Lords, bowling them out for 33 and 19. In this match, Spofforth gained his nickname, the Demon Bowler.

Sadly, this match was not given 'Test' status.

A total of eight tests were played before 1882—seven in Australia and one in the UK. Australia won four tests, England two and two were drawn.

In 1882, England lost at home for the first time and Spofforth won the test for Australia, taking 7 for 44. He bowled his last eleven overs for two runs and four wickets and Australia won by eight runs.

After the match the following poem was published in *Punch*:

Well done, Cornstalks! Whipt us fair and square,
Was it luck that tript us? Was it scare?
Kangaroo Land's 'Demon', or our own
Want of 'devil', coolness, nerve, backbone?

Also, a mock obituary was famously inserted in the *Sporting Times*, which read:

In Affectionate Remembrance of ENGLISH CRICKET, which died at the Oval on 29th AUGUST, 1882, Deeply lamented by a large circle of sorrowing friends and acquaintances R.I.P. N.B.—The body will be cremated and the ashes taken to Australia.

This was the beginning of the Ashes legend.

When the 8th Earl of Darnley, Ivo Bligh, led the English team to Australia in the following English winter, the English press joked that he was going to 'bring back the ashes'.

When his team won two of the three official tests, a group of Melbourne ladies, including Bligh's future wife, Florence Morphy of Beechworth in Victoria, and Lady Clarke, who had, along with her husband, entertained the English team in Melbourne, made a presentation to him of a terracotta scent bottle, which contained some ashes.

In 1998, Darnley's eighty-two-year-old daughter-in-law said they were the remains of one of her mother-in-law's veils, probably from a hat. MCC officials still claim, however, that it is 'ninety-five per cent certain' that the urn contains the ashes of a cricket bail, most likely one used in a social game between the English team and one chosen by Sir W.J. Clarke.

While 'bail' and 'veil' are very close in sound, and a misunderstanding is plausible, anyone understanding the nature of the joke presentation (and how hard it is to actually cremate a cricket bail and recover the ashes) will realise that the ashes are, in all likelihood, derived from something much easier to incinerate than a wooden bail. At least, that's my opinion.

The Countess of Darnley presented the urn to the MCC after her husband's death. She died in August 1944. Replicas of the urn are often used as trophies for the Ashes Series but the original remains with the MCC in London. **JH**

SACKCLOTH AND–
C.J. DENNIS

Ashes? What ashes? Please don't talk; I'm busy.
Strange how the work piles up to worry you.
Don't turn that wireless on! It makes me dizzy—
I never listen when there's work to do . . .
What's that? Heard I'd been listening all the week?
Who said so? Lot of rot some people speak.

What ashes are you harping on so sadly?
You had a fire? . . . Oh, cricket? Yes. A game.
When I was young I played it not so badly;
But now—well, watching it is rather lame.
Besides, there's work to do; and life is short.
Australians give far too much time to sport.

Far too much time—what ashes? Oh, we've lost 'em.
Well, fancy that. But does it matter much?
A few old ashes? Think how much it cost 'em
In energy and nervous strain and such,
While serious things—what's that? I didn't get—
Oh! So you heard I'd lost a heavy bet?

Well—yes; I did. I mean I—had forgotten.
And listened-in? Well—yes; for quite a while.
Excited? Me? Aw, well; I did feel rotten.
The ashes?—Oh, good lord, man! Raise a smile!
Why that was yesterday. So brighten up.
Ashes!—What's doing in the Davis Cup?

NELLIE MELBA

Nellie Melba was a Melbourne girl. Born Helen Porter Mitchell in 1861, she was the eldest of ten children. Her dad was a builder and actually built Scots Church Melbourne where she sang as a child in the 1870s, and where her state funeral was held, in 1931.

When she was twenty, the family moved to Mackay where her dad bought a sugar mill and she married a baronet's son, Charles Armstrong. They had a son, but then she became bored and left for Melbourne to be a professional singer. The rest is history.

Melba helped the careers of many younger singers. She taught for many years at the Conservatorium in Melbourne, which is named after her, and mentored and promoted some promising young opera singers, including Florence Austral, Gertrude Johnson and Louise Homer.

Yet she was, in the words of the late John Cargher, 'the true traditional prima donna with all the temperament, backbiting, social climbing and spontaneous generosity expected of a diva.'

Melba was a ruthless networker who used adultery, business connections and powerful friends to get ahead and destroy the careers of her rivals. When her husband threatened divorce action, naming the Duke of Orleans as co-respondent in 1890, he was 'talked out of it'. The Duke went on a two-year safari in darkest Africa, but his influence had already helped Melba to attain stardom in the major opera houses of Europe.

Peter Dawson once remarked that, as far as singing at Covent Garden was concerned, any talented young soprano who seemed a threat to Melba 'hadn't a chance of getting in with a tin-opener.'

Blanche Marchesi, the daughter of Mathilde Marchesi, the woman who 'discovered' Melba in Paris, said of Melba,

> She was the worst woman I ever knew . . . Melba's jealousy ruined many lives . . . Some powerful, invisible spirits were hard at work to eliminate artists who might easily have settled in the hearts of the public . . . It is no exaggeration to say that Melba ruled the Edwardian musical and social world with a will of iron.

Oddly, Melba often sang secondary roles to other female singers in major operas, like *Carmen*. But it was always when she knew she could either upstage the lead or when the other singers were no threat to her style of singing.

If she wanted to unsettle a young singer singing a secondary role to her, she would stand in the wings and sing over them so they could hear but the audience could not.

The Polish soprano Janina Korolewicz-Wayda said Melba was, 'by nature unpleasant, off-handed and brutal, very sure of herself, conceited and spoilt.'

All her help and support and mentoring of others came after she had finished her endless farewell tours and no longer felt threatened by young talent.

Sadly, she died, in St Vincent's Hospital Sydney, of septicaemia caused by a botched face lift in Europe when she was sixty-nine. She was attempting to get back to her beloved Melbourne but was too ill to travel the last leg of the journey.

Melba is remembered by a highway, a suburb, two desserts and a conservatorium. She released over one hundred records and helped to establish the popularity of the gramophone.   **JH**

WHEN ENRICO SLIPPED NELLIE THE SAUSAGE

One of the few people who ever got the better of Melba was the great tenor, Enrico Caruso, a man she despised as 'common, coarse and uncultivated' although she realised his importance to her as a partner on stage.

Performing with her in *La Bohème* one night, Caruso, as a joke, took a hot sausage from the backstage buffet and slipped it into her hand as he took it to sing the famous words '*Che gelida manina, se la lasci riscaldar*' (Your tiny hand is frozen, let me warm it).

Melba never spoke a friendly word to the 'vulgar Italian' again.

Legend has it that as Melba, disgusted, threw the offering aside as surreptitiously as possible and began to sing, Caruso whispered, 'You English women don't like the sausage?'

Perhaps he should have asked the Duke of Orleans.   **JH**

MELBA
C.J. DENNIS

Written 6 February 1931, the day after Melba's death.

Born to the sun and smiling skies,
And bird-songs to the morning flung,
To joyousness that never dies
In hearts that stay for ever young—
'Twas here, beneath the shining trees,
She paused to learn the magic rune
Of those unlaboured ecstasies
That keep a weary world in tune.

The grey thrush fluting by the nest,
The golden whistler trilling high—
Their gifts she captured and expressed
In magic notes that may not die.
Then to the old, grey world she gave,

Exultingly, at Art's command,
In songs that live beyond the grave,
Her message from a bright, young land.

With sheer exuberance of Art,
Won from that happy, feathered throng,
She poured our sunshine from her heart,
Translated into magic song.
And tho', alas, the singer dies,
Who bade old continents rejoice,
Not ever from our sunlit skies
Departs the memory of her voice.

A.B. (BANJO) PATERSON

We all know 'The Banjo' as the man who wrote two famous poems and a song. But there are so many other elements to Andrew Barton Paterson's life apart from being the author of 'Clancy', 'Snowy River' and 'Waltzing Matilda'. He was a remarkable man.

I guess most people think Paterson was born and raised in the bush, but he lived there on the family property for just the first decade of his life and left home in 1874, at the age of ten, to live with his literary-minded grandmother in Sydney and attend Sydney Grammar School.

After leaving school, he trained to become a solicitor, and started writing poetry about current affairs, sporting events and tragic bush tales and sending them to *The Bulletin*. His first published poems were about the Sudan War, the Melbourne Cup and a lost child dying in the bush.

He was a very 'sporty' type and a very good rider. He always said the broken arm he suffered as a child was his secret; his shortened arm gave him a light touch on the reins. His 'nurse' was an Aboriginal girl who was too scared to tell the family she'd dropped the baby and the arm had to be treated in several painful operations years later.

Banjo was known as Barty to family and friends; he used the name of a station racehorse as his nom de plume, The Banjo.

Even after 'The Man From Snowy River' caused a stir in *The Bulletin*, no one knew who The Banjo was until his first book was released. Later he was so famous that the pen name The Banjo was shortened to Banjo and added to his name.

He played in the first New South Wales polo team ever assembled and they defeated Victoria 2–0. He won the Polo Challenge Cup, a race for polo ponies, at Rosehill racetrack in 1892. He was a member of the Sydney Hunt Club and rode at Randwick and Rosehill as an amateur jockey.

Paterson was a solicitor by trade and helped Henry Lawson and Breaker Morant with legal matters at times. For six years he was engaged to the daughter of the head of the law firm he worked for, but the marriage never happened and it was many years before he married someone else. He became bored as a solicitor and later worked as a journalist, editor and broadcaster.

He travelled to distant parts of Australia and the Pacific and wrote articles on pearl fishing, hunting, new colonies, racing and many other things.

As a war correspondent at the Boer War, Paterson developed sympathy for the Boers and became opposed to the war.

In 1914, Paterson enlisted, at the age of fifty-one, to fight in World War I and was disappointed when he was made an ambulance driver on the Western Front. He asked to do something more useful and was put in charge of the 2nd Remount Division, in charge of bringing horses from Australia via India to the war. He became a major, saw service in the Middle East and became quite ill, but continued serving until the end of the war.

Paterson travelled to Britain and China and kept writing and broadcasting until his death in 1941.

He was never a part of the bohemian group of writers at *The Bulletin*, but he met Conan Doyle, was friendly with Rudyard Kipling and developed a friendship with artist Norman Lindsay— they went for weekend rides 'through the bushland'—at Cremorne, which is now an inner suburb of Sydney!   **JH**

BANJO
TED HARRINGTON

Don't tell me that The Banjo's dead—oh, yes, I've heard the tale—
But Banjo isn't dead at all, he's caught the Western Mail.
He has a lot of friends you know, among the western men,
He wants to look into their eyes and clasp their hands again;
He longs to spend some quiet nights beneath the western stars
And hear the evening wind again among the green belars.
So if they tell you Banjo's dead just say that it's a lie:
He comes from where they breed 'em tough and Banjo will not die.

They say that Clancy sent him word, he's at the Overflow,
With many more old mates of his who knew him long ago.
The man from Snowy River's there, from Kosciuszko's side,
Who brought the wild mob in alone and taught them how to ride.
He's got his mountain pony, too, as tough and wiry yet
As when he chased the brumby mob and colt from old Regret.
Another chap, now what's his name? He comes from Ironbark,
He thought the barber cut his throat and didn't like the lark.

All these old mates of his are there, with others on the way,
And when he got a call from them, well, how could Banjo stay?
There's Gundagai and Saltbush Bill, a rough and rugged pair,
I bet that there will be some fun when Banjo meets them there.
Old Trooper Scott is coming, too, to represent the force,
And Andy Regan (or his ghost) on Father Riley's horse.
They're making for the Overflow, and when they all arrive,
You'll see that Banjo isn't dead, he's very much alive.

Then glasses clink, and healths are drunk, and many a tale is told
Of roving days and droving days that never will grow old.
The seasons come, the seasons go, and little here abides,
But good old Banjo will not die as long as Clancy rides.
As long as bushmen love a horse or wild, black swans go by,
As long as there's a Southern Cross, the Banjo will not die.
So send the joyous news abroad, through hut and shearing shed,
And tell the bushmen not to grieve, for Banjo is not dead!

WATTLE AND WARATAH

The bush was grey a week today,
Olive green and brown and grey,
But now it's sunny all the way,
For Oh! the Spring has come to stay
With blossom for the Wattle.

Veronica Mason

Acacia pycnantha, Golden Wattle, is a shrub or small tree which grows 4 to 8 metres tall. The brilliant yellow, fragrant flowers make it a popular garden plant. It is moderately frost tolerant and grows well in a wide range of soils providing drainage is effective, but tends to be short-lived in cultivation. It has become a pest in South Africa and in the Stirling Ranges in Western Australia. It is our national flower.

The approach of Federation brought the desire for national symbols. In 1891 a *Melbourne Herald* reader, David Scott, advanced fourteen reasons why Wattle should be the national emblem, suggesting that Golden Wattle, *Acacia pycnantha*, had 'the highest value' because of its importance at that time to the Australian leather industry, which used the tannin-laden bark of that particular species in the tanning process.

Archibald Campbell founded the Wattle Club in Victoria in 1899 to promote Wattle Day. He said 'by numbers, the Wattle is almost exclusively Australian, and should undoubtedly be our National Flower.' Wattle Day was celebrated in Sydney in 1909. Victoria and South Australia participated in 1910, and Queensland in 1912. In 1992, 1 September was formally declared National Wattle Day by the Minister for the Environment, Ros Kelly, at the Australian National Botanic Gardens in Canberra.

The adoption of the wattle as the national flower was confirmed by its introduction into the design of the Australian arms in 1912. But *Acacia pycnantha* was not proclaimed the national floral emblem until 1988, at the National Botanic Gardens by Hazel Hawke.

Many, like botanist R. Baker, advocated the waratah, *Telopea speciosissima*, as the national flower. He wrote: 'The expression "the land of the Waratah", applies to Australia and no other; it is Australia's very own. Africa has over one hundred native wattles, and it also occurs in America, East and West Indies and the Islands . . .'

The waratah, however, does not grow in all states of Australia. *Telopea speciosissima* is found naturally only in New South Wales. Other varieties are found in Victoria and Tasmania and the plant can be cultivated in most parts of Australia. So some other states opposed the waratah as a national flower.

The conflict which existed about the choice of the Australian national flower is seen in the inclusion of both waratah and wattle flowers as decoration on the three golden trowels used by Governor General Lord Denman, Prime Minister Andrew Fisher and Minister for Home Affairs King O'Malley, for the laying of foundation stones in Canberra, the national capital, on 12 March 1913.   **JH**

WARATAH AND WATTLE
HENRY LAWSON

Though poor and in trouble I wander alone,
With rebel cockade in my hat,
Though friends may desert me, and kindred disown,
My country will never do that!
You may sing of the Shamrock, the Thistle, the Rose,
Or the three in a bunch, if you will;
But I know of a country that gathered all those,
And I love the great land where the Waratah grows.
And the Wattle-bough blooms on the hill.

Australia! Australia! so fair to behold—
While the blue sky is arching above;
The stranger should never have need to be told,
That the Wattle-bloom means that her heart is of gold.
And the Waratah's red with her love.

Australia! Australia! most beautiful name,
Most kindly and bountiful land;
I would die every death that might save her from shame,
If a black cloud should rise on the strand;
But whatever the quarrel, whoever her foes,
Let them come! Let them come when they will!
Though the struggle be grim, 'tis Australia that knows
That her children shall fight while the Waratah grows,
And the Wattle blooms out on the hill.

SURF LIFESAVING

A 'Reel' Great Invention

Until 1902, swimming in the ocean in daylight was illegal in NSW. It was thought to be indecent. That year, William Gocher defied the law and swam in daylight at Manly Beach. The resulting court case caused the law to be abandoned.

Soon small groups of experienced, regular surfers began to form themselves into lifesaving bodies to assist those who needed to be rescued from an unfamiliar environment. As these clubs grew in size and numbers, the need for a united front to raise funds and seek assistance from local and state governments resulted in the New South Wales Surf Bathing Association being formed on 18 October 1907.

Although the Bondi Life Saving Club was not officially founded until a meeting was held at the Royal Hotel Bondi in February 1907, there was a well-organised group operating on the beach well before that date.

In 1906, Lyster Ormsby, of the Bondi Surf Bathers Club had an idea for a device to enable safer rescue operations at the beach and built a model from a cotton reel and two bobby pins of a portable horizontal reel for the rope. The first full-size reel was built by Sergeant John Bond of Victoria Barracks in Paddington, and was improved on in the same year by Sydney coachbuilder G.H. Olding, whose final design was used until 1993.

The reel allowed a lifesaver wearing a belt with a rope attached to reach a distressed swimmer. The crew on the beach could then pull them back to the beach. It required discipline and control to carry this out efficiently. The first surf lifesaving reel in the world was demonstrated at Bondi Beach on 23 December 1906.

Several weeks later, the reel was used for a rescue for the first time. *The Sydney Morning Herald* reported the event as, 'Another sensation at Bondi—a narrow escape of two boys':

> The surf bathers at Bondi had another exciting experience yesterday afternoon, when two lads, Rupert Swallow, a resident of Darlinghurst and Chas. Smith living at McMahon's Point, narrowly escaped losing their lives.
>
> About 3 o'clock a number of people on the beach noticed that the boys, both of whom were about 9 years old, had been carried out by the undertow, and that they were unable to make any headway towards the beach. The alarm was given, and immediately many willing hands were ready to grasp the lifeline and go to the assistance of the struggling boys. James McLeod, a resident of Park Parade Waverley, and Wm. Burns, of Mill Hill Road, Waverley, succeeded in bringing Swallow into safety; while James McCarthy, of Rowe Street, Darlington and Warwick Wilce, of Croydon, rescued Smith.
>
> When brought to the shore Smith was in a bad way, having lost consciousness, but Nurse Sweeney, of Quirindi, who happened to be on the scene, applied restorative measures, and shortly after both lads were able to return to their homes.

Little Chas Smith was indeed nine years old; he would celebrate his tenth birthday a month later and go on to become Sir Charles Kingsford-Smith, war hero, pioneer aviator, Australian legend, and the first person ever rescued by Lyster Ormsby's new-fangled lifesaving reel!

Surf lifesaving now has more than 80,000 members in more than 260 clubs around Australia. In New South Wales alone, over 58,000 members of 129 clubs protect 1590 kilometres of coastline and perform an average of 6500 rescues and treat 30,000 first aid cases each year.

Lifesaving competitions still include the use of the reel, but it was phased out of active service for rescues in 1994. Now rubber duckies (inflatable boats with outboard motors) carry out over fifty per cent of all rescues.   **JH**

CHARLES KINGSFORD-SMITH

Tragic and Troubled Hero

Smithy was one of seven children of William Smith and his wife Catherine Kingsford, whose family were well known in Queensland: her father was Mayor of Brisbane in 1876. William went into real estate in Canada in 1903 and worked as a clerk with the Canadian Pacific Railways before the family returned to live in Sydney at the end of 1906.

Not long after the family returned to Australia, Smithy, aged nine, became the first person to be rescued using the new lifesaving reel at Bondi Beach. Charles was partly educated in Vancouver, St Andrew's Cathedral Choir School, Sydney, and Sydney Technical High School. At sixteen, he was apprenticed to the Colonial Sugar Refining Co Ltd.

He was at home in both the USA and Canada and his record-breaking flight across the Pacific was, in fact, an American funded venture and the *Southern Cross* was an American registered aircraft.

Kingsford-Smith served in the first AIF at Gallipoli and on the Western Front before joining the fledgling Australian Flying Corps and, as second lieutenant with the Royal Flying Corps, was shot down and awarded the Military Cross 'for conspicuous gallantry and devotion to duty'. He had brought down four German planes before having several toes shot off when he was shot down. Promoted to lieutenant he served as an RFC instructor until the war ended. He then went to the USA to fly and perform stunts in a flying circus and in early Hollywood movies.

Smithy returned to Australia and flew in Western Australia. He formed a partnership in 1924 with fellow pilot Keith Anderson to form a trucking and aviation business.

Smithy then started raising money for the historic flight across the Pacific. The New South Wales government helped and so did the businessman Sidney Myer, but US oil magnate G.A. Hancock provided most of the money.

With Charles Ulm and two Americans, Harry Lyon and Jim Warner, Smithy took off from Oakland, California, on 31 May 1928. He flew via Hawaii and Suva to Brisbane, completing the historic crossing in 83 hours and 38 minutes of flying time. The fliers received subscriptions of over £20,000 and Smithy was awarded the Air Force Cross and appointed honorary squadron leader, Royal Australian Air Force.

Smithy was a controversial figure. First, Anderson, no longer a partner, sued unsuccessfully for part of the prize money from the flight across the Pacific. Then Smithy caused a scandal by divorcing and remarrying eighteen months later. His aviation company went broke after the *Southern Cloud* crashed in 1931, while taking mail to Melbourne. He was accused of costing the lives of two mates who died during the search for the *Southern Cross*, which he had crash-landed on a deserted beach in Western Australia in 1929. Some in the press said it was a publicity stunt to raise money for his flights. Smithy denied this and an inquiry exonerated him of any misdoing. He was also a member of the extreme right wing militaristic organisation known as the New Guard.

Sadly, fame did not stop his life from being troubled and full of financial worries and he was forced to keep breaking records to raise funds.

Smithy and Tom Pethybridge left England on 6 November 1935, attempting to break the record to Australia in the *Lady Southern Cross*, a Lockheed Altair single-engined aircraft. Smithy had not been well for some time and suffered severe headaches during the two-day flight to Allahabad. The next day, Jim Melrose, who was engaged in an attempt to break the solo Britain to Australia record, sighted the *Lady Southern Cross* over the Bay of Bengal.

'I could see jets of flame spurting from Smithy's plane's exhaust pipe,' Melrose said, 'and I was overcome by an eerie sensation as I watched.'

Despite a huge search, no trace was ever found of *Lady Southern Cross*. **JH**

KINGSFORD-SMITH
WINIFRED TENNANT

Ask the sun; it has watched him pass—
A shadow mirrored on seas of glass;
Ask the stars that he knew so well
If they beheld where a bird-man fell.
Ask the wind that has blown with him
Over the edge of the ocean's rim,
Far from the charted haunts of men,
To the utmost limits and back again.
Ask the clouds on the mountain height,
The echoes that followed him in his flight,
The thunder that prowls the midnight sky,
If a silvered 'plane went riding by.

If the birds could talk, would they tell of the fall
Of a god who winged above them all?
Of an eagle-man, by the world's decrees,
King of the blue immensities.

QANTAS

When World War I flying aces Paul McGinness and Hudson Fysh were given a job scouting out a route and air strips for the 1919 London-to-Sydney Great Air Race, they came into first-hand contact with the difficulties of getting around in the bush.

One hot Sunday afternoon in Cloncurry, driving to a picnic, McGinness met influential grazier, Fergus McMaster.

McMaster's car had broken an axle in the dusty bed of the Cloncurry River and he had walked to town for a replacement. The garage was closed, perhaps its owner was at the picnic, so McGinness cheerfully removed corrugated iron from the garage wall and found an axle.

He drove McMaster back to his car and helped the older man fix it.

The seeds of a future partnership were planted and, as a result, on 20 June 1920, McGinness and Fysh sat with McMaster at a glass-topped table in Brisbane's elegant Gresham Hotel to register a new airline company.

Still young, still feeling displaced by their war experience and too restless for ordinary occupations, McGinness and Fysh were determined to seize their chance. They tried a number of different names for the company and finally chose Queensland and Northern Territory Aerial Services Limited, QANTAS.

On 10 February 1921, the first board meeting was held at Winton, in the Winton Club, which is still there today. It was the only meeting held in Winton, as a decision was promptly taken to shift company headquarters to Longreach. It felt more prudent to be closer to that railhead, with easier access for passengers and spare parts.

On 21 May 1921, the first annual general meeting of shareholders was held at Longreach. The original paid-up capital was £8650. The rest is history, all thanks to a broken axle. JH

THE AUSSIE AIRLINE
JIM HAYNES

There's a hangar out at Longreach, a relic of the past,
That was first home to an airline that, it seems, was built to last.
An airline that was born upon a hot November day
In the year of 1920 and went on to show the way
To every other airline that you just might care to name,
The second oldest in the world, that's just one claim to fame.

The oldest airline anywhere they use the English tongue,
And the safest airline ever, though born when flight was young.
Born out of a necessity, in this great land of ours,
To lessen isolation, turn weeks and months to hours,
To join the city to the bush, to keep the flag unfurled,
And go on to join our isolated nation to the world.

Its symbol is an icon, the flying kangaroo,
It shows what good old Aussie ingenuity can do.
I'm sure Sir Hudson would be proud, that famous flying Fysh,
To see it flying safely still; so here's a final wish;
May QANTAS and the flying kangaroo fly on forever,
And safely bring the whole world, and Australians, together.

HOW TWO CHILDREN'S STORIES SAVED THE KOALA

The koala is a mostly nocturnal marsupial, averaging about 10 kilograms in weight. Koala is an Aboriginal word meaning 'no drink'. The koala only drinks when there is not enough moisture in the gum leaves. They used to be found throughout Australia and they can live in a variety of habitats, from coastal islands to dense eucalypt forests and inland woodland areas.

Koalas were widespread until the 1900s and were hunted indiscriminately until the 1920s when hunting was restricted. When the hunting season was reopened in Queensland in 1927, over 800,000 koalas were killed in less than a month.

Norman Lindsay's drawings and his children's story, *The Magic Pudding* (published in 1918), helped Australians see koalas as not just a food source, but it was New Zealander Dorothy Wall's story *Blinky Bill* that helped popularise the cause of the koala and helped to save our unique Aussie icon. After her famous children's books were published in 1933, there was a public outcry and this finally convinced state governments to shut down the hunting season and declare the koala a protected species.

Koalas look cuddly and fat but are actually long and lean. They share with humans the evolutionary feature of opposable thumbs and carry their own seating in a pad of fur and fat on their bottoms.

Now that eighty per cent of Australia's eucalypt forests have been cleared, koalas are once again a threatened species.   **JH**

THE COATHANGER

Although Uluru and the Opera House have, to a large extent, replaced the Sydney Harbour Bridge as the most recognisable Aussie icons—the history of the Coathanger is still a big part of Sydney's psyche.

A bridge from Dawes Point to Milson's Point was first proposed by Francis Greenway in 1815 and in the 1820s 'Commodore' Billy Blue ran his ferry across the stretch of water the bridge now spans.

After World War I, the plans were made by Dr J.C. Bradfield and officers of the New South Wales Department of Public Works. In 1922, the contract went to Dorman Long and Co of Middlesbrough in the UK and construction began in 1924.

Six million rivets were used in the construction and 800 homes were demolished to make way for the approaches. Sixteen workers died during the building of the bridge. In 1991, author Peter Corris wrote a murder mystery, *Wet Graves*, using those deaths as his subject.

The decision to build the bridge, which was so obviously needed, was not welcomed by one and all. The Country Party complained about the expense and said it was no good to their constituency because farmers couldn't use it to get produce to market. Lord Shelbourne called it 'an unnecessary monstrosity and great waste of money'. *The Bulletin* said it was 'built prematurely at wicked cost on borrowed money'.

The pylons were criticised in letters to the press as being 'useless and ugly'. They are certainly useless, as they perform no structural function, but they have become part of the Sydney landscape.

The opening in 1932 was surrounded by controversy. The Australian bishops objected to the opening ceremony being held during Easter week and Major de Groot, a furniture maker and member of the right wing paramilitary New Guard, objected to Labor Premier Jack Lang opening the bridge. He thought it should be a member of the royal family or the governor, so he famously rode past Lang and slashed the ribbon with his sword—but nothing happened. The cutting of the ribbon did not operate the mechanism for the fireworks and music. A workman watching Lang was to press a button. So the ribbon was re-tied and the ceremony went ahead after de Groot's arrest.

The weight of steel in the bridge is 52,800 tonnes and the span itself weighs 39,000 tonnes. The arch may rise or fall 18 centimetres due to heating or cooling.

Its initial three coats took 272,000 litres of paint and we all know that the painting of the bridge's 485,000 square metres of steel span never ends; the painters complete the task after three years of painting and 30,000 litres of paint, and they immediately start again.

The Harbour Bridge was a part of Sydney's culture from the day construction began. As kids, we had a favourite piece of nonsense verse:

One fine day, in the middle of the night,
The Harbour Bridge it caught alight.
The blind man saw it and was dismayed
And the dumb man rang the fire brigade.
One deaf fireman answered the phone,
Gathered the others and came on his own.
On the way to the fire he hit a dead cat,
Killed it again and squashed it flat.
He got to the bridge before he departed
And put out the fire before it started.   **JH**

'I SAW PHAR LAP'

The story of Phar Lap has been told many times, but then, it is a great yarn!

The 'Red Terror' is an Australasian icon and revered and adored both in New Zealand and Australia.

Phar Lap was a disinterested and lazy track worker as a young horse and kept growing until he stood at seventeen hands, so his trainer Harry Telford had him gelded.

Even so, he ran poorly at eight of his first nine starts as a late two year old and early three year old but finally showed a glimpse of what was to come by winning a Juvenile Maiden at Rosehill at his fifth start, after finishing last at his previous start.

He went on the first of his great winning jaunts by taking the Rosehill Guineas, AJC Derby, Craven Plate and VRC Derby before being sent out at even money favourite for the Melbourne Cup.

Phar Lap ran the same time for both derbies and broke Manfred's record by a quarter of a second. In the Cup, with only 7 stone 6 pounds (47 kilograms), he had to be ridden by lightweight jockey Bobby Lewis.

It is often mistakenly stated that Lewis took the mount from Phar Lap's 'regular jockey' Jim Pike, who could not make the weight. The truth is that the colt had been ridden in his first fourteen races by eight different jockeys, although Pike had ridden him in both derbies and would become his regular jockey, riding him at every one of his sixteen starts as a four year old—for fourteen wins. Pike rode the great chestnut thirty times in total, for twenty-seven wins and two seconds.

The 'Red Terror' could be a real terror to ride and he refused to settle for Lewis in the 1929 Cup. The jockey said later he just could not get the horse's head down or stop him reefing and pulling and so reluctantly he let him lead, only to be run down and finish third behind Nightmarch and Pacquito.

Nightmarch was the first good horse to be sired by Phar Lap's sire, Night Raid. He was from the 'outcast' stallion's first crop and was a year older than Phar Lap.

On his return to racing in the St George Stakes in the autumn, Phar Lap ran third behind Frank McGrath's great stayer Amounis, the only horse to beat him twice.

In the eighteen-month period starting from March 1930 and ending with his eighth placing, carrying 10 stone 10 pounds (68 kilograms), in the Melbourne Cup of 1931, the 'wonder horse' started thirty-two times for thirty wins and two seconds, winning every major race in Sydney and Melbourne from a mile (1.6 kilometres) to 2 miles (3.2 kilometres).

Those wins included the W.S. Cox Plate twice, two more Craven Plates to add to the one he won at the age of three, the Melbourne

Cup with ridiculous ease, carrying 62.5 kilograms and all the other classic races of the spring and autumn carnivals in both cities.

The great horse won weight-for-age races by twenty lengths and broke the existing records for all distances between a mile and a half (2.4 kilometres) and 2 miles (3.2 kilometres).

He started at prices like 14 to 1 on, and it is common knowledge that he remains the shortest priced horse to win the Melbourne Cup and the only ever odds-on winner. What people may not know is that he actually shut down the betting ring on no less than twelve occasions, when no bookmakers would field on the races he won. He also travelled to Adelaide and won two classic races there.

Jim Pike always said his greatest victory was when he took on the sprinters and beat them in the Futurity stakes at Caulfield on a bog track carrying 64.5 kilograms. He missed the start and then took off around the entire field to run down the good sprinter Mystic Peak.

Drama and sensation were part the great horse's career. He was shot at before winning the 1930 Melbourne Stakes (MacKinnon) and then hidden away at St Albans near Geelong before winning the Cup three days later. He almost emulated the greats of former eras, like his ancestor Carbine, by winning four major races over eight days, three major races in a week and four major races in a month several times.

Both his owner, David Davis, and his trainer, Harry Telford, have been accused of over-racing their champion and Davis has been criticised for starting Phar Lap, against Telford's wishes, in the Melbourne Cup of 1931 with the cruel weight of 68 kilograms and for taking the horse to America.

Davis, however, seems in retrospect to have been a fair-minded man. He was grateful to Telford for finding the horse and allowed him to remain as part owner for a modest £4000 when the lease expired. It was also Davis who had the great horse's skin, heart and skeleton returned to Australia after his tragic death. It is also worth remembering that Telford, who leased Phar Lap from Davis for the first three years of his career, had already won a Melbourne Cup with him, while Davis, who actually owned him, had not.

Myths develop quickly in racing and the truth is often forgotten when fiction and films are created from fact. Telford has been criticised for leaving young Tommy Woodcock in charge of the valuable champion in the USA, but the fact is that Telford's daughter had just died and he was organising her funeral.

It is also true that a team of four, which included jockey Bill Elliott and vet Bill Nielsen, travelled to the USA with Woodcock and Phar Lap. His owner, David Davis, who was an American, was also in the USA, managing the campaign.

It is a mark of Phar Lap's greatness that the VRC changed the weight-for-age rules in 1931 to include allowances and penalties, in an attempt to bring the great horse 'back to the field'. They also gave him a massive 10 kilograms over weight-for-age in the 1931 Cup.

Further testaments to Phar Lap's greatness are the sensation he caused in the USA and the ease of his win in the invitational Agua Caliente Handicap in Tijuana, Mexico, at his first start on dirt after a long sea journey and a 1300 kilometre road trip. He was also recovering from a bad stone bruise to a heel and raced in bar plates for the first time, and he broke the track record. That win, his only start outside the relatively minor racing arena of Australia, made him the third greatest stakes winning racehorse of all time, in the world.

Phar Lap's tragic death and the theories surrounding it have been well documented. The nation mourned and the autopsy showed a severe gastric inflammation from duodenitis-proximal jejunitis, a condition exacerbated by stress.

Later studies, as recently as 2008, showed the presence of arsenic in large quantities which has led to all sorts of theories, ranging from Percy Sykes' statement that all horses at that time had arsenic in their systems to theories of deliberate poisoning. Phar Lap had evidently been fed foliage cut down after being sprayed with arsenic-based insecticide.

Two things seem certain, the well-documented symptoms the horse suffered are totally consistent with duodenitis-proximal jejunitis, and there was a lot of arsenic in his system. The rest is conjecture.

Phar Lap's spectacular career has been continually documented and mythologised in books and films for eighty years, and his tragic end has been analysed and debated again and again.

Phar Lap was such a towering figure that the history of thoroughbred racing in Australia is divided into 'before' and 'after' Phar Lap. All champions since him have only ever been 'the best since Phar Lap'.

Comparing horses of different eras is silly, but people keep doing it. The exercise was described as 'folly' by the US *Blood-Horse Magazine*, which nevertheless in 1999 ranked the top hundred horses ever to race in America. The panel placed Phar Lap, on the strength of one start in Mexico, twenty-second.

When the findings were published, one of the panel recalled a conversation with Francis Dunne, who had been a placings judge at Agua Caliente and later a senior racing administrator in New York State. Dunne was asked, after Secretariat's Triple Crown win in 1973, whether Man O' War or Secretariat was the greatest horse of them all. He replied, 'Neither, I saw Phar Lap.'   **JH**

PHAR LAP
ANONYMOUS

How you thrilled the racing public with your matchless strength
    and grace;
With your peerless staying power and your dazzling burst of pace.
You toyed with your opponents with a confidence so rare,
Flashing past the winning post with lengths and lengths to spare.
No distance ever proved too great, no horse or handicap,
Could stop you winning races like a champion—Phar Lap.

With a minimum of effort you would simply bowl along
With a stride so devastating and an action smooth and strong.
And you vied with the immortals when, on Flemington's green track,
You won the Melbourne Cup with nine-stone-twelve upon your back.

How the hearts of thousands quickened as you cantered back old
    chap,
With your grand head proudly nodding to the crowd that yelled,
    'Phar Lap'.

Who that saw it could forget it—how you won the Craven Plate?
When a mighty son of Rosedale, whom we'd justly labelled 'great',
Clapped the pace on from the start in a middle-distance race,
Just to test you to the limit of endurance, grit and pace.
He was galloping so strongly that the stands began to clap,
For it seemed as though your lustre would be dimmed at last,
    Phar Lap.

But you trailed him like a bloodhound till your nostrils touched
    his rump
Then your jockey asked the question and, with one tremendous jump,
Something like a chestnut meteor hurtled past a blur of black
And, before the crowd stopped gasping, you were halfway down
    the track,
And, the further that you travelled, ever wider grew the gap,
And you broke another record—one you'd set yourself, Phar Lap.

The hopes of all Australians travelled with you overseas,
Wishing to inspire you to further victories.
And at Agua Caliente you proved you were the best,
Then your great heart stopped beating—so they brought it home
    to rest.
And Australians won't forget you while the roots of life hold sap;
For the greatest racehorse that was ever foaled was you, Phar Lap.

CHESTY BOND

The Cartoon Hero with the Premier's Jaw

Aussie cartoons have been very successful—and Aussie cartoonists
were pioneers of both the single frame and strip cartoon.

Great artists like Nicholas Chevalier and Norman and Lionel
Lindsay drew cartoons for magazines like *Melbourne Punch* and

The Bulletin in order to make a living early in their careers and Norman Lindsay continued as a cartoonist until the demise of *The Bulletin* in the 1940s.

Felix the Cat, the world's first international cartoon superstar, was the brainchild of New York based Australian filmmaker and entrepreneur Pat Sullivan, although he was drawn by artist Otto Mesmer.

Ginger Meggs, Fatty Finn, Wally and the Major, The Potts, Bluey and Curly and *Uncle's Joe's Horse Radish* were all ground-breaking Aussie cartoon strips.

But there was another Aussie first in cartooning—we had the world's first advertising cartoon strip—*Chesty Bond*.

It all began in 1915 when American immigrant George Bond started importing underwear from the USA. After World War I, import shortages forced him to begin making clothing locally, in the inner city Sydney suburb of Camperdown.

All went well for George until the economic crash of 1929 sent him broke and he lost the company. The brand survived, however, and Bonds Industries began 1930 as a public company.

Having survived the Depression, the company needed a boost and they turned to J. Walter Thompson Advertising for help and ideas in 1938. The idea for the Chesty Bond character came from Ted Moloney and Syd Millar was commissioned to draw the iconic bronzed Aussie who was never seen without his Bond's singlet.

Syd Miller was told to draw Chesty as 'a kind, loveable, good-looking Aussie—strong but not the lumpy weight lifting type'.

After a few intermittent appearances, the strip was soon running three days a week from 1940 and was the world's first advertising comic strip, eventually running for over twenty years. Chesty, with his characteristically powerful jutting jaw and impressive physique, became a superhero when he pulled on his trusty Chesty Bond athletic vest.

As a result of the successful campaign, Chesty Bond became the archetypal Australian hero synonymous with Australian masculinity and an icon that was recognised Australia wide.

Chesty was so successful, appearing several times a week in syndicated newspapers across the land, that Syd Miller was commissioned to draw another 'advercartoon' for Scotch Tape in 1950. It was a cartoon bear who did amazing things with 'Bear Tape' and even had a slogan—'a little bear will fix it'.

Chesty made a comeback of sorts in the 1990s when Paul Mercurio danced with him in a television ad and Trevor Barnabas gave him a new degree of fame in the form of a very successful 18 footer yacht.

Although there are many who claim otherwise, Syd Miller always said that Chesty's famous jaw was the only part of the character modelled on a real person.

Whose chin was it?

Chesty's chin was modelled on that of the 'Big Fella'—controversial New South Wales Premier Jack Lang.   **JH**

SLIM DUSTY

Slim Dusty made 107 albums, won 37 Golden Guitar Awards and was an Aussie icon. He also had some great yarns about touring in the early days.

Slim was the most enthusiastic and energetic person I ever toured with. When we had shows in country towns, he was always first up and, as he knew I didn't party on after a show like some of the others, he'd sometimes tap on my motel room door and say, 'Come and I'll show you where we used to put up the tent in the old days.'

Slim would sit backstage and yarn until it was time for one of us to go on. He always saw the show in terms of a set structure with a female singer, comic, bush balladeer, maybe even a sight act in the old days, like a knife thrower or whip cracker or acrobats.

Once on tour I recall that he was so rapt in the story he was telling me that he forgot that I was there as part of the show. Slim and I knew each other in another context, as board members of the Country Music Association and, as we sat yarning backstage, Slim asked, 'Who's on now, the comic?'

I had to reply, 'Errr, no Slim —I'm the comic!'

Photographer John Elliott, who travelled more miles with Slim than most of the artists on the show in the last few years of Slim's career, has written some of the best stories about those days.

Slim's first tour was in 1954, from Sydney to Toowoomba and back. The show consisted of four people. The 'stars' were Slim and his wife Joy McKean, who was much more famous than Slim at that stage. Joy and her sister Heather, as The McKean Sisters, had their own radio show and magazine in the early 1950s.

The other two in the first touring show were guitarist Barry Thornton and whip cracker Larry Mason, who doubled as the other musician on bass. The tours were all about multi-tasking: setting up, selling tickets; there were no roadies then.

Slim and Joy had a 1938 Ford and a caravan. 'The caravan took four of us to lift,' Slim said, 'and we'd put it on the back of that poor old Ford and she'd just about lift off the ground.'

Usually, they just camped outside the halls where they performed, with some of the crew bunking down in the dressing rooms or in swags.

Now and then there was trouble with drunks and someone had to be the bouncer or 'chucker-outer'. Joy's Auntie Una was part of the show for many years and had a fearsome reputation. She joined the show to take care of front of house and look after the kids as the show got bigger.

Slim called Auntie Una 'the Best Bloody Bouncer in the Business' but the story I was told was that Auntie Una's reputation was achieved partly by mistake.

One night in a country hall, a bloke was being a nuisance. Auntie Una had chucked him out several times but he'd run around to another door to get back in again. When she ejected him on the third or fourth occasion, she ran to the other door and closed it from the inside. What she didn't know was that he was racing towards the door on the other side and, as she slammed the door shut, she flattened the poor bloke and broke his nose and knocked out a few teeth.

When the crowd rushed to see what was going on, there was the diminutive Auntie Una standing over an unconscious big lump of a bloke with a broken nose!

Slim never had audience trouble in that area again.

Barry Thornton's daughter, Meryl Davis, has terrific yarns about those days and remembers Auntie Una saving her life when she swallowed a threepence.

'She picked me up and shook it back out and saved my life,' said Meryl, 'I must have been three or four because I was sent off to school when I was five and left the tour. She was a fearsome lady!'

In later years, the show grew and Slim used better caravans and trucks. The famous Thunder and Lightning were two Internationals; Thunder was bigger than Lightning and they took the Slim Dusty Show all over Australia with Slim and Barry Thornton as the drivers.

When Slim took off his hat, he became a different person. Meryl remembers a story her father, Barry Thornton, told about one time he and Slim were repairing one of the trucks.

Slim was under one of the Internationals when a young reporter arrived and asked could he interview Slim Dusty.

Slim slid out from under the truck covered in grease and oil and dirt and said, 'He's not here, mate, come back in half an hour.'

He then went and cleaned up, put on the famous hat and waited for the reporter. They did the interview and the reporter never knew it was the same bloke.

Although they were stranded a few times, they never had many breakdowns.

'We were only ever held up twice on the track,' Slim remembered, 'once at Rowena, a little town south of Walgett with no pub—fancy being stuck for four days in a town with no pub.

'Another time we got stuck on a stretch up the top of Western Australia at a place called the Pardoo Sands, which was a big boggy flat below Roebourne.

'There were trucks and tourists in caravans all stuck there with us and luckily for them we always carried supplies of fruit juices, tinned meats and things under the bunks in the caravans. We ended up supplying a lot of people with a bit of tucker.'

Slim, and wife Joy, always felt close to truckies. 'We had a lot in common with the truck drivers in those early days. Just like the truckies, we had to really watch ourselves.

'Some of those roads were pretty isolated in the mid to late sixties; the truck stops were at the old-time stations. They were pretty wild and woolly places.'

Slim remembered one of the trips across the Nullarbor.

'We treasured Sunday nights when we'd pull our vans way off the road and park them in a circle.

'One of these camps I remember well. We were about 80 or 90 miles out of Norseman and we'd pulled off the road to have our night off.

'We had a good time, a barbecue and a few beers. The next afternoon in Norseman, one of the blokes on our tour said, 'I can't find my wallet, it must have fallen out when I was lounging around the fire last night.'

'We couldn't go back because we had a two and a half month tour ahead of us.

'Well, we did our tour and, on the way back, we camped at the same spot. We drove to the spot and the coals from our camp fire were still there and right next to them was the wallet, and the money was still there.   **JH**

THE OPERA HOUSE

Bennelong Point or Wynyard?

The Sydney Opera House is built on Bennelong Point, the east bank of Sydney Cove. Bennelong was an Aborigine who lived there after being captured by Governor Phillip in 1789 and taken to the UK in 1792. When he returned, he was rejected by his two wives and lived on James Squire's property at Ryde until he was killed in a tribal fight in 1813.

The first known concert on Bennelong Point was held in March 1791 when Bennelong and some friends provided an evening of entertainment for the Governor and his party.

Bennelong Point was a tidal island when the First Fleet arrived. The narrow strait was later filled in with rubble and connected to the shore when Francis Greenway built Fort Macquarie in 1817.

The fort was demolished in 1901 and a tram depot was constructed in the design of a fortress with ramparts in homage to the previous building. The depot operated from 1902 to 1955 and was demolished in 1958 to make way for the Opera House.

As early as 1947, Eugene Goossens, conductor of the Sydney Symphony Orchestra, had called for 'a musical home for a symphony orchestra and an opera company'. In 1955, New South Wales Premier, Joe Cahill, announced a competition for the design of 'an opera house'.

Out of 233 entries from thirty-two countries, Jørn Utzon won first prize in 1957 and work began in 1959. The first performance at the Opera House was a concert given for the workers by Paul Robeson in 1960, thirteen years before it opened. Utzon resigned from the project in 1966.

The first test concert, in December 1972, was the Sydney Symphony Orchestra conducted by Sir Bernard Heinze. The first opera staged was *War and Peace* by Prokofiev on 28 September 1973 and the first public concert in the Concert Hall the next evening was Birgit Nilsson singing Wagner with the Sydney Symphony Orchestra under Charles Mackerras.

On 20 October 1973, Queen Elizabeth finally opened the Opera House. The final cost was $102 million.

Premier Joe Cahill had to be talked out of building the opera house in 'a better location for transport', near Wynyard Station!

JH

AUSSIES AT WAR

This section merely contains a bunch of yarns—a mix of factual stories and apocryphal yarns about our involvement in the Boer War, World War I and World War II.

It's a grab bag of yarns about Australians at war in roughly chronological order. I have made no attempt to be comprehensive or to balance the stories, yarns and anecdotes into equal sections for each major conflict.

The only real invasion of our continent occurred with British settlement and we have no borders with any other nation. Yet Australia has a remarkably 'war-conscious' heritage. Perhaps this is because the Boer War and World War I occurred just before and after Federation. The Boer War was the first time we thought of our soldiers as 'Australian' rather than residents of separate colonies.

The experience at Anzac Cove has been called a defining moment for our nation, a baptism of blood and fire that gave birth to the concept of an Australia that was no longer a British colony but a nation apart whose attitudes and interests could be quite different from those of Britain.

In World War II, the threat of invasion emphasised our geographical distance from Europe and forced us to accept the idea that we were culturally different from Britain. Many of these yarns demonstrate that cultural difference

THE FIGHTING 29

The Boer War was the first time Aussies fought as 'Australians', as our nation federated and was born during the course of the conflict.

The first contingents sent to fight in South Africa were raised by the Australian colonies in response to the outbreak of war in 1899. Mostly these contingents were men in the militia of the various colonial forces.

The next lot to go were what were called the 'bushmen' contingents, recruited from more diverse sources and paid for by public subscription or by gifts from wealthy individuals.

The next groups to be recruited were the 'Imperial bushmen' contingents, which were raised in a similar way, but paid for by the government in London.

Then there were 'draft contingents', which were raised by the state governments after Federation on behalf of the new Commonwealth government, which as yet didn't have the infrastructure to do so.

A group of New South Wales horsemen had set off for London to train at the Cavalry School, Aldershot, in February 1899, and some of them helped defeat the Boers at Elandslaagte on 21 October 1899, as part of the Irregular Troops of the Imperial Light Horse.

The New South Wales Lancers landed at Cape Town on 2 November 1899. Most of this contingent joined General John French's force at Colesberg, in the Border District of the Cape Colony.

Twenty-nine of the Lancers, however, led by Lieutenant John Osborne, were sent as part of an advance force of seventy-two to take part in the Battles of Belmont and Graspan and went into action as part of Field Marshall Methuen's force on 23 November 1899.

Two days later, the same twenty-nine men were part of the follow-up action to Belmont, the hard-fought Battle of Graspan Siding. Methuen bungled both battles and there were heavy losses and fierce hand-to-hand fighting at Graspan. The Lancers held a small gully against a determined Boer advance and earned the nickname 'the Fighting 29'.

About 16,000 Australians fought in the Boer War. They were under British command and contingents were often broken up and attached to British forces.

Towards the end of the war, Australian Commonwealth horse contingents were raised by the new federal government. These contingents fought in the counter-offensive of 1900, when the Boer capitals fell, and then on through the guerrilla phases of the war, which lasted until 1902.

During the Boer War, 282 Australians died in action or from wounds sustained in battle, while 286 died from disease and another 38 died in accidents or of unknown causes.

Six Australians received the Victoria Cross during the fighting in South Africa.   **JH**

GET HOLD OF THAT BRUSH

There is an old yarn about Lord Kitchener visiting a small field hospital during the Boer War.

There were only four beds in the small canvas hospital situated behind the lines, and Kitchener decided to boost morale by cheering up the four soldiers who occupied the beds.

In company with the commanding officer and the Field Ambulance officer, Kitchener entered the tent and smiled at the soldier in the first bed.

'Hello there, young man,' said the Field Marshal, 'what regiment are you with?'

'South Lancashires, sir,' the soldier replied, briskly.

'And what seems to be the trouble with you?'

'Lost part of my leg and gangrene set in, sir,' was the reply.

'Dear, dear, that's no good at all,' replied Kitchener, 'and what is the treatment?'

'Take the tablets and scrub the affected parts three times a day with the brush, sir.'

'That's the way, lad, don't despair, eh? Tell me, what's your ambition now?'

'To get back into action and fight for Queen and country, sir.'

'Jolly good!' was the Field Marshall's reply, 'that's the spirit!'

The party moved to the next bed and found a very sad looking young soldier sitting up rather awkwardly, waiting to be addressed.

'Hello, lad,' said the Field Marshal, 'and what regiment are you with?'

'Loyal North Lancashires, sir,' said the soldier.

'And what seems to be the trouble with you?'

There was an embarrassed silence, and then the soldier replied softly, 'I'm afraid I've had a rather bad case of pubic lice, sir, which resulted in a rather painful and nasty infection.'

'Oh, dear, that's . . . that's dreadful,' replied Kitchener sympathetically, 'hard to get treatment while you're busy fighting. I'm glad we got you in here to fix you up. Tell me, what's the treatment?'

'Take the tablets and scrub the affected parts three times a day with the brush, sir.'

'Jolly good! Now, tell me, lad, what's your ambition?'

'To get back into action and fight for Queen and country, sir.'

'That's the spirit!' said Kitchener and the party moved on.

In the next bed was a sergeant, a middle-aged veteran, lying on his side. The party moved around till they were facing him.

'Hello,' said Kitchener, 'and what regiment are you with?'

'Royal Artillery, sir,' said the sergeant.

'And what's the trouble with you?'

'Well, it's a severe case of haemorrhoids, I'm afraid,' replied the sergeant. 'It's constipation from the dry rations they said, what caused it.'

'Oh, dear, that's nasty!' remarked Kitchener. 'Tell me, what's the treatment?'

'Take the tablets and scrub the affected parts three times a day with the brush, sir.'

'Jolly good! And what's your ambition?'

'To get back into action and fight for Queen and country, sir.'

'That's the way,' said the Field Marshall.

Sitting there despondently in the last bed was an Aussie soldier who looked quite healthy.

'And who have we here?' asked Kitchener.

The soldier appeared to have trouble speaking. He swallowed twice and then answered, in a tiny, husky voice, 'Private Riley, sir, Queensland Lighthorse.'

'Ahhh, a young colonial chappie,' said Kitchener, ' and why are you in here?'

'Well, sir,' croaked the bushman, 'I've got a severe case of laryngitis—can hardly talk, and the officer thought it might be infectious, so he sent me here for a few days.'

'Oh, dear, laryngitis, eh, that's no good at all,' replied Kitchener, 'can't have you fighting those Boers when you're sick. Tell me, what's the treatment?'

'Take the tablets and scrub the affected parts three times a day with the brush.'

'Jolly good show, that's the way,' said the Field Marshall. 'Now, tell me, lad, what's your ambition?'

The Aussie croaked his reply.

'To get hold of that brush before those other bastards . . . sir.'

JH

BEFORE GALLIPOLI—THERE WAS ELANDS RIVER

'When the ballad makers of Australia seek for a subject, let them turn to Elands River . . .' Sir Arthur Conan Doyle

Elands River was a staging post on a rocky ridge in the Western Transvaal. A massive build up of stores accumulated there in 1900, to supply British columns moving through the area. The camp contained 1500 horses, oxen and mules, together with 100 wagons and enough supplies to maintain a force of 3000 for a month.

The Boers desperately wanted the supplies, which were valued at over £100,000. On 4 August 1900, Colonel De La Rey's commando force of around 3000 men surrounded and laid siege to the post which was defended by 200 Rhodesian militiamen and 300 Australians from the various colonies, fighting as Australian Imperial Bushmen. There were 141 Queenslanders commanded by Major Walter Tunbridge, 105 from New South Wales, 42 Victorians, 9 Western Australians and 2 Tasmanians. Most of these men had never been shot at before.

Captain Butters led the Rhodesian contingent and the overall commander was the British Lieutenant Colonel, Charles Hore. He was suffering from malaria at the time.

The Boers had twelve modern artillery pieces, which pounded the post in its exposed position. They also had snipers positioned on three sides of the camp.

The defenders had one Maxim gun and one old seven-pound muzzle-loader. Unfortunately, the supplies at Eland River Post did not include ammunition. The defenders had just enough shells to take an occasional pot shot at the Boer guns and it was necessary to sneak out of the camp to scout the Boer gun positions.

Lieutenant James Annat scouted out several times with other Queenslanders and was fatally wounded after he'd succeeded in forcing one Boer gun crew to retire.

Over 2500 shells landed on the post during the first two days of the siege. Most of the 1500 horses, mules and oxen were killed in the horrific bombardment.

The one gun the defenders had was old and faulty. Major Tunbridge had to dismantle it for repairs and reassemble it four times during the siege. The shells they had were also damaged and Tunbridge spent days and nights reshaping them with a file.

On the third day, a force commanded by General Carrington arrived to relieve them but was driven back by the Boers and retreated all the way back to Mafeking. The men defending the post saw them come and go.

Five hundred men were trapped without cover under the blazing sun, with the stench of 1500 dead animals in the air. They had no access to water except by night patrol and they had seen their 'rescuers' retreat.

On 8 August, the Boer commander, De La Rey, sent a messenger under a flag of truce to advise that the whole area was in Boer hands. He offered to escort the force to the nearest British post provided that none of the supplies within the camp were destroyed, 'in recognition of your courage in defence of your camp'. He even offered to let the officers retain their weapons.

There was a conference among the officers. Apparently Hore was willing to surrender and asked Butters and Tunbridge what they thought.

Butters said he could not go back to his Rhodesian troops who had fought so bravely and tell them to surrender. Tunbridge consulted the various Australian colonial forces' officers and they made a written reply, which read:

> If De La Rey wants our camp, why does he not come and take it? We will be pleased to meet him and his men, and promise them a great reception at the end of a toasting fork. Australians will never surrender. Australia forever!

Our nation was exactly eight months old at the time. The 'Australians' fighting were actually soldiers from different colonies who had left home before Federation.

A few days later, on 12 August, De La Rey sent a second offer of honourable surrender and safe passage. He was keen to get the stores without further bombardment and damage. Colonel Hore replied: 'Even if I wished to surrender to you—and I don't—I am commanding Australians who would cut my throat if I accepted your terms.'

Another relief column commanded by General Baden-Powell came within 30 kilometres of the besieged post from the east. But because headquarters thought it impossible that the garrison had held out and presumed that the Australians and Rhodesians had been killed or surrendered, Baden-Powell was ordered to turn back.

Finally, when a message from De La Rey to Boer Commander De Wet, stating that the garrison was still holding out, fell into the hands of one of Kitchener's scouts, Kitchener himself, who had been leading a huge force of near 20,000 men chasing De Wet, detoured to Elands River and the siege was lifted.

A British officer with the relieving force wrote to the *London Times*, 'I do hope that Great Britain will show its gratitude to those Australians for the brightest page in the history of the war.'

General Smuts, who later became Prime Minister of South Africa, said of the men at Elands River, 'There can only be one opinion about the fine determination and pluck of these stalwart Colonials . . . deserted by their friends . . . they simply sat tight until Kitchener's column finally disinterred them from the carcass-covered Kopje.'

Losses were twelve dead and fifty-eight wounded.

Fifteen years later, the Anzacs landed at Gallipoli and the Battle of Elands River faded from the memory of most Australians. **JH**

ELANDS RIVER
GEORGE ESSEX EVANS

It was on the fourth of August, as five hundred of us lay
In the camp at Elands River, came a shell from De La Rey.
We were dreaming of home faces, of the old familiar places,
And the gum trees and the sunny plains five thousand miles away.
But the challenge woke and found us
With four thousand rifles round us;
And Death stood laughing at us at the breaking of the day.

Hell belched upon our borders, and the battle had begun.
Our Maxim jammed: We faced them with one muzzle-loading gun.
East, south, and west, and nor'ward
Their shells came screaming forward
As we threw the sconces round us in the first light of the sun.
The thin air shook with thunder
As they raked us fore and under,
And the cordon closed around us, as they held us—eight to one.

We got the Maxim going, and the field gun into place
(She stilled the growling of the Krupp upon our southern face);
Round the crimson ring of battle
Swiftly ran the deadly rattle
As our rifles searched their fore-lines with a desperate menace;
Who would wish himself away
Fighting in our ranks that day
For the glory of Australia and the honour of the race?

But our horse-lines soon were shambles, and our cattle lying dead
(When twelve guns rake two acres there is little room to tread)

All day long we heard the drumming
Of the Mauser bullets humming,
And at night their guns, day-sighted, rained fierce havoc overhead.
Twelve long days and nights together,
Through the cold and bitter weather,
We lay grim behind the sconces, and returned them lead for lead.

They called on us to surrender, and they let their cannon lag;
They offered us our freedom for the striking of the flag—
Army stores were there in mounds,
Worth a hundred thousand pounds,
And we lay battered round them behind trench and sconce and crag.
But we sent the answer in,
They could take what they could win—
We hadn't come five thousand miles to fly the coward's rag.

We saw the guns of Carrington come on and fall away;
We saw the ranks of Kitchener across the kopje grey—
For the sun was shining then
Upon twenty thousand men—
And we laughed, because we knew, in spite of hell-fire and delay,
On Australia's page forever
We had written Elands River—
We had written it for ever and a day.

RECRUITED AT THE TOWN HALL
'HAYSTACK' HANMAN

A Yarn about Enlisting in 1914

I found myself at Lismore on the 18th September 1914. The town itself seemed deserted, save for a few rumbling, grumbling farmers' carts, groaning on their way to some distant little homestead in the bush.

In one of the sleepy, lazy-looking streets, I found myself in front of the recruiting hall—one of a crowd, all intent upon the same purpose—taking the oath to serve their 'King and Country till the termination of the War and four months after'.

The crowd consisted of lawyers, bank clerks, drapers, labourers—mostly big, strapping fellows who looked as though they had every chance of becoming food for powder and shot.

On every face could be seen anxiety—anxiety that the owner was suffering from some complaint of which he was unaware—fearful lest he be found unfit. When a chap knows he is to be examined by a medical man, he becomes afraid, he imagines he has a weak heart, lung trouble, or any other of the too numerous diseases which afflict mankind. Assure him as fervently as you like to the contrary, and his brain will run to imaginary complaints until he feels quite ill. Waiting for the doctor is nearly as bad as awaiting the command for a bayonet charge.

Every man is sizing up his neighbour and weighing him in the balance, when the doctor puts in an appearance. What a relief!

Who are these chaps with such smart uniforms, such a magnificent martial bearing and such pretty little bits of red and gold on their hats, shoulders and sleeves? Surely they are captains; but no, by their voice, and pompous manner, they must surely be no less than generals! Wait, worried recruit. When you have been in the army one little week, you will know, only too well, that they are after all only sergeant-majors on the instructional staff.

' 'Tion!!! 'tion, 'tion, look here, you chumps, fall in, fall in, we can't wait here all day, stand over there. No, come over here—that's right, no—damn it—that's wrong. Ah! Now, fall in.'

Some of us were beginning to think that we had fallen in right enough, but not in the way the drill instructor meant.

Then came the order to strip. What a funny sight!

The doors of the hall were wide open, and a rather fresh breeze blowing in, and there stand or sit in every self-conscious attitude about fifty fellows, all wondering what Adam did in cold weather!

One by one we were called to face the doctor, and it is no exaggeration to state that these same fellows were more frightened then than they were on that never-to-be-forgotten dawn of April 25th 1915.

At last my turn came. I hopped, jumped, stepped sideways, backwards, forwards, touched toes, waved my arms madly about, so much so, that if a stranger had seen me he would have imagined he was beholding a rehearsal for a corroboree or the dance of the seven veils.

I was tapped here, punched there, asked to cough—though that request is superfluous, because by now I was coughing pretty regularly.

Then you are brought to your senses by 'Halt, about turn.'

And you walk forth a soldier whose battles have already commenced, for ten to one, someone has admired your shirt and taken off with it, or shown a preference for your socks.

CALL THE COOK

This story has several versions but is supposed to have occurred at Mena Camp where the Australian troops were under the command of British officers.

There was not as much respect shown to officers by the Australians as the British would have liked and comments about the food were aired quite loudly and openly in the mess hall. British army food was not to the liking of most of the Aussie bushmen of the first AIF, and they often said so, loudly.

Finally, it came to a head and comments about the cooks' ancestry were heard in a manner that could not be ignored. After one such incident, the officer in charge of the mess called a parade of the Australian troops.

The men stood under the blazing sun waiting for an hour before the officer addressed them.

'Now, listen here, you men, I will not tolerate this insubordinate attitude towards the cooks. Today at lunch one of you actually called one of the cooks a "bastard". I heard it clearly and I intend to punish that man. I want to know who called the cook a bastard!'

One digger immediately stepped forward from the front rank.

'Ahh,' said the officer, 'so, we have some honesty here, I see. Are you stepping forward to confess that it was you who called the cook a bastard?'

'No. Sir,' replied the Aussie loudly.

'Well, I want to know who called the cook a bastard, why did you come forward?'

'Because, sir, we'd like to know who called the bastard a cook!'

JH

PEACEABLE-LOOKING MEN
JOSEPH L. BEESTON

The truce at Gallipoli was one of the strangest and most telling events of the whole campaign. It was the start of a strange relationship between Australians and Turks which has led to a friendship that is still palpable in the twenty-first century. The respect shown by the often racist Australians towards their Turkish foes was the start of an understanding of different ways of life that often occurs when people travel outside their own comfort zone. This yarn is a fascinating insight into how the Aussies first saw the Turks as men, not caricatures.

On 23 May 1915, anyone looking down the coast could see a man on Gaba Tepe waving a white flag. He was soon joined by another occupied in a like manner.

Some officers came into the Ambulance and asked for the loan of some towels; we gave them two, which were pinned together with safety pins. White flags don't form part of the equipment of Australia's army.

Seven mounted men had been observed coming down Gaba Tepe, and they were joined on the beach by our four. The upshot was that one was brought in blindfolded to General Birdwood. Shortly after, we heard it announced that a truce had been arranged for the following day in order to bury the dead.

The following morning, Major Millard and I started from our right and walked up and across the battlefield. It was a stretch of country between our lines and those of the Turks, and was designated no-man's-land. At the extreme right, there was a small farm; the owner's house occupied part of it, and was just as the man had left it. Our guns had knocked it about a good deal.

In close proximity was a field of wheat, in which there were scores of dead Turks. As these had been dead anything from a fortnight to three weeks, their condition may be better imagined than described.

One body I saw was lying with the leg shattered. He had crawled into a depression in the ground and lay with his greatcoat rolled up for a pillow; the stains on the ground showed that he had bled to death, and it can only be conjectured how long he lay there before death relieved him of his sufferings.

Scores of the bodies were simply riddled with bullets. Midway between the trenches, a line of Turkish sentries were posted. Each was in a natty blue uniform with gold braid and top boots, and all were 'done up to the nines'. Each stood by a white flag on a pole stuck in the ground. We buried all the dead on our side of this line and they performed a similar office for those on their side.

Stretchers were used to carry the bodies, which were all placed in large trenches. The stench was awful, and many of our men wore handkerchiefs over their mouths in their endeavour to escape it. I counted 2000 dead Turks. One I judged to be an officer of rank, for the bearers carried him shoulder-high down a gully to the rear.

The ground was absolutely covered with rifles and equipment of all kinds, shell-cases and caps, and ammunition clips. The rifles were all collected and the bolts removed to prevent their being used again. Some of the Turks were lying right on our trenches, almost in some of them.

The Turkish sentries were peaceable-looking men, stolid in type and of the peasant class mostly. We fraternised with them and gave them cigarettes and tobacco.

Some Germans were there, but they viewed us with malignant eyes. When I talked to Colonel Pope about it afterwards, he said the Germans were a mean lot of beggars.

'Why,' said he most indignantly, 'they came and had a look into my trenches.'

I asked, 'What did you do?'

He replied, 'Well, I had a look at theirs.'

JH

SHRAPNEL
TOM SKEYHILL

Tom Skeyhill wrote a large amount of rhymed verse that was popular at the time, although his fame as a poet was fleeting and his volumes of verse are now long forgotten. Skeyhill fought as a regimental signaller of the 2nd Infantry Brigade and was blinded at the second battle of Krithia on 8 May 1915.

He was hospitalised in Egypt, and later at the Base Hospital in Melbourne. His patriotic, stirring doggerel was published both here and in New York and he was something of a celebrity during and after the war. Later, he recovered his sight and went to the USA where he went on the speaking circuit. He later went to Hollywood and worked on the script of the famous movie Sergeant York, *which made Gary Cooper a star.*

In this poem, written in 1915, he rather spookily describes the phenomena of shell-shock and post-war syndrome which were not properly diagnosed and dealt with until after World War II.

I was sittin' in me dugout and was feelin' dinkum good,
Chewin' Queensland bully beef and biscuits hard as wood.
When, 'Boom!' I nearly choked meself, I spilt me bloomin' tea,
I saw about a million stars and me dugout fell on me!

They dug me out with picks and spades, I felt an awful wreck,
By that bloomin' Turkish shrapnel I was buried to the neck,
Me mouth was full of bully beef, me eyes were full of dust,
I rose up to me bloomin' feet and shook me fist and cussed.

The Sergeant says, 'You're lucky lad, it might have got your head,
You ought to thank your lucky stars!' I says, 'Well, strike me dead!
It smashed me bloomin' dugout, it buried all me kit,
Spoilt me tea and bully beef—I'll revenge that little bit!'

I was walkin' to the water barge along the busy shore,
Listenin' to the Maxims bark and our Big Lizzie roar,
When I heard a loud explosion above me bloomin' head,

And a bloke, not ten yards distant, flopped sudden down, stone
  dead.

I crawled out from the debris and lay pantin' on the sand,
I cussed that Turkish shrap and every Turk upon the land.
We cussed it when it busted a yard or two outside,
We cussed it when it missed us, a hundred yards out wide.

It's always bloomin' shrapnel, wherever you may be,
Sittin' in your dugout, or bathin' in the sea.
At Shrapnel Gully, Deadman's Gully, Courtney's Post and Quinn's,
At Pope's Hill and Johnson's Jolly—that deadly shrapnel spins.

I don't mind bombs and rifles, and I like a bayonet charge,
But I'm hangin' out the white flag when shrapnel is at large.
When I get back to Australia and I hear a whistlin' train,
It's the nearest pub, for shelter from that shrapnel once again!

SERGEANT MAJOR MURPHY

A dear friend of mine, Alan Murphy, who sadly passed away in
2012, gave me a copy of his grandfather's diary from Gallipoli.
Alan's grandfather was Sergeant Major Thomas Murphy, a cook
with the 1st Battalion who was badly wounded and lost an eye
at Gallipoli.

His diary is full of extraordinarily matter-of-fact observations
and comments such as:

27/5/15 Wounded at Shrapnel Gully in the head. Shrapnel shell
bursts over me while taking ammunition on mules up the gully.
Mules play up and I am dragged down the hillside and badly
bruised.

29/6/15 Leave Anzac for rest at Imbros.

6/7/15 Return to Gallipoli on SS *El Kahira*. Cooking resumes
under heavy shellfire.

7/7/15 Receive letters and news of Mother's death. Send letters home. Turkish night attack; heavy losses on their side.

31/7/15 Aeroplane drops bomb on cookhouse; food spoilt, no one hurt.

7/8/15 Captain Shout and Pte. Keyzor earn V.C. Cookhouse shelled heavily. Wounded in right eye.

16/8/15 Sent to hospital ship *Rewa* in barge . . . supplied with cocoa and food. Sleep on deck. Bullets fall on deck; shift bed to port side and go to bed.

I am in awe of men like Sergeant Major Murphy, they don't make men like him any more.   **JH**

AN ANZAC MEETS A LORD

The whole Gallipoli campaign was created because the British and French fleets failed to force a passage through the Dardanelles in March 1915.

This failure was laid partly at the door of the First Sea Lord, Lord Fisher. He had been First Sea Lord from 1904 to 1910 and came out of retirement to take up the position again in 1914.

Fisher resigned seven months after the failed attempt to break through the Dardanelles, in frustration over Churchill's decisions at Gallipoli. He then served as chairman of the British Government's Board of Invention and Research until the end of the war.

This story concerns Lord Fisher's visit to a military hospital to 'cheer up the wounded soldiers'.

A young Australian, wounded in the Gallipoli fighting, had been taken to England to recover his strength.

During his convalescence, a social event was organised at which Lord Fisher came to mingle with the veterans. The Right Honourable Gentleman was in the company of his political chiefs and was interested in acquiring a few impressions from the men of Anzac.

He asked this particular Anzac what he thought of the campaign on Gallipoli.

With the hammering of the British fleet against the Dardanelles all through March in mind, the Anzac answered, 'Well, you know, if I'd been a burglar, and wanted to break into a place, I wouldn't have spent several nights before pelting stones on the roof.'

The Right Honourable Gentleman immediately terminated the conversation then and there and moved on with his smiling entourage.

'Didn't you know who that was?' a horrified bystander asked the Anzac.

'Yeah, usen't he to be the First Sea Lord?' replied the Anzac, unperturbed.

JH

HORSES AND VIEWING PLATFORMS
JOSEPH L. BEESTON

Joseph Beeston was born in Newcastle, NSW, in 1859, studied medicine in London and later attended the Dublin College of Surgeons.

Beeston practised medicine in Newcastle and was Honorary Surgeon at Newcastle Hospital. He was also president of the Newcastle School of Arts and the Newcastle Agricultural and Horticultural Society. In 1908, he was appointed a lifetime Liberal member to the New South Wales Parliamentary Upper House.

He served as Honorary Captain in the Army Medical Staff Corps from 1891 and enlisted on the outbreak of war in September 1914. As Lieutenant Colonel, he was Officer in Charge of the 4th Field Ambulance at Gallipoli and was awarded the CMG. He contracted malaria and returned to Australia in 1916. He died in 1921. The last story is particularly amusing because Beeston was very short, only just over 1.5 metres.

There were very few horses on the Peninsula, and those few belonged to the artillery. But at the time I speak of, we had one attached to the New Zealand and Australian headquarters, to be used by the despatch rider.

Anzac, the headquarters of General Birdwood, was about two and a half miles away; and, being a true Australian, the despatch-carrier declined to walk when he could ride, so he rode every day with despatches. Part of the journey had to be made across a position open to fire from Walker's Ridge.

We used to watch for the man every day, and make bets whether he would be hit. Directly he entered the fire zone, he started as if he were riding in the Melbourne Cup, sitting low in the saddle, while the bullets kicked up dust all round him.

One day, the horse returned alone, and everyone thought the man had been hit at last; but in about an hour's time he walked in. The saddle had slipped, and he came off and rolled into a sap, whence he made his way to us on foot.

When going through the trenches, it is not a disadvantage to be small of stature. It is not good form to put one's head over the sandbags; the Turks invariably objected, and even entered their protest against periscopes, which are very small in size. Numbers of observers were cut about the face and a few lost their eyes through the mirror at the top being smashed by a bullet.

On one occasion, I was in a trench which the men were making deeper. A rise in the bottom of the trench just enabled me, by standing on it, to peer through the loophole.

On commending the man for leaving this lump in the floor of the trench, he replied, 'That's a dead Turk, sir!'

MY LITTLE WET HOME IN THE TRENCH
TOM SKEYHILL

I've a Little Wet Home in the Trench,
Which the rainstorms continually drench.
Blue sky overhead, mud and sand for a bed,
And a stone that we use for a bench.
Bully beef and hard biscuit we chew,
It seems years since we tasted a stew,

Shells crackle and scare, there's no place can compare
With My Little Wet Home in the Trench.

Our friends in the trench o'er the way
Seem to know that we've come here to stay.
They rush and they shout, but they can't get us out,
Though there's no dirty trick they won't play.
They rushed us a few nights ago,
But we don't like intruders, and so,
Some departed quite sore, others sleep evermore,
Near My Little Wet Home in the Trench.

There's a Little Wet Home in the Trench,
Which the raindrops continually drench,
There's a dead Turk close by, with his toes to the sky,
Who causes a terrible stench.
There are snipers who keep on the go,
So we all keep our heads pretty low,
But with shells dropping there, there's no place can compare,
With My Little Wet Home in the Trench.

PRIVATE DONNELLY'S YARNS
ANONYMOUS

These first-hand accounts of day-to-day events at Gallipoli were reported in the Sydney Sun *in 1917. The reporter visited wounded Anzacs at Randwick Hospital, sadly his name was not used in the article.*

'Allow me to introduce Private Donnelly, 1st Battalion.'

'I'm afraid I've forgotten everything since I had shell-shock,' he tells me, bringing his wheelchair to a standstill.

'Did you really suffer from shell-shock?' I asked.

'Yes, from eating peanuts!'

I learn that after four months on Gallipoli, he got so badly peppered by a machine-gun that his mates suspected him of having tried to eat it.

He was taken off to Malta with a complement of thirty-two bullets. He marks off the joint of his first finger to show the length of them.

His right arm is of use only when lifted in a certain way, and it will be a week or two yet before he is able to discard the wheelchair. His legs show several crevices where bullets entered.

'This was a bull's-eye,' he continues, opening his tunic so that I can see a cup-shaped wound in his chest. The bullet came out through the shoulder.

During the Gallipoli campaign, Private Donnelly went from a Friday afternoon until the following Tuesday with five hours' sleep. 'In action,' he says, 'you never feel tired, even when you've been at it for as long as three or four days; but as soon as you come off duty you go flop.

'I remember being sent into the trenches. There were regular rooms where you could lie down. They were shell-proof, and, as you may imagine, very dim. I went along the trench looking for a place to rest, and I met one of my pals. "Oh," he said, "the big room along here is all right. I'll wake you when your time's up."

'I stumbled along, and when I got there the place was full except for one bit of floor just big enough for me. I tiptoed over the others to it, and lay down, with my water-bottle for a pillow. There were two big chaps either side of me, and as they'd been there before me I took it they'd had a pretty fair innings, so made myself more comfortable by shoving one of them against the wall. My pal woke me at 9 p.m. I asked him for a cigarette, and when I struck the match I said to him, "My word, those fellows are doing well, sleeping so long."

'He laughed, and I took another look at them. I had been sleeping between two dead Turks! But you didn't take any notice of things like that out there!

'On the day of the armistice, I made friends with a Turk. He spoke perfect English. He had been coming out to Sydney to join his uncle and nephew in business, but five days before his departure he was called up. We exchanged cigarettes—I gave him a box of those awful Scotch things we used to get out there, and he gave me the real Turkish article, which, I can tell you, I enjoyed.

'While we smoked, he said, "Strange, you know! Today we smoke, chat and are happy together; tomorrow we shall probably pour lead into each other!" He was taken prisoner afterwards, and I never saw him again. He was a really good fellow, like many of the other rural Turks against whom we fought.

'Life in the trenches? Well, there wasn't any dinner bell! We took bully beef and biscuits with us, and opened the beef whenever we were hungry and had the chance of eating.

'There was one fellow who had been a shearer's cook. He made a sort of grater by piercing a piece of tin with holes. He used to grate the biscuits and beef, and make rissoles and cutlets and things. My word, we wouldn't have lost him for a fortune. We were the envy of the lines.

'One day, someone shot a hare (the first and last I saw on the peninsula). It was a lord mayor's banquet! We grilled it, and as soon as a bit was cooked it would be hacked off, and it was "Goodbye, hare".'

Private Donnelly was in London for Anzac Day 1916. He says that most of the Australians had fresh tunics made for the occasion, more smartly cut than usual. He and several others were in a theatre during the day. In the seat in front was a broad-shouldered Australian in khaki. They recognised him as a pal.

'How 'bout it, Nugget?' said one of the soldiers, laying his hand on the shoulder of the Anzac in front. 'Nugget' turned round, and, to their dismay, they saw the crown of a general on his shoulder.

'Beg pardon, sir,' said they, 'thought you were one of ourselves.'

'Well, damn it all, aren't I?' said the general. 'Come out and have a drink.'

He refused to tell them his name, and they have never discovered it.

WHO GOES THERE?

During World War I, the Australian troops were renowned for not saluting officers and generally not giving respect unless it was earned.

This story is told of a sentry on the Western Front who was obviously used to the Aussies' way of dealing with army protocol.

One dark and foggy night the sentry was standing on duty where several communication trenches met, going about his duties to the best of his ability.

Two figures appeared in the gloom and the sentry took his stance with rifle pointed right at them.

'Halt, who goes there?'

'Sappers of the Suffolk Regiment, Third Brigade,' came the crisp reply.

The sentry knew those were the sappers on duty that night.

'Pass, Suffolk Regiment,' he announced, lowering his weapon.

Sometime later, a group of a dozen or so figures in trench coats approached the sentry post.

'Halt, who goes there?'

'Duty patrol of the Welsh Guards, Fifth Regiment.'

The sentry knew the Fifth Regiment was patrolling that night.

'Pass, Welsh Guards,' he announced, formally, again lowering his rifle.

Twenty minutes later, a group of four men came walking along, chatting casually and smoking cigarettes.

'Halt, who goes there?'

'Who fucking well wants to bloody know?' came the reply.

The sentry lowered his rifle and replied, 'Pass, Australians.'

JH

HOW SOME AUSSIE SOLDIERS GOT THE HUMP

The Imperial Camel Corps was one of the oddest fighting forces in World War I. It was originally formed in early 1916, in response to an uprising of tribesmen in Egypt's Western Desert. The rebels were men of the Senussi tribe, who were sympathetic to the Turkish cause.

Most of the 'cameleers' were recruited from the Australian infantry and lighthorse battalions who were back in Egypt recuperating after the Gallipoli campaign. Eventually, there were four battalions and the first and third were entirely Australian. The second was British, and the fourth was a mix of Australians and New Zealanders. The Camel Corps also had a machine-gun unit, and a battery of light artillery manned by recruits from Hong Kong and Singapore.

The operations of the Corps against the rebels were characterised by long desert patrols and surprise attacks, ambushes and skirmishes.

Late in 1916, the Camel Corps transferred to the Sinai desert to fight against the Turkish army alongside the Australian Light Horse. They served with distinction at Romani, Magdhaba and Rafa and remained an integral part of the British and Dominion force during the advance north through Palestine in 1917 and 1918.

The Corps suffered heavy casualties and losses at the Second Battle of Gaza on 19 April 1917, and in the battles fought in November as part of the campaign to destroy the Turkish desert defences and capture Beersheba.

The Camel Corps had a tough reputation. Not only were the camels cantankerous and feared by other troops, their riders were, too!

There was a good reason for this. When the Corps was originally formed, the Australian battalion commanders saw an opportunity to offload some of the more difficult, unruly and insubordinate members of their battalions.

It was common practice for British headquarters to warn other British officers if the Camel Corps were to be stationed nearby. In 1917, officers commanding the supply dump at Rafa were warned to double their guards as the Camel Corps was going to be camped nearby.

The cameleers were tough, resourceful and effective fighting men. While defending a hill called Musallabeh in April 1918, they ran out of hand grenades and began heaving boulders down upon the attacking Turks. The plan worked and the Turks retreated and the hill became known as the Camel's Hump.

As the fighting moved into the more fertile country of northern Palestine, horses could move much faster and this odd fighting force was disbanded in June 1918. The Australian cameleers swapped their camels for horses and became the 14th and 15th Light Horse Regiments. **JH**

PALESTINE AND POETS
ANONYMOUS

Where the tracks are hard and dreary,
The tracks are long and dry,
The tropic sun is beating down
From out a cloudless sky;
There's naught to see but sand
And now and then you'll see a clump
Of palm trees—it's no wonder
That the camel's got the hump.

Never-ending sands that stretch
To where the sky and land
Meet in a line of blue and brown—
And poets say it's grand!
But poets stay at home in ease
And travel not afar,
To where the way is lighted
By a 'pale unwavering star'.

Poets never rise at dawn
And feed a blinking horse,
And poets never eat our grub,
Plain bully-beef, of course.
They never scorch or swelter,
At the desert never swear,
The reason why's not hard to find;
They never have been there!

Now, when you hear the poet rave
Of 'vast encircling sands
Whose magnitude is circumscribed
By cloudless azure bands
Of Heaven's vault' (his poesy's
Imagination grows)
Just think of all these scorching sands—
And bash him on the nose!

IT'S NOT CRICKET!

World War II saw Aussies back in the deserts of North Africa
once again.

The Australians who served against the Axis Forces in North
Africa, the Mediterranean and the Middle East were all volunteers.
They were members of three of the four divisions which made up
the 2nd AIF.

The siege of Tobruk was a very Australian affair. Almost two
thirds of the troops defending the garrison were Australians,
15,000 of them. They provided virtually the whole of the infantry
at Tobruk with the 12,000 British troops making up four artillery
brigades.

The name 'Rats of Tobruk' was taken from phrases used in a
propaganda move that backfired. Lord Haw-Haw, in the German
propaganda radio broadcasts, had referred to the garrison troops
as 'poor desert rats of Tobruk' during radio broadcasts.

The name was appropriate as the troops defending the garrison dug extensive tunnel networks and were 'caught like rats in a trap' during the siege.

What the German propaganda machine didn't realise, and perhaps could not ever understand, was the characteristic Australian affection for self-deprecating and ironic humour. The men of the 9th Division removed metal from a German bomber, one they had shot down with a salvaged German gun, and made their own unofficial medal with a rat emblem. The 9th Division was officially allowed to have all its badges and flashes shaped in the form of a 'T' after the siege of Tobruk.

The Australian media and general public loved the Rats of Tobruk. The siege helped Australians at home to feel that the nation was playing a vital role in the war effort against Nazism. Their dry wit and unmistakable 'Australianess' were a source of pride and inspiration.

Here are the 'official' Rules of Cricket for a game played between Australia's 20th Brigade and Britain's 107 Royal Horse Artillery at Tobruk on 30 July 1941:

Rule 2. Play to be continuous until 1800 hours, except by inter- ference by air raids. Play will NOT, repeat NOT cease during shellfire.

Rule 4. Shirts, shorts, long socks, sand shoes if available. ITI helmets will not be worn or any other fancy headgear. Umpires will wear white coat (if available) and will carry loaded rifle with fixed bayonet.

Rule 6. All players to be searched for concealed weapons before start of play, and all weapons found, other than ST grenades, Mills bombs, & revolvers will be confiscated. (This does not apply to umpires.)

Rule 8. Manager will make medical arrangements & have ambu- lance in attendance.

I have no idea what happened to rules 1, 3, 5 and 7!

Ten months after they were replaced at Tobruk the famous Rats were again called upon to take the main brunt of the Axis attack at El Alamein, while other elements of the Eighth Army fumbled and stumbled their way to victory further south.

During the entire El Alamein Campaign, the 9th Division suffered 22 per cent of the Eighth Army's casualties; 1177 Australians were killed, while 3629 were wounded, 795 were captured and 193 were missing. Axis casualties of 37,000 amounted to one third of their total force. Allied casualties of 13,500 were small by comparison at around 6 per cent.

As soon as it was obvious that the battle was won at El Alamein, Montgomery made his way to 9th Division Headquarters to thank General Morshead for the Australian role in the victory.

Perhaps the ultimate tribute came on D-day, by which time the 9th Division had fought a campaign against the Japanese in New Guinea. Just before the Allies landed in Normandy, Monty, now Viscount Field Marshall Montgomery, asked his Chief of Staff, Major-General Francis de Guingand, what he thought of the prospects for victory.

'I only wish,' the General replied, 'that we had the 9th Australian Division with us this morning.'   **JH**

FREIGHTER
TIP KELAHER

I found The Digger Hat, *a collection of verse by Tip Kelaher, in a second-hand bookshop. The slim volume was published just three months after Kelaher's death and the verses are a soldier's honest expressions of humour, patriotism and homesickness for the bush life he knew and the Sydney he loved. Coincidentally, I had lived in the same suburbs of Sydney and the same area of north-west New South Wales as he had. He and I had attended the same school and I happen to share his enthusiasm for Randwick Racecourse and Coogee beach, enthusiasms he expressed in his verse. He refused to leave his machine gun in the face of a German advance and died at the Battle of Tel El Eisa, in Egypt, in 1942.*

Now the days were long and dismal,
Though the wildflowers blossomed bright
And Spring's warm sun made living glad for some.
There was plenty good tobacco,
But we felt the 'drought' at night,
When in our tents we'd smoke and yarn of home.

And the big, bare slopes seemed cheerless
With their camel bush and rocks,
And barley, golden in the morning light;
But a happy rumour's reached us,
Hailing from the Suez docks,
That has somehow changed life's prospects over-night.

For a freighter's berthed in Tewfik,
That has sailed from southern seas,
A-laden to the decks with cargo rare.
And each mulga mail's confirmed it,
Borne in on the southern breeze—
She's beat the Japs and anchored safely there.

No, she's not an ocean liner,
Just a rusty, battered tramp,
With a tired stoker leaning on the rail;
But she's heaved the green seas from her,
And we reckon she's a champ,
For she's brought a load of Aussie beer and mail!

JACK EDMONDSON

Jack Edmondson was born in Wagga Wagga, New South Wales, later moving to Liverpool where he attended Austral Public School and Hurlstone Park Agricultural high School.

After he left school, Edmondson worked on his parents' farm. He joined the 4th CMF militia when war broke out and enlisted in the AIF in May 1940. He was promoted to corporal and embarked for the Middle East with the 2/17th Infantry Battalion, as reinforcements for the 9th Division.

After training in Palestine, his battalion were sent to relieve the 6th Australian Division at Marsa Brega and became part of the Australian contingent defending Tobruk.

In April 1941, German tanks and infantry breached the defences on the southern desert side of Tobruk and established machine-gun posts as well as positions for mortars and field guns.

A seven-man Australian patrol attacked a strategic German position. Edmondson was wounded in the neck and stomach but ran to the German position under heavy fire and killed the German gunner with his bayonet.

He continued to advance and saved the life of his commanding officer who was attempting to bayonet one of the enemy when the man grabbed his legs and another German soldier attacked him from behind. Although severely wounded, Corporal Edmondson ran to his assistance and killed both of the Germans, saving his officer's life.

Jack Edmondson died from his wounds soon after the German attack was repelled.

An hour later, the post they had captured was re-taken by a force of two hundred German infantry and the Australians were forced to withdraw,

The Germans then established a bridgehead in the outer defensive line at Tobruk. The ferocious Australian defence and counterattack, however, forced Rommel to change plans and the Australian tactic of letting German tanks pass and then following and destroying them from behind forced Rommel's army to retreat with heavy casualties.

Corporal John Edmondson was the first Australian to be awarded the Victoria Cross in World War II and is buried in the Tobruk War Cemetery.

His mother accepted his VC from the Governor-General on 27 September 1941 and, in 1969, she presented her son's medals and military belongings to the Australian War Memorial. You can see them there today.

A school, a park and a street in Sydney, a suburb of Wagga Wagga, a rest area on the road to Canberra, and a street near the War Memorial are named in memory of Jack Edmondson, VC.

JH

LEST WE FORGET

The Rats of Tobruk hold an almost sacred place within the ranks of returned servicemen in Australia. There is the Rats of Tobruk Memorial in Canberra and the international Rats of Tobruk Association was responsible for official memorial services and the erection of numerous other monuments in Australia and the UK. The association also organised with the Royal Mint of Australia the striking of a fifty-year anniversary medallion in 1991.

A big part of the legend being firmly established in Australian minds and hearts was the 1944 movie *The Rats of Tobruk*, starring Peter Finch and Chips Rafferty and directed by Charles Chauvel. The Rats were remembered with almost the same reverence as the original Anzacs and traditionally received the loudest cheer at every Anzac Day march.

An incident which occurred sixty-seven years after the siege is indicative of the respect Australians give to the memory of the Rats.

In April 2007, the Victorian contingent of the Rats of Tobruk Association reluctantly decided that it could no longer afford the upkeep of Tobruk House, the inner-city Melbourne meeting hall purchased by the association in the 1950s, when the Victorian association had 2000 members.

In 2007, the eighty who were left, all aged in their eighties and nineties, decided they had to sell the hall. From the sale, they hoped to raise a million dollars to be used for research at the Royal Children's Hospital, Melbourne, where there is a Rats of Tobruk Neuroscience Ward.

Bill Gibbons, who made his wealth out of trucking, had seen reports of the Rats deciding it was time to sell the Victoria Street property and felt it was a shame they should lose the home they had bought in the 1950s. At the auction, he beat off four other bidders for the hall, but had to pay $400,000 above what anyone expected. He then told the veterans they could keep the hall as long as they liked.

Bill Gibbons, whose father had served three years in the Middle East, but not at Tobruk, said, 'I went down there, shot my hand up and paid more than I ever intended, as you do at auctions—but everyone in Australia would have a feeling they should retain this place.'   **JH**

TOBRUK
ANONYMOUS

There's places that I've been in
That I didn't like too well;
Scotland's far too bloody cold
And Cairo's hot as hell.
English beer is always warm,
Each place has something crook.
But each is perfect when compared
To the place they call Tobruk.

I've seen some dust storms back at home
That made poor housewives work,
But there's enough inside our shirts
To smother all of Bourke.
Two diggers cleaned their dugout,
Their blankets out they shook;
Two colonels perished in the dust,
In this place they call Tobruk.

There's centipedes like pythons,
And there's countless hordes of fleas;
As big as poodle dogs they are,
All snapping round your knees,
And scorpions like lobsters
Come round to have a look,
There's lots of bloody livestock
In this place they call Tobruk.

Now there's militant teetotallers,
Who abhor all kinds of drink.
There's wives who break good bottles
And pour grog down the sink.
This place would suit them to the ground,
We've searched in every nook,
But booze is scarce as hen's teeth
In this place they call Tobruk.

The shelling's nice and frequent,
They whistle overhead.
You go into your dugout
And find shrapnel in your bed;
And when the stukas dive on us
We never stop to look,
We go down our holes like rabbits
In this place they call Tobruk.

Sometimes we go in swimming
And we float about at ease,
The water's clear as crystal,
There's a lovely ocean breeze,
Then down comes bloody Herman
And we have to sling our hook;
We dive right to the bottom
In this place they call Tobruk.

I really do not think this place
Was made for me and you,
Let's leave it to the Arab,
And he knows what he can do.
We'll leave this god-forsaken place
Without one backward look,
We've called it lots of other names,
This place they call Tobruk.

HOW WOULD I BE?

This is the archetypal Aussie yarn and has usually been attached to Tobruk. It is sometimes known as 'The World's Worst Whinger'.

The deadpan, self-deprecating black humour of the story somehow seems to fit the dry Aussie humour that sustained the troops at the Siege of Tobruk. The Aussies took the German insults and attempts to destroy their morale and used them to boost their morale and thumb their noses at their enemies.

I struck him first in a shearing shed near Longreach in far western Queensland. He had a smoke stuck to his bottom lip and was wearing a dirty old blue 'Jackie Howe' singlet. He'd just shoved a cranky old ewe down the shute and was taking a deep breath when I nodded and asked the usual Aussie question by way of greeting.

'How'd ya be?'

He didn't answer for a few seconds, he just looked at me as if I'd crawled out from under a log, took the roll-your-own smoke out of his mouth and scratched his head.

'How would I be?' he said slowly, 'how would I bloody well be!?'

'How the bloody hell do you think I'd be? Get a look at me, will you? I'm covered in dags and burrs, these bloody shears are blunt and the shearing engine only works when it feels like it.

'The boss of this place is the lousiest bastard in Australia, me missus is chasing me for maintenance on three kids that aren't mine and I haven't had a beer for weeks.

'Last time I got a beer in me mitt some dopey bastard knocked it out of me hand and then the publican threw me out of the pub for hitting the dopey bugger!

'The cook in this shed should be cooking for murderers in some prison, his gravy and his custard taste exactly the same and he's the only bloke I know who can make eggs taste like India rubber!

'How would I be!? How do you bloody well think I'd be!?'

Next time I saw him, he was sitting outside the recruiting office in Brisbane with a pile of army gear in his lap.

I should have known better, but the words were out before I could stop myself, 'How'd ya be, cobber?'

'How would I bloody well be?' he said, 'Take a gander at me, would ya! Get a load of this bloody outfit; look at me bloody hat—size nine and a half and I take a six and a half; get a bloody eyeful of these strides, you could hide a brewery horse in the bloody things and still have room for me; they gave me one shirt four sizes too big and one three sizes too small and look at these boots, there's enough leather in the bastards to make a full set of saddle and harness; and they told me this was a man's outfit!

'How'd I be? How do you bloody well think I'd be!?'

I next saw him in Tobruk. He was seated on an upturned ammunition box; tin hat over one eye, cigarette butt hanging out from his bottom lip, rifle leaning against one knee, trying to clean his fingernails with the tip of his bayonet.

I should have known better, but I asked him: 'How'd ya be, digger?'

He swallowed the butt and fixed me with a fearsome look. 'How'd I be? How would I bloody well be? How would you expect me to be? Six months in this bloody place being shot at by every Fritz in Africa and used as target practice by the bloody Luftwaffe ten times a day!

'I'm eating bloody sand with every meal; there's flies in me hair and eyes, frightened to sleep a bloody wink, expecting to die in this bloody godforsaken place and copping crow every time there's a handout of a job to anybody. How'd I be? How the bloody hell do you expect I'd be?'

Well, he must have died at Tobruk, because the last time I saw him I was dreaming—and he was in Heaven.

I know I should have known better, but I said, 'G'day old mate, how'd you be?'

'How'd I be? How in bloody Heaven's name do ya reckon I'd be?

'Get a look at this bloody regulation nightgown, would you! A man trips over the bloody thing fifty times a bloody day and it takes me ten minutes to lift the bloody thing when I want to scratch my shin.

THE BEST AUSTRALIAN YARNS

'And get a gander at this bloody right wing, feathers missing everywhere—a man must be bloody well moulting!

'Get an eyeful of this halo—only me bloody ears keep the rotten thing on me skull.

'How would I bloody well be? Cast your eyes over me bloody harp; five strings missing and there's band practice in ten minutes.

'How'd I be? How do you bloody well think I'd be!?'   JH

MIDDLE EAST SONG
ANONYMOUS

Oh, they took us out to Egypt, that God-forsaken land,
It's filled with bloody nothing and covered up with sand.
They fed us on stale biscuits, camel piss and stew,
And we wandered round in circles with bugger-all to do.

The generals that they sent us had not a bloody clue,
They ought to round the bastards up and put them in a zoo.
They said, 'Keep your eye on Rommel, don't let the bastard pass.'
But he'd sneak around behind them and kick them in the arse!

Then out came Montgomery, his prayerbook in his hand.
He said, 'Now men, the time has come to make a bloody stand.
We've got the Lord on our side and Rommel's cupboard's bare.
Now then men, down on your knees and say a bloody prayer!'

And we prayed, 'Oh, Jesus save us, 'tis not the Hun we fear,
Save us from the crazy bastards Churchill sends out here!'

BIGGER THAN PEARL HARBOR

The Darwin raids on 19 February involved more Japanese aircraft than the Pearl Harbor raid and more bombs were dropped than at Pearl Harbor.

The two separate air raids carried out against Darwin on 19 February 1942 were planned and led by Japanese Naval Air Service

Captain Mitsuo Fuchida, who also famously planned and led the attack on Pearl Harbor two months earlier.

It was the first time since European settlement that mainland Australia had been attacked by a foreign enemy. The operation has often been described by military historians in retrospect as 'using a sledgehammer to crack an egg (or a walnut)' and even Fuchida himself said later in his report that the operation 'seemed hardly worthy' of his highly trained strike force.

Fuchida led the first group of 188 attack aircraft, which were launched from four Japanese carriers stationed 350 kilometres from Darwin in the Arafura Sea near Timor.

In the first attack, which began at 9.58 a.m., heavy bombers pattern-bombed the harbour and town while dive-bombers and Zero fighters attacked shipping in the harbour and bombed the military and civil airfields. The first victim of the raid was a US Catalina flying near Bathurst Island, which was spotted and attacked by nine Zeroes.

The pilot was Lieutenant Tom Moorer, who would survive to later become an admiral and eventually Chairman of the US Joint Chiefs of Staff. Moorer crash-landed into the sea and, although the passing freighter that rescued him, the *Florence D.*, was later attacked and sunk, Moorer and most of his crew survived.

Once the pattern-bombing runs of the town and harbour were completed, eighty torpedo bombers attacked the ships in the harbour, while seventy dive-bombers, escorted by thirty-six Zeroes, attacked the RAAF bases, other airfields and public buildings, including a hospital.

Eight ships were sunk in Darwin Harbour, including a large American troop carrier and the destroyer USS *Peary*, which lost eighty crew in the attack. The merchant ship SS *Zealandia*, which was being used as a troop transport, also sank. Not long after the raid was over, MV *Neptuna* exploded spectacularly when 200 depth charges she was transporting blew up as a result of fires caused by the bombing.

The HMAS *Mavie*, a patrol boat, was also sunk, along with an American freighter, a British refuelling vessel and a coal transport ship. A locomotive, which was on the pier, was blown into the harbour and the jetty was partly destroyed.

The seaplane tender USS *William B. Preston* was badly damaged but managed to make a run to the open sea and was later repaired at Fremantle.

The hospital ship *Manunda* was attacked and damaged in spite of her obvious white hospital colour and signage, and the mine-sweeper HMAS *Gunbar* was damaged by strafing as she left port. A crewman was killed and five others were wounded.

Three ships were saved from sinking only by being beached after suffering severe damage and another ten were badly damaged in the raid.

In total, the air force hardware damage included ten Kittyhawks, a B24 bomber, and three transport planes. The US navy lost four flying boats and the RAAF lost all six Hudsons and the Wirraway training planes.

Most civil and military facilities in Darwin, along with most essential services including water and electricity, were badly damaged or totally destroyed.

The attack lasted forty minutes and was followed, an hour later, by the second wave of fifty-four land-based heavy bombers, flying out of recently captured airfields at Ambon and Kendari, which attacked the RAAF base from high altitude for about twenty minutes.

While Darwin was devastated and the population was left in chaos, the Japanese were dismissive of their easy target. Captain Fuchida noted derisively that:

> a single pier and a few waterfront buildings appeared to be the only port installations. The airfield on the outskirts of the town ... had no more than two or three small hangars, and twenty-odd planes of various types scattered about the field ... were destroyed where they stood. Anti-aircraft fire was intense but largely ineffectual, and we quickly accomplished our objectives.

Two aircraft were acknowledged as lost by the Japanese, but Allied reports claimed five Japanese aircraft were definitely destroyed and another five probably shot down. One Japanese Zero pilot who crash-landed on Melville Island was captured by a local Tiwi Islander and handed over to the army to become the first prisoner of war captured on Australian soil.

The two raids on 19 February, the first of sixty-four that Darwin would suffer, claimed at least 243 lives and around 400 more people were badly wounded. Some estimates by rescue workers of up to 1100 dead have never been substantiated. Darwin Mayor Jack Burton estimated 900 people were killed while the official government figure, given by the censor as fifteen several days later in order to prevent panic, was obviously nonsense. The best official count possible after the war estimated the number at 292 to 297 dead.

While the number of those killed in the raids remains unknown, partly due to the fact that the Aboriginal population was not accurately recorded at that time or even included in the census, the number of injured hospitalised is known reasonably accurately and the figure of around 300 dead seems to make sense in light of the number injured. **JH**

MITSUO FUCHIDA, SKY PILOT

Captain Fuchida, the architect and leader of the Darwin and Pearl Harbor raids, was about to be involved in the Battle of Midway when he had to undergo an emergency appendix operation onboard the carrier *Akagi*.

Akagi was hit and exploded and sank during the battle and Fuchida broke both ankles when the explosions threw him from a rope ladder he was using to leave the ship onto a deck metres below. He survived and spent the rest of the war as a staff officer.

Fuchida was again apparently singled out by fate to survive against the odds when he was part of a group sent to Hiroshima the day after the atomic explosion to assess the damage. While all other members of Fuchida's party died of radiation poisoning, Fuchida suffered no symptoms.

In 1947, Fuchida met a group of returning Japanese prisoners of war and among them was his former flight engineer, Kazuo Kanegasaki, who was believed to have died at Midway.

Kanegasaki told Fuchida that, as prisoners of war, Japanese soldiers captured by the Allies were well treated and not tortured or abused. He related how a woman whose missionary parents had been murdered by Japanese troops in the Philippines had cared for the Japanese POWs.

Hearing this, Fuchida, raised in the Bushido belief of revenge for honour, was stunned and became obsessed with trying to understand Christianity, although at first he couldn't find a Bible translated into Japanese.

His obsession eventually led to a meeting with the Christian evangelist Jacob De Shazer and conversion to Christianity.

Fuchida became a member of the Worldwide Christian Missionary Army of Sky Pilots and spent the rest of his life evangelising in the United States, becoming a US citizen in 1960. He died of a diabetes-related illness in 1976, aged 74. **JH**

JAPAN'S FIRST DEFEAT—MILNE BAY

While the outnumbered Australian militia were being pushed back along the Kokoda Track by a massive, well-trained Japanese army in August 1942, and the 500 soldiers of the 39th battalion at Deniki were holding back an enemy force ten times larger, the Japanese were planning an invasion around the eastern end of New Guinea. They planned to take Milne Bay at the eastern tip of the island and then get to Port Moresby and surround the Australian forces.

The Japanese had regularly bombed the three Allied airstrips that were being constructed at Milne Bay since 4 August.

Japanese intelligence reports mistakenly indicated a small force of Allied infantry constructing the three airfields at Milne Bay. There were, in fact, almost 9000 Allied troops at Milne Bay. About half of them were infantry, the rest were made up of over 1300 US engineer and construction troops and anti-aircraft and RAAF personnel.

The Australian infantry stationed at Milne Bay included militia from the 7th Brigade and the 55th Battalion along with the men of the 18th Brigade 7th Division 2nd AIF, who had famously served alongside the 9th Division at Tobruk.

On 24 August, a force of some 2000 Japanese troops, including 850 from the elite Marine Landing Corps, left Rabaul on three transports escorted by two cruisers and three destroyers. Another convoy left Buna to land further along the north coast and attack overland. Both convoys were spotted and subsequently attacked by the RAAF.

The only Australian naval vessels in the deepwater bay were a destroyer and a transport. Both were able to leave before the superior Japanese force arrived.

The RAAF effectively stranded the convoy from Buna on Goodenough Island by destroying the convoy's landing barges. Air strikes against the larger convoy inflicted little damage but were partly the reason the troops were landed well away from the airstrips.

The Japanese had complete naval supremacy at Milne Bay and were able to move troops up and down the coast at night. The RAAF had control of the air and were able to land and take off even when the airstrips were under heavy attack.

The Japanese landed 2000 marines and two tanks 11 kilometres east of their intended landing place. These troops faced a long march through swamp and jungle but made a concerted attack on one of the airfields after pushing Allied defenders westward. The tanks simply bogged and were abandoned.

The Japanese then landed 800 more marines and the big attack came, with artillery support from the warships, on the night of 31 August.

The 25th and 61st Australian Militia Battalions, along with the 43rd US Engineers, took the brunt of this attack, which included three waves of frenzied Japanese troops attacking across open ground. The Allied troops held firm in a furious battle and the Japanese were repulsed.

The Japanese were forced to withdraw back to the east and were pursued along the peninsular back to their base and again defeated by the 2/12th and 2/9th Battalions of the AIF on 4 September.

The Japanese retreated from Milne Bay after sinking a British merchant ship on 6 September. It was the first time the Japanese had been defeated in a land battle and forced to withdraw after attempting an amphibious landing.

At Milne Bay, 167 Australians died, along with fourteen men of the 43rd US Engineers. The RAAF were magnificent in their defence of the bay, taking off under fire and attacking Japanese ships and artillery without thought for their own safety.

Only half of the expeditionary forces landed by the Japanese managed to evacuate. About 750 were killed in the battles and the rest attempted to retreat overland to the Japanese base at Buna, only to be hunted down by Allied patrols.

Australian forces had inflicted the first defeat on the German army in World War II at Tobruk, and followed it up with the first defeat of Japanese forces—at Milne Bay.   **JH**

THE BRAVE 39TH

On 25 August 1942, the Australian militia fighting on the Kokoda Track at Isurava received news that men of the AIF 2/16th Battalion were coming to relieve them and were only a day's march away.

Meanwhile, the commander of Japan's elite South Seas Detachment, Major General Tomitaro Horii, an odd, obsessive man who rode a white horse during the Kokoda campaign, had placed his troops in the mountains for the attack on Isurava.

The Japanese had landed 13,500 troops by 21 August and Horii had assembled about 6000 seasoned combat troops between Kokoda and Isurava ready for the push towards Port Moresby. Specialist units, including mountain artillery and engineers, supported these troops.

The attack on Isurava began on the morning of 26 August. Horii sent the bulk of his combat troops in repeated attacks on the Australian positions at Isurava while a battalion of Japanese troops moved along the roughly parallel eastern track between Deniki and Alola to outflank the Australians.

While the attack at Isurava was taking place, Australian commander Brigadier Potts established his headquarters at Alola, the first village south on the track from Isurava. Potts believed that the 1100 troops of his two AIF rifle battalions would be facing 4000 Japanese and had no idea that 10,000 of Japan's best combat troops were encamped to the north.

The 2/16th Battalion was on its way and the 2/27th Battalion was being held at Port Moresby until the outcome of the battle of Milne Bay was known.

Early on 27 August, after heavy bombardment of Australian positions, the Japanese rushed the Australian perimeter from the north-west. Fresh troops replaced the Japanese soldiers who fell as wave after wave attacked the defensive line held by B Company 39th Brigade.

Just when it appeared that all was lost, troops of 2/14th AIF Battalion arrived at Isurava and the Japanese withdrew into the jungle.

The defence of Isurava by the young militiamen of the 39th Battalion against a massive elite Japanese army on 27 August 1942 ranks as one of the bravest actions in Australia's military history.

With all companies of the 2/14th AIF Battalion now at Isurava, the 39th Battalion were due to be relieved and return to Port Moresby, but their commander persuaded Brigadier Potts to allow the 39th to stay and support the troops who had come to their aid.

JH

THE 39TH BATTALION
DENNIS O'KEEFFE

I stood with my grandpa one cold April morn.
As we heard a trumpeter bugle the dawn.
I said, 'Grandpa, what are those medals you wear,
Were you a brave soldier, is that why they're there?'
He pointed and said, 'See those names carved in stone,

They were the bravest, they never came home.
So stand with me now and salute them today,
They lie buried in soil in a land far away.'

Later I sat on my grandfather's knee,
In the park where the start of the march was to be,
He talked of Kokoda, and told me the story
And ended by saying, 'There wasn't much glory,
Just young Aussies dying, so you could be free.'
Then he un-pinned his medals and pinned them on me,
And I stood up with grandpa and we formed in line,
I held his hand as we marched to the shrine.

Grandpa has gone now and since then I've grown,
To be so bloody thankful that he made it home.
For the young men who died had no chance to have sons,
It's a high price to pay to make boys carry guns.
So I wear grandpa's medals on each Anzac day,
For I know, even now, there's a debt to repay
To the brave 39th, on a track called Kokoda,
'Bloody heroes,' who fought till the battle was over.

PRIVATE KINGSBURY

At daybreak on 28 August 1942, three fresh AIF companies faced the Japanese on the north-west Australian defensive perimeter at Isurava.

As each company of the 39th Battalion was relieved, they were moved to the eastern and southern perimeters where cliffs and jungle made Japanese attack less likely.

At first light on 29 August, Japanese troops began massing at the northern and western perimeters. They attacked in waves throughout the day and, despite heavy losses, penetrated the western perimeter, forcing the Australians to fall back towards the village.

The right forward perimeter, facing Deniki, was also under threat of a breakthrough when Lieutenant Clements of C Company gathered men for a counterattack that was led by Sergeant Bob

Thompson from Headquarters Company and Private Bruce Kingsbury from A Company.

Kingsbury's platoon had been overrun and wiped out in fierce fighting north of battalion headquarters and he volunteered to immediately join another platoon heading to the front line.

Kingsbury had taken over the platoon's Bren gun and was checking it when the Japanese attacked again. He rushed forward, firing the Bren gun from his hip and calling, 'Follow me, we can turn them back!'

Having succeeded in clearing a path through the enemy, which halted the Japanese advance, Private Kingsbury was shot dead by a sniper hiding on top of a large rock at the edge of the jungle. Kingsbury's action turned the tide of the battle that day and saved the battalion headquarters from being overrun.

Bruce Kingsbury became the first soldier to be awarded a Victoria Cross while defending an Australian territory. His was also the first VC awarded in the South Pacific.   **JH**

PRIVATE KELLIHER

On 13 September 1943, at Heath's Plantation just west of Lae, Private Richard Kelliher of the 2/25th Brigade 7th Division, whose platoon had come under heavy fire, saw his platoon leader, Corporal William Richards, shot down ahead of the platoon.

Kelliher suddenly broke cover, ran 70 metres towards a Japanese machine-gun post and hurled two grenades at it; he then ran back, seized a Bren gun, returned to the enemy post and silenced it.

He then asked permission to go out again to rescue Richards, which he did successfully under heavy fire from other enemy positions, undoubtedly saving the severely wounded corporal's life. Nine Japanese dead were later found in the machine-gun post.

In an interesting twist to this heroic story, Kelliher, an Irishman by birth, had been court-martialled for cowardice in the face of the enemy during the battle for Gona. He had always claimed his platoon commander, who was killed in the action, had sent him back from the front line to obtain orders and information.

After he was found guilty, but later acquitted due to lack of evidence, Kelliher said he would prove one day that he was no coward.

He did so at Heath's Plantation ten months later, and was awarded the Victoria Cross for bravery. **JH**

A MYSTERY SOLVED
HMAS *SYDNEY*

A few years back, in a book I wrote about the Australian experiences of World War II, I discussed the sinking of HMAS Sydney and decided to write what I thought had happened.

I'd always had a feeling that the German captain, Theodor Detmers, had told the truth about the encounter, and I had an idea why the captain of the Sydney acted as he did.

This was a very risky thing to do as the wreck had not been found and many theories still existed. To make matters worse, the wrecks of the Sydney and Kormoran were discovered in between me writing the book and it being published.

Sometimes, however, you get lucky.

On 11 December 1941, the battle cruiser HMAS *Sydney*, the second ship of that name, built in 1933, was returning from escort duty to Fremantle when she sighted a strange ship off the coast of Western Australia, west of Geraldton.

The vessel was the German raider *Kormoran*, disguised as a Dutch freighter, the *Straat Malakka*. Built in 1938 as the merchant ship *Steiermark*, and refitted in October 1940 as a *hilfskreuzer* or 'auxiliary cruiser', she was renamed *Schiff 41* for operational purposes and named *Kormoran* by her new captain, Theodor Detmers.

Detmers was the youngest of the German raider captains and had visited Australia on the training cruiser *Koln* in 1932. He liked Australians and celebrated at sea his thirty-ninth birthday, in August 1941, by issuing rum to the captured Australian crew members of a freighter he had sunk, the *Mareeba*, and singing songs with them.

Between December 1940 and November 1941, *Kormoran* sank seven merchant ships in the South Atlantic and three in the Indian

Ocean. She was cruising off the west coast of Australia when HMAS *Sydney* sighted her.

Detmers knew he had to rely on disguise; his ship was no match for a battle cruiser. When the *Sydney* flashed 'What ship?' he deliberately replied by flag signals, rather than morse code, realising the more confusion he created and the more slowly he replied to signals, the longer he had to make a plan.

He replied by hoisting the signal-code pennant halfway, meaning, 'I can see your signal, but I can't make out what it is'. When the signal was repeated, *Kormoran* replied, clumsily and slowly, first with one flag missing, and then with several tangled flags, that she now understood.

The *Sydney*, 12 kilometres away, flashed a further signal asking 'Port of destination?' Detmers, who couldn't understand why the enemy ship was maintaining radio silence and why he hadn't yet been told to heave to, replied 'Batavia' (now Jakarta).

The cruiser continued to close in on the *Kormoran*, flashing another signal, 'Nature of cargo?' The misspelled answer, 'Piece goods', was so poorly and slowly signalled it was probably unreadable.

About 5 p.m., Detmers raised the Dutch flag and twice transmitted a distress signal 'QQQ *Straat Malakka*' ('suspicious ship approaching'), impersonating the Dutch ship the *Straat Malakka*.

This message was designed to be picked by the HMAS *Sydney*, confuse the situation and buy more time. It was picked up at several places on the mainland and acknowledged by the Perth station.

Detmers waited for the cruiser to call his bluff by requesting the secret call sign letters for the *Straat Malakka*, which, of course, he did not know. Finally, the request came and Detmers hoisted the letters 'IK', which he had correctly guessed was part of *Straat Malakka*'s four-letter secret call sign.

HMAS *Sydney* was now less than 1000 metres away, moving slowly directly abeam of the *Kormoran*.

At 5.30 p.m., *Sydney* again demanded the secret call sign letters and Detmers struck the Dutch flag, ran up the German colours, removed his camouflage and opened fire with all six of the *Kormoran*'s 150-mm guns.

It all happened in less than ten seconds.

Because HMAS *Sydney* was so close, Detmers was also able to use his anti-aircraft guns and torpedoes. The first salvo from the *Kormoran* took out *Sydney*'s bridge and gun control tower.

In the ensuing battle, both ships were sunk. The *Sydney* attempted to steam away after pounding the *Kormoran* until she was crippled. Detmers stated that there was an explosion on the *Sydney* as she disappeared over the horizon towards Geraldton.

The surviving Germans then abandoned ship and the crippled *Kormoran* exploded and sank later that night.

There were no survivors from the *Sydney*; all 645 men on board died and were never found. There were 317 survivors from the *Kormoran*. They remained prisoners of war in Australia until January 1947, twenty-one months after the war ended.

Detmers gave a full account of the battle, but many Australians did not believe his story until the wrecks were found in 2005.

Australians remained obsessed by the mystery of the tragic loss of the HMAS *Sydney*.

Many theories were put forward over the years about the way HMAS *Sydney* was lost. One theory blamed a lurking Japanese submarine, although Japan had not entered the war at that point. Others blamed a second German raider or U-boat.

But one question remains, why did Captain Burnett take the *Sydney* so close to a suspect ship? The theory I subscribed to was that he mistook the disguised raider for an unarmed German supply ship.

HMAS *Sydney*, like all warships, carried a book of information on enemy warships, supplied by naval intelligence. It contained a photo of the *Schiff 41/Kormoran*, but the photo was taken before she was converted to an auxiliary cruiser. It was a photo of her when she was the *Steiermark*.

It was not a good photo. It showed a ship riding high in the water, where the *Kormoran* sat low. It showed the wrong number of Sampson poles and a stern that looked like a half-counter half-cruiser stern, not the full cruiser stern the *Kormoran* actually had in 1941.

Perhaps the photo caused Burnett to think the *Kormoran* was the Japan-based supply ship, the *Kulmerland*, he knew was working in the area, supplying U-boats and raiders.

The *Kulmerland* was a very similar ship to the *Kormoran* with a full cruiser stern. The *Kulmerland* was known to be unarmed and operating in the area where the Sydney found the *Kormoran*, usually disguised as the Japanese steamer *Tokyo Maru*.

The *Kulmerland* was the *Kormoran*'s Indian Ocean 'mother ship'. A few weeks before, she had spent a week re-supplying the *Kormoran* at sea near Cape Leeuwin. She had also taken all the prisoners, survivors of the ships Detmers had sunk, to be sent back to Germany.

British Naval Intelligence issued a report on German raiders in May 1941. It described each ship, giving the original identity, alternative names and known disguises.

Descriptions of most of the raiders were quite comprehensive, but the report gave little information on the *Schiff 41/Kormoran*, which was quite wrongly described as having a 'squat funnel in the centre of a rather high superstructure', with a 'half-cruiser, half-counter' stern. In fact, the *Kormoran* was specifically reported to resemble 'a modified *Kulmerland*'.

I believed the poor photo and misleading description caused the *Kormoran* to be misidentified as the *Kulmerland*.

If Captain Burnett believed the *Kormoran* was the *Kulmerland*, everything he did makes sense.

The pretence about identity and the unreadable signal would have been logical. It would have been a quite normal and expected ploy to gain time to scuttle the ship and prevent her falling into enemy hands. This was a common practice and explains Burnett's haste to get to the vessel, to prevent it being scuttled and take her as a prize. It also explains why the warship came along broadside to the raider; this would have been the normal practice when sending a boarding party.

It even explains why HMAS *Sydney*'s first salvo missed completely, as her guns would have been set to miss in order to scare an unarmed enemy ship into surrendering and not attempting to scuttle. As there were no officially reported messages from HMAS *Sydney* at all, it will never be known what Captain Burnett believed.

After the wrecks were discovered and explored, the investigation showed that Detmers had told the truth—and my theory was very plausible.

Phew!　　　　　　　　　　　　　　　　　　　　**JH**

LOST WITH ALL HANDS
PETER MACE

Her hull was laid down on a far distant shore,
When the threat to world peace was too great to ignore,
Designed for a purpose, and that purpose was war,
The dockyards were building the *Sydney*.

Launched when the Great Depression held sway,
In action to keep the Italians at bay,
By blockading the ports in the Med, far away,
From her namesake, the city of *Sydney*.

With the world now at war the real work has begun,
Against Germany now, soon Japan's rising sun,
The *Bartollomeo* felt her twin six-inch guns,
The day she was sunk by the *Sydney*.

Steaming down south to the west of Shark Bay,
A freighter is seen at the close of the day,
With the flag of the Dutch flying there on display,
But a raider is stalking the *Sydney*.

The Captain approached what he thought was a friend,
But the one thousand yards is too close to defend,
Then the flag of the Reich on the mast did ascend,
And all hell breaks loose on the *Sydney*.

Taking water and burning she turns on the Hun,
Returning her fire, 'These colours won't run',

Determined to finish what she has begun,
She fought to the end did the *Sydney*.

The battle is over, both ships drift in haze,
The *Kormoran* scuttled and *Sydney* ablaze.
The painful conclusion, made after six days,
All hands have gone down on the *Sydney*.

. . .

The bronze woman stands gazing, grief etched on her face,
Symbolising the mothers and wives who, with grace,
Had waited for news on the last resting place,
Of their loved ones who served on the *Sydney*.

. . .

It was just a dark smudge on a video screen,
But the hunters were cheering for what they had seen,
Then the thoughtful reflection on what it may mean
Had they found the wreck of the *Sydney*?

A nation had waited sixty-seven long years,
Long after the loved ones had shed all their tears,
Then a shadowy shape on the sonar appears
And reveals the wreck of the *Sydney*.

A cold watery grave for captain and crew.
No one will ever know what they went through,
When the *Kormoran*'s guns and torpedoes flew,
Straight into the heart of the *Sydney*.

The fate of six hundred and forty-five men
Remembered in silence by the Navy, and when
The wreaths were cast out, the priest whispered, 'Amen,'
And they prayed for the souls of the *Sydney*.

The wreaths were cast out, the priest whispered, 'Amen,'
And they prayed for the souls of the *Sydney*.

RACING YARNS

The racetrack is a rich source of great yarns and there is something very Australian about the yarns that come from the racing game. I guess they often emphasise the stoic, deadpan nature of Aussie humour, that dry self-deprecating style we seem to enjoy—laughing at ourselves.

I have enough racing yarns to fill a book on their own. Come to think of it, I have filled two books already with racing history, yarns and true stories. But this book is strictly for good yarns, so we will stick to the most interesting and amusing yarns.

As settlements spread out into the bush in the nineteenth century, horses were an essential part of life; they were virtually the only means of transport. Whether it was a good saddle horse or a sulky, buggy, dray or Cobb & Co coach, horses were the only alternative to walking.

Entertainment in the bush was limited and the race meeting became the most common way to let your hair down after a spell of hard work, a way to socialise after living in isolation for a while. Along with this came the love of a long weekend or a holiday, the belief that handicapping the more talented performers makes things 'more interesting', and the Australian love of gambling.

The racing industry is so full of colourful true stories that there seems to be no reason for exaggeration or make-believe, but, Australians being what we are, there are plenty of tall tales told about the races.

So, this section mixes totally factual yarns about racing with make-believe, tall stories and often-told yarns and jokes. You can guess which is which!

Banjo Paterson loved the races and was a very good rider himself, winning races at Rosehill as an amateur rider on several occasions and being a member of the first ever New South Wales polo team, which defeated Victoria 2–0 in the first ever interstate polo match. Banjo had a great store of humorous yarns about racing—so he gets a good look-in in this section.

NOT BAD

Stoicism is a common element in racetrack humour. One of my
favourite stories concerns the old battling punter who heads off
to the races with $20 in his pocket.

The old battler, let's call him Jim, backs the first winner at 10
to 1 and then goes all up on the next three favourites, who duly
salute the judge, giving him a bank of $500 when the fifth race
comes around.

Now, Jim has done the form carefully on this race and has a
'special' which opens at 6 to 1 and drifts out to 8 to 1. Unperturbed,
Jim steps in, backs his 'special' and watches it win with his hands
in his pockets and no emotion on his face.

Two more all-up bets on successful favourites take Jim's bank
to almost $20,000 before the final race on the card.

This race features Jim's second 'good thing' for the day, a track
specialist named Wire Knot, third up from a spell over his pet
distance.

Jim extracts a $50 note from his wad, tucks it into his back
pocket and puts the rest on his second 'special', Wire Knot, on
the nose at 3 to 1.

Wire Knot misses the kick, flies down the outside late and it's
a photo finish. The judge calls for a second print before awarding
the race to the rank outsider, Mitre Guest. Wire Knot misses by
a nose.

On his way to the bus stop, Jim meets a mate who says, "Hello,
Jim, how'd you go today?'

'Not bad,' says Jim, deadpan, 'I won $30.'   **JH**

WHAT'S IN A NAME?

I have often been amazed and amused by the wonderful cryptic
and appropriate names owners come up with for racehorses.

Some favourites of mine over the years here in Australia have
been Itchy Feet which raced in Sydney in the 1960s and was by

an imported French stallion named Le Cordonnier which means 'the shoemaker' in French, out of a mare called Ticklish.

And as a kid, I was amazed that race callers didn't 'get' the name of a well-performed Sydney horse. The name was spelled C U R F T A and race callers always said 'Kerff-tar' but, of course, with Curfta being sired by Arrivederci, which means 'goodbye' in Italian, the name should have been pronounced C U R fta—'see you after'.

A few of the more imaginative and amusing names of recent years have been None for the Road, which was by Noalcoholic out of Road to Gold; Greenie by Naturalism out of Ozone Friendly; and Rumpus Room by Shemozzle out of Downstairs.

Some of the most clever Aussie names I can remember are Bowled Lillee, which was out of a mare named Courtmarsh, and VRC Derby winner Plastered, a Western Australian colt whose mother was called Tipples.

Some names are quite obscure and the majority of racegoers may never see the cryptic joke or reference involved. Caulfield Cup winner Railings, for instance, was out of a mare called Suffragette who was a daughter of Emancipation, and the name was a reference to the early suffragettes chaining themselves to the railings in Downing Street.

Suzanne Philcox, who works at Woodlands Stud, has to find names for up to 300 foals a year. 'I try to use the dam's name,' she says. 'I also try to keep names short for the callers. Crawl is out of a mare called Traipse whose mother was Elegant Walk; another of her foals was named Swagger.'

Phar Lap is Malay for 'lightning' spelled with a P H because trainer Harry Telford thought seven letters was lucky and horses with two-word names comprising seven letters won the most Melbourne Cups!

With so many opportunities to be clever with names, I often bemoan the fact that owners miss golden opportunities to be inventive, coming up with unimaginative names when some thought could have produced a real beauty.

An imaginary horse by Bogtrotter out of Cakewalk, for instance, often ends up being labelled with Bogwalk or Caketrotter or, even worse, Bogtrotter Lad or Cakewalk's Lass. Lad, Lass, Boy, Girl, Star, Prince, Lord, Lady, King and Queen are thrown onto the end of sires' and dams' names with reckless abandon to create names which, it seems to me, are harder to carry than topweight in a welter handicap.

The best and funniest racing name story comes from the early days of thoroughbred racing and is a true story—the best yarns are always the true ones.

The horse was named Potoooooooo or Pot-8-Os (truly!). He was foaled in 1773 and was a quite well-performed racehorse who defeated some of the greatest horses of his day and later became an influential sire. He was sired by the great Eclipse and bred by a bloke with an wonderfully posh name, Willoughby Bertie, 4th Earl of Abingdon.

Pot-8-Os acquired the strange spelling of his name, Potatoes, when a stable lad was asked to write it on a feed bin. The lad's version, Potoooooooo, was said to amuse his lordship so much that he kept it, and it appears in the Stud Book.

Pot-8-Os won thirty-four races over the span of seven years, including the Jockey Club Purse three times, and the prestigious Craven Stakes. He retired in 1783 to stand at stud and sired 172 winners including Champion, the first horse to win both the Derby and the St Leger (in 1800); Waxy, who won the Derby Stakes in 1793; and Tyrant, the 1799 Derby winner.

Pot-8-Os was finally 'planted' when he died at Upper Hare Park in November 1800. **JH**

WHAT PRICE POSSUMUM?

One of the strangest true stories of the Australian turf concerns the uncanny punting ability of a Chinese market gardener from Bankstown, Jimmy Ah Poon. The odd thing about this story is that, to the best of anyone's knowledge, Jimmy only ever backed one horse, and only when he won.

You see, Jimmy Ah Poon's appearance on Sydney's racetracks coincided with the career of the mighty champion Poseidon in the early years of the twentieth century.

Poseidon won eighteen times from twenty-six starts as a three and four year old. His wins included two Derbies, two Caulfield Cups, the Melbourne Cup and the AJC and VRC St Legers, and it seems that Jimmy backed him on every occasion that he won but never when he ran second or worse.

Jimmy was known as 'Louis the Possum' by bookmakers because he could not pronounce the name of the horse which won him an untold fortune. Every time Poseidon was due to win, Jimmy would turn up at the track and ask the bookmakers, 'What price Possumum?'

Jimmy disappears from Australian racetrack history after Poseidon's four-year-old season. Legend has it that he returned to China and lived like a mandarin for the rest of his days on the estimated £35,000 fortune he acquired due to his uncanny prescience about the future successes of 'Possumum'.

Punters used to follow Jimmy around and treat him as kindly as possible to see if he was going to bet or not. I believe this is the origin of that odd saying still heard on Aussie racetracks when a punter cannot pick a winner for love or money—'My luck's lousy today, I must have killed a Chinaman.'   **JH**

YOU CAN'T LOSE—AT LEAST, NOT TO A HORSE

Back in the days before doping tests came in, a trainer was spotted by a steward slipping a pre-prepared 'speed-ball' to his horse before a race.

'What did you give that horse?' demanded the steward.

The trainer, who had several more of the pills in his pocket, replied, 'Oh, they're just home-made boiled lollies,' and he popped one into his mouth and went on, 'my Missus makes 'em and the horse loves them. I'm having one myself,' he says, 'here, do you wanna try one?'

'Okay,' said the steward as he took the pill, looked at it and put it in his mouth, 'but I've got my eye on you.'

Minutes later, as the trainer legged him aboard, the stable jockey asked, 'Are we all set, boss, everything as planned?'

'Yes,' the trainer replied, 'money's on and he'll win. If anything passes you, don't worry, it'll just be the Chief Steward or me!' **JH**

THE MAN WHO LIKED LOT 41

There was once a battling trainer in Sydney who was addicted to studying bloodlines. He was born in Australia, in Bendigo in fact, but had lived most of his life in New Zealand before returning to Sydney to try to make it as a trainer.

He spent a lot of time reading through auction catalogues. He always found the time to do that, but he didn't have the budget to do much else.

He had an uncanny knack of looking at a horse's breeding and making an assessment of its ability, while completely ignoring the racing history and results achieved by its immediate forebears.

To the uninitiated (and that's 99.99 per cent of the population) a horse's pedigree is a jumble of names. To people like the battling trainer, however, a horse's family tree can be a treasure map showing how certain great ancestors' DNA, in conjunction with that of certain others, can produce an alchemy of characteristics and innate abilities unseen by those without the 'sixth sense' and encyclopaedic knowledge to calculate and spot such things.

One day, while browsing a New Zealand auction catalogue, the battling trainer noticed a yearling being offered for sale as the despised last lot of the day—Lot 41. The last few lots at any sale are not horses that the auctioneer expects to do well in the sale ring.

The sire of this particular lot was bred in England but had poor conformation and, although he was well bred, his breeder 'got rid of' him for a mere 100 guineas as a yearling. He was trained by a good trainer named Tom Hogg but only ever ran third in a poor 'selling' class race and Hogg 'got rid of' him to Australia where he was trained in Sydney by Peter Keith. The horse only managed one win in a restricted race at Randwick, and even that was a dead heat, not a stand-alone win.

Keith then 'got rid of' him to breeder Paddy Wade who stood him at stud in the bush at Wagga Wagga. Even there the horse could not attract mares from local owners and so Wade decided to 'get rid of' him to a New Zealand breeder and sold him for half what he had paid for him.

This battling trainer, however, perusing the family tree of this racetrack failure, saw that he was a grandson of two great champion sires Bend Or and Spearmint. He also had the blood of the great St Simon and the well-known champion sire Galopin on both sides of his family tree. Having Spearmint as a grandsire meant he also had the blood of champions Carbine and Musket in his veins.

All this aroused the battling trainer's interest.

The mother of the yearling for sale had damaged a shoulder as a young horse and raced once only, at five, and performed poorly. She was then left in the paddock and forgotten by her owners until they heard that a local stud was looking for second-rate mares to be served by a poorly performed cast-off stallion brought over from Australia. So her owners then 'got rid of' her to the stud owner for 60 guineas.

The battling trainer then looked a little further; he looked at the dam's mother's bloodlines. He ignored the fact that this mare was also an abject failure on the track and a failure at stud, being culled from the breeding stock of the Trelawney Park Stud at the age of fifteen and sold for 20 guineas, having produced no foals of any consequence. It was not even known if she was in foal at the time she was sold for the insulting price of £20, but she was, to an imported stallion.

The battling trainer noticed that the £20 reject had Musket blood on her dam side.

He began to get excited.

He became obsessed by Lot 41 in the catalogue for the 1928 Trentham sales, and implored his brother in New Zealand to attend the sale and buy the colt no matter what he looked like—'as long as he was sound'. His limit was a paltry 200 guineas.

The battling trainer's main problem was that he didn't even have the 200 guineas to back his judgement. He had to convince one of the owners he had trained a few horses for to pay for the horse.

The owner reluctantly agreed to fund the purchase and the trainer's brother was at the sale when the last lot of the day, Lot 41, came into the ring. He was not quite alone, one other bidder was present in the near empty arena, but he was acting as agent for a buyer who had gone home, like everyone else, and he was unsure about how much his buyer wanted to spend, so the colt was knocked down to the battling trainer's brother for 160 guineas on a day when 2300 guineas had been paid for one lot and the average prices had hovered between 1000 and 2000 guineas.

When the horse arrived in Sydney, it was suffering from seasickness and had broken out in pimples. The colt was ugly, over-tall, under-developed, awkward and gangly.

It was such a poor looking creature that the owner refused to pay for its feed and training and the battling trainer was forced to lease the horse himself and train it and race it in his own colours.

In case you're still wondering—the £20 reject was an old mare named Prayer Wheel and her poorly performed daughter was a small black mare named Entreaty. The racetrack failure and breeding reject who sired Lot 41 was Night Raid. The battling trainer was Harry Telford—and Lot 41 was the chestnut horse we all know as Phar Lap!   **JH**

WEIGHT WAS RIGHT
A.B. (BANJO) PATERSON

Banjo Paterson was well placed to gather great yarns. Well-known and well connected in both Sydney and the bush he was often told yarns by friends and acquaintances. He used the anecdotes on his regular radio broadcasts and in his newspaper articles. Here's an example.

Once, years ago, a son of the then Governor of New South Wales secured a ride in a picnic race. Intensely enthusiastic and a very lightweight, this young gentleman turned up, full of hope, to ride his first race.

He got on the scales with his saddle, and it turned out that he was 2 stone short of making the weight!

Not one of the amateurs had a lead bag to lend him, but no one would dream of leaving the Governor's son out. He was the main attraction of the meeting.

The officials had never been confronted with anything like this, but the caretaker was a man of resource. He shovelled a lot of sand into a sack and strapped it firmly on the pommel of a big saddle; weight was right, and away the field went.

It was an amateur hurdle race and, every time that the horse jumped, a puff of sand flew up, like the miniature spouts blown into the air by killer whales.

Simultaneously jumping and spouting, the vice-regal contender saw the race out, unsuccessfully, it is true; but he got more applause than the winner.

THE AMATEUR RIDER
A.B. (BANJO) PATERSON

Amateur jockeys were able to ride in registered meetings until the 1960s; there was still a race for 'gentleman riders' at Randwick on Bank Holiday when I was a kid. In Banjo's day it was very common and both Breaker Morant and Banjo himself rode in Sydney at Rosehill and Randwick. This poem, told from the point of view of the bloke strapping the horse, is all about not judging a book by its cover—and being cunning enough to change your mind 'after the event'.

Him going to ride for us! Him—with the pants and the eyeglass
    and all.
Amateur! don't he just look it—it's twenty to one on a fall.
Boss must be gone off his head to be sending our steeplechase crack
Out over fences like these with an object like that on his back.

Ride! Don't tell me he can ride. With his pants just as loose as
  balloons,
How can he sit on his horse? And his spurs like a pair of harpoons;
Ought to be under the Dog Act, he ought, and be kept off the
  course.
Fall! why, he'd fall off a cart, let alone off a steeplechase horse.

Yessir! the 'orse is all ready—I wish you'd have rode him before;
Nothing like knowing your 'orse, sir, and this chap's a terror to bore;
Battleaxe always could pull, and he rushes his fences like fun—
Stands off his jump twenty feet, and then springs like a shot from
  a gun.

Oh, he can jump 'em all right, sir, you make no mistake, 'e's a toff;
Clouts 'em in earnest, too, sometimes, you mind that he don't
  clout you off—
Don't seem to mind how he hits 'em, his shins is as hard as a nail,
Sometimes you'll see the fence shake and the splinters fly up from
  the rail.

All you can do is to hold him and just let him jump as he likes,
Give him his head at the fences, and hang on like death if he strikes;
Don't let him run himself out—you can lie third or fourth in the
  race—
Until you clear the stone wall, and from that you can put on the
  pace.

Fell at that wall once, he did, and it gave him a regular spread,
Ever since that time he flies it—he'll stop if you pull at his head,
Just let him race—you can trust him—he'll take first-class care
  he don't fall,
And I think that's the lot—but remember, he must have his head
  at the wall.

Well, he's down safe as far as the start, and he seems to sit on
  pretty neat,
Only his baggified breeches would ruinate anyone's seat.

They're away—here they come—the first fence, and he's head over
    heels for a crown!
Good for the new chum, he's over, and two of the others are down!

Now for the treble, my hearty—By Jove, he can ride, after all;
Whoop, that's your sort—let him fly them! He hasn't much fear
    of a fall.
Who in the world would have thought it? And aren't they just
    going a pace?
Little Recruit in the lead there will make it a stoutly run race.

Lord! But they're racing in earnest—and down goes Recruit on
    his head,
Rolling clean over his boy—it's a miracle if he ain't dead.
Battleaxe, Battleaxe yet! By the Lord, he's got most of 'em beat—
Ho! did you see how he struck, and the swell never moved in his
    seat?

Second time round, and, by Jingo! he's holding his lead of 'em well;
Hark to him clouting the timber! It don't seem to trouble the swell.
Now for the wall—let him rush it. A thirty-foot leap, I declare—
Never a shift in his seat, and he's racing for home like a hare.

What's that that's chasing him—Rataplan—regular demon to stay!
Sit down and ride for your life now! Oh, good, that's the style—come
    away!
Rataplan's certain to beat you, unless you can give him the slip;
Sit down and rub in the whalebone now—give him the spurs and
    the whip!

Battleaxe, Battleaxe, yet—and it's Battleaxe wins for a crown;
Look at him rushing the fences, he wants to bring t'other chap
    down.
Rataplan never will catch him if only he keeps on his pins;
Now! the last fence! and he's over it! Battleaxe, Battleaxe wins!

Well, sir, you rode him just perfect—I knew from the first you
    could ride.

Some of the chaps said you couldn't, an' I says just like this a'
    one side:

Mark me, I says, that's a tradesman—the saddle is where he was
    bred.

Weight! you're all right, sir, and thank you; and them was the
    words that I said.

A-MAIZING ESCAPE
A.B. (BANJO) PATERSON

*Here is another of Banjo Paterson's yarns about country race meet-
ings. This time it's a memory of a meeting on the south coast of
New South Wales.*

The most vivid memory that abides with me of south-coast racing
is of a meeting held many years ago in the Shoalhaven District.

The attendance consisted mostly of the local agriculturalists,
horny-handed sons of the soil quite formidable in appearance
and character. The foreign element was provided by a group of
welshers, sideshow artists, prize-fighters and acrobats who followed
the southern meetings as hawks follow a plague of mice.

The centre of the course consisted of a field of maize fully 10
feet high and when one bookmaker decided to 'take a sherry with
the dook and guy-a-whack' (a slang expression meaning to abscond
without paying), he melted into the maize and took cover like a
wounded black duck.

The hefty agriculturalists went in after him like South African
natives after a lion in the jungle. For a time, nothing could be seen
but the waving of the maize and nothing could be heard but the
shouts of the 'beaters' when they thought they caught sound or
scent of their prey.

After a time, all and sundry took a hand in the hunt; so the
'wanted man' simply slipped off his coat and joined in the search

for himself, shouting and waving his arms just as vigorously as anybody else.

When the searchers got tired of the business and started to straggle out of the maize he straggled out, too, on the far side, and kept putting one foot in front of the other till he struck the coach road to Sydney.

THE STUTTERING STABLEHAND

One of my favourite politically incorrect racetrack stories concerns an old stablehand, the iconic desperate old battler, who was a victim of *alalia syllabaris*, that is, he stuttered. This character appears in front of a bookmaker who is frantically writing out tickets and taking money hand-over-fist just before a big race.

'Waddya want, mate?' asks the bookie.

'I b-b-b-b-b-backed . . .' stammers the stablehand.

'Come on, mate,' says the bookie, 'you backed what?'

'I b-b-b-b-b-backed . . . a f-f-f-f-f-f-f-five t-t-t-t-t-t-t . . . ,' the flustered stablehand manages to get out, his face growing red in the process.

' 'Struth, mate,' says the impatient and insensitive bookie, 'you backed what!?'

'I b-b-b-b-b-backed . . . a f-f-f-f-f-f-f-five t-t-t-t-t-t-to . . .' comes the slow stuttering reply.

'Look, mate,' says the bookmaker, 'I haven't got time to hear your story now. You backed a five-to-one winner and lost your ticket or something—here's $50, I hope that's near enough, now get out of the way will you?'

The old stablehand is walking back to the horse stalls when he meets the trainer he works for. The trainer sees the $50 in his hand and asks, 'Bloody hell, where did you get $50?'

'W-w-w-w-w-w-well,' replies the stutterer, 'I w-w-w-w-went t-t-t-to t-t-t-tell that b-b-b-bookie, old M-M-M-Mr S-S-S-Samuels I b-b-b-b backed . . . your f-f-f-five t-t-t-t-ton h-h-h-horse float over his M-M-M-Mercedes . . . and he gave me f-f-f-fifty b-b-b-bucks!'

JH

BOTTLE QUEEN
TRADITIONAL/JIM HAYNES

*Here is a yarn which I heard often as a kid. It concerns the 'ponies'—
a term which may need some explaining for readers who cannot
remember the heyday of unregistered racing in our larger cities.*

*Prior to World War II, there were six racetracks between the
CBD and Botany Bay in Sydney. Apart from Randwick, there was
Kensington, where the University of New South Wales is now;
Rosebery, which became a housing estate in the 1960s; Ascot, which
made way for the expanding airport, Victoria Park, which is now
another housing estate near Moore Park; and Moorfields out towards
Kogarah. Other racetracks which provided events for unregistered
horses were to be found at Glebe, Menangle, Parramatta, Hornsby
and other suburbs.*

*These tracks operated from the late nineteenth century as 'pony
tracks'. Pony racing is a forgotten part of our racing history. Many
people today assume that thoroughbred racing is the only form of
horseracing we've ever had, but 'unregistered' or pony racing was
huge in Sydney and Melbourne from the 1890s to the 1930s and
many horses were trained in suburban backyards for these races,
although many 'pony' trainers had huge stables.*

*This yarn about a 'pony' which was trained by a couple of
'bottle-ohs' and used on the bottle cart when not racing, is a classic
tale which I heard decades ago and put to verse. My version is based
in Botany or Mascot. Obviously the joke is that the horse was also
trained to stop to collect bottles!*

We bred her in the suburbs and we trained her after dark,
Sometimes down the Botany Road and sometimes in the park,
And the way we used to feed her, it often led to rows,
We pinched the chaff from stables and the green stuff from the
    Chows.

Now her sire was imported but we never knew from where
And her mother, Black Moria, was a bottle dealer's mare.

We bought a set of colours, they were second hand and green,
And we had to call her something, so we called her Bottle Queen.

In the evenings when we galloped her I usually took the mount,
We didn't have a stopwatch, so me mate, he used to count.
She showed us four in forty-nine, one-forty for the mile,
But she coulda done much better, she was pulling all the while.

Now that's something like a gallop, on the sand with 10 stone up,
It'd win the English Derby! Or the Wagga Wagga Cup!
And when we thought we had her just as fit as she could be,
Me mate, he bit his sheila for the nomination fee.

We bunged her in a maiden and they dobbed her 7 stone,
Talk about a 'jacky', she was in it on her own!
So we worked her on the bottles when the cart was good and light,
It was bottles every morning and training every night.

We walked her down to Kenso on the morning of the race,
The books had never heard of her, we backed her win and place,
Then we rubbed her down and saddled her and led her to the track,
And told that hoop his fee was good . . . if he brought a winner back!

Well, they jumped away together but The Queen was soon in front,
As for all the others, they were never in the hunt!
She was romping past the leger, she was fighting for her head,
When some bastard waved a bottle . . . and our certainty stopped
    dead!
Now when folks who know hear, 'Bottle-Oh', they say, 'There's
    poor old Jim,
He mighta made a fortune, but the bottle did him in.'
Yes, we shoulda made a motza, my bloody oath we should,
Except I guess you might say that The Queen was trained too good!

So, don't talk to me of racing, you can see I've had enough.
It's a game for men with money and for blokes who know their stuff.
And if someone tries to tell you that the racing game is clean . . .
Just remember what I told you, my tale of Bottle Queen.

THE ONLY UNDEFEATED MELBOURNE CUP WINNER

Grand Flaneur holds a unique place in racing history; he is the only Melbourne Cup winner who was never defeated on a racetrack, starting nine times for nine wins. Added to this is the fact that he was a very successful and influential sire, whose son won England's two greatest races.

Grand Flaneur was a Sydney horse, owned by AJC Chairman Mr W.A. Long at a time when colonial rivalry was intense. He was by the great colonial sire Yattendon, out of an imported mare, First Lady. He won at Flemington over five furlongs as a two year old and then was rested until the Sydney Spring Carnival of 1880. He duly took out the AJC Derby and Mares Produce Stakes and then returned to Melbourne to win the Victoria Derby, Melbourne Cup and Mares Produce Stakes within a week, defeating the local champion, Progress, each time.

Grand Flaneur was the horse who finally gave one of the greatest jockeys of the time, Tom Hales, his one and only Melbourne Cup win. The colt then won the 1881 VRC Champion Stakes and VRC St Leger Stakes and ended his career by winning the 1881 VRC Town Plate.

He was taken back to Sydney for the AJC Autumn Carnival but broke down and was retired to stand at stud. Bravo, the 1889 Melbourne Cup winner, was from his first crop of foals and he also sired the 1894 Cup winner Patron and was the leading Australian sire in 1894–95.

Grand Flaneur's son, Merman, won the prestigious Williamstown Cup in 1896 and then went to race in Britain. Owned by the famous actress Lily Langtry, Merman won the Goodwood Cup in 1899 and the Ascot Gold Cup in 1900, the same year that his sire Grand Flaneur died, aged twenty-two, at the Chipping Norton Stud near Liverpool in Sydney.

You might spare a thought for the good Victorian colt Progress, who ran second to Grand Flaneur five times in classic races

in Melbourne. If you're from New South Wales, of course, you
probably won't bother!   **JH**

THE GROG-AN'-GRUMBLE STEEPLECHASE
HENRY LAWSON

*Although he wasn't a 'horsey' type by any stretch of the imagina-
tion, even Henry Lawson found time to spin a yarn about the
unscrupulous locals who made it near impossible for outsiders to
succeed at race meetings in the bush. He named this parochial little
town 'Grog and Grumble'.*

*While yarns about training horses to stop for bottles, or return
home after being sold, may seem far-fetched—Lawson went one
better in this yarn about a horse who was trained to stick out his
tongue in close finishes.*

'Twixt the coastline and the border lay the town of Grog-an'-Grumble
In the days before the bushman was a dull 'n' heartless drudge,
An' they say the local meeting was a drunken rough-and-tumble,
Which was ended pretty often by an inquest on the judge.
An' 'tis said the city talent very often caught a tartar
In the Grog-an'-Grumble sportsman, 'n' returned with broken heads,
For the fortune, life, and safety of the Grog-an'-Grumble starter
Mostly hung upon the finish of the local thoroughbreds.

Pat McDurmer was the owner of a horse they called the Screamer,
Which he called 'the quickest shtepper 'twixt the Darling and
    the sea',
And I think it's very doubtful if the stomach-troubled dreamer
Ever saw a more outrageous piece of equine scenery;
For his points were most decided, from his end to his beginning,
He had eyes of different colour, and his legs they wasn't mates.
Pat McDurmer said he always came 'within a flip of winnin' ',
An' his sire had come from England, 'n' his dam was from the States.

Friends would argue with McDurmer, and they said he was in error
To put up his horse the Screamer, for he'd lose in any case,
And they said a city racer by the name of Holy Terror
Was regarded as the winner of the coming steeplechase;
But he said he had the knowledge to come in when it was raining,
And irrelevantly mentioned that he knew the time of day,
So he rose in their opinion. It was noticed that the training
Of the Screamer was conducted in a dark, mysterious way.

Well, the day arrived in glory; 'twas a day of jubilation
With careless-hearted bushmen for a hundred miles around,
An' the rum 'n' beer 'n' whisky came in wagons from the station,
An' the Holy Terror talent were the first upon the ground.
Judge McArd, with whose opinion it was scarcely safe to wrestle,
Took his dangerous position on the bark-and-sapling stand:
He was what the local Stiggins used to speak of as a 'vessel
Of wrath', and he'd a bludgeon that he carried in his hand.

'Off ye go!' the starter shouted, as down fell a stupid jockey—
Off they started in disorder—left the jockey where he lay—
And they fell and rolled and galloped down the crooked course
        and rocky,
Till the pumping of the Screamer could be heard a mile away.
But he kept his legs and galloped; he was used to rugged courses,
And he lumbered down the gully till the ridge began to quake:
And he ploughed along the siding, raising earth till other horses
An' their riders, too, were blinded by the dust-cloud in his wake.

From the ruck he'd struggled slowly—they were much surprised
        to find him
Close abeam the Holy Terror as along the flat they tore—
Even higher still and denser rose the cloud of dust behind him,
While in more divided splinters flew the shattered rails before.
'Terror!' 'Dead heat!' they were shouting—'Terror!' but the Screamer
        hung out
Nose to nose with Holy Terror as across the creek they swung,

An' McDurmer shouted loudly, 'Put yer tongue out! put yer tongue out!'

An' the Screamer put his tongue out . . . and he won by half-a-tongue.

THE HORSE WHO COULDN'T GET HIS SHOES ON

The greatest racehorse of all time, in my humble opinion, was Carbine, who won thirty-three of his forty-three starts and was only unplaced once, when suffering from a badly cracked hoof. He won fifteen races in succession, and seventeen of his last eighteen races.

Carbine was bred in New Zealand. His sire was the English Ascot Stakes winner Musket and his dam, Mersey, was also imported from England.

After five wins in New Zealand, he was sent to Melbourne for the VRC Derby in 1888 but finished second when his jockey, New Zealander Bob Derret, dropped a rein in the tight finish.

Urged on by astute Melbourne trainer Walter Hickenbotham, VRC committeeman Donald Wallace bought Carbine for 3000 guineas.

Walter Hickenbotham took over training Carbine and, after a third in the Newmarket Handicap and a second in the Australian Cup, he went on a winning spree, taking first place seven times from eight starts as a three year old, at distances from 7 furlongs (1.4 kilometres) to 3 miles (4.8 kilometres), including the Sydney Cup, in which he carried 15.4 kilograms over weight-for-age.

As a three year old, Carbine won four races in four days during the Sydney Autumn Carnival in 1890, including the Sydney Cup on the second day. The next day he won the All-Aged Stakes over a mile and the Cumberland Stakes over 2 miles and, two days later, he won the AJC Plate over 3 miles.

While in training for his four-year-old season, Carbine cracked a heel so badly that he could not race without a special binding of beeswax and cloth and a special bar shoe.

He ran a brave second to Bravo in the Melbourne Cup of 1889. Carrying 63 kilograms to Bravo's 54 kilograms, Carbine's damaged hoof opened up during the race and he was beaten by a length by the son of Grand Flaneur.

Two days later, with his hoof repaired, he won the Flying Stakes over 7 furlongs (1400 metres) but, two days after that, he ran last in the Canterbury Plate over 2 miles (3200 metres) when the binding on his hoof completely fell apart. It was the only unplaced run of his career.

With a good rest and his hoof patched up again, Carbine returned to racing in March 1890 and won three of his four starts in Melbourne before heading to Sydney for the Autumn Carnival.

As a four year old, Carbine went one better than the previous year. This time he won five races at distances from 1 mile to 3 miles in seven days: the Autumn Stakes, on 5 April; the Sydney Cup, carrying 61.2 kilograms; on 7 April; the All-Aged Stakes and the Cumberland Stakes on 10 April; and the AJC Plate on 12 April.

Carbine then won another eight races before racing into immortality in the Melbourne Cup of 1890, carrying the biggest winning weight in history, 66.5 kilograms.

Carbine raced seven more times for six victories. His narrow defeat came in the All-Aged Stakes at Randwick. His hoof was so bad that day that shoes could not be fitted, so he raced without shoes and ran second to Marvel on a slippery wet track.

Unperturbed, Walter Hickenbotham took Carbine back to his stall, persevered and finally managed to get shoes on the champion, who promptly went out a few races later and beat Marvel easily over 2 miles in the Cumberland Stakes.

After a short successful career as a sire in Australia, Carbine was purchased to stand at Welbeck Stud in England as a second string sire to the famous champion St Simon. Because he was so good-natured and placid, Carbine was bred to daughters of St Simon, who had a savage temperament.

In spite of being only 'second fiddle' sire at Welbeck, Carbine became one of the most successful sires in racing history. His

Australian son Wallace was one of the greatest stayers and sires in Australian racing history and between 1902 and 1906 Carbine sired 138 winners in the UK.

Carbine's son Spearmint won the 1906 Epsom Derby and was a great success at stud.

One reason Carbine was sold to Welbeck Stud was that there, on soft English soil, he didn't have to wear shoes!

Carbine died in 1914 at the ripe old age of twenty-nine. His blood has been present in the pedigrees of over fifty Melbourne Cup winners, including Makybe Diva. Phar Lap was Carbine's great great grandson.

Not bad for a horse who couldn't get his shoes on. **JH**

FLYING KATE
ANONYMOUS

If you think Henry's Lawson's yarn about the horse trained to poke out his tongue is well beyond credibility, here is the most outrageous racing yarn of all time. It's about a mare so good that she raced while she was in foal and then . . . oh, look, read it for yourself and find out! It's by that well-known Aussie poet A. Nonymous.

It makes us old hands sick and tired to hear
Them talk of their champions of today,
Eurythmics and Davids (yes, I'll have a beer)
Are only fair hacks in their way.

Now this happened out West before records were took,
And 'tis not to be found in the guide,
But it's honest—Gor' struth, and can't be mistook,
For it happened that I had the ride.

'Twas the Hummer's Creek Cup, and our mare, Flying Kate,
Was allotted eleven stone two;
The race was two miles, you'll agree with me, mate,
It was asking her something to do.

She was heavy in foal, but the owner and me
Decided to give her a spin,
We were right on the rocks, 'twas the end of a spree,
So we needed a bit of a win.

I saddled her up and went down with the rest,
Her movements were clumsy and slow,
The starter to get us in line did his best,
Then swishing his flag he said, 'Go!'

The field jumped away but the mare seemed asleep,
And I thought to myself, 'We've been sold,'
Then I heard something queer, and I felt I could weep,
For strike me if Kate hadn't foaled.

The field by this time had gone half-a-mile,
But I knew what the old mare could do,
So I gave her a cut with the whip—you can smile,
But the game little beast simply flew.

'Twas then she showed them her wonderful speed,
For we mowed down the field one by one,
With a furlong to go we were out in the lead,
And prepared for a last final run.

Then something came at us right on the outside,
And we only just scratched past the pole,
When I had a good look I thought I'd have died,
For I'm blowed if it wasn't the foal.

I HAVE A DREAM!

While we are roaming the realms of pure fantasy, here is a racing
yarn that I have heard years ago but cannot corroborate.

The scene was suburban Melbourne a few years back. A bloke
bumped into a neighbour on the tram going home.

'Hello, Bill,' said the friend, 'where have you been?'

'I've been to the races,' Bill replied.

'You don't usually go to the midweek meetings, do you?' said the neighbour.

'No,' said Bill, 'I only went today because I had a very vivid dream early this morning. I saw sunshine through fluffy clouds and a voice kept repeating "number seven . . . number seven . . .". So I looked in the paper and there was a horse carrying saddlecloth seven, coming out of barrier seven, in the seventh race at Sandown, at seven to one. So I went to the track and put $777 dollars on it.'

'What happened?' asked the neighbour.

'It ran seventh,' replied Bill.   JH

FLASH JACK'S LAST RACE
A.B. (BANJO) PATERSON

Here is another yarn from the pen of Banjo Paterson. This incident took place not far from where Banjo spent his childhood. He went to school at Binalong, not far from Jugiong.

It was at the hamlet of Jugiong that an event occurred, which is perhaps unique in turf history.

It was a publican's meeting, which means that the promoter was less concerned with gate money than with the sale of strong liquor.

The unfenced course was laid out alongside the Murrumbidgee River and one of the Osborne family, graziers in the district, had entered a mare which was fed and looked after on the other side of the river.

Off they went, and the mare made straight for home, jumping into the river and nearly drowning the jockey, who was rescued by a young Aboriginal boy.

Meanwhile, Mr Osborne, under a pardonable mistake, was cheering on another runner in the belief that it was his mare.

Then there came a splashing sound at the back of the wagonette and Mr Osborne, looking around, was astonished to see his jockey.

'Well, I'll be damned,' he said. 'What are you doing here? Where's the mare?'

'She's home by now,' said the boy, a bush youngster known locally as 'Flash Jack from Gundagai'.

'And I'm going home, too,' he added, 'I've had enough of it. In the last race my moke fell in front of the field and there was me lying on the track with nothing but horses' heels going over my head for half an hour and this time I was nearly drowned. I'd sunk four times when that black boy came in after me.

'I'd like a job, Mr Osborne, picking up fleeces in the shed if you ain't full up; but Flash Jack has rode his last race.'

ASK THE HORSE
A.B. (BANJO) PATERSON

Banjo Paterson was a successful amateur jockey and knew most of the great jockeys and trainers of his day. As a journalist with the Sportsman *newspaper, he spent much of his time studying the racing game and even wrote a detailed treatise explaining betting and other aspects of the complex world of racing. Here he is reminiscing about a famous old trainer, Sydney's Bill Kelso Senior.*

Bill Kelso was an old-time trainer, a very direct-spoken man and if you didn't like what he said you could leave it.

I was doing some amateur riding and falling about over steeplechase fences and, like a lot of other young fellows, I began to fancy myself as a judge of racing. So, one day I asked old Kelso, 'Mr Kelso, what will win this race?'

'Well,' he said, 'I'll tell you something. Do you know what I was before I went in for training?'

I said, 'No.'

He said, 'I was working for a pound a week and I might be working for a pound a week still, only for young fools like you that will go betting. You leave it alone or get somebody to sew your pockets up before you come to the races.'

Well, it wasn't very polite but it was good advice.

The committee had him in once to explain the running of the race, before the days of stipendiary stewards. It took them a lot of trouble to get the committee together and they sat down, prepared for a good long explanation.

'Mr Kelso,' said the chairman, 'can you tell us why your horse ran so badly today?'

'No, I'm afraid I can't,' he said, 'you'll have to ask the horse. He's the only one that knows.'

THE TWO FALCONS

Here are two trivia questions for you:

When did Falcon run third and eleventh in the Melbourne Cup?
When did Falcon run third but didn't finish third in the Melbourne Cup?

Confusing? You bet it is, but it's true.

The Melbourne Cup of 1866, won by The Barb as a three year old, was a controversial race. There were two horses named Falcon engaged. One of them, from Sydney, also trained by The Barb's trainer, 'Honest' John Tait, finished third behind The Barb but the judge would not declare a third place, as the colours carried by the 'Sydney Falcon', yellow jacket and red cap, did not match any of those of the entries given to the judges on the official race card.

Tait had substituted a red cap on his second runner to differentiate the colours from those carried by The Barb, but evidently he didn't notify the judge officially. The following day at four o'clock, the stewards declared 'Sydney Falcon' had been placed third, but many bookmakers refused to pay out on the horse, arguing that only the judge had the power to 'place' horses officially.

So Falcon, from Sydney, ran third according to the stewards but wasn't officially third according to the judges and Falcon, from Melbourne, ran eleventh—officially!

JH

TOO MANY TIM WHIFFLERS!

Before the registration of names was properly controlled, different horses often raced with the same names. There were three Tim Whifflers in the Australian colonies in the 1860s, one was an imported stallion who sired the 1876 Melbourne Cup winner Briseis and the other two Tim Whifflers both raced in the Melbourne Cup of 1867. 'Sydney Tim', trained by Etienne de Mestre, won the Cup and 'Melbourne Tim' ran fifth.   **JH**

ROBINSON CRUSOE

In 1876, the steamer *City of Melbourne* ran into a savage storm taking the Sydney horses to Melbourne for the Spring Carnival and all but one were washed overboard and drowned.

One of the Sydney champions lost on that sad night was Robin Hood. According to the great trainer Etienne de Mestre, he was the best horse he ever trained.

In a shocking display of poor taste, the bookmakers of Melbourne held a party to celebrate the tragedy and rejoice at all the money they had suddenly gained, for the Sydney horses who perished had been well backed to beat the local Melbourne horses in the big Spring races.

The one surviving horse had already won the AJC Derby but was, strangely, as yet unnamed. He was appropriately named Robinson Crusoe and went on to be a champion and a great sire.

JH

A POST-CUP TALE
C.J. DENNIS

All true 'racing tragics' know the sickening feeling that overwhelms a punter when he has done the form and chosen his horse but for some inexplicable reason changes his mind at the last minute, only to see the horse he originally chose logically and painstakingly win at good odds.

C.J. Dennis was the Aussie poet who best captured the voice and feelings of the common man. Here is his yarn about the punter who picked the Melbourne Cup winner in 1928, the Sydney three year old, Trivalve, and was talked out of backing him at the last minute. It brings a tear to my eye every time I read it!

I 'ad the money in me 'and!
Fair dinkum! Right there, by the stand.
I tole me wife at breakfus' time,
Straight out: 'Trivalve,' I sez 'is prime.
Trivalve,' I sez. An', all the week,
I swear ther's no one 'eard me speak
Another 'orse's name. Why, look,
I 'ad the oil straight from a Book
On Sund'y at me cousin's place
When we was torkin' of the race.
'Trivalve,' 'e sez. 'Is chance is grand.'
I 'ad the money in me 'and!

Fair in me 'and I 'ad the dough!
An' then a man 'as got to go—
Wot? Tough? Look, if I 'adn't met
Jim Smith (I ain't forgave 'im yet)
'E takes an' grabs me be the coat.
'Trivalve!' 'e sez. 'That 'airy goat!'
(I 'ad the money in me 'and
Just makin' for the bookie's stand)
'Trivalve?' 'e sez. 'Ar, turn it up!
'Ow could 'e win a flamin' Cup?'
Of course, I thort 'e muster knoo.
'Im livin' near a trainer, too.

Right 'ere, like that, fair in me fist
I 'ad the notes! An' then I missed—
Missed like a mug fair on the knock
Becos 'is maggin' done me block.
'That airy goat?' 'e sez. 'E's crook!'

Fair knocked me back, 'e did. An' look,
I 'ad the money in me 'and!
Fair in me paw! An', un'erstand,
Sixes at least I coulder got—
Thirty to five, an' made me pot.
Today I mighter been real rich—
Rollin' in dough! Instid o' which,
'Ere's me—Aw! Don't it beat the band?
I 'AD THE MONEY IN ME 'AND!
Put me clean off, that's wot 'e did . . .
Say, could yeh len' us 'arf a quid?

NO CHANCE

It was a country race meeting with small fields and only a few
bookies fielding on the six races.

Just before the last race, a handicap with five starters, a well-
dressed 'squatter' type cockie approaches one of the bookies who
has come up from the big smoke to the meeting.

'I want a hundred on Blue Peter,' he says, 'what are the odds?'

'You can have ten to one,' says the bookie and the bloke is quite
happy with that and hands over the money.

Five minutes later, the cockie is back, having visited the other
five or six bookmakers fielding that day.

'Do you still have Blue Peter at tens?' he asks.

'Look, mate,' says the bookie, 'you can have twelves if you like,
but I have to tell you, I don't think he has a chance.'

'That's okay,' says the cockie, 'I only want the bet, not the advice.'
And he pulls out another hundred and gets his ticket.

Just as the race is about to start, he is back again, 'What price
Blue Peter now?' he asks.

'Mate, you can have twenty to one but I have to tell you, I own
Blue Peter and we brought him up for the run. The horse is running
off weight and being trained for much longer races—he hasn't
much hope at all in this race. I've already got two hundred quid
of your money, I don't want to rob you blind!'

'That's okay,' says the cockie, unperturbed, 'I'll have another hundred at twenties.'

The bookie shrugs and writes the ticket.

The five-horse field is despatched by the starter and, in a very slowly run race, Blue Peter wins by two lengths.

The bookie is stunned; he pays out and says to the cockie, 'How the hell did you work that out? We only brought the horse up here to run him into some condition! I told you I owned him, and you still knew he could win, what did you know that we didn't?'

'Well,' said the cockie, stuffing the money into his pockets, 'I knew that I owned the other four runners.'   JH

WRONG DIAGNOSIS

The Western District of Victoria is a great area for racing. This story was told to me by a great old yarn spinner at Port Fairy, near Warrnambool. He swore it was true but couldn't give me any names or details.

It seems that an old cocky once turned up at a jumps meeting with a tough old steeplechaser, but with no jockey to ride it. As the lad he had engaged for the ride didn't show up, the old trainer approached one of the professional city jockeys and asked if he would take the ride.

The jockey looked the old bloke up and down with a bored expression on his face and said, 'All right, Pop, I'll take him around for you I suppose, the moke I was booked for has been scratched and it will warm me up for the important races later in the day.'

As the old bloke legged the jockey aboard, he whispered urgently, 'Now, listen carefully, this horse will win easily if you remember one thing.'

'I'll do a good job on him, Pop,' the jockey said impatiently, 'don't worry, I do know how to ride, you know.'

The old trainer persisted, 'This is important, listen. As you approach each jump, you must say "one, two, three . . . jump!". If you do that he'll win.'

The jockey was already moving the horse away from the old trainer as this advice was given. 'Sure, Pop, it'll be all right, don't you worry,' he called back over his shoulder.

Of course, the smug city jockey took no notice of the old trainer's advice. Away went the field and the tough old chaser was up with the leaders as they approached the first fence. When the horse made no preparation at all to jump, the jockey desperately attempted to lift him. The horse belatedly rose to the jump, struck heavily and almost dislodged the startled 'professional'.

This incident caused them to fall right back through the field, the horse being lucky to stay on his feet and the jockey using all his skill to stay in the saddle. The jockey's mind was now racing to remember the old man's advice and, at the next jump, he succeeded in calling out, 'One, two, three . . . jump!' and the horse easily accounted for the fence.

The jockey repeated the process at each jump and the horse jumped brilliantly, making up many lengths, but just failing to catch the winner at the post.

On his return to the enclosure, the jockey was confronted by the old trainer who said, 'You didn't listen to me, did you? You didn't say "one, two, three . . . jump" at the first fence.'

'Yes, I did, Pop,' lied the jockey, 'but perhaps I didn't say it loudly enough the first time. He didn't hear me, he must be deaf.'

'He's not deaf, you bloody fool,' replied the old trainer laconically. 'He's blind.' **JH**

WHEN BUSHRANGERS STOLE A MELBOURNE CUP WINNER

In 1864, a large group of valuable horses was taken by bushrangers from the Lee family's farm near Bathurst and driven south. One of the family, Henry Lee, followed them to Monaro where police apprehended them and all the horses except one were recovered.

The missing horse was a black colt foal that the kindly, horse-loving bushrangers had left with a farmer at Caloola when it went lame and could not travel. The loss was reported in the press and the farmer returned the foal to its rightful owners a few weeks later.

That foal grew up to be The Barb.

The Barb was a small jet-black horse who became known in the press as 'the black demon'.

In 1866, the AJC introduced new races at Randwick to rival those run in Melbourne and, in the true spirit of inter-colonial rivalry, the Victorian colt, Fishhook, was purchased for a record sum by famous Victorian racing man C.B. Fisher, and sent to Sydney to win the AJC Derby.

The Barb trounced Fishhook and The Barb's trainer, 'Honest' John Tait, decided to take him to Melbourne and rub salt into the wounds by winning the Melbourne Cup.

The Barb would go on to win the Sydney Cup twice, once carrying the biggest winning weight in the race's history, 10 stone 8 pounds (67 kilograms). He was virtually unbeatable at weight-for-age and was unbeaten as a five year old. He travelled successfully to win the Melbourne Cup at three and took out the VRC Port Phillip Stakes and the Launceston Town Plate in Tasmania as a four year old. The Barb went on to win sixteen of his twenty-three starts.

And all because the kind-hearted, horse-loving bushrangers spared him as a foal and left him with a farmer at Caloola to recover from lameness. The bushrangers, incidentally, were arrested, convicted and served prison sentences.   JH

FATHER RILEY'S HORSE
A.B. (BANJO) PATERSON

This is one of the best ever racehorse yarns. It has everything required of a ripping yarn, a cops-and-robbers chase, an impossible scheme that miraculously works out, cunning plans and deceptions, underdogs triumphant, a 'ghost', tongue-in-cheek humour and a huge dose of Irish sentimentality. Banjo was a genius at telling a good yarn!

'Twas the horse thief, Andy Regan, that was hunted like a dog
By the troopers of the upper Murray side,
They had searched in every gully—they had looked in every log,
But never sight or track of him they spied,
Till the priest at Kiley's Crossing heard a knocking very late
And a whisper, 'Father Riley—come across!'
So his Rev'rence in pyjamas trotted softly to the gate
And admitted Andy Regan—and a horse!

'Now, it's listen, Father Riley, to the words I've got to say,
For it's close upon my death I am tonight.
With the troopers hard behind me I've been hiding all the day
In the gullies keeping close and out of sight.
But they're watching all the ranges till there's not a bird could fly,
And I'm fairly worn to pieces with the strife,
So I'm taking no more trouble, but I'm going home to die,
'Tis the only way I see to save my life.

'Yes, I'm making home to mother's, and I'll die o' Tuesday next
An' be buried on the Thursday—and, of course,
I'm prepared to meet my penance, but with one thing I'm perplexed
And it's—Father, it's this jewel of a horse!
He was never bought nor paid for, and there's not a man can swear
To his owner or his breeder, but I know,
That his sire was by Pedantic from the Old Pretender mare
And his dam was close related to The Roe.

'And there's nothing in the district that can race him for a step,
He could canter while they're going at their top:
He's the king of all the leppers that was ever seen to lep,
A five-foot fence—he'd clear it in a hop!
So I'll leave him with you, Father, till the dead shall rise again,
'Tis yourself that knows a good 'un; and, of course,
You can say he's got by Moonlight out of Paddy Murphy's plain
If you're ever asked the breeding of the horse!

'But it's getting on to daylight and it's time to say goodbye,
For the stars above the east are growing pale.

And I'm making home to mother—and it's hard for me to die!
But it's harder still, is keeping out of gaol!
You can ride the old horse over to my grave across the dip
Where the wattle bloom is waving overhead.
Sure he'll jump them fences easy—you must never raise the whip
Or he'll rush 'em!—now, goodbye!' and he had fled!

So they buried Andy Regan, and they buried him to rights,
In the graveyard at the back of Kiley's Hill;
There were five-and-twenty mourners who had five-and-twenty
    fights
Till the very boldest fighters had their fill.
There were fifty horses racing from the graveyard to the pub,
And their riders flogged each other all the while.
And the lashin's of the liquor! And the lavin's of the grub!
Oh, poor Andy went to rest in proper style.

Then the races came to Kiley's—with a steeplechase and all,
For the folk were mostly Irish round about,
And it takes an Irish rider to be fearless of a fall,
They were training morning in and morning out.
But they never started training till the sun was on the course
For a superstitious story kept 'em back,
That the ghost of Andy Regan on a slashing chestnut horse,
Had been training by the starlight on the track.

And they read the nominations for the races with surprise
And amusement at the Father's little joke,
For a novice had been entered for the steeplechasing prize,
And they found it was Father Riley's moke!
He was neat enough to gallop, he was strong enough to stay!
But his owner's views of training were immense,
For the Reverend Father Riley used to ride him every day,
And he never saw a hurdle nor a fence.

And the priest would join the laughter: 'Oh,' said he, 'I put him in,
For there's five-and-twenty sovereigns to be won.
And the poor would find it useful, if the chestnut chanced to win,

And he'll maybe win when all is said and done!'
He had called him Faugh-a-ballagh, which is French for 'Clear
    the course',
And his colours were a vivid shade of green:
All the Dooleys and O'Donnells were on Father Riley's horse,
While the Orangemen were backing Mandarin!

It was Hogan, the dog poisoner—aged man and very wise,
Who was camping in the racecourse with his swag,
And who ventured the opinion, to the township's great surprise,
That the race would go to Father Riley's nag.
'You can talk about your riders—and the horse has not been schooled,
And the fences is terrific, and the rest!
When the field is fairly going, then ye'll see ye've all been fooled,
And the chestnut horse will battle with the best.

'For there's some has got condition, and they think the race is sure,
And the chestnut horse will fall beneath the weight,
But the hopes of all the helpless, and the prayers of all the poor,
Will be running by his side to keep him straight.
And it's what's the need of schoolin' or of workin' on the track,
When the saints are there to guide him round the course!
I've prayed him over every fence—I've prayed him out and back!
And I'll bet my cash on Father Riley's horse!'

Oh, the steeple was a caution! They went tearin' round and round,
And the fences rang and rattled where they struck.
There was some that cleared the water—there was more fell in
    and drowned,
Some blamed the men and others blamed the luck!
But the whips were flying freely when the field came into view,
For the finish down the long green stretch of course,
And in front of all the flyers—jumpin' like a kangaroo,
Came the rank outsider—Father Riley's horse!

Oh, the shouting and the cheering as he rattled past the post!
For he left the others standing, in the straight;
And the rider—well, they reckoned it was Andy Regan's ghost,

And it beat 'em how a ghost would draw the weight!
But he weighed in, nine stone seven, then he laughed and disappeared,
Like a banshee (which is Spanish for an elf),
And old Hogan muttered sagely, 'If it wasn't for the beard
They'd be thinking it was Andy Regan's self!'

And the poor of Kiley's Crossing drank the health at Christmastide
Of the chestnut and his rider dressed in green.
There was never such a rider, not since Andy Regan died,
And they wondered who on earth he could have been.
But they settled it among 'em, for the story got about,
'Mongst the bushmen and the people on the course,
That the Devil had been ordered to let Andy Regan out
For the steeplechase on Father Riley's horse!

ROUGHNECK

It was Oakbank, 1978. It was a small field for the Great Eastern Steeplechase that year as the track was quite heavy and the weather was wet over Easter.

The atmosphere was a little dampened and the ground was soggy underfoot but it was still Oakbank, the great Easter Racing Carnival in the Adelaide Hills.

In 1978, most of the already small field either fell or retired. Oddly enough, it was mostly the front-runners who fell or dropped out.

Of those left standing towards the end, three were way back in the field and one, a tough little chestnut gelding with the totally appropriate name of Roughneck, ridden by veteran jockey Peter Hely, was left way out in front.

What a fizzer of a race, you might think. How can four horses scattered over a mile of racetrack with one half a miles in front be of any interest?

You might think that.

You might also think these things demonstrate why jumps races hold little interest and are an anachronism.

You'd be wrong on both counts.

You might think, in a race like that, there's no real contest.

You'd be wrong again.

There was no cheering, no roaring of the crowd as Roughneck cleared the fallen log, came down the hill, entered the straight and approached the last two jumps.

There was just an uncanny quiet.

You see—Roughneck was just about out on his feet. He was visibly exhausted and laying in badly.

At the second last, he clipped the jump and almost went down, just about touching his nose on the turf. He regained his footing but staggered sideways as the entire crowd caught its breath.

I'd never heard fifty thousand people catch their breath before. It was a sound that filled the valley.

Hely somehow got him balanced again and approached the last jump.

In those few seconds, I truly came to believe in something akin to Jung's theory of the collective subconscious or the power of prayer. I knew that everyone watching was willing that little chestnut gelding to get over that last fence.

He steadied and approached the fence at a speed just fast enough to gain some momentum for a final jump.

Hely seemed to lift him by the reins and he rose to take the last fence . . . and landed safely,

Then the crowd roared.

And that's the loudest roar I've ever heard on a racetrack anywhere in the world.

Hats flew into the air and the cheering lasted until long after Roughneck had cantered slowly past the winning post.

No one had backed him. He was forty-to-one.

The nearest horse wasn't even in the straight when he cleared the last jump. He won by forty lengths.

But that's the best battle down the straight that I ever saw. **JH**

HOW THE FAVOURITE BEAT US
A.B. (BANJO) PATERSON

*This is a parody of a famous Adam Lindsay Gordon poem called
'How We Beat the Favourite' and it's even written in exactly the
same rhyme and metre as that famous poem. It's the classic yarn
of a bloke who decides to pull up his horse because he can't get a
decent price about her, but gives the jockey the wrong signal by
mistake. A 'brown', incidentally, is a penny, or any copper coin.
The advice 'win when you're able' is still the best advice any owner
or trainer can follow!*

'Aye,' said the boozer, 'I tell you it's true, sir,
I once was a punter with plenty of pelf,
But gone is my glory, I'll tell you the story
How I stiffened my horse and got stiffened myself.

''Twas a mare called the Cracker, I came down to back her,
But found she was favourite all of a rush,
The folk just did pour on to lay six to four on,
And several bookies were killed in the crush.

'It seems old Tomato was stiff, though a starter;
They reckoned him fit for the Caulfield to keep.
The Bloke and the Donah were scratched by their owner,
He only was offered three-fourths of the sweep.

'We knew Salamander was slow as a gander,
The mare could have beat him the length of the straight,
And old Manumission was out of condition,
And most of the others were running off weight.

'No doubt someone "blew it", for everyone knew it,
The bets were all gone, and I muttered in spite,
"If I can't get a copper, by Jingo, I'll stop her,
Let the public fall in, it will serve the brutes right."

'I said to the jockey, "Now, listen, my cocky,
You watch as you're cantering down by the stand,
I'll wait where that toff is and give you the office,
You're only to win if I lift up my hand."

'I then tried to back her—"What price is the Cracker?"
"Our books are all full, sir," each bookie did swear;
My mind, then, I made up, my fortune I played up
I bet every shilling against my own mare.

'I strolled to the gateway, the mare in the straight way
Was shifting and dancing, and pawing the ground,
The boy saw me enter and wheeled for his canter,
When a darned great mosquito came buzzing around.

'They breed 'em et Hexham, it's risky to vex 'em,
They suck a man dry at a sitting, no doubt,
But just as the mare passed, he fluttered my hair past,
I lifted my hand, and I flattened him out.

'I was stunned when they started, the mare simply darted
Away to the front when the flag was let fall,
For none there could match her, and none tried to catch her—
She finished a furlong in front of them all.

'You bet that I went for the boy, whom I sent for
The moment he weighed and came out of the stand—
"Who paid you to win it? Come, own up this minute."
"Lord love yer," said he, "why, you lifted your hand."

''Twas true, by St Peter, that cursed "muskeeter"
Had broke me so broke that I hadn't a brown,
And you'll find the best course is when dealing with horses
To win when you're able, and keep your hands down.'

A CUNNING PLAN

As well as his amazing record of victories, Phar Lap could probably have also easily won the Caulfield Cup of 1930. The fact that he was left in the field so long and scratched quite late was controversial at the time.

It was, indeed, part of a 'cunning plan'.

Nothing outside the rules of racing took place but some, mostly bookmakers, consider the actions of Harry Telford and fellow Sydney trainer Frank McGrath had a tinge of mischief about them, one might even say skulduggery.

Most racing men say it was a stroke of genius.

I have to interrupt the narrative here to say a few things.

Firstly, I have the greatest respect for both men. Harry Telford was the astute 'genius' who had the vision to pick Phar Lap as a future champion based wholly upon his breeding and Frank McGrath was one of the greatest trainers of stayers in our racing history. He trained Prince Foote to win the Melbourne Cup in 1909 and Peter Pan to win two more in the 1930s.

As a punter, I applaud their cunning plan to empty the bookies' bags without any harm being done to man or beast and no interference with the way the races were run.

Indeed, I have it on the best authority that Frank McGrath never knowingly did anything detrimental to any of the great horses he trained. He patiently nursed Peter Pan back to health through two serious illnesses, an infection, caused by running a nail though his hoof as a two year old, and a debilitating form of rheumatism in his shoulders which caused him to miss an entire year of racing.

In each case, patience and kindness prevailed and Peter Pan won two Melbourne Cups, one after each setback.

McGrath's patience and love of the horses he trained was evident again with his stayer Denis Boy, who he nursed back to racing fitness after breaking a knee bone. McGrath kept the horse's leg in a sling until the bone healed. He then trained Denis Boy to win the 1932 AJC Metropolitan Handicap and run fourth behind Peter Pan in the Melbourne Cup.

In 1940, an attempt was made to shoot McGrath's Cup favourite, the Cox Plate and Mackinnon winner Beau Vite. The marksman managed to shoot another of McGrath's horses, El Golea, by mistake. Beau Vite ran fourth behind Old Rowley in the Cup that year and McGrath nursed El Golea back to fitness to run third in the Mackinnon in 1941 and third in the Caulfield Cup in 1942.

Frank McGrath knew horses. He had been a good jockey and was a survivor of the infamous Caulfield Cup race fall of 1885, when sixteen horses fell in a field of forty-one. One jockey was killed and many injured.

As a trainer, he understood how to condition a horse and how to place horses to best advantage, but more than that, he was a trainer who cared for his horses. A trainer of the old school in many ways, Frank McGrath was 'modern' in the sense that he always put the horse's welfare first, and his plans were always long-term plans.

His long-term Cups double plan was one of his best.

McGrath was astute and realistic; he knew his great stayer Amounis was unbeatable in the Caulfield Cup of 1930 if two other particular horses were not there. In early markets, however, Amounis was at long odds.

The cunning plan revolved around three great horses, Amounis, Phar Lap and Nightmarch.

Nightmarch had defeated Phar Lap in the Melbourne Cup of 1929, but, the following spring, Nightmarch was defeated four times in a row by the 'Red Terror', and his owner, Mr A. Louisson, had been heard to say that if Phar Lap contested the Caulfield Cup he would take Nightmarch back to New Zealand for the New Zealand Cup—rather than run against the champion again in the Caulfield Cup.

In a conversation with Harry Telford, Frank McGrath suggested that Amounis, the only horse to defeat Phar Lap twice, would win the Caulfield Cup if Nightmarch and Phar Lap didn't start. He suggested that Telford leave Phar Lap in the Caulfield Cup field until Louisson took his horse home. In that time, they could get very lucrative odds about their two horses winning the Caulfield Cup Melbourne Cup double. Then Telford could scratch Phar Lap from the Caulfield Cup and the two trainers would make a fortune on the Cups doubles betting.

The plan worked perfectly.

Seeing that Phar Lap was set to contest the Caulfield Cup, Louisson took Nightmarch home (and he duly won the New Zealand Cup).

Then Harry Telford scratched Phar Lap, stating that he didn't want to over-race the champion, and Amounis duly won the Caulfield Cup.

Phar Lap, of course, famously and easily won the second leg, the Melbourne Cup, and the two trainers sent a battalion of bookies near bankrupt.

How do I know Frank McGrath was such a kind and patient trainer? Well, I play tennis twice a week with his granddaughter who assures me it's true.

She also tells me that her grandfather bought a very expensive imported motor car—sometime late in 1930.　　　**JH**

THE OLD TIMER'S STEEPLECHASE
A.B. (BANJO) PATERSON

Here is another classic tale from the days when races of 3 and 4 and even 5 miles were common—especially in steeplechasing. This meant that several laps of the track had to be made, and thus the opportunity to 'take a lap off' arose if there was some bush along the course and you were clever enough. Of course, there was always a chance there was someone cleverer than you!

The sheep were shorn and the wool went down
At the time of our local racing:
And I'd earned a spell—I was burnt and brown—
So I rolled my swag for a trip to town
And a look at the steeplechasing.

'Twas rough and ready—an uncleared course
As rough as the pioneers found it;
With barbed-wire fences, topped with gorse,
And a water-jump that would drown a horse,
And the steeple three times round it.

There was never a fence the tracks to guard,
Some straggling posts defined 'em:
And the day was hot, and the drinking hard,
Till none of the stewards could see a yard
Before nor yet behind 'em!

But the bell was rung and the nags were out,
Excepting an old outsider
Whose trainer started an awful rout,
For his boy had gone on a drinking bout
And left him without a rider.

'Is there not one man in the crowd,' he cried,
'In the whole of the crowd so clever,
Is there not one man that will take a ride
On the old white horse from the Northern side
That was bred on the Mooki River?'

'Twas an old white horse that they called The Cow,
And a cow would look well beside him;
But I was pluckier then than now
(And I wanted excitement anyhow),
So at last I agreed to ride him.

And the trainer said, 'Well, he's dreadful slow,
And he hasn't a chance whatever;
But I'm stony broke, so it's time to show
A trick or two that the trainers know
Who train by the Mooki River.

'The first time round at the further side,
With the trees and the scrub about you,

Just pull behind them and run out wide
And then dodge into the scrub and hide,
And let them go round without you.

'At the third time round, for the final spin
With the pace, and the dust to blind 'em,
They'll never notice if you chip in
For the last half-mile—you'll be sure to win,
And they'll think you raced behind 'em.

'At the water-jump you may have to swim—
He hasn't a hope to clear it—
Unless he skims like the swallows skim
At full speed over, but not for him!
He'll never go next or near it.

'But don't you worry—just plunge across,
For he swims like a well-trained setter.
Then hide away in the scrub and gorse
The rest will be far ahead of course—
The further ahead the better.

'You must rush the jumps in the last half-round
For fear that he might refuse 'em;
He'll try to baulk with you, I'll be bound,
Take whip and spurs on the mean old hound,
And don't be afraid to use 'em.

'At the final round, when the field are slow
And you are quite fresh to meet 'em,
Sit down, and hustle him all you know
With the whip and spurs, and he'll have to go—
Remember, you've got to beat 'em!'

The flag went down and we seemed to fly,
And we made the timbers shiver
Of the first big fence, as the stand flashed by,
And I caught the ring of the trainer's cry:
'Go on! For the Mooki River!'

I jammed him in with a well-packed crush,
And recklessly—out for slaughter—
Like a living wave over fence and brush
We swept and swung with a flying rush,
Till we came to the dreaded water.

Ha, ha! I laugh at it now to think
Of the way I contrived to work it.
Shut in amongst them, before you'd wink,
He found himself on the water's brink,
With never a chance to shirk it!

The thought of the horror he felt, beguiles
The heart of this grizzled rover!
He gave a snort you could hear for miles,
And a spring would have cleared the Channel Isles
And carried me safely over!

Then we neared the scrub, and I pulled him back
In the shade where the gum-leaves quiver:
And I waited there in the shadows black
While the rest of the horses, round the track,
Went on like a rushing river!

At the second round, as the field swept by,
I saw that the pace was telling;
But on they thundered, and by-and-bye
As they passed the stand I could hear the cry
Of the folk in the distance, yelling!

Then the last time round! And the hoofbeats rang!
And I said, 'Well, it's now or never!'
And out on the heels of the throng I sprang,
And the spurs bit deep and the whipcord sang
As I rode! For the Mooki River!

We raced for home in a cloud of dust
And the curses rose in chorus.
'Twas flog, and hustle, and jump you must!

And The Cow ran well—but to my disgust
There was one got home before us.

'Twas a big black horse, that I had not seen
In the part of the race I'd ridden;
And his coat was cool and his rider clean,
And I thought that perhaps I had not been
The only one that had hidden.

. . .

And the trainer came with a visage blue
With rage, when the race concluded:
Said he, 'I thought you'd have pulled us through,
But the man on the black horse planted too,
And nearer to home than you did!'

Alas to think that those times so gay
Have vanished and passed for ever!
You don't believe in the yarn you say?
Why, man! 'Twas a matter of every day
When we raced on the Mooki River!

RAILWAY YARNS

t was on 2 August 1854 that Australia's first train journey took place. On that day, the first train puffed its way out of Melbourne Station (now Flinders Street Station) on the short run to Port Melbourne. It was a gala occasion and an important first for Melbourne—one in the eye for rival city Sydney.

When the train reached the astonishing maximum speed of 24 kilometres an hour, a reporter on board noted that 'at that speed the countryside became a blur!' Few among the thousands waving and cheering that day would have realised the effect the railway would have on our growing nation over the next century or so.

The railways were the largest employers in Australia for over a hundred years. There are very few Australians who do not have at least one relative or ancestor who worked on the railways in some capacity.

Large towns grew up because of the railways, and thousands of smaller settlements owed their entire existence to them. Even before the trains ran, townships developed around the navvy camps.

There are thousands of great railway yarns from the early days of steam right down to today. Stories of the railway builders and navvies, engine drivers, railwaymen and station staff, and, of course, the women who ran the Railway Refreshment Rooms!

Almost all the railway yarns and history I know come from my great mate of many years, Russell Hannah, whose Dad, Lyle, was a fireman on the great 38 class locos, including the train that took the Queen on her journeys while in Australia on the first royal tour.

Lyle always said there were only two kinds of people—those who worked on the railways and those who wanted to!

Most of these yarns were collected by, told to me by, or inspired by Russell Hannah.

HOW NEW SOUTH WALES GOT A RAILWAY

The Sydney to Parramatta line had been built by the Sydney Railway Company and opened in 1855. At the same time, there was a line being constructed by the Hunter River Railway Company in the Hunter Valley, from East to West Maitland.

There had been many problems with these railways, however, and, in December 1854, Charles FitzRoy's last act as Governor-General of the colonies had been to give assent to a bill that acquired the railways for the government and made provision for the government to construct and own all future railways in the colony.

New South Wales had been granted responsible government in 1855, and the new government needed an engineer-in-chief, someone with a practical knowledge of railway planning, costing and construction; someone who could deal with inexperienced colonial politicians. They needed 'a thoroughly practical engineer of considerable professional attainments' and 'a gentleman of unquestioned principle and integrity'. That was exactly how the powerful British railway magnate Sir Morgan Peto described John Whitton in his recommendation to Lord Stanley.

Whitton, a Yorkshireman, was engineer on the Manchester, Sheffield and Lincoln Railway when he was just twenty-eight and, at the age of thirty-three, he was chosen to replace the greatest engineer of them all, Isambard Brunel, as resident engineer on the Oxford, Worcester and Wolverhampton Railway.

So, in 1856, John Whitton was offered, and accepted, the commission to become Engineer-in-Chief of the New South Wales Government Railways at an annual salary of £1500.

Sir William Denison was the new governor of New South Wales. He was a professional soldier with a background in engineering. John Whitton would need to display considerable amounts of his Yorkshire stubbornness in the months and years to come.

There were two early battles that Whitton needed to win. Firstly, Denison had suggested a horse-drawn rail system for the more remote areas of the colony. Not long after his arrival, in fact the day after his appointment was officially confirmed by the Railway Board, Whitton stated:

> I would not recommend any line to be made to be worked by horsepower. Any gradient which is bad for locomotives will be bad for horses also. You must take into consideration the immense amount of horse labour you have to employ to execute the same amount of work you would get done by a locomotive engine. I think it would not be by any means a saving but a great additional expense.

Whitton also showed he was a man who was willing to speak his mind, whether Governor Denison liked it or not, on the issue of surveys. Until that time, railway surveys had been conducted by military personnel under the charge of the Surveyor-General, in the same way that land surveys were conducted. In spite of the Governor's military–engineering background, Whitton was blunt in his opinion of the surveys conducted thus far:

> I think they are being carried out in a very objectionable manner so far as the railway is concerned. I think decidedly that they should be under the charge of the Engineer of Railways. I do not see what the Surveyor-General can have to do with them. [You can almost hear the Yorkshire accent.]

Whitton went on to construct a wonderful railway system for New South Wales, but his greatest achievement was the great zig-zag system which took the railway across the Great Dividing Range. It was the first mountain railroad in the world.　　JH

THE GREAT ZIG ZAG

The Zig Zag Railway was one of the greatest engineering and construction feats of the Victorian age. John Whitton began by designing the first zig zag, which raised the line 160 metres to the summit of Lapstone Hill. He had to design and build a three-span bridge over the Nepean River and a massive stone viaduct across Knapsack Gully.

The bridge, named the Victoria Bridge, naturally, had three spans of 61 metres and the viaduct required seven arches and rose 38.4 metres at its centre. The steepest gradient here was one in thirty.

The construction of this zig zag was, however, mere child's play compared to the building of the one which was necessary on the western side of the Great Dividing Range.

The Lithgow Valley zig zag, the Great Zig Zag, carried the line from the Clarence Tunnel down a descent of 209.4 metres to the valley floor in three great sweeps across the mountain sides. The gradient was one in forty-two.

Construction lasted three years, from 1866 to 1869, and the project was a source of fascination in the colony. In January 1867, part of the mountain blocking the line near the first reversing station of the Great Zig Zag needed to be removed by blasting. This was to be the most massive explosion ever seen in Australia. Using the new process of electrical detonation, 40,000 tons of rock was to be cleared in one huge explosion. Twenty-five holes were drilled 9 metres into the mountain face and over three tons of blasting powder was inserted.

In the building of this railway, the colony truly came of age. No longer a quaint colonial backwater, the colony of New South Wales now had an engineering marvel to impress the world, along with all the strange plants, animals and natural wonders.

From 1869 until 1910, every train across the mountains in either direction used John Whitton's zig zags. By 1910, however, traffic was so heavy that a new line was designed to replace it, using what became known as the 'ten-tunnel deviation'.

In 1972, a group of railway enthusiasts started to rebuild the zig zag track and then formed a cooperative and purchased rolling stock. Trains first ran again on part of the track in 1975. The track was extended all the way to Clarence in 1988 with the aid of a bicentennial grant. The railway operates on weekends and in school holidays using steam engines and vintage diesel rail motors.

There is a delightful irony in the Great Zig Zag's rebirth. John Whitton's ghost, I suspect, might express his blunt Yorkshire disapproval at the fact that the line now runs on the narrow 3-foot gauge he so detested, and uses vintage Queensland rolling stock.

The Great Zig Zag was regarded as one of the engineering wonders of the Victorian age. John Whitton has been called 'the father of the New South Wales railways'. When he arrived in 1856, there were just 32 kilometres of railway. When he retired in 1890, there were 3500 kilometres of railways in New South Wales.

Whitton died in February 1898, aged eighty, at his house in St Leonards and was buried in St Thomas' Cemetery, North Sydney.

JH

HOW WE GOT A NATIONAL PARK

Australia has the second oldest national park in the world (Yellowstone in the USA is the oldest). The Royal National Park, south of Sydney, was proclaimed in 1879 and it can be argued that it is, in a strange way, a legacy of John Whitton's honesty. Not that he had any interest in national parks; he was just interested in building railway lines well and efficiently.

Owning land through which a railway line would pass could be lucrative because the government had to resume the land and pay compensation. When the line was being surveyed south of Sydney in the early 1870s, speculation was rife and many politicians and their cronies, thinking the line would go through the Hacking River valley, bought the land that now makes up the Royal National Park.

Whitton, however, selected the Bottle Forest route along the ridges to the west and the speculators were left holding worthless land. It seems that they had enough 'friends' in the government to stop construction of the line for some months when it reached Sutherland, hoping that Whitton could be convinced to change his mind. Whitton's decision prevailed, as it usually did, and the line continued down through the Bottle Forest.

Strange to say, the 'kindly' government purchased the land anyway and saved the speculators from financial loss. Apparently it

was decided that what the colony needed was something unheard
of at the time—a national park.   **JH**

THE FLYING GANG
A.B. (BANJO) PATERSON

*The 'flying gang' were the railway's emergency crew. They sped down
the line in a special train equipped with cranes and equipment to
repair lines and remove damaged rolling stock and repair engines.
Their expertise kept the railway running efficiently in spite of mishaps.*

I served my time, in the days gone by,
In the railway's clash and clang,
And I worked my way to the end, and I
Was the head of the 'flying gang'.
'Twas a chosen band that was kept at hand
In case of an urgent need;
Was it south or north, we were started forth
And away at our utmost speed.
If word reached town that a bridge was down,
The imperious summons rang—
'Come out with the pilot engine sharp,
And away with the flying gang.'

Then a piercing scream and a rush of steam
As the engine moved ahead;
With measured beat by the slum and street
Of the busy town we fled,
By the uplands bright and the homesteads white,
With the rush of the western gale—
And the pilot swayed with the pace we made
As she rocked on the ringing rail.
And the country children clapped their hands
As the engine's echoes rang,
But their elders said: 'There is work ahead
When they send for the flying gang.'

Then across the miles of the saltbush plain
That gleamed with the morning dew,
Where the grasses waved like the ripening grain
The pilot engine flew—
A fiery rush in the open bush
Where the grade marks seemed to fly,
And the order sped on the wires ahead,
The pilot must go by.
The Governor's special must stand aside,
And the fast express go hang;
Let your orders be that the line is free
For the boys in the flying gang.

HOW SHELLHARBOUR BECAME DUNMORE
RUSSELL HANNAH

The railway station serving the south coast town of Shellharbour is known these days as Dunmore (Shellharbour). This has not always been the case, however; it was originally known simply as Shellharbour despite the fact that it is situated in the hamlet of Dunmore. Dunmore is made up of a dozen or so cottages that struggle up one side of Shellharbour Road, with a rural fire station tucked in between them. Dunmore's chief claim to fame is that all the houses in the village back onto the municipal tip.

On the other hand, the much more substantial 'village' of Shellharbour, situated 4 kilometres up the road and well out of sight of the station, is a thriving township and tourist resort. It has a pub, several clubs, restaurants, al fresco dining establishments, takeaways, schools and shops, and it attracts many tourists and travellers of all kinds.

This is the story of how the name change from Shellharbour to Dunmore (Shellharbour) supposedly came about. It concerns David Hill, one-time general manager of the ABC and, for a time, chief executive of New South Wales State Rail.

One day, David Hill had a strange notion for a state government chief executive officer: he decided it would be beneficial to his understanding of his job if he actually went out and experienced the joys of train travel from the point of view of an ordinary paying passenger. So, rather than travelling well-heralded in the pampered luxury of the commissioner's special car, he would, once a month or so, select a destination from the list of stations and travel incognito, making notes and checking on staff, service and comfort as he went.

Inevitably, one day his selection was Shellharbour and, thinking this would be a pleasant trip to a seaside resort, he boarded the train at Sydney's Central Station and enjoyed the scenic trip down the coast.

When he reached Shellharbour Station, however, he alighted from the train and found himself surrounded by cow paddocks. Now, David Hill was no dill. He noticed the straggle of houses on the other side of the road and realised immediately that this couldn't possibly be the famous seaside resort town of Shellharbour, even though the station signs were telling him so. After all, he couldn't even see the sea.

This was back in the days when the railways actually employed a few people to man even the smaller stations. Sure enough, there, clad in an ill-fitting uniform and waiting to collect Hill's ticket was a sixteen-year-old junior station assistant.

'Well,' said David Hill to the kid, 'this clearly isn't Shellharbour township.'

'No, mate,' replied the kid, who had no idea who he was talking to. 'This is Dunmore.'

'Ah, I see,' said Hill. 'Well, where's Shellharbour?'

The kid pointed up the Shellharbour Road and said, 'It's up the road there a bit, just over the hill—it's about 4 kilometres away.'

'That's a bit strange, isn't it?' mused the boss of the railways. 'Wouldn't you think that they'd have built the station a bit closer to the town than this? Shellharbour Station would be much better closer to Shellharbour, wouldn't it?'

The junior station assistant looked at David Hill like he was a bit simple and said, 'No, mate, it's much better to have it down here, near the railway line.'

Within weeks of the supremo's visit the station got a name change to Dunmore (Shellharbour).

THIN ICE
RUSSELL HANNAH/JIM HAYNES
(TOLD TO RUSSELL HANNAH BY A MATE)

'Many years ago, in my youth, I was a painter for the Public Works Department, and one of our jobs was to travel the state painting small bush schools. We worked in gangs of two and, in general, it was a good job. The pay wasn't great, but we received a pretty good living away from home allowance, most of which we were able to save, as the headmaster would generally let us camp in the weather shed. Of course, we got to see the inside of many country pubs, where we happily contributed our living expenses to the Publican's Retirement Fund.

'Now, one time we had to paint the school at a little place called Bardalungra. Bardalungra consisted of a few houses, a pub, a garage and general store combined and the obligatory one-teacher school. Bardalungra was a place destined for oblivion.

'There was, of course, one more building, and that was the railway station. The station was small. A weatherboard waiting room attached to a signal box that contained all those mysterious levers that enable trains to pass when there's a single line. Not that trains ever passed much at Bardalungra. It was a branch line that was serviced by a "mixed"—a goods train with a passenger carriage attached. The carriage was for those travellers who either had plenty of time for their journey or, like us, had a government rail warrant.

'The old trundler was not noted for speed. It was also one of those trains that, for reasons I could never understand, would stop at irregular intervals. It would stop at sidings that barely existed, or even in what seemed to be open paddocks, and just stay there for a while.

'The train only ran four times a week, except in harvest time, when a few trains were used to cart barley and wheat. That was the only time there was any other traffic on the line.

'Well, my mate and myself caught the train to Bardalungra one stinking hot day. It was one of those days when you dream of swimming pools and cold beer. The only "air-conditioning" available was to open the windows, but the air outside was hotter than inside: that dry heat of summer in western New South Wales.

'The irony of it all was that we had six bottles of beer with us that we'd bought the night before at a pub in Moree. We'd bought a dozen and for some reason still had six left when we finally hit the sack. Unfortunately, they were at least as hot as the air in the carriage, so we'd put off drinking them till we could find some suitable refrigeration.

'Not surprisingly, we were the only people in the carriage. We soon struck up a conversation with the guard, as you always did on country trains back then. He was a large friendly character with a florid face, the kind of bloke who looked like he might like a cold drink on a hot day, or any other day for that matter. He soon left the guard's van and joined us. It seemed he liked a bit of company—there being very few people travelling on the line—and it wasn't long before he knew all there was to know about us and we knew all about him.

'It also wasn't long before he noticed our six large bottles of beer sitting on the seat. "I see you boys have got a bit of the good liquid refreshment there," he said. "Are you going teetotal today?"

'Now, our throats were pretty dry and our heads were a bit heavy from the previous night. We explained that, as much as we'd love a beer, we couldn't bring ourselves to drink beer that was quite so hot.

'"I can fix you up, lads," he said. "I've got some ice in the van—next stop I'll pop back and bring some up."

'The guard's van was separated from our carriage by several goods wagons and, as luck would have it, the next stop wasn't far away. He soon disappeared back to his van and returned with a billy can half full of ice. Before too long we had the water glasses down from the carriage wall and were happily into our first bottle of cold beer. Naturally, the guard joined us. After all, it was a hot day.

'It seemed that our new mate the guard had an endless supply of ice. At every stop he'd go back to his van and return with more ice in the billy. He wasn't a bad drinker either. He certainly managed to put away his fair share of our beer.

'After a while, we were on our last bottle and feeling quite affectionate towards our new mate, the railways, and the world in general. We were also regretting that we didn't have another six bottles left over from the night before. When we expressed this opinion to the guard, he remarked that it was probably a good thing—as he was about to run out of ice.

'Perhaps it was about then that I really began to wonder where this seemingly endless supply of ice had come from. It didn't take long to find out.

'The train soon made another of its interminable stops, at a small siding which had a name that thankfully I forget. The guard had left us to do "a bit of work" in his van.

'As I leaned idly out the window, my belly full of cold beer, I noticed a black panel van and two well-dressed blokes standing by the siding. That's funny, I thought to myself. That van looks like a hearse. I soon realised what "bit of work" the guard had returned to his van to do. As I watched, the doors of the guard's van opened. Then, the two well-dressed blokes and the guard lifted a coffin out of the train and into the back of the black panel van.

'It was then that I knew where the ice had come from.'

A FAIR GO FOR NEW AUSTRALIANS
CHRIS HOLLEY

After completing the Intermediate Certificate, I left school and applied to join the New South Wales Government Railways. Like hundreds of other hopefuls, I was sent to Sydney to sit for the entrance examination at the Personnel Centre in Pitt Street.

At that time, there were thousands of new immigrants to this country also endeavouring to obtain employment. It was fascinating for me to observe and be a part of the integration of these 'new Australians' into the Australian lifestyle and way of doing things.

The written examination for entry to a railway career was really a little farcical. The arithmetic and English papers that needed to be taken required a level of knowledge somewhere between the kindergarten and second-class standard of the education system as it was then. Knowing how to manage simple addition and spell basic words seemed to be an indication of superior intelligence in a railway examination.

The system, however, completely discriminated against the poor immigrants. Unable to speak a word of our language, they just sat there totally bewildered.

If they learned nothing else from the exam, the immigrant candidates present when I sat the papers at least learned something about the average Aussie's belief in a 'fair go'. Seeing that I had finished my set papers and noting that I had everything correct, the supervising officer asked me if I would mind 'lending' my answers to a table of Italian lads sitting nearby. This I did, and the 'new Australian' boys copied diligently for over an hour and joined the railways along with me and many other Australians, all with 100 per cent passes. The supervisor was obviously aware that the lingo would come later on.

THE PUB WITH NO RAILWAY
RUSSELL HANNAH/JIM HAYNES

A lot of towns still have a Railway Hotel, though there hasn't been a train for years, but there's one town that's got a Railway Hotel and it's never had a railway line through it, let alone a station.

The place is called Wolumla. I ran across it when I was down the NSW coast fishing a couple of years ago. I was driving between Bega and Merimbula and there it was, out in the middle of nowhere—the Railway Junction Hotel, Wolumla.

There's not a railway line to be seen. There never was a line at Wolumla or anywhere else on the south coast for that matter. The nearest railway lines stopped a couple of hundred kilometres to the north at Bombaderry, and a hundred kilometres up the range at Bombala.

The publican's a decent sort of bloke and he told me the story. It seems that back in the late 1800s, when old Henry Parkes was Premier, he came down the coast campaigning. In those days you didn't promise tax cuts or border security to get votes. What you promised were public buildings and railways.

You couldn't bribe the voters by getting them drunk either, because they used to shut the pubs on election day.

Anyway, old Henry promised a lunatic asylum and a railway to Eden. The line was to come down the mountain from Bombala, and Wolumla was to be the junction where the line would shoot off north to Bega.

So, some enterprising developer decided to beat the crowd, get in first and build a Railway Hotel. The only problem was that the line was never built. So, right there at Wolumla is the only Railway Hotel ever built without a railway. It's a good pub, though.

And the lunatic asylum? Well they never built that either, evidently there weren't enough mad characters down there to warrant one.

BREAKFAST ON THE BANJO
RUSSELL HANNAH/JIM HAYNES

'Banjo' was a common term for a coal shovel used in both coal mining and railways. The name derives from the shape, which facilitated faster unloading of the shovel when the coal had to be thrown a distance. Shovels were classified by size—a number 5 banjo, etc. These shovels made perfect hotplates.

My father always cooked his own meals in the old steam days. One time, Dad and his fireman were working a 'goods' up near Garah on the North West line. The night was terrible cold, as nights are on the Western Plains in winter and this old fellow, a bit down on his luck, asked if he could get a ride with them. There were still swaggies around then, though they'd given up jumping into billabongs, and trains were still their favourite form of transportation.

Now, the night being so cold, my old dad felt a bit sorry for him. So, rather than let him ride back on one of the flat cars where he might catch pneumonia, he invited him into the cabin.

Of course, having unauthorised people in the loco cabin was a breach of several regulations and could lead to all sorts of punishment, including the sack. But they were pretty certain that they wouldn't run into any inspectors—it was a Sunday night and a bit too cold for inspectors to be out and about.

The old fellow was very happy to sit unobtrusively in a corner where he could get very warm. He was still there a few hours later when morning came on and the train was parked in a siding to wait for a 'down goods' to pass, it being a single line.

'Time for breakfast,' says Dad, and the fireman gets the tucker out.

'You'd better join us,' he said to the old fellow. The swaggie was very thankful and said that it was very kind of them to share their sandwiches with him.

'Sandwiches,' laughed my dad, 'no one eats sandwiches for breakfast in my cabin. It's always a good solid Australian feed:

sausages, bacon and eggs, toast, and a spot of Worcestershire sauce for a bit of flavour.'

Well, the old swaggie was delighted. He was amazed to hear that he was about to get some real tucker. Swaggies often had to make do with a 'swaggie's breakfast'—drink of water, a smoke and a pee. He was a bit puzzled, however, and asked Dad how he planned to cook this feast. He didn't see any cooking facilities in the cabin.

The fireman just chuckled and produced his shovel, which, though well used, was as clean and shiny on the action side as the day it was new. The constant scraping of the coal on the surface of a fireman's shovel always kept it clean. 'Instant hotplate!' said the fireman. 'Breakfast on the banjo!'

Dad cracked a few eggs onto the shovel and threw on a bit of bacon and a couple of sausages; then the fireman held the shovel in the firebox and, before long, the three men were tucking into a great breakfast.

'Best breakfast I've had since the ones me old mum cooked before I left home thirty years ago!' said the old swaggie.

By now they were taking the train along at the usual pace that goods trains go and the old fellow settled back in the corner of the cabin out of everyone's way. Before long, he fell asleep as the train chuffed along.

When the train started to pile on speed a couple of hours later, the swaggie woke up. It seems my dad had to make up time to get into the next passing loop and let a passenger train through. It's important that passenger trains aren't late. If they're held up, people are likely to complain, so Dad was in a bit of a hurry and he couldn't stop anywhere.

When the old fellow woke up, he started to squirm a bit. He had a funny look on his face and Dad twigged to the problem at once. 'Are you okay?' he asked.

Well, the old bloke told Dad there was a bit of urgency about him finding a place where he could answer a very severe call of nature.

'Just hang on tight and pee off the back of the engine,' said Dad.

'It's not a pee I need,' said the swaggie, doubling up. His condition was probably due to the first decent feed of rich tucker he'd had in ages.

'Does this loco have a dunny?' he asked.

'Of course we've got a dunny, mate,' my dad says with a grin, 'its a kind of portable one. You use it and we dispose of the results as we steam along, fertilises the bush. Pass him the dunny, Bill.'

At this, the fireman stopped leaning on the banjo and passed it to the old bloke.

'Go for your life,' said Dad, 'but try to make it quick. It's nearly time for crib and I want to cook a couple of pancakes.'

'My dad had no idea how that swaggie managed to hang on till he left them when they parked in the passing loop. 'He didn't even thank us for breakfast,' Dad said.

1174
ANONYMOUS

Railwaymen tell stories about certain engines they loved, ones that always ran well, like the famous 3801, and those they hated. Although all engines in the one class were supposedly identical, some just never seemed to be any good. The most famous of these back in the 1930s was the 1174 ('eleven-seventyfour').

When you're signing on at Enfield and they meet you at the door
And they tell you that your engine is 1174,
You can hear the driver grumble; you can hear the fireman roar—
Why? Just look in the repair book of 1174.

'Faulty valves and pistons', 'burnt-off smoke box door',
'Engine steaming badly'—that's 1174.
God knows why they run her, but the bosses know what's best,
She'll be hours late any time they run her to the west.

And if they put her on a north job, you can always safely bet
That she'll end up in a siding somewhere up near Morisset.

Try to take her 'cross the mountains where she really has to climb!
By the time you get to Glenbrook, you're an hour behind time!

I have struggled, sworn and sweated, I have tried to get her through,
But I always feel like quitting when I get to Warrimoo!
'Cos we're facing those Blue Mountains and we'll do the best we can,
But to make that engine steam well is a task beyond a man!

I take up that damn shovel, off come my overalls,
And I know that I'll be buggered when we get to Wentworth Falls.
As we struggle on to Lithgow, we swear and curse our fate,
And 1174 is just exactly three hours late.

It's a number that will haunt me and haunt me evermore,
For it doesn't matter what I do—it's 1174.
One night my dear wife said to me, 'Your hands are burnt and sore!'
I said, 'Yes, I've been to Lithgow on 1174.'

She gave me perfumed soap for them, the best she could procure,
It's called '4711'—just like 1174!
I bought a ticket in the lottery, thought my luck would change
   for sure,
The winner was 1175—I had 1174!

Disgusted, I enlisted and went off to the war
And my regimental number was 1174.
And when the war was ended, I came back to work once more
And they sent me off to Lithgow on 1174!

STARGAZER JONES AND THE CAT
RUSSELL HANNAH

One of the most famous drivers on the New South Wales railways
was a chap called Stargazer Jones. He was not known as Stargazer
because of any great interest in astronomy, but because he had a
certain vagueness and forgetfulness about him. He was often in
receipt of 'blueys', or 'please explain' directives that led to official
reprimands and fines, for running signals, exceeding speed limits

and other such misdemeanours. Still, he was a good-hearted fellow, and though he was often the victim of practical jokes, he rarely held a grudge.

For some time in the early '50s, the other member of Stargazer's crew was a fireman named Paul O'Brien. Paul was a competent amateur ventriloquist and entertainer. He had, in fact, appeared on the very popular *Amateur Hour* radio show hosted by Terry Dear, winning the first prize one night with an act that consisted of imitating bird and animal noises. There weren't many birds or animals Paul couldn't imitate and workmates often heard kookaburras laughing or horses neighing or even lions roaring in the shower block when Paul was in overnight railway barracks.

Paul also had a wicked sense of humour.

One Saturday night, Stargazer and Paul were working the Honeymoon Express. After several best men from the wedding parties had crossed Stargazer's palm with the appropriate silver coins to ensure the whistle was blown, he was approached by another well-dressed fellow carrying a sugar bag.

'Look,' said the man. 'In this bag is my wife's cat. I am not fond of cats, but I can normally tolerate them, particularly if it keeps my wife happy.

'She loves this cat, but I find it obnoxious, especially when I am eating my dinner, as it has a disturbing habit of jumping on the table and trying to steal whatever I am eating. No matter how well fed the cat is, it persists in this behaviour. I can stand it no longer and I have decided to rid myself of this cat once and for all.'

Though Stargazer Jones and his fireman listened intently, they wondered what all this had to do with them.

'I cannot,' the man continued, 'bring myself to drown the cat or do anything else that may lead to its death. Firstly, I am a bit soft-hearted and, secondly, I would have to lie to my wife.

'Unfortunately my wife always knows when I am lying and my life would be extremely miserable if she knew I had killed her cat. I just want it to disappear, and this is where you can help.'

'What can we do?' asked the bemused Stargazer Jones.

THE BEST AUSTRALIAN YARNS

'What I would like you to do,' the man replied, 'is to release the cat from the bag as you are passing through the national park. That way, the cat can have a good life roaming free and I can truthfully say to my wife that I have not harmed the cat in any way.

'Of course, I would like you to take this five shillings as a token of my appreciation for all your help.'

Well, Stargazer always had a soft spot for animals, especially when there was five bob involved. He thought this was a humane way of solving the problem and took the bag with the cat in it and placed it in the cabin. (This was, of course, in a less environmentally friendly time, when many people thought it was quite all right to let cats loose in national parks, much kinder, in fact, than drowning them.)

Stargazer had quite warmed to the Catman and they were passing the time of day chatting about cats and wives and life in general before the train departed. Meanwhile, Paul O'Brien, who had heard the entire conversation, moved the sugar bag to the other side of the cab, undid the string and released the cat on the other side of the train. In its place, he stuffed a large lump of coal into the bag.

Soon the time came for the train to depart Port Kembla and, to the usual accompaniment of whistles, singing, waving and shouting, the honeymooners were left to hold hands in the carriages and contemplate their future lives as the train puffed towards Sydney via Wollongong.

Up in the cabin all was normal until the train approached Lysaghts. At that point, Paul used his twin talents of ventriloquism and animal noise imitation, and Stargazer believed he heard a plaintive cry come from the bag. The immediate response from the fireman was to give the bag a thorough kick, upon which Stargazer heard an even louder wail.

Stargazer was shocked at what he thought was a wanton act of cruelty to a dumb animal and admonished his fireman. 'Leave that cat alone,' he said. 'Even if it is making a bit of noise, it's not hurting anyone; I'll let it out when we get through Helensburgh.'

Another mile or so up the track, however, the same thing happened again, and the normally easygoing Stargazer was starting to get a bit annoyed with his fireman's apparent cruelty.

'I said, leave that cat alone,' he repeated. 'It'll be gone when we get into the park.'

The final act of the charade occurred as the train was pulling into Wollongong Station. Stargazer again heard a piteous meowing, and this time Paul O'Brien shouted 'I hate bloody cats!', picked up the sugar bag and hurled it into the blazing firebox. As he did so there was one last terrible scream of pain and then the fireman slammed the firebox door shut.

Well, Stargazer was absolutely mortified by Paul's behaviour, so much so that he overshot Wollongong Station and consequently earned himself another bluey. After an initial burst of angry shouting at his fireman, he subsided into a sullen silence.

Apart from the cruelty to the cat, Stargazer felt that he had betrayed the trust of the bloke at Port Kembla Station. After all, he had promised him that no harm would come to the cat and it would be released to live a free life in the Royal National Park.

Paul O'Brien managed to control himself and keep from laughing even though he had to put up with a stony silence from Stargazer all the way to Central Station. It was such a good story that it wasn't long before every driver and fireman in the depot knew about it.

Everyone decided it was such a good story, in fact, that there was no one who would tell Stargazer about the hoax. Instead they milked it for all it was worth. Men would sidle up to him and tell him stories about cat skins being found outside Chinese restaurants, and they'd wonder what roast cat would smell and taste like. Others talked incessantly about cats having nine lives and some wondered aloud if the Port Kembla cat had used up eight of his lives somewhere else.

All this only encouraged Stargazer to hold firm to his one act of retribution: he refused to talk to his fireman. All ensuing journeys were undertaken in deathly silence and any talk was confined to the absolute bare essentials needed to run the train.

It was nearly killing Paul O'Brien not to confess, and the silence at work wasn't very pleasant, but so many people were getting mileage out of the story that he managed to endure the silence until the joke finally ran its course. And soon enough, it did run its course.

Two weeks after the incident, Stargazer and Paul were again at the head of the Honeymoon Express, about to pull out of Port Kembla Station, when Stargazer spotted the Catman striding down towards the loco. It was too late for Stargazer to hide; he had been spotted and he could see that the fellow was not at all happy as he approached.

'You know, I trusted you,' the cranky Catman exclaimed. 'In good faith, I gave you five shillings to get rid of the cat. You promised to let him out at the national park.

'Instead, what happens? I call in at the Commercial for a couple of schooners to celebrate at last being able to eat my tea in peace, and when I get home, what do I find? The bloody cat sitting on the table waiting for me!'

Stargazer was so relieved that the cat hadn't met a fiery fate that he was struck dumb for a minute. In that time, while the Catman waited for a reply, Stargazer at last realised that he'd been had. Then he remembered Paul's win in the amateur hour and the penny dropped—and he started laughing in the poor bloke's face. He was lucky the bloke didn't clock him one.

Stargazer finally gathered his scattered wits and assured the man that he was laughing with *relief.* 'You mustn't have had the bag tied tight enough, mate,' he lied. 'The cat escaped near Coniston. I've been really worried about it—' He finally managed to placate the bloke by promising to give him his five bob back or take the cat on another trip.

THE END OF THE LINE

By 1860, Sydney's population had expanded to the point where a general cemetery was needed. Some 80 hectares were gazetted for the purpose in an area that was then beyond the existing suburbs, near Harlem's Creek Station on the railway line to Parramatta. This became Rookwood Cemetery.

A branch line into the centre of the cemetery was completed at the end of 1864, and funeral trains ran regularly from 1867.

Leaving from the old Sydney Station twice a day at 9.15 a.m. and 3.00 p.m., the funeral trains stopped just short of Harlem's Creek Station and backed along the branch line to the two cemetery platforms.

Having funerals operate from normal railway platforms at Sydney Central soon proved unsuitable. Funeral groups were forced to mix with commuters and a place was also needed to store coffins that arrived by train from the outer areas, so, in 1869, the colonial architect James Barnet designed two church-like sandstone buildings, one at the Sydney end (which became known as the Mortuary Station) and the other at the cemetery.

The sandstone building at the cemetery end was 38 metres by 16 metres and the arch was 17 metres high. The trains backed right in and coffins were unloaded inside the building, which was decorated with angels holding scrolls and trumpets, to represent Judgement and Resurrection.

In the early twentieth century, funeral trains were made up of six of the most basic carriages in operation at the time. Between Mortuary Station and Rookwood, they could be flagged down at any station to pick up coffins and funeral groups. At Homebush, there was a long stop for ticket collection from the living passengers; coming back, the trains again stopped at Homebush for tickets to be checked and to make a list of where people needed the train to stop on its journey back to Sydney.

The coffin carriage could hold up to thirty coffins and the passengers, first- and second-class, rode in the front of the train accompanied by the undertakers.

The trains also picked up at some of the stations on the way. When they reached Rookwood, people would take their dear departed to where the freshly dug graves were waiting.

The length of the graveside eulogy depended on how far the grave was from the station because the train ran to a strict timetable and it took time to get the coffins to the more distant parts of the cemetery. So, the further away the grave was, the shorter the service had to be. Plots near the station were more expensive.

There is a story that one day, an old lady's coffin had been placed in the train when her daughter approached the undertaker. She explained that her mum had always wanted her to have her rings as a keepsake, but when they laid her out they had forgotten to remove them.

The undertaker told the daughter not to worry and, when he had seen that all the mourners were aboard, he hopped into the coffin car with a screwdriver. By the time the train reached the cemetery, he had retrieved the rings and nobody was any the wiser. The daughter was very grateful. Even though everyone was sworn to secrecy, the word soon got around and that undertaker became a minor celebrity in his profession because he was the only person ever to ride in the coffin carriage of a funeral train with a return ticket!

In April 1948, the last funeral train ran and the branch line was closed. Motor vehicles had made the service unnecessary and a new road was planned which cut the branch line and made it impractical to operate.

In 1957, the building at the Rookwood end was purchased by the Anglican Church for the grand sum of £100 and moved stone by stone to Canberra. It still stands as All Saints Church of England, in the suburb of Ainslie.

Mortuary Station still stands today between Central and Redfern stations, which is quite close to the site of old Sydney Station near Regent and Devonshire streets.

JH

SAVED BY A CIGARETTE
RUSSELL HANNAH/JIM HAYNES

The commuter train that left Mount Victoria in the heart of the Blue Mountains at 6.09 a.m. every weekday morning was christened the Slogger by some of the passengers who travelled on it regularly from the mountains. It was due into Central at 8.32 a.m. and, consistent with its name, it generally delivered its human cargo fairly close to time. Just a handful started the trip at Mount Victoria but, after stopping at almost all the stations in the mountains, its passenger complement was often swollen to well over 600, many of them standing, by the time it left Parramatta.

It was no fancy train, just an old workhorse of eight wooden carriages, close to retirement, hauled by an electric loco. Certainly not the sort of train you'd expect people to be talking about for years to come. Yet, on Tuesday 18 January 1977, at 8.13 a.m., the Slogger tragically crashed its way into history.

You see, the Slogger was the train involved in the nation's worst ever railway accident, and the second worst peacetime disaster on Australian soil—what Australians call the Granville Disaster.

A couple of kilometres east of Parramatta, Bold Street crosses the main railway line at Granville. Two concrete-buttressed steel trestles supported the Bold Street Bridge, each with eight steel stanchions. Just prior to passing under the bridge from the west, the railway line takes a long left-hand curve and passes over a set of points. Evidently, the line's gauge had widened as a result of pressure from the heavy traffic; some of the dog spikes were badly worn.

As the Slogger rounded the curve and crossed over the points, the engine left the rails, began to rock and roll sideways and hit the trestles of the bridge, taking out eight of the sixteen steel stanchions.

As it did this, the engine also hit a steel mast that was holding the overhead electric wires and broke it off at the base. The mast swung out like a great sword and sliced the top off the first carriage. For a full twenty seconds, it seemed that the worst was over. Then the unimaginable happened. The bridge began to sag and 255 tonnes of concrete crashed into the old wooden carriages of the train.

It was the worst rail disaster in our history. The final count was 83 killed and 213 injured.

Bob Brain survived the disaster by remarkable chance circumstances.

Every morning he'd catch the bus from his West Guildford home to Parramatta Station and then take the train to Central. He often travelled with his friend Chris, who caught the same bus and train.

The Slogger was Bob's preferred train because, after Parramatta, it stopped only once, at Strathfield, which made it the quickest way of getting to work. As the third carriage stopped near the entrance to the platform, it was the one he always travelled in.

The morning of Tuesday 18 January 1977 began like any other for Bob. The only difference was that his mate Chris had had a bit of a stressful morning and hadn't had time for his morning cigarette. 'What about we get on the first carriage for a change?' Chris suggested, desperate for a smoke. Smoking was permitted in car one, but not in car three of the Slogger.

Bob agreed and they made their way to the front car. As the train was pretty full, they didn't manage to get a seat, so both stood at the rear of the car and Chris managed to light up his smoke. This change to their routine not only meant they weren't in the carriage that suffered the most fatalities—car three—but also, by chance, they were standing in what was to be the 'safest' end of the first carriage.

Bob recollects hearing the bang as the train left the rails. He remembers the carriage rocking to the left about thirty degrees then rocking to the right at about the same angle. At this point he recalls falling onto the floor and having Chris fall over on top of him.

The accountant's next memory is of waking on a stretcher beside the line with an ambulance man wiping blood from his face. His mate Chris was there as well. Bob's main concern was for his briefcase and the work papers he had in it—he kept asking Chris to go back and see if he could find it.

A cigarette saved Bob Brain's life. When he got out of hospital, the first thing he did was to buy Chris the largest carton of cigarettes he could find.

Strangely enough, Bob has since discovered that he is allergic to cigarette smoke—and he's eternally grateful that he didn't know about his allergy before that Tuesday in January 1977.

UNCLE ALEX MEETS TIMETABLE SCOTTIE

ALEX HOOD/JIM HAYNES

My Great Uncle Alex had a very short career on the railways but he always travelled on trains without a ticket.

It started when he met a girl from Perth when she was visiting Sydney and reckoned he'd follow her back when she went home. Great Uncle Alex always was a bit of a romantic. He scrounged around and got the train fare to Perth, then wrote to this girl and told her he was coming and asked her if she could meet him at the station.

Well, she met him at the station all right but she had a bloke with her. Evidently she said, 'Hello Alex; this is my fiancé, Bill.'

Great Uncle Alex was a pretty perceptive bloke. He was quick to get the hint that perhaps he shouldn't hang around. But anyway, there he was, stuck in Perth with no money and with nowhere to live. So, he did the only reasonable thing a young bloke could do in those days. He joined the railway.

There was always plenty of work on the railways in those days, but most of it was out in the bush, and that's where they sent Great Uncle Alex. They gave him a rail pass to Northcliffe, a few hundred kilometres south-west of Perth.

Uncle Alex thought the job would be a featherbed 'cos there were only two or three trains a week, but he was in for a shock. Apart from the summer heat and the flies, he had to lay sleepers by hand, with only a sledgehammer and a crowbar. To top it off, the ganger was a real bastard and when he kicked my uncle up the arse after a fortnight in the job, Uncle Alex jobbed him and then, of course, he had to leave the job.

He had to get back to Perth so he could get back to Sydney, so he got to the marshalling yards in Bunbury. It was night, and he was looking for a goods train that might be going to Perth. One of the problems with jumping rattlers was that you didn't know where the hell they were going.

Anyway, there he was, looking for a likely train, when he heard a voice say, 'Get your head down, ya mug, or someone'll see ya.'

Uncle looked around and couldn't see where the voice was coming from. 'Get down, ya mug,' the voice hissed again, 'or you'll cruel it for me as well.'

'Where are you?' whispered my Uncle Alex, as loud as he dared.

'Over here in the fruit wagon—where are you going?' says the voice.

'Perth!' said Uncle Alex.

'Well, that's where this train's going in fifteen minutes. Jump in here with me, but keep your bloody head down,' said the disembodied voice.

So, Great Uncle Alex climbed into that fruit wagon and that's how he met one of the most famous travellers in Australian railway history, Timetable Scottie.

Timetable Scottie knew everything about everything on the Australian railways. He knew where you could expect to find every loco; he knew how long it took to travel between stations. He knew when was the best time, and best place to get on and off goods trains. Best of all, he knew exactly where every train—passenger or goods—was going and what time it would arrive, allowing for lateness of course.

He was an amazing man. Every railway department in the country should have paid him thousands of dollars and got him to organise their timetables. Trouble was, they could never find him. He'd never paid a fare in his life and reckoned he'd travelled on every line in the country.

By the time that goods train reached Perth, Great Uncle Alex knew more tricks about rail travel than any other bloke in the country. Timetable Scottie was indirectly responsible for Great Uncle Alex becoming the wealthy man he is today.

It happened like this.

Months later, Great Uncle Alex was doing it tough—no money, no job and stuck in Hay. The temperature over a century every day and flies in plague proportions. Great Uncle Alex wanted to head for the coast, but he had no money for a fare. That's when he used a trick that Timetable Scottie had taught him.

He went down to the station and told the stationmaster he was looking for a job on the railways. In those days, there was plenty of work on the railways but everyone had to do a written test. The stationmaster explained that Uncle Alex would have to go to Sydney to do the test. So, the stationmaster wrote him out a rail warrant, and off went Uncle in style.

When he got to Sydney, he did the test and he went pretty well in it. Great Uncle Alex was no dill. The last part of the test was for colour blindness. You can't get a job on the railways if you're colourblind, for obvious reasons. Every time they put a card in front of Uncle Alex and asked him what he saw, he said he saw brown dots. No matter what colour they flashed before him, all he saw was brown dots.

So they asked Uncle Alex to wait outside, and, a few minutes later, one of the examiners came out and told him that, even though he'd done exceptionally well in the test, they were unable to employ him 'cos he was colourblind. Uncle Alex pretended to be devastated and bunged on a blue.

He put on such a turn that they offered him a rail warrant to anywhere that he wanted to go in New South Wales, just to quieten him down.

Uncle Alex thought the north coast sounded a nice spot to spend the summer, so he got a ticket to Murwillumbah, the end of the line north.

He took the old North Coast Mail and got a job on a banana plantation. Then he courted the owner's daughter and married her. When the old fellow died, he inherited the plantation. Now he owns six or seven plantations. He's on the local council and he's the biggest banana grower on the Tweed, all because he met Timetable Scottie.

If he hadn't got that free ticket to Murwillumbah, his life would have been far different. He may still be jumping goods trains, just like Timetable Scottie.

HIT FOR SIX
JIM HAYNES

It was in a little western town,
The day was clear and fine,
And we were playing cricket
Down near the railway line.
The bowler sent a loose one down,
He couldn't stand the strain;
I opened up me shoulders
And it landed in the train.
The driver blew the whistle,
Well, he hadn't seen the ball.
I stared across at square leg
And I waited for the call.
It had the umpires puzzled,
It had 'em in a fix.
See, they found the ball in Broken Hill
But they only gave me 'six'!

THE NEVER-NEVER RAILWAY LINE

The Northern Territory is renowned for its characters. Territorians reckon they are more 'Australian' than the rest of Australia. So, when it comes to trains, it's no surprise to find that Territory trains have always had their own uniquely 'Territorian', and very Australian, character.

The most famous Territory train is, of course, the Ghan, although the old Ghan was technically a South Australian train, running as it did from Port Augusta to Alice Springs. It first ran in 1878, but the line didn't extend to Alice Springs until 1929. When it stopped running in 1980, it was the source of a thousand wonderful yarns and legends. The new Ghan is part of the national rail system and now links Adelaide to Darwin.

The Northern Territory's 'other' train was the one that ran from Darwin down to Pine Creek. As you would expect, this train also had a unique Territory character. In *We of the Never-Never*, Jeannie Gunn described it as 'a delightful train—just a simple-hearted, chivalrous, weather-beaten old bush-whacker, at the service of the entire Territory'.

Her account of her very first journey on the train is one of the highlights of that famous book. She likened the train to a large, friendly prehistoric creature:

> There were no fences to shut us in; and as the train zigzagged through jungle and forest and river-valley—stopping now and then to drink deeply at magnificent rivers ablaze with water-lilies—it almost seemed as though it were some kindly Mammoth creature, wandering at will through the bush . . .

Other accounts of travelling from Darwin on 'the Never-Never Line' seem to suggest that the train was not, perhaps, as tame a creature as Jeannie Gunn would have us believe.

The Palmerston and Pine Creek Railway Bill was passed in 1883 and the line opened in 1888. Thousands of Chinese and Indians provided the labour.

The line was built to take freight but rarely ran at a profit. The gold rush ended, the cattle industry was struggling, cattle stations were too far from the railway line and the wet season meant derailments and washaways. To top it all off, termites ate the sleepers and, in 1897, a cyclone caused massive damage that virtually closed the line for two years.

In 1912, Darwin's non-Aboriginal population was only 3310, made up of 1418 Europeans, 1331 Chinese, 280 Aborigines of mixed race and 281 'others'—so the railway wasn't exactly busy.

At the end of World War I, work began on extending the line to Emungalen, on the banks of the Katherine River. This was so that Vesteys could get their cattle to the Darwin meatworks. As labour was short, Greeks, Russians and even Patagonian migrants were brought in. Many settled in the Territory to add to the melting pot.

The wildness of railway gangs in Katherine was legendary. One gang of thieves, rumoured to be railway workers, built a spur track into the bush, removed the goods in two vans, set the vans alight and covered their tracks by removing the rails.

A newspaper account from 1920, in *The Northern Territory Times and Gazette*, describes a typical trip to Pine Creek. The train was made up of a loco, two passenger carriages and ten goods cars. There were only twenty-two passengers—'the Territory's usual mixed assortment of Britishers, Greeks, Italians, Russians, Swiss, Swedes, Half-castes and Chinese'. The reporter further describes the scene in the carriages: 'every mother's son had a bottle or a case of grog. "Ave a drink" was the password and no one declined—it wasn't manners and it was the only way to avoid arguments.'

Apparently, not one bottle was left when the train pulled into Pine Creek after the nine-and-a-half-hour journey of 235 kilometres.

At one point, while the train was stopped at a remote station, a fight broke out between two drinkers:

As the two combatants worked from the original scene of the action to other parts of the carriage, occupants shifted out onto the platform at the rear or onto the footboard to give them more room. The guard coming along for tickets spoilt the show by promising to throw out the grog unless there was an improvement in prevailing conditions. All hands then had a drink and declared that the guard wasn't a bad sort of poor bastard.

A bridge was finally built across the Katherine River and the first train crossed in 1926. Emungalen then closed and the town of Katherine grew on the new site across the river. The line was meant to continue on to Daly Waters but, when funds ran out in the Depression, it stopped at Birdum, some 515 kilometres from Darwin. There was absolutely nothing at Birdum—except a buffer to indicate the end of the line.

World War II meant moving troops to the north and Darwin became a strategic defence post after the Japanese bombing raid that killed over 200 people. Shipping wasn't safe and there were 120,000 troops in Darwin, so the railway was essential for supplies. The rolling stock had been run down badly by then and the first troops arrived in converted cattle trucks. Soldiers from the eastern states evidently named the train Spirit of Protest in a sarcastic parody of the modern Sydney to Melbourne train Spirit of Progress.

Plans were made to extend the railway from Birdum to Alice Springs. Instead of this, however, the Stuart Highway was sealed between Alice Springs and Darwin.

After the war, despite the introduction of diesel hydraulic rail cars with air-conditioning, the line was not well patronised. It deteriorated until its closure in 1976, following damage from Cyclone Tracy two years before and frequent flooding. The rails were sold off (at $50 a ton) to Taiwan and the Philippines, and the sleepers were donated to Indonesia under the Colombo Plan.

Many Darwin people mourned the loss of their Never-Never Line, as historian James Harvey noted: 'Its trains had run whenever asked, despite enemy bombs, cyclones, floods, economic depressions and recessions, government and public indifference, and the inexorable delays caused by the tropical environment.'

It's an irony that the Never-Never Line has now disappeared into Australian history and folklore. You see, while that great little line no longer exists, the long-promised Adelaide to Darwin Railway, first mooted in 1858 and so long a part of Aussie folklore, is now a reality. The new Ghan ran from Adelaide to Darwin for the first time in February 2004.   **JH**

FARE EVASION
RUSSELL HANNAH/JIM HAYNES

There were many ingenious ways of avoiding paying your fare on the railways, and the most common involved doing it in the relative comfort of a passenger compartment, rather than the dirt and discomfort of a goods van. Hiding in the toilet was a favourite, but any ticket inspector worth his salt would lie in wait if the 'engaged' sign was up. Eventually the scaler would have to come out.

The following story is a favourite among Kiwis living in Australia.

It seems that there were six friends, three New Zealanders and three Australians, who worked in Wagga and decided to catch the South West Mail up to Sydney to watch an Australia–New Zealand Test match. When they got to the station, the Aussie blokes noticed that the Kiwis only bought one ticket between the three of them.

'How are the three of you going to travel on just one ticket?' asked one of the Aussies quizzically.

'Watch and you might learn something,' said one of the Kiwis.

Well, they boarded the train and the journey began. As soon as they saw the inspector enter the carriage, the three Kiwis headed straight for the toilet and crammed into it. The inspector checked the Aussies' tickets and noticed that the 'engaged' sign was showing on the toilet door. He banged on the door and in his most authoritative voice said, 'Tickets, please.'

The toilet door opened about a centimetre, just enough to push the ticket through. The inspector clipped the ticket and moved on.

The Australians were greatly taken by this and thought it was most clever, especially for New Zealanders. They decided that they would do the same on the return trip.

When they arrived at Central for the return trip, the Aussies bought one ticket between them but the Kiwis bought three platform tickets at a penny each. Again, the Aussie blokes were quite perplexed by it all. Perhaps we should mention that Australia had won the Test, so the Kiwis were rather despondent, not too happy with Australians in general and in a mood for revenge.

'How are you three going to travel without any ticket at all?' asked one of the Aussies.

'Watch and you might learn something,' replied one of the Kiwis.

The train pulled out and after a while one of the Kiwis said, 'I think the inspector's coming through.'

The Aussie trio had been keeping an eye on the toilet to make sure it wasn't occupied when they needed it. Now they made a beeline for the cubicle in order to be ensconced before the inspector came through.

After a sufficient break of about ten minutes, one of the Kiwis got up, strode purposefully down the carriage, stood outside the cubicle that all three Aussies were crammed into, and called out, in a most authoritative voice, 'Tickets, please.'

THE RUNAWAY TRAIN
GRAHAME WATT

The train roared down the mountain, the engine driver paled,
He bellowed at the fireman, 'The flaming brakes have failed!'
The train raced on freewheeling, the whistle warned ahead,
Around the bends at breakneck speed, through signals green
   and red.

Faster, ever faster, the driver tried in vain!
He pulled every lever but he couldn't stop that train.
It hurtled across bridges and crossings in a flash,
At a hundred miles an hour upon its downward dash.

Sparks came off the spinning wheels; the guard began to swear,
The driver and the fireman said a silent prayer.
Then slowly, very slowly, for the mountains had now gone,
The speed began to slacken, but still the train rolled on.

The further that it travelled from that mad descent,
The further that the train rolled free, the slower that it went.
For forty miles the train slowed down, on level ground once more,
Till it stopped at Central Station, platform twenty-four.

Well the driver was a hero; they still talk of the day,
The Minister for Railways had quite a lot to say.
'This is a special day,' he said, 'a day of joy sublime,
For it is the first occasion that this train has run *on time!*'

MEAN MIKE
RUSSELL HANNAH/JIM HAYNES

An old railway mate of my dad's, named Ken, was firing a late-night mail train out of Central. It was about 11 p.m. and his driver was Mean Mike, the most miserable bastard on the New South Wales railways, and mean!

Before they even pulled out of Central, Mean Mike said he was starving hungry. So, he grabbed the banjo, took a couple of eggs out of his tucker box and proceeded to fry them on the banjo in the fire. A banjo is a coal shovel, drivers and firemen cooked their meals on a clean coal shovel in the open firebox.

He didn't offer Ken any; Mean Mike wouldn't have offered his own mother any, even if she hadn't eaten for a week.

Mean Mike scoffed his eggs with a bit of toasted bread as they headed out of Central. But soon he turned pale—and then he started to turn a bit green. Next thing, he was leaning out of the cabin, spewing his heart out.

Ken was a bit worried. He decided Mean Mike was probably not fit for work and told him he should go home. Ken said he'd ring ahead for a replacement driver when they pulled into Strathfield.

Mean Mike, however, assured him that everything was okay. Since he had offloaded the eggs, he felt much better. Sure enough, Mean Mike seemed to have made a perfect comeback and was looking much improved. Ken assumed it was just a passing stomach complaint.

When the train reached Valley Heights in the mountains, Mean Mike was evidently feeling a bit peckish again, so he grabbed the banjo and pulled out another couple of eggs. He followed exactly the same procedure—cooking the eggs and eating them and, within a few minutes, he's gone green again and before long he's leaning out of the cabin throwing up that lot of eggs.

Ken figured there must be something seriously wrong with Mean Mike. Maybe he had a duodenal ulcer or terminal stomach cancer. He reckoned that they should get a replacement driver as soon as possible, so Mike could go and see a doctor.

But, once again, Mean Mike said he was quite okay. It was only the eggs that made him feel crook, he said. It was fine now; he didn't have any more eggs in his tucker box, so he'd be okay.

Ken thought this was all a bit strange, but, as Mean Mike once again looked to have recovered, he decided not to insist on getting a replacement driver. 'Do eggs always make you feel crook?' he asked Mean Mike.

'Yeah,' Mike replied, 'I think I'm allergic to eggs.'

Ken was at a loss to understand why anyone would keep eating eggs if they knew they were allergic to them. You see, he had no idea just how mean Mean Mike was. But he found out when he asked, 'Why do you keep eating 'em if you think you're allergic to them?'

Well, Mean Mike looked at Ken and said, 'I've got to eat 'em! You see . . . I've got chooks!'

THE LADIES IN GREY

Women didn't become train drivers, firemen, guards or station-masters until relatively recently. True, some became gatekeepers and carriage cleaners but these were a relatively small proportion of railway workers.

There was one area of the railways, however, where the work-force consisted predominantly of women. This was the catering department that flourished during the age of steam and spawned the great Railway Refreshment Rooms—the RRR.

For many decades 'the Great Triple R' was ruled over by those fearsome 'ladies in grey'.

In pre-railway days, travellers walked or rode. Fifty kilometres was a good distance to travel each day. In colonial Australia, shanties, pubs, boarding houses and roadside inns were scattered along the roads.

The railways changed all that. A week's journey could be compressed into a day, and a series of refreshment rooms grew up on Australian railway stations. In New South Wales alone, at the height of the steam era, there were over 120 such rooms scattered over the stations of the rail system.

The first New South Wales train rolled out of Sydney terminal on 26 September 1855. It went as far as Parramatta. Early growth was slow, and the need to build refreshment rooms into the stations was not a high priority for railway builders.

In fact, the famous engineer John Whitton, the man responsible for the enormous growth in the railway system up until 1890, was actively opposed to building refreshment rooms. It was a waste of precious resources, he said; all available money should go into building the lines.

The official history of the New South Wales railways, published in 1955, tells us:

> The first refreshment room [at Sydney terminal] consisted of a counter and two stools. It was open only shortly before the departure and arrival of trains. Supplies were brought to the station by a kind old lady from her pastry cook shop in Botany Road. It was quite common to see hungry passengers anxiously looking out for Mrs Moon and her basket when she was a little later than usual.

Despite Mrs Moon's recognition as the first purveyor of pastries at Sydney Station, other records indicate that that honour went to a certain Henry William Dudley, who initially operated out of a tent on some wasteland outside the station. His venture proved disastrous. The tent was constantly at risk of burning down due to cinders from the passing steam engines and, on one occasion, it blew away in a strong wind.

The early refreshment rooms were all leased out to private operators. Many of them did not seem to impress Railways Commissioner John Rae; in the early 1870s he wrote:

> There is no part of our railway economy so defective as the arrangements of the supply of refreshments to passengers . . . the keepers of what are facetiously called refreshment rooms on our Railways are little more than apple-stall holders, and vendors of

lollipops and stale pastry, serving out junks of sandwiches and messes of tea and coffee to their customers, without any regard to their accommodation and comfort.

Finally, in 1917, the New South Wales government stepped in, took control of the previously leased refreshment rooms, and thus began the great era of the Great Triple R. Women became part of the railway workforce. Nearly eighty per cent of the staff was female and they earned just under half the wages of men.

Waitresses on the railways earned thirty-five shillings per week. Their male counterparts picked up seventy-five shillings. Women were not classified as permanent workers and had no access to government superannuation, long service leave or sick pay.

Trains stopped at refreshment room stations at any hour of the day or night. Hours of operation for refreshment rooms were often something like 2.30 a.m. to 4.30 a.m., followed by 7 a.m. to 8.30 a.m.; or 9 a.m. to 11.30 a.m. followed by 9.30 p.m. to 11.30 p.m. Though the actual hours worked were the regulation eight, they were spread over twenty-one hours of the day.

Many women lived in the railway accommodation and had compulsory deductions taken from their wages for meals and accommodation. This was a source of much discontent and, together with the irregular hours and broken shifts the women had to work, may have accounted for their legendary grumpiness. Stories of the grumpy 'ladies in grey' abound. This one is typical:

RRR waitress: What do you want?
Weary traveller: How about a cup of tea, a pie and a few kind words?
RRR waitress: There's your tea. There's your pie. That's two and sixpence.
Weary traveller: What about the few kind words?
RRR waitress: Don't eat the pie!

When the train pulled into the station, all hell broke loose as a trainload of hungry and thirsty passengers descended on 'the ref rooms'. They all had to be fed and refreshed within periods of time that ranged from ten to forty minutes.

Working the Great Triple R was a stressful occupation. When the train left, the staff had cleaning-up duties. Then the 'ref room' would revert to its usual somnolence until the next train reignited the frantic activity.

In some places, passengers sat down to silver-service three-course meals in ornate dining rooms. Other stations just had fruit and pie and coffee stalls called 'tearooms'. The humble railway pie was the fast food of the railway era.

It wasn't passengers' needs that made the Railway Refreshment Rooms such a great institution; it was the fact that trains used steam power. Steam locos needed to be changed, watered and re-coaled. This meant that long stops at some stations were inevitable.

These steam maintenance facilities were not necessarily in major towns. They were more likely to be at the junction of several railway lines. Thus the major refreshment rooms existed where there were significant loco yards, like Werris Creek and South Grafton—not Grafton City.

The war years produced some of the RRR's finest hours. Packed troop trains were a regular occurrence but troop movements were secret. The women of the RRR were often given just one hour's notice to feed up to 4000 men. During this time, assistance was provided by the Voluntary Aid Detachment. In the small towns like Gloucester, north of Maitland, the RRR and the VAD would service up to five troop trains a day. During the course of the war, they served over one million meals at that station alone.

Perhaps the finest hour of any refreshment room occurred during the floods of 1955 in Narrabri. Water was lapping over the platform and the surrounding area was one vast inland sea when the last train arrived in from Walgett. The passengers soon realised that they were trapped at the station. The refreshment room cooking facilities were still operational but there was a serious shortage of food supplies.

Jim Madigan, an earth-moving contractor from Gunnedah, who was on the train, would write:

The adaptability of people in an emergency was amazing. Two cows that were tethered near the station were brought onto the platform and milked to supply the babies and children amongst the crowd. Six sheep and a pig seen floating past still alive were rescued from the water only to be slaughtered. This meat plus a bag of potatoes consigned northwest from Narrabri were used to cook meals in the refreshment room facilities. During the first 48 hours of the flood the people stranded on the station were probably the best fed in the whole of Narrabri.

When steam power was replaced by diesel power, trains no longer needed lengthy stops for re-coaling or loco changeovers. Long distance trains carried on-board buffet or dining cars. The rise of road and air transport also meant that the catering services started losing money.

By the 1970s, country passenger services had declined drastically and most branch services were gone by the early 1980s.

These days, XPT services stop just long enough to disgorge their passengers and luggage and pick up those who are boarding.

Some of the old Triple R buildings have been taken over by historical societies. Others have just become part of the station offices and buildings. Several retained their liquor licences and became pubs.

The ladies in grey live only in memories and old photographs, but for fifty years they were an essential part of the great adventure of rail travel. Ahh, nostalgia is the child of progress—

When I was a boy, my greatest joy
Was going away on a train.
In a corridor carriage my parents' marriage
Was lucky to stand the strain.
My brother and I would demand a meat pie,
Mum would wish on a star,
And Dad would say that he blessed the day
When they opened the Great Triple R.

JH

TRIPLE R LADY
JIM HAYNES

I'm a Triple R lady—you'll get no change from me,
Just pies and salad sandwiches and boiling cups of tea.
Don't think that you can jump the queue and if you push or shout,
I'll serve everyone but you—and you can just miss out.

'Cos you've only got ten minutes—then the engine gives a toot,
And if you end up hungry—I couldn't give a hoot,
You can't buy food back on the train and there's no dining car,
And you've got all night to travel to the next Triple R.

And the ladies there are just like me, tough and dressed in grey,
So if you want refreshments you'd best do things my way.
You can push and yell at me but I really wouldn't try it
'Cos if you do I'm warning you, you're going on a diet!

Be rude and I'll ignore you, be polite and I'll be cheerier,
'Cos I'm a Triple R lady—boss of the cafeteria,
If you dare annoy me, that's an easy thing to fix,
I've a hundred ways to sort you out, lots of little tricks.

Last time a bloke was rude to me, know what I did to him?
Gave him the hottest pie I had, filled his teacup to the brim,
And counted his change out slowly so he'd run to make the train,
Gee, that hot tea must have burned his hand, he won't try that again.

For if the train begins to move it's you that has to worry
You want to catch the train, or wait for your change? I'm not in
    a hurry.
I know which pies are cold and stale—it's easy to arrange it,
And once the train pulls out of here you can't come back to change it.

But when I'm in a good mood, I'm an angel dressed in grey,
I'll make your journey pleasant and brighten up your day,
'A nice hot pie? Of course, love, and a nice hot cup of tea.'
But I'm a Triple R lady—so don't try to mess with me!

But just remember, I'm the boss, this is my domain,
Your happiness depends on me when travelling by train.
With my sandwiches and drinks and cakes, my pie rack and my urn,
I'm a Triple R lady, so stand and wait your turn.

PERHAPS I'M SENTIMENTAL
JIM HAYNES

Perhaps I'm sentimental, but, in my mind, I seem
To remember childhood journeys through a veil of smoke and steam.
And, down the tunnel of time, I see a past for which I yearn,
When a train trip was an adventure, a chance to live and learn.

The world passed by those windows, backyards and country scenes,
Just like those on the carriage walls and, in my childhood dreams,
I was an adventurer, like those fettlers on trikes outback,
A battler waiting to jump a freight, a traveller down life's track.

How lucky we were to be alive when a train trip meant a ride
Behind an engine like a living thing, with its insides all outside.
And a platform ticket for a penny was little price to pay
For the joy of those reunions, or the sorrow of going away.

You don't meet many people in a car or bus or plane,
But there was many a friendship made to the rhythm of a train.
If you dream of steam and carriages, card games and conversation,
Well, perhaps you're sentimental too, and I'll see you at the station.

ACKNOWLEDGEMENTS

Many friends have helped with contributions and suggestions for this collection, notably: Russell Hannah, Frank Daniel, Paul B. Kidd, Dennis O'Keeffe, Grahame Watt, Peter Mace, Meryl Davis, John Elliott, Melinda Schneider, Paddy Ryan, Chris Holley, Ellen Montgomery, Max Ellis and Alex Hood. I also acknowledge using information from Allen Peters' website on Police History.

Thanks to Jamie McKew and the Port Fairy Folk Festival for giving me the chance to be involved in spoken word and Aussie folklore at that wonderful event for some twenty years.

Thanks also to George Moore and Paul B. Kidd and Radio 2UE for giving me a reason to collect so many great Aussie yarns and broadcast them every Sunday for over ten years.

My thanks also to Stuart Neal for suggesting the collection and Foong Ling Kong, Laura Mitchell and all at Allen & Unwin for helping to make it a reality.

Many of these yarns have been used as part of radio segments on 2UE's weekend program, *George and Paul on the Weekend*, and I acknowledge research done using the Australian Dictionary of Biography and the National Library of Australia's Trove resources.